T0329711

THE SOLIDARITY ECONOMY

The Solidarity Economy

NONPROFITS AND THE
MAKING OF NEOLIBERALISM
AFTER EMPIRE

Tehila Sasson

PRINCETON UNIVERSITY PRESS

PRINCETON & OXFORD

Published by Princeton University Press
41 William Street, Princeton, New Jersey 08540
99 Banbury Road, Oxford OX2 6JX

press.princeton.edu

ISBN 978-0-691-25038-0
ISBN (e-book) 978-0-691-25512-5

British Library Cataloging-in-Publication Data is available

Editorial: Priya Nelson, Morgan Spehar, and Emma Wagh
Production Editorial: Jenny Wolkowicki
Jacket design: Heather Hansen
Production: Danielle Amatucci
Publicity: William Pagdatoon

This book has been composed in Miller

Printed in the United States of America

10 9 8 7 6 5 4 3 2 1

For my grandmother Yaffa (Jenny, Jamila)

CONTENTS

ABBREVIATIONS

BIM British Institute of Management

CWC Ceylon Workers' Congress

CAP Common Agriculture Policy

CBI Confederation of British Industry

EEC European Economic Community

FAO Food and Agriculture Organization

FCO Foreign & Commonwealth Office

FFHC Freedom From Hunger Campaign

ICP Industry Cooperative Program

IDS Institute of Development Studies

ITDG Intermediate Technology Development Group

ILO International Labour Organization

IMF International Monetary Fund

ICFTU International Confederation of Free Trade Unions

ITC International Trade Centre

LSE London School of Economics

ODM Ministry of Overseas Development

NCB National Coal Board

NIEO New International Economic Order

ODI Overseas Development Institute

SEWA Self Employed Women's Association

TWIN Third World Information Network

TUC Trade Union Congress

UNCTAD United Nations Conference on Trade and Development

ACKNOWLEDGMENTS

THE CONCEPTUAL QUESTION which frames this book—whether capitalism can be ethical—was one that preoccupied me long before I thought I'd become an academic, and one that I've returned to only after I finished my PhD. Yet it's also a question that I wouldn't have been able to fully articulate or develop if it wasn't for my formative years at Tel Aviv University and at the University of California, Berkeley. I'm grateful for the friends and mentors there, as well as in the intellectual communities I've been fortunate to inhabit across Israel/Palestine, Britain, and the United States since then.

At Tel Aviv University, the late Boaz Neumann offered the encouragement and support I, a first-generation college student and high school dropout, needed to become an independent thinker. I often return to his advice. Billie Melman modeled feminist mentorship and showed me what the study of empire and colonialism can reveal about the worlds I inhabit, as much as it can about Britain. At the University of California, Berkeley, Tom Laqueur generously adopted me into his intellectual family and taught me, with many growing pains, how to connect what he calls "the cosmic with the particular." I miss bickering with him in his office about history and theory as well as sharing breakfasts at Saul's. It's hard to express how grateful I am for James Vernon's friendship and mentorship. I often feel like my work is part of a longer conversation with him, one which began on "visit day" in March 2009 sitting on a bench outside of Dwinelle Hall sharing a cigarette. Wendy Brown pushed me to connect the pleasures of archival stories with broader political and theoretical points. I will forever be grateful for the conversations we had in her office about Marx, Foucault, and Weber. Stefan-Ludwig Hoffmann has been the most invigorating reader, who introduced me to the field of the history of human rights and its intellectual payoffs. Studying with and teaching for Marty Jay has shaped how I think about Western Marxism and helped me write some of the chapters in this book. I also owe gratitude to my teachers Carla Hesse, Jonathan Sheehan, and the late Saba Mahmood.

One of the best gifts the academy has given me is the meaningful friendships I've made over the years and which helped me complete this project. I'm especially grateful for Yanay Israeli's emotional and intellectual comradery, as well as for teaching me how to appreciate a bowl of Mashawsha. I'd like to thank Alice Goff for infecting with me with her love for Northern California as well as for doodling some of my best portraits. My deep gratitude also goes to Jennifer Allen, who offered endless emotional support at critical junctures working on this book. The late Philippa Hetherington provided me with some valuable advice about feminist theory and skin care. I miss her terribly. The conversations I've had with Seth Anziska in London have nourished me politically and emotionally. Sam Wetherell has been a brilliant friend, always willing to talk about history and politics and gossip. Hannah Farber, Bathsheba Demuth, Peggy O'Donnell Heffington, and Alice Goff offered the most supportive writing community during a lockdown year in London, when I was also feeling isolated by the experience of early motherhood. Julia Shatz has been a great companion to kvetch with about motherhood and academia. Rebecca Herman Weber's text messages not only offered valuable advice but also included uplifting pictures of San Francisco's beaches. Hilary Falb Kalisman provided endless pep talks. Natasha Wheatley shared with me some of the best Indian food I've ever had while listening to my writing woes. I'm also grateful to Yael Fisch, Liron Mor, and Shira Shmuely for providing much wisdom and cheer from across the Atlantic.

The *Past & Present* Junior Research Fellowship provided me with valuable time and resources to think about the book I want to write and the luxury to ditch my dissertation project. My special gratitude to Matthew Hilton for his professional support and mentorship during this time and the years that followed it. Combined with a Research Associateship at the Centre for History and Economics at the University of Cambridge, the postdoc allowed me to read my way through the history and sociology of economic life and what came to be awkwardly labeled the new histories of capitalism. I also thank Emma Rothschild, Gareth Stedman Jones, Paul Warde, and Inga Huld Markan for this institutional support. Over these years and after, I had the privilege of sharing my ideas with and getting feedback from Priya Satia, David Feldman, Frank Trentmann, Catherine Hall, Manu Goswami, Jessica Reinisch, Paul Kreitman, Martin Daunton, Kevin O'Sullivan, Susan Pederson, Helen McCarthy, Peter Mandler, Andrew Thompson, Seth Koven, Judith Surkis, Sam Fury Childs Daly, Or Rosenboim, Erik Linstrum, Patricia Clavin, Pat Thane, Michelle Tusan, Deborah Valenze, Arianne Chernock, Nadja Durbach, Claire Langhamer, Dominique Marshall, Jed Purdy, and Erika Rappaport. I also had the opportunity to work on an article with Alex Lichtenstein and Robert Schneider at the *American Historical Review* when I was still a graduate student and, although the materials did not end up in the book, what they taught me shaped how I wrote it. The late Marilyn Young, Philippa Levine, Dane Kennedy, Jason Parker, and Roger Lewis hosted a monthlong legendary seminar in Washington, D.C., which became important for how I think about the end of empire.

Emory's Department of History was where I really began writing this book and I am immensely grateful for all the support I've received from my colleagues. Joseph Crespino made sure I had the time and resources to work on the book. Astrid M. Eckert and Brian Vick have been model colleagues and friends who provided warmth and support from the moment I moved to Atlanta. Yanna Yannakakis, Tom Rogers, and Ellie Schainker generously gave their time, advice, and mentorship when I struggled to wrap up the manuscript. Clifton Crais offered support and feedback on drafts. Pamela Scully talked me through how to juggle writing a book, teaching, and motherhood. My sincere thanks also to Jeff Lesser, Mariana Candido, Malinda Maynor Lowery, Jamie Melton, Matt Payne, Jonathan Prude, Daniel LaChance, Judith Miller, Eric Goldstein, Jason Ward, Walter Rucker, Gyan Pandey, Allen Tullos, Tonio Andrade, Sharon Strocchia, Michelle Armstrong Partida, Becky E. Hering, Katie Wilson, Allison Rollins, Jazlyn Jones, and Kelly Richmond Yates. For their comradery journeying through the years of the tenure track I'm thankful to Chris Suh, Dawn Pederson, Adriana Chira, Carl Suddler, Yami Rodrigez, and Maria Montalvo. I'm also grateful to Allison Adams at the Centre for Faculty Development and Excellence. My brilliant undergraduate and graduate students have been the best gift Emory has given me. I'm especially thankful to Edina Herstein, Olivia Cocking, Madelyn Stone, Hannah Halmey, Alex Levine, Hugo Hansen, Joam Jeannite, Georgia Brunner, Anjuli Webster, and Alexander Compton. I'm also thankful to Teresa Davis, Xochitl Marsilli-Vargas, and Pablo Palomino for offering some of the best company and food I've had during these past few years. My thanks also to Geoff, Jenny, and Gaby Levine for their friendship. Mary L. Dudziak has been the most generous mentor and friend. I'm immensely grateful to her and Bill for their encouragement.

I'm thankful to the National Endowment for the Humanities for awarding me a fellowship that supported a yearlong sabbatical and the writing of the first chapters of this book. A subsequent fellowship from the Bodleian Libraries, Oxford allowed me to collect additional materials for chapters 3 and 6. The Oliver Smithies Visiting Lectureship at Balliol College, Oxford allowed me to finish writing them. I'm grateful to Martin Conway and John-Paul Ghobrial for their hospitality while living at Balliol as well as Richard Overton at the Bodleian Library.

My special thanks to Sam Moyn and Jordanna Bailkin for generously supporting me professionally through the years. I'm also grateful to Vanessa Ogle for her friendship as well as to Glenda Sluga and Stefanos Geroulanos for their support and advice. Over the years, I've met some fellow travelers of the mind and the archives. For their friendship and comradery and for sharing a laugh, I thank: Liz Fink, Sheer Ganor, Samantha Iyer, Penny Ismay, Des Fitzgibbon, Radhika Natarjan, Sarah Stoller Carrie Ritter, Jeff Schauer, Caroline Shaw, Chris Casey, Katie Harper, Sam Robinson, Jason Rosumolski, Mattie Armstrong, Jon Connolly, Melissa Turoff, Gene Zubovich, Nicole Eaton, Alberto García, Terry Renaud, Udi Greenberg, Daniel Steinmetz-Jenkins, Zachary Manfredi, Ben Siegal, Sarah Shortall, Josh Specht, Alessandro Landolo, Mira Siegelberg, Katrina Forrester, Jamie Martin, Sophie Smith, Amia Srinivasan, Tom Meaney, Alden Young, Jeff Byrne, Ari Dubnov, Daniel Immerwahr, Quinn Slobodian, Stephen Wertheim, Kristin Loveland, Mircea Raianu, Tareq Baconi, Anna Bocking Welch, Brian Drohan, Christienna Fryar,

Liz Marcus, Daniel Lee, Camilla Schofield, Natalie Thomlinson, Mo Molton, Lise Butler, and Daisy Payling. My special thanks to Charlotte Lydia Riley and Emily Baughan for the comradery and sisterhood in the archives and outside of them. I'd also like to thank Florence Sutcliffe-Braithwaite for taking me on walks around Brockwell Park, while I was stuck in my own head during the cold months of lockdown. My deep gratitude to Simon Jackson for encouraging texts and chats; they helped me get to the finish line and submit this manuscript.

Many people read and engaged with the manuscript and I'm so grateful for their generosity and insightful suggestions. I would particularly like to thank Ben Jackson, Quinn Slobodian, and James Vernon for an invigorating manuscript workshop, supported by Emory's Department of History. I've learned so much from their expansive comments and deep engagement with the manuscript. I'd like to also thank my generous colleagues Astrid M. Eckert, Tom Rogers, Ellie Schainker, Chris Suh, and Joseph Crespino for participating in the workshop and for providing me with such excellent feedback. The fantastic comments offered by the three peer review readers for Princeton University Press, who subsequently revealed themselves as Jordanna Bailkin, Emily Baughan, and Kevin O'Sullivan, were immensely helpful as I revised the manuscript. Thanks so much also to Jennifer Allen, Hilary Kalisman Falb, Simon Jackson, Lise Butler, Ben Siegel, Clifton Crais, Wendy Brown, and Michel Feher, who read parts of the manuscript and gave me encouragement and useful feedback.

Various people invited me to workshop parts of this manuscript and help me sharpen its arguments. I'm grateful to Erik Linstrum at the University of Virginia and to Krishan Kumar, Stuart Ward, Atossa Araxia Abrahamian, Mircea Raianu, and Freddy Foks for their helpful feedback. Maribel Morey invited me to a workshop at the Center for Advanced Study in the Behavioral Sciences at Stanford University, where I had helpful conversations with Nils Gilman, Lily Geismer, and Angus Burgin. Berkeley's Global History Seminar allowed me to workshop an earlier version of the introduction. My thanks to Rebecca Herman Weber, Brian DeLay, David Henkin, Caitlin Rosenthal, Stefan-Ludwig Hoffman, James Vernon, Kyle Jackson, Daniel Sargent, and Claire Wrigley for their useful feedback. Thanks to Princeton's Modern Europe Workshop and especially Laine M. Hewitt, Jeremy Adelman, Yair Mintzker, Natasha Wheatley, and Matt Karp for their questions and suggestions. Yale's Modern Europe Seminar and particularly Rohit De, Surabhi Ranganathan, Jennifer Allen, Terry Renaud, Paul Kennedy, and Charles Troup provided excellent comments. My sincere thanks to Stefanos Geroulanos and the participants of the Intellectual History Workshop of the Consortium for Intellectual and Cultural History, who provided an invigorating discussion. Thanks also to Alexia Yates and the participants of the Manchester History Research Seminar Series as well as Geoff Jones, Sabine Pitteloud, and the participants of the Harvard Business School's seminar for their terrific questions on an early version of the introduction.

At Princeton University Press, Priya Nelson has been a dream editor, who supported the project throughout. I thank her and the team at Princeton University Press, including Emma Wagh, Morgan Spehar, Eric Crahan, Jenny Wolkowicki, Heather Hansen, and Jenn Backer. John Pallatella helped me bring this manuscript into shape. Teresa Davis provided additional edits at crucial moments as well as creating the index.

Writing this book wouldn't have been possible without the help of archivists and librarians. I'd especially like to thank Chrissie Webb, who generously helped me work my way through some of Oxfam's materials before they were fully catalogued in 2012, as well as the kind and generous John Gagnon at the Schumacher Center for a New Economics. The multiple archivists at SOAS and Cadbury Research Library in Birmingham helped me through some catalogued and uncatalogued collections of War on Want, Christian Aid, and Save the Children. My thanks also go to Sophie Bridges and Tom Davies at the Churchill Archives Centre; James King and the rest of the team at Modern Records Centre at Warwick; Fabio Ciccarello at the Food and Agriculture Organization; Tom Rosenbaum at the Rockefeller Archive Center; and Theo Jackson-Cole for allowing me to read through her late husband's papers at West Sussex Record Office.

Some friends outside the academy played a vital role in keeping me sane and happy. My thanks go to: Talia Beck for providing endless love and support through the years; Knomes McKerl for her warmth and delicious cakes; Jennifer and David Dodge for helping us feel at home in Atlanta and for generously providing us with childcare.

My family, especially my sister Dafna Sasson, my brother Iftah Sasson, and my mother, Sarah Sasson, have always been a source of care and encouragement. My parents-in-law, Wilhelmina Kraemer-Zurné and Sebastian Kraemer, have cheered me along when I felt like I'd never manage to wrap up this project. I'm grateful to my brother-in-law and friend William Kraemer for providing long-distance writing advice and the etymology of some of the words used here. The book is dedicated to my maternal grandmother, Yaffa Haleva, once called Jamila, who has shaped the person that I am today. Thank you for everything you have done for me, Savta.

Linus Kraemer has been the most caring and loving partner. I'm immensely thankful for everything he has given me: for the endless emotional support, for moving to a different country, and for countless childcare Saturdays. And last, to my beautiful son Jonathan, who has been with me through writing this book: thank you for your patience these past few years and for giving me such a brilliant second childhood.

THE SOLIDARITY ECONOMY

Introduction

THE SEARCH FOR ethical practices has become a central feature of contemporary capitalism. From ethical consumption and fair labor practices to conscientious investments, an increasing number of businesses, activists, and economists seek to intertwine profit with a concern for social and environmental impact. In this approach, coffee cups and leisure wear become more than just household objects or clothing. Adorned with powerful images of coffee growers in Kenya or textile workers in Bangladesh, such commodities are sold to consumers as a means of supporting fair labor practices and environmental responsibility in the communities that produced them. Fair trade constitutes only part of the story. Equally important is the increasing centrality of ESG (environmental, social, and governance) investments, which encourage investors to fund responsible and sustainable business. This approach entrusts consumers to make virtuous choices about the products and services they finance and puts pressure on businesses to reconcile the pursuit of profit with their obligation to have a positive impact on society and the world at large. It upends the conventional notion that the function of a business is solely to maximize returns for shareholders and instead embraces what some have called "capitalism with a human face."[1]

How can we make sense of this so-called ethical capitalism and what do we know about its origins? Numerous chronologies seek to explain the phenomenon of ethical capitalism and how it transformed consumption, production, and finance. Two stand out in particular. On the one hand, there are those who suggest that the roots of this ethic can be traced back to the advent of capitalism itself. They point especially to the British antislavery movement of the late eighteenth and early nineteenth centuries as the first instance in which ethical considerations became intertwined with free-trade ideals, calling upon consumers to boycott slave-made goods. The shift toward free-market economics, in their view, brought with it humanitarian sensibilities—in this case a preference for free labor—and imbued capitalism with an ethical thrust from the start.[2] On the other hand, those who are more skeptical of ethical capitalism lay out a different chronology for its emergence. In this view, ethical incentives to consumers emerged as a branding strategy employed by corporations to increase shareholder value in the years following the collapse of communism.[3] Such strategies appealed to well-meaning consumers in the absence of viable alternatives to capitalism. The skeptics argue that no real ethics is possible under capitalism.[4]

These views inhabit opposite poles, but they share similar drawbacks: both assume an inherent logic of capital and neglect the role that historical agency played in shaping the ideas and actions that linked ethical principles to various forms of accumulation. They also limit our understanding of why some ethical values have endured while others have not. As new histories of capitalism have suggested, there is much to gain if we forgo fixed definitions of capitalism and instead track specific capitalist constellations or formations.[5] What happens, then, if we tell the story of the search for ethical capitalism from the perspective of unexpected protagonists such as nonprofits and nongovernmental organizations? What might such a focus tell us about the standard heroes of the history of capitalism—that is, the corporation, the state, the consumer, and the producer? And, perhaps most importantly, what can nonprofits teach us about the politics of ethical capitalism and its role in driving deregulation? As we shall see, the story of ethical capitalism was as much about the transformation of the relationship between state and nonstate actors in the economy as it was about changes in consumer habits and labor practices. Understanding the politics of ethical capitalism and its limits requires us to analyze the history of its ideas and institutions as well as the types of political economy it ended up shaping on the ground. It offers important insights into the politics of contemporary capitalism and its future: from the politics of consumer activism and the transformation of work to the limits of corporate social responsibility and the possibilities within structural, state-led labor reforms.

This book recovers a crucial chapter in the longer quest for ethical capitalism, focusing on Britain and its empire in the years of decolonization and their aftermath. It follows the nonprofit sector and the economists, activists, aid workers, and businesspeople who played a key role in it. Between the 1950s and the 1990s, the nonprofit sector in Britain—and particularly the self-proclaimed humanitarians who dominated it—developed their own ideas and theories about how to make global capitalism ethical. They did so through a series of welfare and development programs, from fair trade of handicrafts and foods via consumer boycotts and microfinance. These programs were designed to connect British consumers directly with producers across imperial and postimperial spaces. They were aimed at creating a grassroots global economy that would be both profitable and moral, supporting fair labor practices, sustainable consumption, and conscientious investments. Some called it a "solidarity economy." While the postwar economy relied on state-led welfare and developmental initiatives, British nonprofits articulated their own vision of decentralized, fair-trade markets as a means of instilling morality in economic lives, thereby circumventing the purview of the state. These nonprofits saw fair-trade markets as an autonomous and humanizing space where ethical relationships could emerge beyond the impersonal realm of the state. Their vision contributed to the growth of a newfound faith in the ethical potential of capitalism.

The search for a capitalism with a human face was, of course, not exclusively a British story. In the United States, Western Europe, and the Soviet Bloc parallel movements focused on ethical shopping, fair labor practices, and responsible business. But in Britain the story of ethical capitalism was distinct in the degree to which it was animated by the politics of decolonization. The British economy has long depended on its colonies; the protracted process of losing its empire posed a fundamental challenge to economic life in the former imperial metropole as much as it shaped postcolonial economies and international politics.[6] Decolonization generated new visions of the sustainability of a postimperial British economy and of Britain's role in the world, while postcolonial economies afforded Britons new spaces to test long-standing ideas about antistatism, decentralization, and corporate paternalism. The British story in fact sheds light on decolonization as an important economic event that restructured British capitalism and its engagement with the world after empire. While the history of British capitalism in this period has often been told as a domestic tale, my book shows that the process of decolonization was integral to the postwar transformation of British economic life. Just as empire was crucial for the emergence and expansion of British capitalism in the eighteenth and nineteenth centuries, so too did empire's demise play a significant role in shaping British capitalism in the latter half of the twentieth century. We cannot understand this quest for ethical capitalism without considering the legacies of decolonization.

My narrative covers the long period of decolonization and the global Cold War, starting with the years after India's independence and ending with the loss of the Hong Kong colony. In these decades, Britain reinvented its role within the global economy through its nonprofit sector and particularly though its nongovernmental aid organizations. As empire was ending, these organizations expanded in size and mission, using the old imperial networks and colonial bureaucracy. Historians have located the work of these organizations within the story of British and international politics. This book approaches them differently.[7] It shows that nongovernmental organizations and nonprofits were not just political players but also important economic actors who shaped British capitalism through their welfare and development programs. In the 1960s—the "development era," as one scholar dubbed it—nonprofits devised their own economic philosophy, which emphasized small-scale, grassroots development projects.[8] By the 1970s, they had connected this economic vision with the idea of fair-trade markets and ethical consumerism. In the 1980s the economic philosophy of these nonprofits became the basis for a broader critique of financialized markets in Britain and beyond. These organizations were also instrumental in the formation of alternative trade organizations and a new "people-centered" approach to development. By the 1990s, these ideas had come back home, as nonprofits helped New Labour place its domestic ideas about multiculturalism and redistribution within a global and postimperial context. The postimperial history of these organizations, their economic philosophy, and the markets they have created are a crucial chapter in the transnational story of the pursuit of ethical capitalism.

The program for ethical capitalism developed by the nonprofit sector has had lasting legacies in both the British and global economies of the late twentieth and early twenty-first centuries. It influenced the business culture and the transformations of financial capitalism in the early 2000s, including corporate engagement in humanitarian, social, and environmental issues, as well as the formation of fair trade more generally. In the aftermath of the Covid-19 pandemic, many politicians and economists in contemporary Britain and outside of it have returned to the nonprofit sector's decentralized vision as a model for how to structure the national economy. Today, its legacy still shapes everything from the landscape of shopping centers and tax exemptions to trade networks and labor arrangements in the global economy. While we know much about the demise of the welfare state and the rise of neoliberal and financial policies in the period, this book tells a crucial story that deserves to be more widely known: how and why the nonprofit sector built a new, market-based order out of the ashes of empire and the rubble of mid-century statism.

In and Against the Market

The history of the economy in the twentieth century is often told as one of transition between the era of welfarism and the age of neoliberalism.[9] In such scholarship, concerns for public interests, social democracy, and elaborate infrastructures of social services were overturned by austerity, privatization, and social conservatism.[10] State-led economies were overtaken by the "encasement" of markets.[11] Individualism elbowed aside communitarian ideas about the public good.[12] Keynesianism, the story goes, was dethroned by the intellectual and political rise of monetarism, amid the neoliberal vogue for an authoritarian globalism.[13] It is a narrative that often spotlights the rise of the conservative right over the disappearance of the socialist left.[14] For some, the fall of the Soviet Union in the early 1990s became the coda to this transformation, the moment when neoliberalism went from "being a political movement to being a political order."[15]

This book tells a different story. Unlike the more commonly told tale about the neoliberal and conservative right, it focuses on the role of the British left—and the nonprofit sector that grew out of it—in this transformation. It shows that many of the features often associated with conservative policies were also a product of a left-wing alternative to mid-century welfare capitalism and the role of the state within it. Haunted by the specter of Cold War and imperial politics, British nonprofits developed their vision of ethical capitalism in response to the primacy of the nation-state in the economy. Strikingly, they saw the state, not the marketplace, as morally vacant. As a result, they sought to overturn the nation-state as the primary organizer of economic life and instead hoped to foster decentralized market participation by directly connecting consumers, producers, and the global community. They advocated for individualism, entrepreneurship, and privatization of aid and welfare in the name of a more humane form of capitalism. Their choice for individualism reflected a commitment to grassroots market participation over state-led economies. "Centralization is mainly an idea of order; decentralization, one of freedom," wrote the economist E. F. Schumacher, who provided much of the inspiration for the nonprofit vision.[16] This antistatism was not premised on protecting markets from democracy, as was the case in the neoliberal penchant for authoritarianism. Rather, it saw itself as operating in democracy's service. In fact, by the 1980s, the nonprofit sector's emphasis on decentralized markets would be used to counter the top-down, neoliberal approach of the Thatcherite state and of organizations like the International Monetary Fund (IMF). British nonprofits were, in the words of one economist, "in and against markets": they critiqued the free market but also sought to operate within it.[17]

Of course, not all nonprofits were an extension of the British left, but many especially key international aid organizations such as Oxfam, War on Want, Christian Aid, and Intermediate Technology Development Group, emerged from the British left generally and the Labour Party in particular.[18] Their story was embedded within a larger transformation of the British left in the second half of the twentieth century. From the 1960s onward these nonprofits became populated by a younger generation of aid workers and activists, who were preoccupied with questions of fairness, justice, and redistribution. They were inspired by the Labour Party's moral commitment to overseas aid and postimperial relations.[19] Some nonprofits, like War on Want, were directly supported by the party. Many of the thinkers who informed their intellectual project—E. F. Schumacher, Barbara Ward, Michael Young, Richard Titmuss, and Michael Barret Brown, among others—belonged to the Labour Party, and some even identified with the New Left. Understanding the story of the left through the lens of the nonprofit sector that grew from it illuminates the relationship of the British left to the neoliberal project.

My narrative helps explain the transformations in British socialism over the course of this period. In the 1950s, the nonprofit sector's critique of the mid-century developmental and welfarist project emerged from debates within the Labour Party over welfare, development, and Keynesianism. By the late 1990s, the sector's embrace of the logic of "in and against the market" came to characterize the New Labour government. This book thus offers insights into how and why the British left abandoned the broader socialist goals of public ownership and state-led economies in favor of market-based socialism. Historians of the British left have largely explained this transition by focusing exclusively on domestic debates within the Labour Party. Whether as a response to the economic crises of the 1970s or the decrease in party membership in the 1980s, the so-called "modernization" of the Labour Party has been analyzed as part of an internal conversation about the future of socialism.[20] Looking at the nonprofit sector, however, I show that the turn to markets also came from ideas and practices connected to development economics and international aid. The dissociation of the liberal left from public ownership and the turn to market socialism was in fact tested by the nonprofit sector in colonial and postcolonial economies during the years of decolonization and its aftermath.

I locate the intellectual origins of this vision in the 1950s within socialist and ethical debates of the British left about the future of British capitalism.[21] In the heyday of modernization theories, Labour politicians and economists sought alternatives to the economic model of public ownership. Their critique of the state-led economy was driven by humanist concerns about both trickle-down economics and centralized planning. They believed that Keynesian macroeconomics, with its focus on quantitative measures of incomes, demand, and gross national product (GNP), could not fully solve the problem of inequality in Britain and newly independent economies. Instead, inspired by anticolonial critiques—especially Gandhian thought—these ethical socialists sought welfare models that would valorize individuals and their communities at the level of the "grassroots." They, in turn, emphasized the role of the consumer, the entrepreneur, and the community in the global economy.

Ethical socialists developed their ideas beyond domestic spaces, often testing them in imperial and postimperial economies. For these socialists, postimperial societies offered the perfect laboratory for experimenting with economic alternatives. The new economies of India and Tanzania, for example, provided them with the ideal grounds to consider the role of decentralization, community development, entrepreneurship, and intermediate technologies in shaping welfare and mitigating inequalities. Between the 1960s and the 1990s, the burgeoning sector of British nonprofits sought to connect the project of domestic welfare with a postimperial quest for community development in the decolonizing empire. Tracing both the imperial and domestic formations of their programs, this book draws the histories of welfare and development into one frame.[22] It argues that welfare and development ideas were interwoven in a single project that aimed to create ethical capitalism on a global scale.

Britons were not alone in their search for alternatives to large-scale state-led development. In the landscape of mid-century international development, American, Indian, and international-based organizations were also thinking about what the historian Amy Offner calls a "mixed economy."[23] Across multiple geographies, economists, welfare thinkers, and activists searched for models that would solidify new relationships between the private and public sectors through welfare and development initiatives. In the British case, this search for an alternative to national ownership was led by nonprofits. For its economists and aid workers, Britain had a particular role to play in the global economy. As Britain gradually lost its place in the world economy, they sought in Schumacher's words to find a "Middle Way" in approaches to economic and social development.[24] This British "third way" would hew a path between the centralized, authoritarian economic planning of the Soviet Union and the hyper-individualist economy of the United States. Nonprofits hoped the British approach would offer an alternative path for newly independent countries to organize their economies.

Nonprofits articulated this British third way in part through the now ubiquitous concept of "stakeholder capitalism." The concept essentially meant organizing the capitalist enterprise around shared governance by its multiple stakeholders, from workers to consumers and finally the larger community within which businesses operated. This type of ownership fused both private and public interests but without state intervention and positioned itself against the more traditional division between trade unions and industry. The concept was not unique to Britons; it appeared across Western Europe in the 1950s and 1960s. In 1971 stakeholder capitalism was popularized by the German economist and founder of the World Economic Forum, Klaus Schwab.[25] By the 1990s the concept came to be associated with the rise of New Labour.[26] This book underscores, however, that we must also understand the rise of stakeholder capitalism in terms of the nongovernmental work enabled by the confluence of the global Cold War and decolonization.

British nonprofits took the idea of stakeholder capitalism and scaled it up to the global economy. They used it to define their own paternalist role as mediators, sometimes even as representatives of different stakeholders in the global economy, including consumers, producers, and private businesses. From the 1960s onward, this idea became the basis for development projects and campaigns. In some cases, nonprofits went so far as to create their own nongovernmental fair-trade enterprises that would represent these stakeholders through shared nongovernmental markets. In other cases, the concept helped them devise campaigns that would advocate on behalf of stakeholders for fairer trading agreements, consumer protections, and labor rights in national and international forums like the United Nations Conference on Trade and Development (UNCTAD) and the Trade Union Congress (TUC). For British nonprofits, the concept of stakeholder capitalism facilitated a more democratic participation in the global economy. They saw it not only as a fairer way to organize industrial democracy from the grassroots but also as applicable on a global scale.

In telling the story of this nonprofit alternative, this book advances a more capacious understanding of what, today, we would label "fair trade." At their most ambitious, nongovernmental campaigns in the 1970s sought to embed programs for community development in the former empire within a wholesale reform of the global economy. From importing handicrafts and revising commodity agreements for sugar growers to linking their handicraft and fair-trade imports to credit and saving schemes, activists saw the goal of their development work as transnational and international in scope. They sought to boost the welfare as well as the income of Third World citizens, and they placed this goal above the traditional aim of growing the national economy.[27] Fairer trade would provide an alternative form of grassroots development, promote participation by indigenous communities, and support "technologies which encourage self-reliance." Their approach would serve as "a reaction against the neo-classical modernists."[28] Using the model of stakeholder capitalism, nonprofits aimed to generate markets independent of the state and international organizations, "a real alternative to mainstream commercial trade."[29]

The nonprofit sector's embrace of stakeholder capitalism was aimed at generating popular forms of participation in the global economy. Charity shopping, fair-trade production, boycotting, and consumer practices more generally became commonplace during this period. By considering these kinds of practices as part of a broader global narrative about the economy, and as elements of the search for ethical capitalism in particular, I aim to expand our understanding of who counts as an economic subject and where that thing called "the economy" is located.[30] Although the role of economists and policy-makers in shaping the state's relationship with the economy constitutes part of this story, the book's overarching narrative centers the nongovernmental arena as constitutive of economic life and as the space in which this project was actually realized.[31]

Throughout the twentieth century, Britons had been called upon to participate in the imperial economy as both consumers and producers of imperial goods. When Britain began to lose its empire, older notions of the patriotic imperial consumer and producer were replaced by a set of postimperial relationships between Britain and the world.[32] Some of these relationships emerged out of both new trade agreements and political alliances with the European Economic Community, as well as through the spread of American ideas about value, entrepreneurship, and financialization. In other cases, especially in the decolonizing world, these new relationships were haunted by the specters of empire, paternalist assumptions about non-British peoples, and enduring racial hierarchies. The nonprofit sector sought to thread its way between the postcolonial economic revolt of the so-called Third World and the changing nature of Britain's own political economy.[33] To do so, it created an economic infrastructure for public engagement that was based on an individualized form of popular participation in the global economy. It aspired to represent the "people"—British consumers and Third World producers—beyond the official strictures of the state.[34] "Economics as if people mattered" was its slogan, which constituted part of the moral response to the dehumanizing nature of the postimperial state.[35] And yet this focus on individuals rather than states also elided the structural conditions that generated economic inequalities and shifted the onus onto consumers and producers to regulate them—a process some have termed "responsibilization," in which the burden for fixing the economy falls on individuals.[36]

This book in fact explains why and how ethical capitalism became a project that operated on the level of the individual consumer rather than that of organized labor and state regulation. Nonprofits aimed to generate a new type of citizen-consumer on a global scale. The consumer had been a political figure since at least the late nineteenth century, but during the last three decades of the twentieth century, nongovernmental activists called upon citizens— especially housewives—to include ethical considerations and global concern in their everyday shopping.[37] They argued that the mundane act of shopping could satisfy both material needs and global moral imperatives. This practice could connect British citizens directly to Third World producers without aid from the state and build solidarities through decentralized markets rather than diplomatic channels. By the 1990s, as one aid worker claimed, there was "a fundamental change in consumer behaviour. Ethical shopping is becoming a mainstream marketing concept. It is already affecting product presentation and promotion, and, more slowly, production methods."[38] By using it to reform Britons' fashion and diet, British nonprofits treated the market as an economic space that could mirror a global moral community. Ethical consumerism sold the promise—albeit a false one—of forming an authentic connection between British consumers and producers in places like India and Bangladesh. It aimed to resolve the capitalist alienation between producer and consumer in everyday economic life, creating a humane capitalism in the process.

At the same time, this book shows that the story of these fair-trade ventures reshaped labor after empire. Nonprofits sought to connect ethical consumerism with various community development projects, cooperatives, and eventually individual entrepreneurs and to move away from state-led development initiatives to more local and grassroots forms of employment. Their fair trade was as much about reshaping supply as it was about demand. They encouraged intermediate technologies in rural communities over the traditional development model that focused on large-scale industrial projects in urban centers. In some cases, British nonprofits even taught postcolonial producers, especially women, to make "indigenous" craft goods, convincing Britons to engage in what they presented as the ethical consumption of such handicrafts and foods. They sought to unleash "the creative freedom" of Third World producers as entrepreneurs.[39] Nonprofits, in fact, came to celebrate entrepreneurship as a solution to inequality. Entrepreneurship fit within their larger philosophy of self-reliance, decentralization, and small scale. It was seen as a way to liberate Third World producers from the strictures and limits of the wage economy and allow them independence. Fair-trade ventures wove together the consumption and production of fair-trade goods as well as the credit structures necessary to sustain them. In this vision, postcolonial entrepreneurs would make handicraft products tailored to the taste of the British customer. These products would then be sold as part of a large network of fair-trade markets managed and regulated by nongovernmental enterprises.

Despite their aspirations to create grassroots cooperatives and industries, many of the campaigns for fair-trade markets did not manage to reform labor standards and working conditions. In the 1970s, amid a global unemployment crisis and deindustrialization, these fair-trade ventures helped cement a global division of labor between Britain and the Third World, particularly its former South Asian empire. Nonprofits' aversion to state intervention meant that fair-trade ventures remained unregulated and often compromised labor rights. Producers worked under poor conditions while profit margins for nonprofits grew exploitatively high. Nonprofits almost exclusively provided indirect support for flexible labor and self-employment in the so-called "informal sector," in which many workers remained outside the official labor force. Informal producers became the key link in a chain of interactions that included charity shops, fair trade, self-employment assistance, and, eventually, microfinance. As nonprofits abandoned such traditional concerns as unionization and state-level labor legislation, they contributed to the growing precarity of labor in postimperial spaces. Nonprofits, in short, ended up becoming drivers of inequality rather than the solution to it.

By the 1980s, when the debt crisis hit many postcolonial economies, nonprofits had to recalibrate their ethical vision and adapt their fair-trade ventures through microenterprise schemes. Influenced by the vogue of financialization throughout the development sector, British nonprofits joined the World Bank and USAID in tying their aid programs to initiatives that offered small loans and financial advice to Third World entrepreneurs engaged in fair-trade ventures.[40] Among the many attractions of this vision was its self-sustaining quality: instead of selling goods to fundraise for their fair-trade programs, nonprofits realized that they could use financial tools like credit to help producers make and export fair-trade goods, whose sale would in turn underwrite the work of nonprofit organizations. They taught producers how to market themselves as Third World producers and to valorize their "human capital."[41] In this financialized model, nonprofits transformed Third World producers into the commodifiers of their own self-worth, purveyors of an authentic "Third World" tradition ready to be sold and marketed as a fair-trade good. This model cemented a view of the Third World as a uniform space of exotic, traditional crafts. By the late 1990s, nonprofits imported this model back to Britain, introducing microfinance as a solution to the financial marginalization of the Black British community and the unemployed.

Nonprofits' project of making capitalism ethical was, in fact, never one-directional. The ideas and schemes that may have originated as part of a development project to remake postcolonial economies also eventually shaped economic life in Britain. We cannot understand the history of the British economy in isolation from its imperial and postimperial formations. Rather than telling a story about British exceptionalism, this book focuses on the postimperial formations of Britain and its economy, transformations that continue to have lingering effects in contemporary Britain.[42] Ethical capitalism was a mutually constitutive story for both the metropole and its former colonies, even after formal decolonization.[43] By showing the relevance of British postimperial history to the broad arc of the postwar, the chapters that follow offer a global history attentive to the specific national and imperial histories and formations often lost in existing accounts of the period.

The Third Sector of the Economy

Looking at the history of the economy in Britain in the second half of the twentieth century from the vantage point of the nonprofit sector affords a novel perspective on the period. Instead of telling a story about the challenges to mid-century capitalism posed by the domestic welfare cuts of Margaret Thatcher's government and the rise of New Labour, I underscore the key role of the nonprofit sector as a locus of alternative visions of capitalism. Beginning in the 1950s, British nonprofits—or charities as they are more commonly called in Britain—laid the foundation for new types of markets and economic ideas. A central thread of this book argues that we should understand the role of nongovernmental organizations and charities in Britain as a central part of the history of the economy. These nonprofits became economic actors in their own right, shaping a new political economy in Britain and the world and, with it, new economic ideas and subjectivities.

My book follows the story of self-proclaimed humanitarian aid organizations such as Oxfam, War on Want, Christian Aid, ActionAid, and Save the Children, as well as smaller development groups such as the Intermediate Technology Development Group (today called Practical Action). Instead of focusing on a collective or individual biography of these organizations, I set out to study their economic ideas and programs as illustrative of a set of broader social and economic changes. While not all British nonprofits were international in their orientation, these organizations played a particularly important role in British capitalism in the second half of the twentieth century. Many of them were founded within the context of total wars. Save the Children, the most liberal leaning of the group, was famously established in 1919 to respond to the Allied powers' blockade of Germany.[44] Oxfam was founded in 1942 and Christian Aid in 1945 in response to World War II. Others were founded during the era of decolonization. War on Want, the most radical of the group, was launched in 1951 as an international antipoverty organization and received the backing of anticolonial activists and Labour politicians, including Harold Wilson, who became prime minister in 1964. The Intermediate Technology Development Group was established in 1966, ActionAid in 1973. These organizations were created in a variety of contexts and circumstances, but it was during the long process of decolonization that they became central actors in the British and the international economy through their development and welfare programs.

My study builds on the work of social and political historians who have demonstrated the role of these organizations within a broader history of internationalism, humanitarianism, and empire.[45] At the same time, it also departs from them, showing that the history of British aid need not be bound to questions of politics and diplomacy. I utilize the newly available archives of these organizations and read them alongside trade union and business archives, the archives of international organizations, and national archives in order to understand their activities, politics, and ideas within the broader political economy of the period. I trace how they moved from Victorian- and Edwardian-style charities to modern economic ventures, forming limited liability companies, pushing for tax exemptions, and devising their own development philosophy. I argue that these organizations played a key role in Britain's transition from an imperial to a postimperial economy.

Methodologically, I classify these organizations as "nonprofits," instead of as charities, NGOs, or humanitarian organizations, in order to emphasize the economic role all such organizations played. We cannot understand the activities of these organizations in the international order without analyzing them as the distinctively capitalist organizations that they were. Considering these organizations as central parts of the economy allows me to ask questions about their economic ideas as well as follow important protagonists, like the economists, businesspeople, and even policymakers who played a critical role in shaping them. It also allows me to analyze their work alongside the British and global for-profit sector and to question the degree to which their activities were, in fact, "nonprofit." In short, in treating these aid organizations as nonprofits, my study writes them into the history of British capitalism.

It may seem counterintuitive to speak of the role of nonprofits as capitalist organizations, since by definition nonprofits are designed to work outside the sphere of accumulation. Since the Elizabethan era British nonprofits have worked alongside local and later state authorities, but they have been defined as serving a social or charitable purpose, rather than that of generating profits for owners or shareholders. Beginning in at least the nineteenth century, their nonprofit status won them special exemptions from British taxation laws and freed them from government intervention.[46] But in the second half of the twentieth century, nonprofits carved out a space for economic exchange that was neither privatized nor fully public, one that became a third sector in the economy. They devised economic approaches, pushes for new tax breaks, and shaped economic policies. Perhaps most strikingly, nonprofits began to manage their own fair-trade enterprises, supporting local cooperatives, small businesses, and individual entrepreneurs in the former empire and importing their products back to British consumers. Nonprofits, in short, were becoming big business.

Part of this story was rooted in the larger political narrative that saw the rise of a number of rivals to the nation-state, to use the historian Charles Maier's formulation, in the second half of the twentieth century.[47] In this period, the sheer number of domestic and international charities grew exponentially, from 56,000 registered charities in 1948 to about 189,530 charities in 2003. The pace of that growth was especially rapid between the late 1960s and the early 1990s.[48] Nongovernmental organizations came to shape the nature of British politics, as the British public broke away from the traditional spaces of churches, trade unions, and political parties to cause-based nongovernmental organizations. The growth of the nongovernmental sector occurred in parallel elsewhere, across Western Europe and the United States, and nonprofits became one of the various alternatives that came to replace the "long century of modern statehood."[49] Nongovernmental organizations stood for a new transnational, and in some cases grassroots, politics. They became a central force in globalization.[50] Their advocates positioned themselves against the British state, although in practice they were never fully separated from it.[51]

At the same time, nonprofits also played a part in the story of global economic governance. From the 1960s onward, British nonprofits developed an economic alternative to international organizations like the IMF and the World Bank. Their fair-trade and microenterprise programs were meant to counteract top-down restructuring of the global economy via commodity agreements, large modernization investments, and structural adjustment programs. Nonprofits devised their own economic approach to growth, which aimed to foment "participatory development" and to involve "the beneficiaries as partners, as co-workers in action and in research," connecting British consumers and Third World producers globally.[52] It was an approach that, by the 1980s, had won British aid organizations a central position in the international aid industry, working alongside and advising the World Bank, the IMF, and the International Labour Organization (ILO). Many aid workers who began their careers in the British nonprofit sector were later employed by these organizations, as the nonprofit sector became a feeder of economic experts and aid workers to international organizations. By the 1990s, some nonprofits called for a revision of international economic mechanisms that originated in the Bretton Woods system, seeking to remake those organizations in their own image. "Over the past fifty years the activities of the World Bank and the IMF," argued one 1994 Oxfam report, for example, "evolved in a way which is contrary to their founding objectives—and to the task of reducing poverty. . . . [T]he policies of the Bretton Woods institutions do not sufficiently reflect the needs of the majority of the world's citizens."[53] Nonprofits represented people rather than governments, which dictated the interests of international organizations. They fashioned themselves as democratic forces that could hold international organizations accountable for their "meddling" in postcolonial economies.[54]

A perhaps more mundane yet important product of this political transformation was that the voluntary sector became a major employer in the British economy. As nonprofits became a third sector in the economy, they competed with private and public industry for the labor force. By the first two decades of the twenty-first century, nonprofits had around six hundred thousand employees and probably twice as many volunteers.[55] Both domestic charities and international and development aid organizations had to recruit from an expanding and highly professionalized technocratic class of experts to administer their programs. Many of these professionals, crucially, were recruited from the Colonial Office.[56] Their imperial experience, expertise, and connections with local elites in postcolonial countries made them highly desirable workers and, in turn, helped expand many international aid programs. The process of decolonization, in other words, fed the exponential growth of the voluntary sector. This book joins a growing literature that shows how NGOs acted as "surrogates" of the imperial state even after empire.[57] Through these nonprofits, Britons found a new moral role in the world after empire as a nation of do-gooders.

But these former colonial experts constitute only a fraction of the story about how nonprofits became capitalist organizations. Just as important were the increasingly large numbers of business experts, trade consultants, banking and financial advisors, and marketing specialists nonprofits recruited into their ranks from the 1960s onward. This new class of financial and economic professionals either came with a degree in economics, marketing, and finance or came from the for-profit sector. They served the nonprofit sector by leading fundraising activities, but they also played a significant role in development and welfare programs, which increasingly focused on fair-trade enterprise, handicraft markets, and eventually microfinance; they led training workshops with fair-trade producers and taught them how to package, market, and sell their products, as well as how to label them as fair trade; they developed their own economic ideas and theories about the place of nongovernmental intervention in postcolonial economies; and, in turn, their economic thinking shaped Britain's own economic and financial engagements with the former empire.

Many of these experts even helped establish new collaborations between nonprofits and the for-profit world. As I show, these collaborations became a testing ground for broader ideas about corporate social responsibility, worker participation, and stakeholder capitalism. While nongovernmental organizations have long relied on the for-profit sector, in the 1980s many organizations established their own corporate relations units, focused on outreach to the for-profit sector in Britain and outside of it. By the late 1980s more than half of British businesses had experience using nonprofits to achieve corporate objectives.[58] Nonprofits, in fact, often worked alongside rather than against the for-profit world in establishing new ethical codes of conduct. They encouraged privatization in the name of industrial democracy and transference of technology. They saw themselves as intermediaries between consumers, producers, and capital.

Importantly, using both former colonial experts and business professionals, nonprofits were transformed into the third sector in the economy through new institutions such as subsidiary trading companies. Over the course of the 1970s, many of the large nonprofits expanded their activities and established their own nongovernmental limited liability companies under the umbrella of fair trade. Since the late Victorian period, philanthropic campaigns had included small-scale production of needlework by poor colonial subjects for the purpose of fundraising from wealthy Britons in the metropole.[59] But from the 1960s onward, aid organizations made these works into an integral part of their development programs. Using newly created limited liability companies, nonprofits began to produce, import, market, and sell fair-trade goods from the former empire to Britons to generate value in the for-profit system. These trading companies became the basis of the nonprofits' economic vision of a capitalism capable of being both humane and profitable.

This vision of ethical capitalism was only made possible through a series of new tax breaks introduced in the 1960s and the 1970s. In these decades, British nonprofits and nongovernmental aid organizations—Oxfam in particular—pushed for these new exemptions as they were setting up their own commercial activities over the course of the decade. From the sales tax to the property tax to deeds of covenant, nonprofits connected these special exemptions to a postimperial mission of helping newly independent economies. These exemptions in turn enabled nonprofits to carve out a special status for their trading ventures. Exemptions forged the material conditions for the ethical capitalism of the nonprofit sector and allowed nonprofits to generate new streams of revenue that would fund more experiments in development globally. Today, thanks to some of these exemptions, many nonprofits are able to compete with the private sector in the retail market and, in some cases, even contribute to the decline of small traders.[60] To understand the limits of the nonprofit project, then, we must analyze them as part of the history of capitalism.

Organization of the Book

Can capitalism be ethical? While the question was a recurring one for the British left at the end of the twentieth century, in the 1950s and 1960s it was at the heart of national political debates. Britain was losing its empire, and with it its preeminent place in the global economy. Many industries had been nationalized, while Britain still relied on many of its African and Caribbean colonies for key resources. From the East, the Cold War brought new challenges to old assumptions about economic management and the role of the state in the economy. Economists, welfare theorists, Labour politicians, and intellectuals of the liberal and Marxist left in Britain heatedly debated the possibility of an ethical capitalism, one that would fit, as one historian called it, a "postcapitalist society."[61] And, for all their different answers, each of these actors shared a deep suspicion of the role of the state in promoting the goals of fairness and solidarity.

Chapter 1 suggests that these early debates about the nature of capitalism were the intellectual and cultural background for the solidarity economy. Domestic debates were inseparable from the experience of the Cold War and decolonization. They self-consciously drew on ideas percolating in the decolonizing world: politicians and intellectuals of the British left were especially attentive to Indian and Tanzanian critiques of British imperialism. It was from anticolonial nationalists like Mahatma Gandhi and Julius Nyerere that British welfare and development theorists, economists, and politicians learned about decentralized economies, the importance of a small, community-based organization of economic relationships, and even the role of altruism in economics. Focusing on three key figures—the sociologist and Labour MP Michael Young, the welfare theorist Richard Titmuss, and the economist E. F. Schumacher—the chapter recovers the broad ethical critique of capitalism that swept through Britain in the 1950s and 1960s and shows how it was enmeshed in the politics of the late empire. Embracing the alternative ownership model of stakeholder capitalism, community development, and market socialism, these critiques became central to the new nonprofit imaginary of a global moral economy by the late 1960s.

The following chapters examine how the nonprofit sector took these ideas of ethical capitalism and experimented in adapting them to different domains and scales. Chapter 2 chronicles how in the 1960s the nonprofit sector adapted these ideas to the world of charity trading. A new cadre of charity organizers, especially at Oxfam, began to weave together the infrastructure of the solidarity economy. These experts had colonial experience and used their connections in the former empire to facilitate philanthropic markets that built upon the

tradition of imperial humanitarianism. They offered British consumers products that would connect them to various international, economic, and development causes. Charity trading, and with it brick-and-mortar charity shops,
focused first on organizing associational life within Britain. This movement
generated a large body of volunteer workers—mostly women—who did the
emotional work of suturing a faltering empire and raising funds for development in the colonies through sales of secondhand goods. Importantly, the
new arena of charity trading was boosted by the growing consumer culture
and the place of the consumer in British politics. Charity trading created the
economic infrastructure—from tax breaks to a new body of limited liability
nonprofit trading companies—for the solidarity economy. It made international aid NGOs into economic actors with stakes in the domestic and postimperial economy.

By the early 1970s, when most of Britain's imperial territories had achieved
political independence, activists transformed these community development
projects into fair-trade workshops. As chapter 3 shows, many nonprofits hoped
to emulate the model of a "cooperative society" comprising Britain and its former empire. They began to import Third World products to Britain and sell
them in their charity shops, especially handicrafts. The idea was to form a
"bridge" between consumers and handicraft producers without the intervention of states and international organizations. Charity trading was thus established to create a direct, ethical market for indigenous goods. Amid a global
unemployment crisis, however, charity trading turned away from its cooperative promise. They offered business opportunities and marketing advice geared
toward satisfying consumer demand in Britain rather than addressing structural inequalities in the labor market in the Third World. They nurtured and
developed a new enterprise culture and emphasized the value of flexible work
through development projects. The chapter untangles the failed promise of
these handicraft markets and how they shaped labor in the 1970s.

Fair-trade markets, however, were not limited to handicrafts. Chapter 4
explains how fair-trade markets were part of a broad project to create a "welfare planet," as one activist termed it. This vision responded to the political
and economic crises of the 1970s and was bolstered by the environmental and
anticolonial critiques they generated. The chapter focuses on the politics of
sustainability as a central object of a nongovernmental, environmentalist
vision of a fairer global economy. The decade saw a variety of campaigns aimed
at facilitating ethical markets for food between Britain and its former empire.
These projects drew upon a then-prevalent postcolonial critique of economic
growth as well as on ecological anxieties over diminishing resources. Some
called for the structural reform of international trade through commodity
agreements on sales of tea and sugar. Others focused on consumer action,
reforming consumption patterns through diets and fair-trade labels. In the
midst of Britain's own changing political economy—its transformation from

imperial metropole to a member of the European Economic Community—these campaigns oscillated between the language of economic justice and emotional pleas for humanitarian compassion. The persistence of compassion-based campaigns and the collapse of those devoted to economic justice demonstrates the possibilities that were opened and then later lost in the 1970s.

The idea of the fair-trade market, as chapter 5 demonstrates, also bolstered a critique of the growing presence of other nongovernmental agents in the global economy, namely big businesses and multinational companies. The nonprofit sector has long had an alliance with the for-profit sector. Before and during decolonization, many NGOs collaborated with private companies on multiple aid schemes. But in the 1970s, many activists in the nonprofit sector embraced a new economic philosophy of corporate social responsibility, one that developed as an alternative to nationalization and state ownership in Britain. It drew upon a wide array of ideas: from Gandhian notions of trusteeship and American management theory to Christian concepts of social auditing. The chapter highlights the enduring influence of Christian ethics on British capitalism. The turn to corporate responsibility transformed private corporations into agents of welfare, capable of better representing the stakeholders in the global economy—workers, consumers, and the community—than the state or the trade union. By the early 1980s, these ideas shaped a new form of nongovernmental activism though international corporate codes of conduct. The chapter tracks the emergence of campaigns for corporate social responsibility and stakeholder activism from their more radical origins in Britain in the 1960s—as projects about the remaking of public ownership—to their more minimal applications like the social audit, which were anchored in the critique of trade unions in the 1980s.

By the 1980s, when the debt crisis hit many Third World economies, nonprofits had to recalibrate their original vision of making capitalism ethical and fit in an increasingly financialized global economy. Chapter 6 charts how British activists responded to the debt crisis and the neoliberal IMF's structural adjustment programs that were meant to mitigate it. Drawing on Judeo-Christian theology, British nonprofits and church activists launched transnational campaigns that critiqued the IMF's programs and called for the cancellation of debt by the new millennium. While these campaigns began as a radical envisioning of the financialized global economy, by the late 1990s they became part of more minimal humanitarian campaigns that garnered support of pop singers, celebrities, and Third Way politicians. Instead of structural adjustments, nonprofits embraced microenterprise as a microeconomic tool that promised to solve inequalities from the "bottom up." It was a solution to the crisis of industrialization and the labor shortage that followed; instead of generating employment through macroeconomic restructuring of industry and fair-trade programs, it made the poor the engine of growth. In doing so, these programs in fact moved the burden of solving the crisis to Third World individuals and cemented the precarization of the poor.

By the late 1990s, microfinance was imported to Britain, becoming part of the repertoire of welfare services. Drawing on a nonprofit model created by Oxfam and other organizations in international aid, Third Way politicians offered microfinancial services to ethnic minorities within Britain's own economy. What started in the 1970s as an antistatist project to reclaim and empower economic subjects in the former empire had by the late 1990s become a state-led strategy by the New Labour government for managing the promise of multiculturalism and the integration of ethnic minorities in Britain itself. The solidarity economy shrank from the project of creating fairness within the global economy to the limited effort of molding subjects—British and non-British alike—into human capital. The legacies of this nonprofit story continue to shape economic and racialized inequalities in both the British and global economies.

CHAPTER ONE

Beyond State Capitalism

IN 1961, ERNST Friedrich Schumacher, a German-born economist and the chief economic advisor of the British National Coal Board, declared that development "cannot be simply [about] economics." For Schumacher, who had recently visited Burma and India as an economic advisor to the newly independent nations, development had become too reliant on quantitative approaches, which had "extremely limited applicability" in solving the problem of poverty and inequality in the Third World.[1] The period was characterized by state-led modernization projects that drew on Keynesian economics and industrialization in order to bolster the newly independent economies.[2] Schumacher, however, thought these projects had missed the main purpose of development: creating a better, more prosperous society, one built on mutual aid. He proposed that proponents of development needed to move away from forcing every social institution "into the service of purely material aims." He urged international development agencies such as the World Bank to adopt a different approach to development, setting aside its long-standing fixed menu of centralized planning, increased incomes, and the growth of gross national product (GNP). He thought that development aid should embrace "an approach more humane and much more compassionate than anything inspired by economism."[3] He called this approach "economics as if people mattered."[4]

In little more than a decade, Schumacher would be hailed as "the philosopher of the western NGO movement."[5] His ideas became the intellectual touchstones for a dizzying array of new approaches to development, from fair-trade schemes and campaigns for corporate social responsibility to microfinance. Schumacher's work—and the movements it inspired—eschewed the prevailing model of development, with its focus on state-led economy, GNP growth, and industrialization. No less notably, if Schumacher's work changed development, it was because his own thinking had changed as well. In the 1940s, he was not only an ardent follower of Keynes but also one of the authors of the Beveridge report on unemployment; by the 1960s, however, a decade often characterized as one of "Keynesian consensus," he had become one of Keynesianism's critics. Against what he identified as the Keynesian emphasis on large-scale development projects, centralized planning, demand-side economics, and data-driven growth, Schumacher articulated an economic vision beginning at the grassroots. This more ethical economic model would focus on decentralized development at the level of the local community and the entrepreneur and would be premised on small-scale technology, which Schumacher declared capable of creating enduring ties of social solidarity.

The few historians who have noted Schumacher's importance have mostly singled out his book *Small Is Beautiful* (originally published in 1973) and its emphasis on small-scale development programs. Yet historians in general have not explained the genesis of Schumacher's thinking nor explored the broader intellectual milieu of British socialism within which his critique emerged.[6] As it happened, Schumacher was not a soloist in his critique of the economy. His ideas about development were part of a broader ethical critique of Keynesian macroeconomics, public ownership, and welfare thinking that emerged as early as the 1950s and 1960s.[7] In these decades, socialists, economists, and welfare theorists in Britain became vocal critics of centralized planning, demand-side economics, and modernization, especially its focus on GNP growth.

During those two decades, many of the critiques of modernization and centralized planning were not limited to Britain.[8] In the British context, however, they were argued in distinctly ethical and socialist terms. Ethics, of course, has always been integral to economics, but in the 1950s some on the British left applied it to "the economy."[9] Key economists began to debate the importance of ethical reasoning to what the political theorist Timothy Mitchell has described as an increasingly consolidated sphere of knowledge about economic life.[10] For some, welfare and development economics needed to offer external values such as fairness that were capable of shaping the market toward the common good. Others suggested that the single-minded focus on macroeconomics had hollowed out the moral purpose of development and welfare work. What was needed was to make the economy focus on people rather than goods. Tabulations and calculations of income generation could not capture the breadth of human experience or quantify the experience of social growth. For Schumacher, the purpose of economics was to help bolster social relationships and encourage solidarity. His people-centered economics was one of various alternatives for a new economic ethics formulated in the 1950s and 1960s.

The critique of state-led economy has commonly been associated with conservative, neoliberal economics. In this account, the neoliberals launched an assault against state-led development and welfare projects in favor of private enterprise, free markets, and entrepreneurial initiative as the key to wealth creation.[11] But that is only part of the story, because some of the most cogent early challenges to state-led development in the 1950s and 1960s originated on the British left. Those challenges were never in favor of simply "liberating the market and individuals from government control."[12] Instead, the critique of state-led economy rested upon the belief in the community as the primary unit of economic and social growth. Ethical socialists preached decentralization of the economy as the path to a humane capitalism. And they sought to implement this vision in both Britain and the new postcolonial economies.

To understand the nonprofit efforts to make capitalism ethical in the 1970s as a distinctly nongovernmental project, we must first consider the ethical critique of the economy that originated in Britain in the 1950s and 1960s and its main theorist, Schumacher.[13] In this chapter I trace Schumacher's own critique of the economy as part of broader debates about ethical socialism in the period. In the midst of the global Cold War, a climate of late imperial tensions, and a growing call for decolonization, many British socialists turned away from centralized planning and Keynesian macroeconomic models toward a more localized, community-based approach to economic development.[14] What gave ethical critiques of the economy such power was that they could be imagined and tested within the newly independent economies of the decolonized world. The theory may have been developed in Britain, but Britain, for all its economic problems, was not the best proving ground for it. In the eyes of many British socialists, decolonization heightened the sense of Britain's role in providing a "middle path" between centralized, totalitarian Soviet planning and America's hyper-individualism. For many economists and welfare theorists, independent postcolonial economies offered the perfect microcosm in which to formulate and evaluate economic alternatives based on socialist ethics.

Among the many theorists and policy hands on the British left who were involved in the experiment, two stand out: the Labour policymaker and social reformer Michael Young and the welfare theorist Richard Titmuss. While British historians have considered Young and Titmuss as part of a domestic debate over ethical socialism in Britain, it is actually the case that along with Schumacher, each formulated his own alternative to what they saw as the ethical problem of capitalism in a period of decolonization, when Britain's moral role on the international stage was changing. Young famously focused on community studies, Titmuss on altruism and reciprocity, and Schumacher on people-centered economics. And there were clear commonalities in their writing: dissatisfaction with what they framed as Keynesian macroeconomics; a turn away from centralized planning toward decentralization; and an emphasis on forging solidarities through capitalism. The alternative social arrangements they proposed were appropriated by and became key tenets for the nonprofit sector and a nongovernmental imaginary of the experiments in humane capitalism in the 1970s.

Village Economics

The idea that the economy should be organized to enhance solidarity between its members was not novel in 1950s Britain. The socialism of the postwar period built on an ethical critique of the economy dating back to the nineteenth century. Social solidarity, for example, was at the heart of the cooperative ideal. In 1844, the Rochdale Pioneers established the first cooperative society for the "benefit and the improvement of the social and domestic conditions of its members."[15] In late nineteenth-century India and early twentieth-century East Africa, where the Cooperative Movement developed into a tool for imperial rule, the cooperative model itself was framed as means of establishing a grassroots community though economic exchange and mutual aid.[16] Human fellowship was also central to the Victorian moralism and socialist utopianism of figures like William Morris. Already in 1894, Morris claimed that wage labor was alienating to workers. The cultivation of their creativity and craft, he suggested, would enhance not only their own humanity but also their mutual sense of fraternity: "Fellowship is life, and lack of fellowship is death," he stressed.[17] The Arts and Crafts Movement that Morris established was designed to generate solidarity among its members.

In the 1910s, when poverty and inequality became connected to larger political and imperial crises in Ireland and India, this ethical tradition of socialism inspired the economic historian R. H. Tawney to investigate the historical origins of capitalism in the quest for alternative models of societies that had been "closer than individualism admitted yet freer than collectivism allowed."[18] Against technocratic welfarism and scientific solutions to poverty, Tawney argued that the problem with the economy was "a question of moral relationships."[19]

The search for an alternative model of a humane yet productive economy was also at the heart of the experimental community of Dartington Hall.[20] Founded by the philanthropist and agronomist Leonard Elmhirst and his wife, Dorothy, in the 1920s, Dartington aimed at reversing the "breakdown of co-operative village life in competition for profits" and instilling the feeling of "life in its completeness" among its members.[21] Elmhirst drew upon the idea of his friend, Rabindranath Tagore, the Bengali philosopher, poet, and nationalist whose Institute of Rural Reconstruction in Bengal was meant to liberate Indians from imperial rule by reviving village life though self-help and community development.[22] Within its first decade, Dartington became an important place for Tawney and socialist-pluralist thinkers like Harold Laski and G.D.H. Cole as well as postwar thinkers like Michael Young and E. F. Schumacher.[23]

These ideas were shunted to the margins in the 1930s by the global economic crisis and mass unemployment across Britain and its empire.[24] For many socialists, mounting unemployment numbers and growing inequality in

Britain heightened the urgency of adopting a more systematic notion of welfare, one where the state itself rather than local communities would be the main agent of change. Socialism became about delivering material goods rather than cultivating ethereal ideals of solidarity and fellowship. In the 1940s, the Keynesian macroeconomic vision that became the basis for the British welfare state was focused on state ownership as the primary method of redistribution.[25] Growth was measured against GNP, the primary measure of economic progress. Debates about ethics were sidelined by discussions of public spending on defense and welfare in "the national economy."[26] British politicians drew up plans for economic management that would increase economic efficacy. Civilian involvement in the war generated new expectations of the British government, from providing full employment to universal access to education and health care. Working-class demands made not only Labourites but also Conservatives more attuned to material expectations of fair distribution in the postwar period.

It was only in the 1950s, at a tumultuous moment for Britain and its empire, that discussions about solidarity returned to the British socialist agenda. British society was changing, and so was its electorate. Labour lost the elections of 1951, 1955, and 1959. White working-class voters were becoming more affluent and more deferential to the language of class conflict.[27] To many, the Keynesian focus on material growth was too technocratic and narrow in its scope to capture the aim of Labour's politics.[28] It was time to rearticulate a new program for the British left, one that transcended the basic contradictions of the capitalist order and offered a socialist politics for an affluent British society.[29] As the historian Ben Jackson has argued, the liberal left turned to thinking about equality in nonmaterial terms. Led by the MP Hugh Gaitskell (who became the leader of the Labour Party in 1955) and spurred on by Anthony Crosland, who wrote the party's manifesto, Labour revisionists redrew a new egalitarian model that would fit a "postcapitalist society," moving it away from socialism's Marxist historical origins toward a model of mixed economy.[30] Nationalization had falsely promised and ultimately failed to end inequalities. For revisionists, the goal of socialism was not to abolish individual property but rather to highlight the importance of "social and economic security, and the virtue of cooperative action."[31]

The liberal left was not the only one that turned to ethics. The New Left similarly began considering socialism in nonmaterial terms.[32] The entire concept of "moral economy" underwent a revival in this period.[33] Many New Left activists were influenced by the arrival of socialist and communist Caribbean immigrants during the 1950s, who turned to community development as a solution to an informal color bar and increasing violence against them.[34] Community development had already been taken up by anticolonial movements in various countries in Africa and the Caribbean as they were reclaiming their economies as part of broader calls for independence.[35] After arriving in Britain in the 1950s, socialist Commonwealth activists reappropriated community development as a tool to defend social rights and welfare in local areas in Britain. Community development offered this new generation of New Left activists—many of them Commonwealth immigrants—a concrete space to rework notions of solidarity into the fabric of social welfare.[36] It brought new meaning to the somewhat old Tawney idea of "moral economy."

The turn toward ethical socialism by both liberals and the New Left was a consequence of the country's changing role in the world. Since the 1956 Suez Crisis, international critique had questioned Britain's moral authority in the world. For the United States, the Suez invasion ran against its Cold War agenda in the Third World and strained the Anglo-American relationship. For countries in the Third World, the crisis exposed Britain's colonial agenda. At the United Nations, postcolonial statesmen like Nehru were challenging the country's legitimacy over its empire.[37] In the wake of colonial violence in the 1950s, many of Britain's territories claimed independence, including Ghana, Malaya, Nigeria, and Cyprus, with countries like Sierra Leone, Tanganyika, Jamaica, and Uganda soon to follow. As the American lawyer and statesman Dean Acheson phrased it, Britain had "lost an empire but not yet found a role."[38]

Cold War ideologies were suddenly doing battle within the newly independent economies of South Asia and later Africa. On the continent, the failed revolution in Hungary cracked the model of a state-led socialism, leading to revaluations within Britain itself. "We have now to rethink the philosophical foundations of our socialism under highly unfavourable conditions," G.D.H. Cole lamented, "because we must square our philosophy with the conditions of the world of today and tomorrow, unless we are content to be merely the dying advocates of a lost cause."[39] British liberals and Marxists alike searched for new models that would redefine the meaning and goals of socialism. It is perhaps no coincidence that there was a revival of a Tawneyite tradition epitomized in the publication of two new editions—one in 1952 and another in 1964—of Tawney's magnum opus, *Equality*. With "his historian's eye to the future," wrote Richard Titmuss, Tawney offered the contemporary British left a relevant framework for understanding inequality beyond the Keynesian "determinism of growth."[40] The turn to ethical socialism in the period meant the return of solidarity as a central goal of the socialist project rather than an exclusive focus on material redistribution and national ownership.

Instead of ideas of national ownership, the British left embraced the community as the primary organizing unit of economic life. Community, it was hoped, could better balance individualism with solidarity, reciprocity, and mutual aid, and at the same time avoid the problem of overcentralization.[41] To some extent, this turn to the small group was not unique to Britain. American sociologists, urban planners, and policymakers were also thinking about the small group as a unit for development of the economy and governance.[42] In Britain, the project of the small group was part of a socialist alternative to nationalization that framed the role of the community in ethical terms. For British socialists, the focus on community offered the moral glue that bonded individuals against the perils of modernization and industrialization. Community encouraged solidarity beyond the state.

No one has been associated more closely with the turn to community than the Labour policymaker and social researcher Michael Young, who argued that the community emulated the kinship bonds of the family and allowed individuals to develop a feeling of solidarity. "A community is not only a body of people living in buildings situated fairly close to each other; it is a body of people possessing the 'spirit' of community, that is having towards each other a certain attitude described as a sense of solidarity, of oneness, of belonging together," he wrote in 1952. "Solidarity does not come just from living in the same locality; it comes from doing things together."[43] From his work at the Institute for Community Studies in East London to the foundation of the Consumers' Association, Young devoted himself to understanding how to revive that sense of solidarity within modern, industrialized economies despite their tendencies toward atomization. His work was highly influential for British socialists but also, as we will see in later chapters, for NGOs like Oxfam and the nonprofit sector more generally.

In his 1949 pamphlet "Small Man, Big World," Young argued that a socialist democracy depended on "solidarity among neighbours."[44] In the spring of 1950, after Labour's narrow victory in national elections, he noted that the idea of community stood in direct opposition to the technical economism of Labour policy in the 1940s. He proposed that the party should focus on designing welfare services that would support the community and neighborhood units as well as local government, thereby strengthening emotional bonds and instilling a spirit of familial obligation. Young echoed the ideas of guild socialism developed by Cole and Tawney in the previous decades but also clearly departed from them.[45] As the historian Lise Butler has argued, Young's project of community revival embraced social science and particularly sociological and psychological research on familial bonds in industrialized Britain as the center of its analysis and the role of women within it.[46] At the very moment when women were turning against Labour at the ballot box, Young articulated an alternative economic vision that recognized the home and not only the factory as important spaces of production. His attack on Labourism was also an attack on the male-dominated culture of the trade union movement. "The same forces have been operating in the economy of the home as in the economy of the nation," he declared.[47] The family, and with it the household economy, was therefore the basis for the social and economic life of the community, and with it the nation. By 1957, Young would famously uncover the familial ties of the traditional, working-class communities in Bethnal Green as the one place where this type of solidarity flourished in Britain, despite the alienating experience of industrial life.[48]

But even before the 1957 publication of his coauthored study with Peter Willmott, *Family and Kinship in East London*, Young found inspiration in the traditional communities of rural India. Historians have explored his ideas in the context of the political disillusionment that haunted Labour after its narrow victory in 1950. They have also highlighted the importance of his critique of the hyper-individualism of American liberalism and his embrace of the social sciences, especially psychology.[49] But just as important for Young was a sabbatical trip he took in 1951 to India and Pakistan, following his mentor and teacher Leonard Elmhirst. The sabbatical was part of a world tour that included, among other places, Israel, where he nearly joined another communal experiment, the kibbutz.[50] But it was in postindependence India where Young encountered different forms of kinship relations that linked economic and communal lives. He also learned about mass poverty and the limits of Keynesian economics in solving it. These were conclusions he would ultimately apply to Britain itself.

In India in the early 1950s, Young saw ideas of community development in practice. He visited Tagore's Institute of Rural Reconstruction in Bengal, which had inspired Dartington Hall (where Young was educated). He also went to the "improved village" of Laldaha, which ran an experimental project of community development, and compared it to neighboring villages. Young learned about Indian land-reform programs and was introduced to cottage industries as possible avenues to development beyond the high-modernist, centralized version of it practiced by the Indian Congress and in Britain. Most importantly, the visit taught Young that the purpose of community development went far beyond modernizing agriculture or eradicating disease and ignorance. Health cooperatives and education served a much more ambitious goal of self-help and cooperation. They were "not to be something abstract, should always be closely connected with the life of the villagers," he wrote in his notes.[51] Further, "the impetus [for development] was to come from [within] the villages." The purpose was nothing less than "to change the mentality of the people, their habits, their whole way of life," he reported back to Elmhirst.[52]

In India, moreover, Young discovered alternatives to British socialism in the antistatist thought of Gandhi, who emphasized village life as the space for national and economic revival:[53] "Gandhi stated again and again that what mattered in India was the point of view of the man behind the hoe. India is a land of villages—550,000 villages. The towns don't matter," the general secretary of the Indian Socialist Party, Asoka Mehta, told him. This was a direct challenge to the Keynesian emphasis on industry and the state, one that suggested multiple paths to development. Another meeting, with J. M. Kumarappa, the director of

the Tata Institute of Social Sciences and the brother of the Gandhian economist J. C. Kumarappa, had taught Young the limits of "Western Modernism."[54]
The meeting left Young skeptical that the high-modernist development model,
which focused on investment in heavy industry as a way to generate growth,
was right for India. Young took note, comparing the conditions of poverty and
unemployment in India to those in Britain in the 1930s, and declared them so
different as to require uniquely different models. Industrial development in
India was not only inadequate but, more gallingly, had contributed to the persistence of poverty by forcing urbanization and eliminating traditional agrarian livelihoods. Young's notes were thick with a vivid, humanitarian narrative
of mass humanity and collective squalor: "There are so many people, so many
many people, so poor, so dirty, so diseased . . . unemployment is colossal in
India."[55] "The beggars are haunting," he remarked at another point.[56] A sense
of acute poverty, hunger, and unemployment permeated *Fifty Million Unemployed*, the fifteen-page report that Young filed with the Labour Party after his
return to Britain in 1952 and which anticipated, in the words of Lise Butler,
"the localist and communitarian turn that would characterize his work in
Bethnal Green."[57]

Fifty Million Unemployed also expressed new doubts about Keynes. "A
good many Western economists seem to have taken it almost for granted that
unemployment is a problem of the industrial countries alone," Young stated.[58]
Two of the classic works on the subject—Keynes's *General Theory of Employment, Interest and Money* and Beveridge's *Full Employment in a Free Society*—
failed to offer solutions for agrarian economies like India's: "Keynes will not
work in a bullock-cart economy."[59] Young made the case that the focus on community as the primary unit of development offered a more effective and substantial solution to mass unemployment in India: "The great questions are not
what can be done with interest rates, prices, purchasing power, or sources of
savings, but what can be done to help the peasants help themselves."[60] The
report emphasized the small-scale, associational life at the level of the family
and the village as the path to solving not only hunger and unemployment but
also "unhappiness" and misery.[61] The lessons Young learned about the emotional as well as economic role of community development in India became
critical to how he came to value the grassroots, small-scale unit of communal
and associational life in Britain. Young offered the examples of both Tagore and
Elmhirst's long development program at the Institute of Rural Reconstruction,
as well as the more nascent American-led project for community development
he saw in Etawah and Gorakhpur in Uttar Pradesh. In both cases, he argued,
"villagers have the remedy in their own hands."[62] The role of the West, and
particularly of Britain, was to offer expertise to organize such communities and
help them develop their local, cottage industries rather than to simply transfer
large funds and equipment. British socialism, he argued, had a responsibility to
facilitate such projects not only domestically but also globally.

Young's discovery of the village community in India afforded him more than an appreciation of the small group in economic life. His postcolonial travels also helped him conceive a new, global role for Britain. "There is yet a further purpose in reviving community and that is to restore hope to a world which knows too little," he later argued.[63] Young connected what he had learned in India and Pakistan to a socialist foreign policy. For Young, Britain had an ethical responsibility to facilitate community development through mutual aid. "Mutualization," a word he used in the party program in 1950 instead of "nationalization," was not only a local but also a global character of British socialism, a way to empower people "against the giant State."[64] Mutual aid shaped his work in the Consumers' Association, which he saw as a form of aid against the acquisitive society, as well as his work at the Institute for Community Development in Bethnal Green.[65] But it also offered Young a way to understand the role of British socialism globally, at the junction of the Cold War and the end of empire.

Throughout his trip to South Asia, Young was confronted by Britain's imperial legacy and its responsibility for the economic and political conditions in postindependence India and Pakistan, from Kashmir to the problem of food production. Although he embraced at no point the radical, liberational language of independence, his trip nevertheless convinced him that British socialism had an international obligation in the Cold War. "The British Labour Party had a special duty," he argued. Britain's long tradition of ethical socialism, and its emphasis on mutual aid, was what made the country a "Third Force" against the totalitarianism of the East and the individualism of the West. British socialism was to lead the decolonizing countries in a "World Plan for Mutual Aid."[66]

Young's vision for the "World Plan" was part of a broader attempt by the Labour Party to establish a socialist foreign policy agenda in the 1950s as it scrambled to garner the support of constituencies at home. It was advocated by the Labour MP and party idealogue Anthony Crosland, who called Labour to embrace a socialist project that would transcend the boundaries of the state and advance a "World Plan for Mutual Aid and a movement toward world equalisation of income."[67] The policy was in no way anticolonial but rather was aimed to fuse a socialist, Cold War agenda with the late imperial focus on development aid. The idea was to connect the new ethical emphasis on solidarity with an internationalist agenda for British primacy in a changing, decolonizing world.

Despite the lack of broad interest in colonial issues during the 1950 general election, in November 1951 the British Labour Party drafted a proposal for a socialist development policy and presented it in Vienna at the Seventh Conference of Economic Experts of the International. Initially focused on newly independent India, Pakistan, Sri Lanka, and Myanmar, the proposal was presented by British Labour in a Cold War key, as a moral project against "capitalist imperialism" and "communist imperialism."[68] "The guiding purpose of such a plan would be to help the poor help themselves, and the extension of democracy, and self-government would accompany economic progress."[69] Here "self-help" did not refer to Gandhian notions of community empowerment as much as a geopolitical, Cold War policy to secure British interests in and partnership with newly independent economies. The proposal was not exactly endorsed by Asian socialists, and the Indian Socialist Party managed to alter it, inserting a passage that expressed support and sympathy for the liberation movements in the dependent territories. The revised version was approved by the Milan Congress of the International in October 1952 and became the basis for the "Special United Nations Fund for Economic Development" in 1954–55.[70] This was one area where ideas of solidarity and mutual aid came to inform discussions both within and outside Britain about economic development and Britain's role in the world. By the 1960s, many of these ideas of mutual aid and economic development would come to shape Labour's own policy for foreign aid and would be framed as part of its "moral crusade."[71]

The Economics of Altruism

If Young represented one approach taken by British intellectuals to frame an ethical vision for British socialism that was local as well as international, his teacher Richard Titmuss, the social administrator and "ideologue of the welfare state," represented another.[72] Titmuss was never as skeptical of the state as Young and Schumacher were, but his focus on the role of altruism in welfare economics provided some of the foundations for the nongovernmental and humanitarian imaginary of the 1970s and its turn away from state-led economies. It also became the basis for lively philosophical and economic debates about the economics of altruism.

Since the 1930s Titmuss had been writing and teaching within the field of social welfare on topics such as childbirth, family planning, and health. He was closely connected to the Labour Party and even served as historian of the Cabinet Office before he took the Chair in Social Administration at the London School of Economics (LSE).[73] His work—which encompassed declining birth rates, child poverty, and, most importantly, health care—was devoted to making modern social services more equitable than the preceding system of poor law. Together with his students at the LSE, the economist Brian Abel-Smith, and the sociologist Peter Townsend, Titmuss wrote about the importance of community and social relations to the well-being of the worker and cautioned against the narrow economism of industrial life.[74]

In the early 1960s, Titmuss became particularly critical of approaches that limited welfare economics to the metrics of GNP growth. In the famous study *The Poor and the Poorest*, Townsend and Abel-Smith had shown that, despite the promise of affluence, the number of those in poverty had risen in Britain from 4 to 7.5 million between 1953 and 1960.[75] In the United States, similar research showed that "two nations," one rich and one poor, coexisted in a country with "the highest standard of life the world has ever known."[76] For Titmuss, the rediscovery of poverty in Britain and the United States proved that the single-minded Keynesian focus on GNP failed to account for increasing disparities in income distribution. In his 1962 *Income Distribution and Social Change*, Titmuss demonstrated that, due to strategies of tax evasion, rising incomes in Britain had increased inequality and ended up benefiting only a few. Promoting GNP growth over social "needs," he emphasized, not only failed to promote welfare but was detrimental to it.[77] " 'Welfare statism,' managed economies and economic growth have made little impression on the holding of great fortunes in at least two of the largest industrial nations, the United States and Britain, and similar trends are probably in operation in de Gaulle's France and Erhard's Germany," he argued in 1965.[78]

But Titmuss did not think of the problem of welfare solely within a domestic context or even as an exclusively Anglo-American one. Like Young, Titmuss's ideas were shaped by the global politics of decolonization. He was particularly attuned to the growing material connections between Britain and its former colonies, especially because of skyrocketing immigration from the Commonwealth. Although shocked that eight million people lived in poverty in Britain, Titmuss also highlighted increasing domestic racial tensions in the aftermath of the 1958 Notting Hill race riots, where white working-class residents attacked Afro-Caribbean migrants. Coupled with increasing calls for political and economic independence from the decolonizing world, these events made Titmuss acutely aware that notions of community were themselves changing. Consequently, "welfare" required attention to matters of social cohesion well beyond merely growing the GNP. "What makes this problem of redistribution such a formidable challenge," he claimed, was that in places like Britain and the United States social and civil rights were "mixed up" in multiethnic communities.[79] The metrics of growth had given the false promise of equality for all, but the market alone could not "resolve the problem of ethnic integration and accommodation."[80] Titmuss sought to formulate a vision of welfare that could meet the needs not only of white working-class communities in England but also of ethnic minorities and people of color who had been excluded from welfare systems in both Britain and the United States. This, in turn, required a shift in social policy "from *ad hoc* programs to integrated social rights, from economic growth to social growth."[81]

Drawing on the ideas of T. H. Marshall, Titmuss mobilized the idea of "social rights" to describe welfare as a universal right of all citizens in the nation, a type of right comparable to—yet nonetheless distinct from—civil, political, and even human rights.[82] For Titmuss, social rights were a type of normative value judgment that exceeded utilitarian economic calculations and made welfare services into an instrument for forging solidarity between every individual in society. The welfare state thus had an ethical mandate to promote "community, integration and equality."[83] In turn, the extension of social rights would be for all members of society, including "the politically obscure" ethnic minorities,[84] and would promote altruistic duties between them. In so doing, Titmuss believed, the welfare state would promote democratic values and moral leadership within Britain and the world.

Titmuss suggested that in its present state of affluence, British society had a responsibility to facilitate solidarity at home and abroad. "More of us, as individuals, can now afford to be moral in our attitude to the great problems of world inequality and racial intolerance," he wrote; "our society should set examples for the younger generation in moral leadership and higher standards of social responsibility."[85] Titmuss's international approach to welfare was informed by his work at the LSE and as an advisor on welfare in the Third World and in the United States. In the 1950s, Titmuss established the first course in Britain on development administration. Based on this experience, he later served as an external examiner for a new degree in social administration at Makerere University College in Uganda. In the late 1950s, Titmuss was also asked by the governor of Mauritius (when it was still a British colony) to help advise on a family planning program during an unemployment crisis in the country.[86]

These experiences further shaped his thinking about welfare. "We can no longer consider welfare systems solely within the limited framework of the nation state," he wrote in 1967, because "what we do or fail to do in changing systems of welfare affects other countries besides ourselves." He framed the problem of distribution in social policy in a transnational and comparative perspective, thinking of welfare, migration, and labor in the global North and South. A "Welfare Society," he suggested, could provide aid to "the poorer nations" by training doctors, nurses, social workers, and scientists.[87] His internationalist vision was not unlike his friend Gunnar Myrdal's notion of a "welfare world," although—shaped in the context of the late British empire—it was rife with paternalism.[88] Titmuss suggested that as a decolonizing metropole and a leader in welfare and health services, Britain's welfare state had the moral duty to help establish welfare systems across its former empire. The British welfare state therefore had a late imperial and even postimperial ethical role to play in international relations.

During the 1960s, Titmuss had two exchanges with newly independent countries that helped him solidify some of these ideas. The first was in Tanzania, where he traveled to advise on building its health services. Against large modernization schemes, Titmuss emphasized the importance of creating "a health service . . . which will not be separate and aloof from the life of the nation but an expression and reinforcement of national unity."[89] The report he wrote after his first visit to the country became the basis for a community development project run by Dartington Hall during the 1960s.[90] Additionally, Titmuss formed a working relationship with the anticolonial activist and Tanzanian prime minister Julius Nyerere while the latter was working on his own village-based vision for socialism. Their exchange, Titmuss reported, was "most stimulating," and he personally received from Nyerere a copy of the Arusha Declaration and other related documents.[91] One historian has even suggested that Titmuss's work had a major effect on Nyerere, who used his colleague's ideas to redesign social and health services in rural Tanzania in support of his villagization project.[92]

Concurrently, Titmuss also helped set up welfare services in Israel. During this decade, Israel was transitioning its own welfare services from an informal system managed mostly by German Jewish migrants, the majority of them women, to a more formal health-care and social security system overseen almost exclusively by male experts.[93] Titmuss's advice and collaboration had a profound effect on the country's welfare discourse which, at least in rhetoric, embraced a language of equality in welfare, ethics, and redistribution. Titmuss developed a special relationship with the Israeli Zionist left and especially with Itzhak Kanev, the founder of the Israeli health-care system. He visited the country four times (including some of its kibbutzim communities) and even met two of Israel's prime ministers, Levi Eshkol and Golda Meir. Some Israelis, like the former Israeli minister of labor and social affairs Israel Katz, considered him a special ally of the "Jewish people, who based on their own suffering, discrimination and socio-political injustices were prone to build a more just society in either West or East."[94] Titmuss's archives remain silent on his own feeling toward the "Jewish people," but he did have a sense of Israel as "a society brimming with opportunity," according to one of his biographers.[95] In the preface to the translation of his book *The Gift Relationship*, he wrote that "Israel, like many new countries around the world, is still young, still struggling to avoid the mistakes of others; still searching for the generous path to social justice. It is my belief that the idea of the 'social man' would prosper and grow in Israel, based on what I have learned in my four visits in the country and the many friendships I have forged in it."[96] Titmuss saw Israel as an emerging nation comparable to other postcolonial nations, potentially an excellent venue for implementing new, ethically driven welfare policies. Nowhere did he mention, however, what that model would look like for the country's Israeli Palestinian population or for the Palestinian population in the occupied West Bank after 1967.

Overall, Titmuss's ideas linked him to a broad transatlantic conversation about the role of altruism in markets, one that responded directly to the challenge of postwar ideological polarization. Perhaps his most influential argument in the 1960s was made in the context of a comparison of British and American health-care services. It was a critical juncture for both countries. In the United States, President Lyndon Johnson was launching his War on

Poverty and expanding the nation's social security system with the Medicare Bill of 1965.[97] In Britain, the Guillebaud Report of the Committee of Enquiry into the cost of the National Health Service (NHS) at its tenth anniversary praised the NHS and called for greater investment in it.[98] The decade saw a broader turn in welfare policies toward transfer payment, fusing tax policies with welfare benefits.[99]

In 1971, Titmuss published his last and most widely read work, *The Gift Relationship*, in which he compared voluntary blood donation in Britain with the commercialized donor system of the United States. For Titmuss, blood donation raised crucial questions about altruism and economics. It arose, he wrote, "from a series of value questions formulated within the context of attempts to distinguish the 'social' from the 'economic' in public policies and in those institutions and services with declared 'welfare' goals."[100] Although he did not systematically follow economic theories, Titmuss used economic concepts to argue that Britain's altruistic model of blood donations was statistically more successful and more effective than the commercialized American system. Altruism involves self-love, as social theorists suggested, but it is also a generator of "economic wealth," Titmuss stressed.[101] The commercialization of blood, moreover, posed a high risk to society as a whole because it encouraged donations on the basis of monetary rewards rather than communal solidarities. Titmuss, for example, showed that the commercialized system had higher rates of infections such as hepatitis B because it encouraged donations from residents of poorer neighborhoods. The commercialized system, in other words, generated negative externalities—the effects of commercial transactions on third parties.[102] Moreover, the commercialization of blood also restricted positive externalities that would arise from acts of solidarity.

The Gift Relationship emerged from a hostile exchange between Titmuss and the Institute for Economic Affairs (IEA), a neoliberal British think tank, and was written against what he described as "the theories of private social policy."[103] It was meant as a direct response to the neoliberal ideas of choice in welfare advanced by the IEA and the American neoliberal Milton Friedman, both of whom are cited repeatedly in the book. For Titmuss, the entire "myth of consumer sovereignty" advanced by neoliberal thinkers was based on false assumptions. "In commercial blood markets the consumer is not a king," Titmuss declared. "Far from being sovereign, he is often exploited."[104]

Responding to what he saw as the failure of market systems to provide basic protections, Titmuss used the case of blood donation to mark a broader point central to his work: that market economies could only work in conjunction with policies protecting "uneconomic" commitments to social rights and altruistic solidarity. As he later explained, the case study of blood donations was about altruism and welfare as much as it was about "the definition of freedom."[105] The role of the welfare state was to secure these social bonds, stimulate ethical behavior between strangers, and protect them against nega-tive externalities. It offered citizens the "Right to Give" to "unnamed strangers," an important liberty neglected by free marketeers. The welfare state, he argued, was founded on a mutual sense of reciprocity as much as it was on trust among strangers. This was an important and controversial intervention in mainstream economic thought, which distinguished between unselfishness in the family and selfishness in the marketplace. In contrast, Titmuss claimed that impersonal forms of altruism offered a more efficient working of the mar-ket. The welfare state therefore had the duty to protect the "Right to Give" in order to secure the workings of an economy of strangers.

Like an array of economists and political philosophers writing in the con-text of Cold War polarization, Titmuss argued that the exclusive focus on mar-kets and productivity had left even welfare capitalism without an ethical core. Consequently, the economic calculus must be shaped by external principles "set to universalize humanistic ethics and the social rights of citizenship." Fol-lowing Karl Polanyi, Titmuss was wary of "disembedding" the economy from social relations, thereby allowing market rationality to dictate all human ends.[106] He called for a new social policy "unrelated to the productivity princi-ple" that would encourage reciprocity and altruism.[107] In addition to provid-ing material equality, the welfare state had a social responsibility to foster organic community and to forge solidarity among its members.[108]

The Gift Relationship became a bestseller in Britain and the United States and was widely read among politicians, economists, and intellectuals.[109] In a favorable review of the book, Robert Solow, one of the primary economists in the United States associated with the GNP growth model, wrote, "There is a lesson here for everyone interested in social policy, because some economists do have a way of drifting into sharp propositions that cannot be fully sup-ported even on narrowly economic grounds."[110] *The Gift Relationship* joined a broader shift within the fields of economics and moral philosophy toward analyses of solidarity in economics. Throughout the decade, economists on both sides of the Atlantic turned to thinking about the contribution of philan-thropy and altruism to welfare economics. American economists like the British-born Kenneth Boulding—whom Titmuss cited in the book and who would come to be most closely associated with environmental economics—as well as economists with such diverse approaches as Gary Becker and William Vickery developed theories aimed at understanding the economic benefits of unselfish behavior and the role of philanthropic foundations in welfare eco-nomics.[111] By 1968, Boulding went so far as to suggest that "there is a minimum degree of benevolence" in every economic exchange, implying that economics itself might be a moral science.[112]

The Gift Relationship also shaped thinking about markets and altruism in the realm of political philosophy. In 1972, a year after the book's publication, philosophers and economists came together at the Russell Sage Foundation in Manhattan to discuss Titmuss's book as part of a symposium on the economics of altruism organized by the economist Edmund Phelps.[113] Among the contributions to that symposium was a paper by the social choice theorist Kenneth Arrow, who had recently published a review of *The Gift Relationship* in *Philosophy and Public Affairs*.[114] While accepting some of his claims, Arrow disagreed fundamentally with Titmuss over the role of altruism in delivering public goods. For over a decade Arrow had been thinking about the relationship between individual choice, social judgment, and the common good. His main intervention in welfare economics, what came to be called the "Impossibility Theorem," was to show that individual choices—or for that matter virtues—could not determine public utility or collective good.[115] For Arrow, welfare economics should include external ethical criteria that would be independent of personal interest, although the conclusions of his thesis had neoconservative implications about the legitimacy of participant democracy, as it mistrusted the individual citizen (what came to be called the "paradox of democracy").[116] Responding to Arrow, the philosopher Thomas Nagel, a student of John Rawls, posited an alternative critique: Titmuss was too quick to associate altruism with a feeling. Both Nagel and Rawls drew upon the idea that altruism was, in fact, a rational stance that recognized one's status "as merely another inhabitant of the world."[117] This, indeed, was the core idea of Rawls's—and later Nagel's—attempt to reestablish American political philosophy during the Cold War. While paralleling Titmuss's concerns for moral regeneration, Rawls and Nagel suggested that, far from a sentiment of social solidarity, altruism was what allowed economic and social life to function efficiently.[118]

But there were other philosophers who agreed with Titmuss's conclusions about the economics of altruism and sought to spread them beyond the national community, with profound effects for thinking about solidarity and giving into the present. In the 1970s, Titmuss's argument about the "Right to Give" joined a broader discussion about moral obligations toward strangers in a global community.[119] In 1973, for instance, the moral philosopher Peter Singer responded to Arrow's review of *The Gift Relationship*, offering a strong defense of Titmuss's thesis. He stated that "the nature of a community's blood supply cannot be considered a purely economic issue."[120] When Singer picked up Titmuss's book, he was already engaged in thinking about moral obligations and duties. For him, altruism and morality more broadly were innate parts of our structure of feeling. Drawing on a series of biological and psychological studies, he argued that altruism was a mental disposition.[121] The introduction of monetary exchanges closed any possibilities for the exchange of "fellow-feeling." By contrast, Singer suggested, "a voluntary system fosters attitudes of altruism and a desire to relate to, and help, strangers in one's community."[122] Singer's adaptation of Titmuss's thesis placed the idea of the solidarity economy within a tradition of individual charity.

Singer's famous essay "Famine, Affluence, and Morality," published in 1972, made the case for extending altruism to aid strangers beyond one's political community. Singer argued that "the development of the world into a 'global village' has made an important, though still unrecognized, difference to our moral situation."[123] There was no moral difference, he argued, between feeling compelled to help our neighbor's child who lives "ten yards from me or a Bengali whose name I shall never know, ten thousand miles away."[124] Moral duties were no longer confined to specific geographies or borders because we have the technologies and the means to reach faraway places. Written in response to the famine in East Bengal, in the aftermath of a series of natural disasters and on the eve of the creation of Bangladesh, Singer's essay proposed a new moral imperative: "if it is in our power to prevent something bad from happening without thereby sacrificing anything of comparable moral importance . . . we ought, morally, to do it."[125] "Without sacrifice" remained a somewhat ambiguous and open-ended qualification, but Singer aimed to offer a utilitarian minimum that would apply to individuals as much as it would to governments and institutions.

According to Singer, the obligation of individuals in affluent nations to act globally through proliferating networks of NGOs and voluntary associations was so strong that to do nothing was the moral equivalent of murder. "If, then, allowing someone to die is not intrinsically different from killing someone," Singer wrote, "it would seem that we are all murderers."[126] This meant that individuals—and not just governments—were all implicated within or liable for the persistence of absolute poverty. To act was not a charitable impulse but a moral obligation. What had for Titmuss been part of the infrastructure of welfare communities and a social right was for Singer an ethical imperative toward a global community represented in the work of British nongovernmental organizations. By the 1970s, Titmuss's call for an ethical framework for welfare, and his critique of pure economism, was embraced by many nongovernmental activists and aid workers who, like Singer, read it as part of an ethical imperative of individuals toward a global community. His economics of altruism became part of their ethical basis of development aid.

People-Centered Economics

"To say that our economic future is being determined by the economists would be an exaggeration; but that their influence, or in any case the influence of economics, is far-reaching can hardly be doubted." So wrote Schumacher in 1968. According to him, the problem with economics was that it divided the world into "economic" and "uneconomic" domains. He argued that "there is no other set of criteria that exercises a greater influence over the action of individuals and groups as well as over those governments."[127] From the late 1950s onward, Schumacher called for the overthrow of prevailing economic thought through an economics focused on social solidarity and local community.

Schumacher's moral critique of the economy paralleled contemporaneous debates about welfare economics. It emphasized the importance of solidarity and self-help in organizing economic life; social over material growth; and the grassroots role of the community. But unlike Young's and Titmuss's, Schumacher's critique emerged not only from welfare thinking but from the new field of development economics. While not himself trained in the field, Schumacher became one of its most ardent critics, decrying the fact that economic development was confined to the Western, industrialized model, one rooted in modernization theory and GNP growth. As one economist phrased it, Schumacher formulated an economic critique of "modernity, inspired by a deep skepticism of the entire Western idea of science, industry, and progress."[128] He called for a more humane model, one in which development would nourish social and environmental relationships.

Schumacher was an unlikely candidate to become a prophet of the antistatism of the 1970s. Born in Bonn in 1911, the son of a German political economist, he was trained in a classical, liberal economic tradition. Like his contemporary the development economist Hans Singer, he studied with Joseph Schumpeter at the University of Bonn. In 1937, Schumacher emigrated to Britain, although he had already formed important connections in the country through his year abroad at the LSE (where he took a class with Harold Laski) and in Oxford as a Rhodes scholar. There he met Dennis Robertson and A. C. Pigou, among others. Perhaps most importantly, Schumacher befriended Keynes, who invited him to Cambridge to attend his Political Economy Club and left a profound mark on him. "A man of genius," Schumacher called Keynes in an obituary he wrote for *The Times* in 1946.[129] So close was their intellectual connection that Schumacher famously wrote a paper about international clearing even before Keynes wrote his own proposal for an International Clearing Union.[130] Though the young Schumacher gestured toward the global economy, his early thinking was centered on the state and developed economies.[131]

Though a foreigner in Britain, Schumacher nonetheless belonged to the economic elite. In the late 1930s, he became friends with David Astor, the heir of the Astor fortune and eventually the editor of the *Observer*, who helped him get a job in 1940 and later a position at *The Times*. He also invited him to the Shanghai Club, a discussion group Astor organized and where Schumacher met economists and progressive journalists like Geoffrey Crowther and Barbara Ward.[132] Schumacher also worked at the Institute of Statistics and as a colonel with the Allied Control Commission in Germany. A Fabian and Labour Party member, Schumacher was invited in 1943 to work with William Beveridge alongside Nicholas Kaldor, Joan Robinson, and Barbara Wootton on *Full Employment in a Free Society* (1944). By 1950, Hugh Gaitskell had recommended him as the economic advisor to the National Coal Board, a post that Schumacher held until his retirement in 1971. In 1963, Schumacher became its director of statistics and in 1967 its chief of planning. He was, as one Conservative MP called him, "a perfectly orthodox Fabian."[133] It is an apt characterization, but it cannot convey the complexity of Schumacher's views.

To some degree, Schumacher's thinking was shaped by his personal experience of World War II. Schumacher was probably a utopian even before the war, working on various "world improvement plans," but the war forced him out of his routine intellectual engagements and challenged him to forgo some of his privileges, at least temporarily. As an enemy alien, Schumacher had to shelter in London before he was interned in the summer of 1940, and he spent several months in Prees Heath, a temporary internment camp in Shropshire. He read Marx and Tawney—the latter having a tremendous influence on his thinking about ethics and socialism. When he was released from the camp in late 1940, he worked as a farm laborer, a position that was "an important formative experience," according to his daughter.[134] He came to connect his "newly acquired left-wing ideas" with agricultural policies and became interested in the organic movement.[135] He also joined the Soil Association, which would eventually have an important influence on his environmental thought. When after eighteen months he concluded his work on the farm, he declared, "I should much rather be a farmer than an economist. The trouble is that I am not a farmer (and have no farm) but an economist." The experience was "not merely an episode but a turning point."[136] Thirty years later, he would still draw lessons from what he had learned at the farm about development, agriculture, and technology.[137]

As late as the 1940s, however, Schumacher remained committed to centralized planning, demand-side economics, and Keynesian macroeconomics. He saw British socialism, fusing economic planning and individual freedoms, as the best application of "Western Politics and Eastern Economics" and as the model for postwar European reconstruction, especially in West Germany. For him, Beveridge's *Full Employment* represented the right balance between "planning and freedom." He was not without criticisms: echoing Tawney, he later admitted he would have "liked Beveridge to have taken an even wider view of the matter" and to include in his planning "not merely the old issues of efficiency, enterprise, and social justice" but also "a new and wider issue—the value of the individual human personality."[138] Schumacher nevertheless called for the full embrace of British socialism, one that combined personal liberties and freedoms with socialist economic planning.[139]

It was in the 1950s, after he joined the National Coal Board (NCB) as its chief economic advisor, that Schumacher began to turn away from state-led economies. He joined the NCB at a crucial time for the industry. Coal was at the heart of what one historian called Britain's "developmental state."[140] It was the basis of Britain's electrification project—from heating houses and powering washing machines to fueling trains and industries—and was viewed as key to modernizing the national economy.[141] Created under Attlee's government in 1946, the NCB was tasked with making the industry more efficient and promised "great economies" through modernizing investment and redeploying labor.[142] It rationalized the industry, closed unproductive pits, redeployed labor, and invested in new technology.[143] It was the capstone of national ownership.

Throughout Schumacher's tenure, however, the NCB was regularly pressed to defend its existence. Many of its Conservative and Labour opponents argued that the NCB could not keep up with demand or offer a reasonable price to the consumer. To be sure, in the 1950s coal remained king "despite the best effort of planners."[144] But from the mid-1950s, when the NCB had to import coal from Europe, the Conservative government called for the replacement of coal by oil, gas, and nuclear energy.[145] Market competition was a key objective for the minister of power, Geoffrey Lloyd, who had a background in oil administration. In 1955, he addressed Parliament on a coal price increase, portraying it as "the most powerful stroke for fuel efficiency since the war."[146] The Fleck Committee, responsible for assessing the industry's productivity and the NCB's work in managing it, suggested that "the industry at large continues to lack true cost consciousness" and that "the colliery manager has been taught how to mine, but not how to manage."[147] The approach of the Labour government that came to power by 1964 was not much different. While it was much more sympathetic to the claims of the National Union of Mineworkers, it nonetheless continued to shrink its workforce, close mines, and move to supplementing coal with oil, natural gas, and nuclear power. Coal was seen by many as an expensive, inefficient source of energy. Oil was promoted as a cheaper, more efficient alternative. Its relative abundance, and the ease with which it was shipped from the wells and pipelines of the Middle East, created an impression of inexhaustible energy. As the political theorist Timothy Mitchell has put it, oil "contributed to the new conception of the economy as an object that could grow without limit in several ways."[148] This vision of limitless growth—measured by GNP—was thus at the heart of both Keynesianism and neoliberalism.

During the 1950s and 1960s, Schumacher was an ardent defender of the NCB against both free traders and what he saw as crude applications of Keynesianism. Nevertheless, his support of the board's mandate in turn shifted his views on economic planning. What Schumacher learned at the NCB was that the economics of extractive industries, and especially of nonrenewable resources, were substantially different from those of manufacturing industries and required different metrics. At the same time, the dependence of manufacturing industries on extractive industries required an economy that would be organized on long-term planning and limited expansion rather than infinite growth and profit. Such planning needed to reconcile the different time frames of manufacturing and extractive industries: you "can build a new factory or refinery in two or three years. But you cannot develop a new colliery, or reconstruct an old one in that period," he argued.[149] Within the economics of extractive industries, he suggested, the NCB had been doing "more constructive and enterprising work" than ever before.[150]

In the late 1950s, Schumacher further developed this view. Counter to visions of infinite growth, nonrenewable resources required planners to pay attention to "uneconomic" factors such as "the problem of conservation."[151] They also necessitated different forecasting models, "looking much further ahead than would normally be required."[152] Conservation, in fact, became a major part of his economic thinking. In the early 1960s, Schumacher warned of the problem of depleting natural resources.[153] "Nature's deposits of concentrated carbon are a unique and irreplaceable bounty," he intoned in a speech to the NCB. He asked his audience to understand that such resources are "a once-for-all endowment to mankind to ease its task of living, and that no generation has the right to abandon and ruin any of them for the sake of a small, fleeting convivence."[154]

A major part of Schumacher's economic critique at the NCB was his opposition to the introduction of oil as a cheap alternative to coal. While he acknowledged that coal could not be the sole source of Britain's energy, Schumacher argued that oil only gave the illusion of being a cheap resource with limitless abundance. In practice, as an imported commodity, oil "impose[d] severe strain on the balance of payments of the United Kingdom."[155] What looked like a low-cost commodity was, in reality, a bad investment. The expenditure of foreign exchange on oil imports, he suggested, would continue to burden the balance of payments. More than a decade before the 1973 oil crisis, Schumacher warned against dependency on an imported resource that was based in the Middle East, "politically the most unstable part of the world."[156] Furthermore, its foundation was an economic model that did not account for the depletion of energy resources or for residual growth; economists measured only the accumulation of capital and labor, which in the case of oil was relatively low. The economics of oil—and for that matter nuclear energy—were based on a mismeasurement of progress that did not account for its extraction, depletion, and environmental consequences.[157] Schumacher came to the conclusion that the discipline of economics "fails to study meta-economics" and *"man's dependence on the natural world."*[158]

Through his work at the NCB Schumacher came to reflect on the project of public ownership. While he had already been thinking about the question of ownership during his days working with Beveridge on *Full Employment*, the work at the NCB challenged Schumacher to develop his ideas especially in light of threats of cuts to public spending in the mid-1950s. His own defense of public ownership moved away from prevailing Keynesian ideas, drawing again on the work of Tawney. "The idea of efficiency," Schumacher wrote in

1958, "is meaningful only in relation to one's purposes. If one's purpose is simply to make money, one's efficiency can be gauged directly from the profit and loss account."[159] Echoing Tawney's *Acquisitive Society* (1921), Schumacher argued that efficiency could only be meaningful if considered as part of a broader moral order.[160] Although Schumacher believed that the NCB should still seek to generate a profit, he nonetheless argued that it had additional economic considerations beyond the characteristics of private business. The NCB's mandate, he noted repeatedly, was "to further the national interest in all respect[s]."[161] This meant calculating "social consideration[s]," such as protecting full employment and delivering coal to the public, over profit, even if at a loss for the board. There is "really no strong case for public ownership if the objectives to be pursued by nationalized industry are to be just as narrow, just as limited as those of capitalist production. . . . Economics and the standard of living can just as well be looked after by a capitalist system, moderated by a bit of Keynesian planning and redistributive taxation."[162] What made the project of public ownership different was that it offered "a more democratic and dignified system of industrial administration, a more humane employment of machinery, and a more intelligent utilization of the fruits of human ingenuity and effort."[163] Schumacher's time at the NCB had cemented his move from Keynes to the ethical economy.

If Schumacher's work at the NCB challenged him to question some of the basic assumptions of centralized planning, it was his experience working as an economic advisor in the newly independent economies of Burma in 1955 and India in 1959 that afforded him with an alternative. In Burma, and later in India, Schumacher formulated his ethical critique of economics, one that would emphasize decentralization and the local community, as well as economic organization from the grassroots rather than the state. He forged his ideas in response to his encounter with the new field of development economics and its application of Keynesian ideas. He had already been reading some works of Traditionalists like Ananda Coomaraswamy and became familiar with Eastern philosophers like Gurdjieff and Buddhism, but in South Asia he learned about Gandhian economics and its vision of economic organization.[164] Their ideas led Schumacher to reformulate his own ideas about labor, centralized planning, and public ownership, arriving at the vision that would influence NGOs in the 1970s.

Schumacher was in South Asia during the heyday of state-led development. During the "Age of Economic Development," as Eugene Black, the president of the World Bank, called it, both international and bilateral aid programs defined their goals vis-à-vis the growth of the newly independent national economies in African and South Asian states.[165] Economic development originated in the interwar period (if not before), when the British, and later French, imperial states began a series of campaigns in South Asia and Africa to support the metropolitan economy during a time of economic crisis.

After World War II, economic development was appropriated by African independence movements and incorporated into the vocabulary of the post-colonial state. In the 1950s, the successes and failures of the welfare and developmentalist states were measured and compared by the same national metric, the GNP. By December 1961, GNP growth became an official target of the United Nations. The goal of the UN's First Development Decade, as it came to be called, was a minimum annual growth rate of 5 percent in aggregate national income.[166] The UN General Assembly called on all member states to accelerate progress toward self-sustaining economic growth and social advancement in the developing countries.

Schumacher's visit to Burma had convinced him that this orthodoxy was wrong. He initially arrived there in 1954, as economic advisor to the Burmese government under the auspices of the United Nations' Technical Assistance Administration. The purpose of the appointment was to advise Burma "on economic policies to facilitate the balanced expansion of economic activity contemplated under the Government's development plans."[167] In particular, Schumacher was tasked with assessing the development plans put forward by a group of American economists and consultants at the World Bank. The plans were extensive. In line with many development programs at the time, they focused on modernization and industrialization, aiming to triple the size of the economy by 1960.[168]

Schumacher was deeply skeptical. In his report he declared such ambitions rife with "unnecessary complications and harmful simplifications."[169] In his private correspondence with his wife he was even more blunt: the American experts were all "materialists without any understanding for the precious heritage of a Buddhist country."[170] As he would later recall, "within a few weeks of my arrival in Rangoon and after visiting a few villages and towns, I realised that the Burmese needed little advice from a Western economist like me. In fact, we Western economists could learn a thing or two from the Burmese."[171] Schumacher began considering a different development model that would not be based on a Western experience of industrialization and would suit newly independent Asian (and later African) economies.

Schumacher was not alone in searching for alternative models of development. From the 1960s onward, he was joined by a group of economists, activists, and intellectuals who pointed to the limits of GNP growth as the best measure of economic development. By the late 1960s, these "growth critics," as the historian Stephen Macekura calls them, formed an alternative to mainstream development thinking.[172] They suggested measuring other parameters—like employment or ecological sustainability—as indicators of economic progress. Economists like Ezra Mishan argued against the costs of economic growth in terms of social welfare and environmental degradation.[173] Others, like the economist Dudley Seers and his colleagues Hans Singer and Richard Jolly at the Institute of Development Studies, which knew and collaborated with Schumacher, focused on the problems of employment, poverty, and inequality and the meeting of "basic needs"—a humanitarian minimum—as alternative targets for development programs. These critics argued that growth had not led to the reduction of poverty and had, moreover, contributed to high unemployment rates because it was concentrated in "relatively limited parts of the economy, mostly those using capital-intensive techniques."[174] By the early 1970s, their findings became the basis of the "basic-needs" approach, which came to define the work of aid agencies like the World Bank and the International Labour Organization.[175]

But Schumacher's critique differed in key ways from those of the growth critics. For him, the problem with economic development was not only its manner of measuring progress. A developmental approach also lacked a clear sense of ethics. In Burma, Schumacher had undergone a spiritual transformation alongside an intellectual one. For one, Schumacher's host, Minister of National Planning and Religious Affairs U Win, introduced him to Buddhism, and he had attended the sixth Buddhist Congress in Rangoon. Schumacher also embraced yoga and practiced Vipassana with U Ba Khin, formerly the accountant general of Burma and a meditation master and founder of the International Meditation Centre. His spiritual transformation extended beyond Buddhism to reading the Gospels. It was also in Burma that he first extensively explored the writings of Gandhi, whom he termed "the greatest man of our age." It was through Gandhi that he learned that there was not "a sharp or any distinction between economics and ethics."[176] This transformation took Schumacher well beyond the critiques covered by his contemporaries.

In February 1955, Schumacher drafted an essay based on what he had learned from his Burmese experience. He argued against the idea of "one size fits all" in economic development. A diatribe against "*the* 'science' of Economics" and its "materialist" approach, the essay suggested that even "welfare" itself was "a term rooted within materialism—although [in] a slightly more subtle fashion."[177] Against the primacy of economic expertise, Schumacher proposed a new approach to economic development, which he called "Buddhist economics."[178]

Schumacher's "Buddhist economics" highlighted that economic development should draw from Gandhian and Buddhist philosophies, especially their emphasis on organizing economic life around the village community. Fused with skepticism about the authority of the economic expert, "Buddhist economics" would become the foundation of the nongovernmental imaginary in the 1970s. Instead of big modernization programs focused on high industry, heavy technology, and massive infrastructure, Schumacher's "Buddhist economics" emphasized sustainable models of development rooted in cottage industries, indigenous manufacturing, and small-scale farming. It aimed to empower local communities to define the ends of their own development.

Schumacher's development model drew, in particular, on Gandhi's ideas of "swadeshi" and "khaddar," and it emphasized the dignity of indigenous manufacturing.[179] Swadeshi was a "religious principle" as much as an economic one. It called for the revival of local, indigenous, and small-scale industries over centralized ones, promoting investment in things produced nearby rather than in large-scale national markets. Khaddar—handspun garment production—fulfilled the kind of service envisaged in swadeshi. It represented the decentralization of both the production and distribution of the necessities of life. Politically and historically, both swadeshi and khaddar became connected to "swaraj," or self-rule. Both ideas had developed as part of the Indian anticolonial movement earlier in the century and included not only the valorization of indigenous handicrafts but also the boycott of foreign commodities.[180]

In Schumacher's reading, however, swadeshi and khaddar were more ethical and economic concepts than political ones. They offered rich possibilities for the entire field of economic development because labor, industry, and capital were not reduced to their materialist value; they were embedded within the dignity of social life. Schumacher's "Buddhist economics" thus navigated a "middle way" between economic progress and self-help. Such a path, Schumacher hoped, would fortify local communities instead of promoting "the growth of a rootless proletariat."[181] In the 1970s these ideas would become particularly important for the transnational fair trade of food and handicraft programs run by British nongovernmental organizations, as well as for Schumacher's concept of "intermediate technology."

By the late 1950s, Schumacher had developed his Buddhist economics further as he learned more about Indian anticolonialism. In 1959, he discovered Bhoodan, or rather the welfare movement "Sarvodaya" of which it was a part. Sarvodaya was an anticolonial and, importantly, antistatist movement led by Vinoba Bhave, one of Gandhi's pupils. It sought the collective uplift of village communities without state intervention, relying instead on donations of money, labor, and skills.[182] Sarvodaya inspired a new form of grassroots development based in the village. The model was adopted not only across India but globally: from Israel to West Germany and Australia. Its philosophy fit well with Schumacher's own "Buddhist economics" and reinforced ideas he had gleaned from his experience at the NCB. It offered him an alternative to public ownership, one that encouraged decentralization and grassroots solidarities. For Bhave, the village rather than the state was the central unit of development. Consequently, his economic models avoided the abstractions that Schumacher saw in the Keynesian project while nonetheless maintaining its commitment to community welfare and economic progress.

Schumacher's experience in Burma won him an invitation to join a group of British journalists and activists who had worked in India in the 1950s, the British Bhoodan campaign. The movement was mostly symbolic, but it helped bring together two types of nongovernmental activism aimed at importing Gandhian ideas of Sarvodaya to Britain. The first type was an international collaboration between Bhoodan and the War on Want, a British NGO with which Schumacher had been involved from its founding in 1951 and would become important for the experiments in ethical capitalism of the 1970s.[183] The organization had already been active in forging an alternative to mainstream liberal humanitarian charities like Save the Children. In the late 1950s, it launched an international grassroots program led by the British Quaker and Gandhian activist Donald Groom, who was also a key figure in setting up the British Bhoodan movement.[184] Groom had been living in India for more than a decade and had known Gandhi, Bhave, Tagore, Nehru, and Jayaprakash Narayan. He was particularly influenced by Bhave and saw a close connection between his own Quaker faith and the Sarvodaya philosophy.[185] For Groom, the collaboration between War on Want and the Indian Bhoodan movement encouraged "sharing between the economically developed and underdeveloped nations and as a means of promoting understanding between the peoples of the United Kingdom and India." Bhave himself reportedly declared on several occasions that the War on Want program had given practical shape to his concept of "Jai Jagat," or universal good.[186] At an abstract level, the idea of nongovernmental organization meshed well with the Bhoodan ideals of village-based development. In practice, activists like Groom proposed aiding and funding Bhoodan initiatives such as the cooperative, village-based agro-industrial development work of the Agrindus project, for which Schumacher would become a consultant in the 1960s. Such aid included technical support, education, and small-scale machinery for farming, as well as the "Adopt a Village Scheme," which invited British citizens to directly support an Indian village in order to "spring one community" through donations that went to technical education and farming.[187]

The Bhoodan campaign in Britain also helped connect Schumacher with Ernest Bader and his development initiatives across the Third World. Bader was a Swiss-born Quaker and an entrepreneur who, like Donald Groom, was influenced by Gandhian ideas about swadeshi and Sarvodaya and saw a connection between his own Quaker pacifism and Gandhi's philosophy. In 1951, Bader decided to gift his own successful chemical manufacturing company, Scott Bader Ltd., to his employees. The cooperative enterprise Scott Bader Commonwealth became the first collectively owned private enterprise to seek a "third way" for capitalism, in which industrial relationships were egalitarian and where labor employed capital.[188] After Bader gave his company away, he attempted to globalize some of its experience and create "a world government" of new industrial relations. To that end, together with the radical Labour MP Wilfred Wellock he founded the Association for the Democratic Integration of Industry (Demintry), aimed at globalizing the idea of common ownership. It was this experience that led him in the late 1950s to join the British Bhoodan campaign and to become friends with Schumacher, who joined Demintry. As we will see in chapter 5, their friendship was crucial for the development of ideas about corporate social responsibility in the 1960s and a nongovernmental organization that would aim to facilitate it.

Importantly, through the Bhoodan campaign, Schumacher met with the Indian independence activist and Gandhi student Jayaprakash Narayan, who invited him in the late 1950s to join the Gandhian Institute of Studies in Varanasi, which Narayan founded to fuse Gandhian thought and the modern social sciences. In India, and through his collaboration with Narayan, Schumacher developed his "Buddhist economics" further, reading the works of Indian economists like J. C. Kumarappa and D. R. Gadgil and meeting Nehru, who prompted him to think even further about alternative models of development. Narayan invited Schumacher to Poona, India, where Schumacher furthered his critique of modernization theory and its advocates in organizations like the World Bank. He began to formulate an alternative development theory based on small-scale technologies and self-help—with which he would be most closely identified in the 1970s.

Many of the initial ideas behind intermediate technology had their origins in Schumacher's 1955 essay "Economics in a Buddhist Country," but it was in Varanasi in the late 1950s that Schumacher fully developed the concept. The movement's name might sound like a technological solution to development aid, but it captured the full scope of Schumacher's moral economy. Most foundationally, Schumacher argued that there was no single Westernized path to economic growth and that countries with more rural and traditional economies needed to find a more "appropriate" path to economic development, one slower in pace and that emerged from the ground up. Intermediate technology was the means to achieving this path to development. It was a model that went against modernization theory, which was geared toward the transfer of labor from rural areas to the urban center in order to support heavy industry. Intermediate technology was meant instead as "the conscious preservation of the *viability* of [traditional] society."[189] The concept encapsulated Schumacher's devotion to an ethical development capable of maintaining social solidarities.

Like his "Buddhist economics," Schumacher's concept of intermediate technology drew heavily on Gandhi's notions of swadeshi and indigenous manufacturing and added to it what Schumacher had learned from the Bhoodan campaign. Here, the village must act "as the planning unit." Additionally, Schumacher suggested a middle, intermediate structure to organize economic development. This meant a "district" of about "one or two million inhabitants, consisting of a thousand or so villages, a number of towns, and a fairly substantial district center or capital."[190] Each district would be geared toward nurturing and developing its own indigenous markets rather than being subjected to targets set by a centralized government. In this model, the central government and aid organizations were tasked with providing technical assistance—in the form of small-scale technology, for example—that would help employ potters, weavers, and farmers, with the aim of making them self-reliant.[191]

Controversially, Schumacher argued that the roots of Indian poverty were not its underdeveloped economy but the imposition of Western development thinking. Countries like India could not afford the advanced technology and heavy industry required by modernization theory, not only because they were pricey but also because they nullified indigenous labor. Such a view suggested that efficiency might be of limited use in assessing development programs. According to Schumacher, if *"the 'high cost' producer* [the indigenous manu-facturer] *has no 'opportunity' of engaging in 'alternative' production, the opportunity cost of his labour is nil."*[192] Social gains, according to him, were just as important as material ones and should be calculated accordingly: "As long as Khadi [khaddar] is produced (preponderantly) by labour which would otherwise do nothing at all, it is, for the economy as a whole, the cheapest cloth of all."[193] Citing Gandhi, Schumacher urged economists, aid agencies, and policymakers to invest in swadeshi rather than the exports of primary commodities and to concentrate their efforts on employing potters, farmers, and weavers by providing them with the technologies and means for expand-ing their markets. "The test is simply whether 'the people'—that is, a substan-tial proportion of the population—are with the planners or not," Schumacher suggested. "If they are not, the planners can do nothing, and it is no use blam-ing the people."[194] This was the idea of economics—as he would later call it—"as if people mattered."[195] It was an ethical path to measure and advance social in addition to economic growth.

More than the social aspect concerned Schumacher. Utilizing appropri-ate technology was also connected to plenary welfare, yet he suggested an alternative model that utilized "uneconomic" aspects such as conservation rather than perpetual growth in order to protect the limited availability of nonrenewable natural resources. Schumacher had already been thinking about the economics of resources as part of his work at the NCB in the 1950s. By the mid-1960s, he connected these ideas about coal to his broader cri-tique of the materialism of economics, where "all goods are treated the same."[196] Beyond coal, economic life should be organized on the principle of conservation rather than infinite growth and profit, thus protecting nonre-newable resources. Schumacher's concept of intermediate technology thus also offered a sustainable model of economic growth, one that utilized renewable energy: people "will have to learn again that it is possible to have a highly productive agriculture by means of 'green manure' and other organic methods and that chemical fertilizers may not be the ready answer at all."[197] Drawing once more on Gandhi's theory of nonviolence, Schumacher argued that the excessive use of nonrenewable goods like coal and oil constituted an act against man as well as nature. By the 1970s, he would even connect these ideas to a Christian ethics, one that spoke against "man['s] 'domination' over all creatures of the earth."[198]

In May 1965, Schumacher approached his colleague from the NCB George McRobie and together they founded the Intermediate Technology Development Group (today called Practical Action). McRobie himself had experience with development work in India, having been active there in 1955 on a Ford Foundation small industries project.[199] Schumacher and McRobie invited around twenty economists and business experts to join the group, including Alfred Latham-Koenig, an economic advisor to one of the consulting companies involved in development work for McKinsey, and Mansur Hoda, an Indian development and business expert who would eventually run the appropriate technology unit at the Gandhian Institute in Varanasi.[200] The economist Dudley Seers and the centrist Tori MP George Sinclair (former deputy governor of Cyprus during the emergency period) were two of its vice presidents. Julia Porter, who was a fundraiser for the UN Freedom From Hunger Campaign in the west country as well as the head of the Africa Development Trust, became the operational organizer and, in the first year, ran the entire operation from her flat in Covent Garden.[201] A year after the formation of the group, she married Robert Porter, the senior economic advisor to the then Ministry of Overseas Development, which won the group a close connection with the UK's formal overseas aid policy.

The Intermediate Technology Development Group (ITDG) was meant to disseminate Schumacher's "Buddhist economics" and change how economists, development workers, and governments thought about economic progress. The central idea was "encouraging development at the 'grass-roots' level" through four core criteria: "(a) smallness; (b) simplicity; (c) capital cheapness; and (d) non-violence."[202] ITDG, in fact, acted more like a consulting company for development aid agencies than a traditional nongovernmental organization. Although Schumacher himself had written extensively against the tyranny of the expert, ITDG itself employed a voluntary panel of experts—from architects to engineers—to focus on designing and developing small-scale projects that would utilize low-skills, low-cost equipment for development and work closely with local indigenous communities at the level of the village. By 1973, there were around two hundred such experts working on myriad projects in such areas as agriculture, building, chemical engineering, cooperatives, forestry, health, power, transportation, and water treatment.[203]

Decentralized Development

In 1973, when Schumacher published *Small Is Beautiful: Economics as if People Mattered*, many of his ideas had already been circulating in the British media as well as in India and the United States. The book was a collection of his essays from the previous decade, and while reviews of it were somewhat slow to come, by the mid-1970s it was being widely read. Schumacher received a CBE honor and an invitation to meet the queen. The book also won him an invitation to meet the Indian president Indira Gandhi, as well as audiences with President Jimmy Carter and the U.S. House of Representatives. The ideas in *Small Is Beautiful* inspired economists like Leopold Khor, activists like Satish Kumar, and ordinary citizens worldwide, and the term became a catchphrase associated with grassroots, community-based organization.

The book arrived in the midst of a series of international economic and energy crises. The ideas were not new, but a new international context gave them a renewed purpose. The fight "against economic misery," the book argued, should be focused on social growth, elaborating a new economic ethics rooted in "democracy, freedom, human dignity, standard of living, self-realization [and] fulfilment."[204] The book resonated with the general malaise of the period, from environmental and population concerns to an international food crisis, stagflation, and a global unemployment crisis. As the decade progressed, the book also helped explain emergent deindustrialization. It spoke directly to growing anxieties among citizens and some public officials about the power of multinational corporations. By the late 1970s, it was a bestseller.

Schumacher's ideas were widely influential on the work of NGOs, especially in Britain, not least because they championed decentralized, nongovernmental, community-based activism and development. To some extent, as in other domains, it was due to the ITDG itself. The agency—probably thanks to Julia Porter's own professional connections—secured funding and collaborated with Freedom From Hunger (a UN campaign that massively engaged British NGOs in the 1960s) as well as with the major humanitarian agencies at the time: Oxfam, Christian Aid, and War on Want. In 1975, ITDG worked with Christian Aid on a boat-building project in South Sudan.[205] It also collaborated with Oxfam on numerous projects, including providing guidance in the mid-1970s on how to design its own low-cost spinning wheel and hand-looms.[206] War on Want and Christian Aid even had representatives within ITDG's directorate.

More generally, Schumacher's economic philosophy gave British NGOs the language to conceptualize their work, one that corresponded to their own ethos and self-perception—misleading as it may be—as grassroots bodies working "against the centralised models of bureaucracy."[207] As an Oxfam pamphlet stated, "Oxfam has preferred to work with voluntary bodies rather than government or international agencies, thereby avoiding formality and benefitting from person-to-person communication at the project level."[208] Schumacher became widely read in the NGO world. For technical as well as ideological reasons, his ideas of small-scale development worked well for British nongovernmental organizations. By the 1960s, organizations like Oxfam, War on Want, and Save the Children had invested in small-scale development initiatives, from the Grameen project in India to Julius Nyerere's experiments with *Ujamaa* in Tanzania. Schumacher's philosophy offered British NGOs a new way of framing their work as ethical, enabling them to be recognized by international and national agencies as such. National governments were increasingly channeling funds for aid through NGOs because the latter were seen as more effective in reaching local populations. This was especially true for the British government, which had a shrinking aid budget during the recession and was a former imperial metropole. The 1980s "became something of a golden age" for the grassroots, small-scale ethos of nongovernmental organizations.[209] Based on Schumacher's ideas, NGOs were seen to have been part of a "barefoot revolution" and a "moving force behind what are often termed 'microprojects', small-scale, community- or village-based development projects under way in a hundred different countries."[210] It came to be called "people-centered development," a new, nongovernmental approach to aid.

But as this chapter has argued, Schumacher's ideas should be understood within a broader debate on the British left in the 1950s and 1960s about the nature of capitalism and the role of the state in economic development and planning. These debates had emerged from a discussion about the purpose of the socialist project in the nexus of decolonization and the global Cold War. For over two decades, visions of "post-capitalist" society proposed alternatives to the mainstream understandings of the role of the welfare state in fostering private markets and promoting economic development beyond the GNP model of growth. For all their different versions, these alternatives were critical of the postwar project of a centralized economy and state-led development models. They emphasized the role of the local as well as the global community in managing economic life, one in which people rather than the Leviathan were the agents of economic growth.

Historians of the British left have examined the ethical turn in socialist thought of the 1950s within domestic debates about affluence and the future of the Labour Party. As this chapter has shown, however, we cannot understand this turn in isolation from the postimperial politics, challenges, and critiques of Keynesianism and development brought about by decolonization. While ethical socialism had a long tradition in British political thought, its return in the 1950s and the 1960s was marked by the political economy of a weakening and shrinking empire. In this context, old ideas about moral economies and grassroots community development became linked to a set of debates about centralized planning, modernization programs, and the Keynesian macroeconomic potential of delivering social goods. Decolonization, in fact, enabled socialists to think outside the confines of British socialism. It challenged some of their insular assumptions about economic management and the role of the state within it.

In the 1970s, when a series of economic crises hit, these ideas became the basis for nongovernmental experiments in ethical capitalism. From the village and the high street to the household and the firm, nonprofits drew on postwar ideas of ethical models for development in search of alternative social arrangements beyond state-led economies. The following chapters track some of the central nongovernmental pathways of decentralized development.

CHAPTER TWO

The Charity Business

WHEN BRITISH NONPROFITS embraced E. F. Schumacher's ideas about the ethics of capitalism in the late 1960s, the nature of their work had already undergone a radical transformation. As a 1965 *Times* article declared, "Charity is now big business."[1] The *Times* reported that "the conception of well-intentioned souls—the vicar's wife of the cartoons multiplied many times over—working in cramped offices and with only the vaguest idea of how money works, is wholly mistaken today."[2] Nonprofits, especially the big international aid organizations—Oxfam, Save the Children, Christian Aid, and War on Want—metamorphosed from Victorian- and Edwardian-style fundraisers to sophisticated business ventures with established permanent charity shops, limited liability companies, and expanded tax exemptions. They had also started to hire employees with professional training, from development workers to public relations specialists. Internationally, they began operating small community development initiatives of their own, especially in locales across the former British empire, that imported handicraft work to Britain. In this "commercial age," the *Times* explained,[3] nonprofits were not only doubling their revenues through a new set of practices but also creating a new humanitarian "business." Today, nonprofits are considered a third sector in the economy.

How did that transformation happen, and what were its social and economic consequences? During the 1960s, nonprofits underwent what sociologists Koray Çalışkan and Michel Callon have called a "process of economization."[4] They were transformed into economic and market actors with particular stakes in the British and former colonial economies, developing new economic expertise, new patterns of consumption and production, and new forms of labor relations. This transformation was accompanied by rapid growth of the number of NGOs in Britain. While in 1948 there were about 56,000 registered charities, by 1975 that number had almost doubled to 120,000.[5] The voluntary sector has long played a key role in Britain's social services,[6] but from the

1960s onward the nonprofit sector pivoted toward more direct political campaigning, lobbying, and antipoverty aid work. NGOs grew in both size and scope.[7]

Historians have described the growth of the nonprofit sector in this period as rooted within domestic British politics: when politics moved from the ballot box and became part of everyday culture in the form of single-issue nongovernmental campaigning.[8] But as this chapter argues, the growth of the sector was also rooted in the expansion of the "mixed economy" of British capitalism at a moment of heightened decolonization.[9] At the same time that British socialists were debating the ethics of the British economy beyond the state, activists and campaigners were reconsidering the role of nongovernmental organizations in the economy. During a period of relative affluence and rapid decolonization, nongovernmental organizations became not only a way for citizens to express their politics but also a training camp: for consumers to be trained as advocates, for ex-colonial experts to be trained as development workers, and for a new generation to hone new skills in marketing and retail. By 1991, 76 percent of the British population claimed to have done some form of work in the voluntary sector.[10] Nonprofits, in short, increasingly took on an important place in Britain's postimperial economy.

This chapter traces the economization of the nonprofit sector through the story of charity trading and one of Britain's most famous institutions, the charity shop. At first glance, the history of charity shops may seem like a marginal tale within the broader transformation of the sector in the 1960s. But, in fact, it is illuminating for what it teaches us about the growth of the nonprofits and their transition from Victorian philanthropy to becoming the third sector in the British economy. In the 1960s, charity shops became distinct economic spaces, shaping new labor practices through volunteer work as well as an important space for consumer action, generating a new taxation system for charity retail. They paved the way for the creation of a new business model: charitable trading companies. In contemporary Britain, charity shops and charity retail serve an even broader range of causes: they sell donated secondhand clothing and household goods as well as, in some cases, fair-trade products to the British public, the proceeds of which go to domestic and international charities.

Charity trade took Schumacher, Titmuss, and Young's abstract ideas about solidarity, altruism, and mutual aid and materialized them into high-street retail practices. Trading ventures aimed to be both ethical and profitable, shaping consumer ethics to support a variety of welfare and developmentalist causes. Charity trade promoted new consumption patterns that helped nonprofits move from a local to a national philanthropic market. It represented a novel development in capitalist enterprise that was neither exactly private nor entirely public. It invited citizens to participate in their causes as stakeholders in the domestic and the global economy.

Crucially, what sustained the nongovernmental vision of ethical trade was the series of tax breaks created during the 1960s. These tax breaks enabled nonprofits to carve out a special status for their trading ventures. From income tax and VAT to property tax, the tax breaks forged the material conditions for the ethical capitalism of the nonprofit sector. The visions of humane capitalism of the nonprofit sector, in fact, hinged upon the tax relief created in this period. We cannot understand the ideals and programs of the ethical capitalism of the nonprofit sector outside the political economy and the history of the charity business and its special tax benefits.

By the late 1960s, the emergence of a growing cadre of aid experts enabled nonprofits to expand charity business to postcolonial economies. Nonprofits used charity trading companies to increasingly support development projects rooted in fair trade and handicraft production and began importing such goods to be sold in charity shops across Britain. The new aid experts had colonial experience and used their connections in the former empire to facilitate philanthropic markets that built upon the tradition of imperial humanitarianism. They offered British consumers products that would connect them to various international, economic, and development causes. While the products they brought to Britain formed only part of shops' supply chain, they represented an important transformation in their character, from local philanthropic markets that served Britain's own domestic community to stores linked to larger postimperial markets.

Although the story of charity trading is not exclusively one of so-called international aid organizations, these NGOs did play a critical role in it. Oxfam in particular became a central protagonist, pioneering a business model for modern charity retail—and new trade and marketing knowledge—that would be imitated by other organizations, both international and domestic. In the 1960s, Oxfam became a sophisticated enterprise selling secondhand goods—like jewelry, books, and toys—and using the profits to support charitable causes. Its trading ventures created local philanthropic markets, fundraising for aid at home and abroad. In this way, the charity shop enterprise was linked to a variety of aid programs in the Third World. Across Britain, the White Dominions, and the United States, charity trading became intertwined with the production of fair-trade goods. The charity business suddenly formed an alternative market that sought to connect consumers and producers through ethical shopping and tax breaks.

The Business Model of the Charity Shop

When the first modern charity shop was erected in Oxford in 1948, charity retailing was not entirely new. Since the 1820s, philanthropists, missionaries, and social reformers had used charity bazaars and fun fairs as fundraising venues.[11] Held in concert halls and banquet rooms, they raised an average of around £1,000 per event ($150,000 in today's currency).[12] Some bazaars sold items produced in Britain and then shipped to imperial domains like India, Australia, Africa, and North America. By the mid-nineteenth century there were more than 1,000 bazaars and jumble sales held across Britain and its empire, with items ranging from secondhand clothing to handicrafts and needlework.[13]

With the opening of the first retail depot in Oxted, Surrey, in 1875, the purpose of charity retail expanded in order to collect donations for the poor in a more permanent way.[14] By the turn of the century, clothing and shopping became an integral part of charity work through a new network of Salvation Army stores, which collected quality secondhand goods from affluent homes as well as repairing broken goods in order to make them serviceable for further use.[15] They were then sold by "salvage stores" to customers unable to buy them new.[16] Salvation Army stores soon opened across the empire and what would be called the White Dominions—Australia, Canada, and to some extent the United States—as part of community organizations for the "undesirable."[17]

This trend continued during the two world wars. While new aid organizations were founded in their aftermath (Save the Children, established in 1919, was one of the most prominent ventures), they nonetheless relied on Victorian methods of charity fundraising.[18] "You are asked to go through your wardrobe, to remember the all-but-naked condition of these unhappy, starving people, with the bitter cold of winter in front of them, and to turn out all you can possibly spare," implored one Save the Children pamphlet.[19] In an empire-wide campaign, charity appeals included a variety of fundraising events, from local concerts to street campaigns and ad hoc bazaar shops. Unlike later efforts, these events collected items to send to the needy rather than to generate profit.

The creation of the first permanent charity shop by the Oxford Committee for Famine Relief (later Oxfam) in 1948 took these Victorian fundraising methods and moved them into a more formal business model. Since its founding in 1942, Oxfam had been a relatively minor charity in the landscape of humanitarian organizations. It joined dozens of aid organizations across Britain and the United States that provided relief to civilian populations in war-stricken Europe.[20] It was comprised of local elites in Oxford including Lord Robert Cecil the Viscount Chelwood, George Bell the Bishop of Chichester, and notable figures like Dr. Henry Gillett and Professor Gilbert Murray of Oxford University.[21] In 1943, together with Dr. Leo Liepmann, a refugee from Nazi Germany, and Sir Alan Pirn, a former Indian Civil Service official, they formed a committee with the goal of aiding German-controlled or occupied countries like Greece. The Oxfam shop at Broad Street became the embodiment of humanitarian ideals. It was created

FIGURE 2.1. The first Oxfam shop on Broad Street, c. 1948.

out of a storage space for donated goods that was repurposed when Oxfam expanded its operations in 1948.[22] Oxfam's original idea was that the shop would generate an additional source of income, even if only a minor one, to contribute to the "relief of suffering arising as a result of war or any other cause in any part of the world."[23]

From its modest beginnings, the Oxfam shop at Broad Street introduced a model that would later be replicated by tens of thousands of nongovernmental organizations in the 1960s. It was the first to collect donated goods and convert them into commodities to sell back to the British public. Purchase was not connected to any particular campaign or cause but instead generated a fund for responding to all humanitarian appeals, current and future, whether in Europe, the empire, or elsewhere. Charity shops created local philanthropic markets, raising funds by selling secondhand goods to the community rather than collecting items for the needy.

The managerial and organizational force behind this model was Cecil Jackson-Cole, a successful businessman with a real estate empire who in 1943 was appointed Oxfam's first honorary secretary. In the 1950s, Jackson-Cole developed a unique approach to philanthropy that combined ideas about altruism and business, a prototype for what we would today call "philanthrocapitalism."[24] Jackson-Cole applied the tools of economic efficiency, business management, and financial solvency to the charitable sector, which he believed could "either finance itself or . . . actually have a financial surplus."[25] There was no reason why philanthropy could not generate a profit. This approach became the heart of Jackson-Cole's work with Oxfam and as a founder of Help the Aged in 1961 (initially called Help the Aged Refugees Appeal) and Action in Distress in 1972 (today ActionAid).

Jackson-Cole was not a typical liberal internationalist, nor was he fully at home in the community of scholars and politicians who initially founded the Oxford Committee for Famine Relief. He was a self-made man and a devoted Christian who at the age of twelve had gone to work to support his family and never finished his formal education. He became interested in philanthropic work only in his forties, after he moved to Oxford in the early 1940s and was exposed, as he himself later described it, to the city's "altruistic climate."[26] One of Oxfam's biographers once called him an "eccentric philanthropist."[27]

In Oxford, Jackson-Cole befriended his neighbors, the classics scholar Professor Gilbert Murray and his wife, Lady Murray, who were already active in the founding of aid organizations like the League of Nations Union and Save the Children Fund in the 1920s. It was Murray who got Jackson-Cole involved with the work of the Oxford Committee for Famine Relief. He suggested to Jackson-Cole that "there is a responsible spirit behind the universe who is seeking to remedy the [sic] suffering." He connected the work of the Oxford Committee to Jackson-Cole's strong Christian ethical commitments.

Oxford was a lively place during the war. Home to organizations like the evangelical Moral Re-armament and the Quaker Society of Friends, the city was engaged with internationalist debates about the moral crisis of the war and its effect on British politics and the economy.[28] Liberals like Murray actively criticized the moral foundation of British conduct during the war, especially the civilian blockade in Greece and Belgium.[29] Socialists like G.D.H. Cole, who had tutored Jackson-Cole, grappled with the moral impact of internationalism on socialist politics.[30] He had even called for the British government to support the humanitarian plight of Europeans, including the Germans.[31] "Most of one's friends," Jackson-Cole himself testified, "seemed to be in support of some good cause or other."[32]

Joining the Oxford Committee gave Jackson-Cole a sense of mission. "My own life for some time had been following a pattern of half-time Christian charity work and half-time business," he later reflected.[33] Jackson-Cole brought his business expertise to Oxfam and pushed it in a direction more lucrative than amateur philanthropic fundraising. Already during the war, he organized a successful event, including a gift shop, that raised £10,000 to support the Greek population. "My function," he wrote, was "to conceive and master-mind the operation and to make sure that the whole was financially successful."[34] When the charity was registered as a permanent organization in 1947, Jackson-Cole was handed the responsibility of building up its fundraising operations.[35] "We are not out to establish an 'Empire,'" Jackson-Cole stated, "but to see that the Cause is carried throughout the world."[36]

Jackson-Cole saw no reason why charities should not be run like any other business enterprise. Charity, he claimed, could rely on "the tools of venture capital to create social benefit on a huge scale."[37] They could be efficient as well as altruistic in their aims. One of the first things that Jackson-Cole did, therefore, was hire a full-time employee to run the business smoothly. Whereas Oxfam, following the nineteenth-century model of charity retailing, insisted on staffing its charity operations primarily with volunteers, Jackson-Cole hired Joe Mitty as the shop manager.

Mitty's arrival in 1949 signaled the making of a professional class of charity workers, an enterprise as well as an industry.[38] "I joined Oxfam because I thought it was something I would like to be associated with," he declared in 1971. Mitty was a former lieutenant in the army's Hampshire Regiment, an experience he linked directly to his work at Oxfam: "I'd seen poverty on service in the East, on railway stations in Bengal and Calcutta. It strengthened my conviction to try and do something to help them."[39] As with many aid experts who joined Oxfam and other international aid organizations during the 1950s and 1960s, Mitty's perspective was shaped by his time in the empire during a period of decolonization.[40] It was this experience that gave charity workers in the 1950s and 1960s a global yet paternalistic imaginary.

Like Jackson-Cole, Mitty was not a traditional charity worker. As one journalist put it, he was "a super-salesman on the side of the angels."[41] In his hands, the shop at 17 Broad Street became a thriving business: its income doubled to £3,000 a year and climbed to over £10,000 by 1953.[42] By 1958, the shop was such a success that Mitty expanded its premises to two roomy display floors. It became one of "the busiest shops in Oxford."[43]

Mitty was also behind the creation of the Oxfam Christmas cards in 1957, which served as a model for domestic and international charities alike. Sold through the shops and by mail order, the cards quickly became a flourishing business, bringing in £18,500 in profits by 1963.[44] At Mitty's instigation, the shop front was dressed to provide a window on the "hundreds of smiling faces—the faces of what were hungry, homeless despairing people who have been helped" through the shop's sales.[45] Throughout the 1950s Mitty ran the shop as his own, writing letters to wealthy housewives trying to solicit items that could be sold. He accepted every donation: from golf clubs to candlesticks to fur coats, from "Cartridge" Kodak cameras and ski poles to coffee cups, lace, and electric saucepans. It was jewelry and silverware that Mitty sought, like a bear seeking honey.[46] Donations of secondhand clothing and shoes were still given directly to refugees, as in the Victorian charity model. More valuable items—like a diamond ring valued at £300, silver and plated articles, bicycles, and even a car—were sold in the shop.[47] "If you and I went into business," he once told the journalist Byron Rogers in an interview, "I think I could have made us a hell of a lot of money. I've got the energy."[48]

If hiring Mitty was the first departure from the old model of charity work, the second was investing in advertising. In the late 1940s, Jackson-Cole started working with a professional advertising agency in order to target broad sections

FIGURE 2.2. Margaret Thatcher talking to Joe Mitty at the thirtieth birthday celebration of the Broad Street shop in Oxford, November 11, 1977.

of the population and publicize charity campaigns.[49] Charities can be more effective, Jackson-Cole claimed, by putting out advertising appeals in the press rather than exclusively in local churches.[50] "We were, in fact, the first ones to initiate large-scale display advertising for the charitable world," he later stated.[51] Fundraising, according to Jackson-Cole, was a key method for forming public opinion and developing the "public desire to ease distressing needs for the poorest people."[52] It could educate the public and disseminate the message of compassion and sympathy.

Jackson-Cole collaborated with Harold Sumption, a Quaker and an advertising agent, to help create a new type of charity enterprise that would rely on marketing strategies. As Sumption would later explain, "We don't just want donors, we need to offer involvement in the problem. We need to raise funds, but we also need to educate public opinion and that is the biggest single change in charity work—getting the donor to identify with the recipient, developing passive, receiving charity into active participation."[53] For Sumption, the new charity venture was a revolution of the heart as well as the purse.

Sumption suggested that nonprofits should, in fact, borrow methods from the marketing world, with aid being branded just like any other product. He wrote new rules of charity publicity that aimed to shock, provoke, and stimulate an emotional response to charity appeals.[54] Sumption even created a mini "Gift Shop News" signed by Mitty that reported to consumers and donors on the shop's activities in addition to announcing local fundraising events.[55]

By the 1950s, Sumption also invented the "off-the-page" ad, which invited the reader to respond directly to the campaign. Sumption introduced a system of "coupons" so responses could be "measured precisely."[56] Ads were "keyed" in such a manner that the responses could be traced to specific newspapers, thereby testing their efficiency. It was, as one newspaper argued, "a pioneering technique that was later applied by mail order catalogues."[57] Ads were carried as banners in various charity events; they became part of the branding of the entire organization. The idea was to deliver a clear sound bite of the charity's message in the media as well as on the streets of Britain.

This new marketing strategy connected the shop on Broad Street with a network of consumers and donors across Britain and the White Dominions.[58] During the 1950s, Jackson-Cole and Mitty received dozens of letters from well-to-do supporters—primarily women—who saw Oxfam's leaflets and advertisements. The majority of the letters offered donations of goods: lace scarves, fur coats, and old artwork. Some letters even enclosed donations of embroidered handkerchiefs, which had been specifically made for the shop.[59] Other donations came from small British businesses such as the Crown Staffordshire China Company Limited at Burslem, which donated pottery and coffee sets.[60] The shop at Broad Street often received letters from consumers seeking to purchase, not just sell, jewelry and antiques.[61] To each letter with an inquiry or donation, Mitty wrote a thank-you note. His personalized method of charity retailing replicated that of successful small businesses that aimed to forge an emotional, intimate connection with consumers. By the late 1950s, the Broad Street shop had set up a business model for charity retailing more generally, one that fused Victorian ideals with more contemporary retail practices. However, it took a deeper structural change to expand Jackson-Cole's charity business model into a market that by the late 1960s would generate around £1 million in revenue for Oxfam alone.

Consumer Politics and the Third Sector

In the 1960s there was a boom in charity stores that moved away from ad hoc campaigning to sophisticated forms of retail business across Britain and its Commonwealth. From that one Oxfam shop in 1958, their numbers grew such that by 1967 there were more than 100 operated by Oxfam alone. By 1971, there were more than 350 Oxfam shops across Britain. By way of comparison, that was 103 more shops than Marks & Spencer had that year.[62] Similarly, the organization moved from one salaried employee in the early 1950s to around 200 paid staff in 1963; 120 of them were stationed in a designated "Oxfam House" in Oxford and the rest were scattered around the country in regional shops.[63] Following Oxfam's model, both international and domestic charities began employing a professional network of business specialists, including local organizers, advertising agencies, and media experts. In turn, shop businesses generated new forms of economic exchange, labor practices, and taxation systems. By the early 1970s, one headline could trumpet that "business is booming in the tragedy trade."[64]

Oxfam led the way, building on the business model Jackson-Cole had developed in the preceding decade. In the first three years of the 1960s, Oxfam opened three more gift shops in Guildford, Leeds, and Cheltenham, serving primarily a middle-class clientele. In the financial year 1963, these shops brought in £79,000, nearly doubling their proceeds in just two years. By 1971, the shops provided a third of the organization's total income. With the development and growth of mail-order catalogues, Britons could sit in the comfort of their home and participate in a culture of ethical shopping.[65] "Charity," the journalist Shirley Lewis put it, "really begins at home."[66]

Influenced by the success of the Oxfam shops, other nonprofits began opening shops of their own across Britain as well as in South Africa, Australia, New Zealand, and Canada. For instance, War on Want, founded in 1951 by members of the Labour Party, including Harold Wilson and E. F. Schumacher, opened its first shop in 1962. Save the Children followed suit in 1963. Help the Aged, a nongovernmental organization led by Oxfam's Jackson-Cole, opened a shop in 1963 to fundraise for its campaigns to help older populations across Britain and the globe. Not only international charities adopted this model. When the NGO Shelter was founded in 1966 to end homelessness in Britain, it too adopted the Oxfam model and opened its own charity shop in London.[67] By the late 1960s, what began as a small fundraising strategy for one humanitarian aid organization had developed into a culture of consumer activism for both domestic and international causes.

The growth of charity retail was rooted within a broader expansion of the nonprofit sector across Britain in the 1960s. The period saw the proliferation of NGOs focused on various issues: from antipoverty to environmentalism to development aid. Some historians have explained this transformation as the "privatization of politics,"[68] but this line of analysis obscures more than clarifies what was new about the 1960s, not least because it seriously underplays the long tradition of voluntary associations in British politics. Instead, we must consider how the growth of NGOs, and with them the nonprofit sector, was embedded within changes in British capitalism. What was distinct about the period were the ways in which the nonprofit sector acted as a substitute for the project of national ownership. It was not only politics but also the British economy that was becoming nongovernmental. The new business of charity invited citizens to participate in various causes as stakeholders in the economy; instead of state-led industries, citizens could now choose to contribute to and fund various welfare and development causes. NGOs were becoming a third sector in the economy.

The rise of consumer culture in the 1960s gave charity businesses a boost. Britain, together with other Western European countries, was loosening or dropping austerity measures and becoming an affluence economy. "Affluence" was a contested term; while some stressed that the standard of living had risen, others emphasized the deplorable poverty in some parts of the country and the importance of working-class identity in Britain. Yet between the 1950s and 1966 Britain's GDP did rise by 40 percent, unemployment stayed under 2 percent, and real incomes and consumption increased.[69] By 1964, British citizens had increased their spending on consumer goods by 45 percent, purchasing items like refrigerators, washing machines, and televisions.[70] By 1965 car ownership, which made shopping easier, doubled.[71] The formation of a new consumer society in Britain was not limited to domestic spending. It also altered the meaning of social housing, economic disparities, and notions of the rights and duties of citizenship.[72] Middle-class Britons had more money to spend on charity retail and more leisure time to volunteer in and run charity shops. "Politics," as the historian Lawrence Black once put it, became "increasingly about rights, tastes, culture, morality, environmental, post-industrial, even anti-materialist, desires and self-expression."[73]

The relative increase in affluence placed the consumer at the heart of the mixed economy of welfare and developmental project. For many the economy was becoming more organized around consumption rather than production. Some—like Michael Young—even called for the establishment of a new political party that would represent the interests of consumers instead of workers. Consumer politics was influenced and shaped by its counterpart in North America, not least by activists like Ralph Nader.[74] But in Britain it also helped redefine the project of social democracy and the meaning of ownership. The turn to consumerism was part of a broader disillusionment with the welfare and development state, as it was unable to represent its citizens and deliver material goods for all its members. While the welfare state and trade unions considered the male breadwinner the primary "worker" in the British economy, consumerism included women and the entire family.[75] Consumer politics in fact became the focus of new nongovernmental agencies such as the Consumers' Association (1957) and the Consumer Council (1963), as well as new magazines like the Consumers' Association's *Which?* (1957). These agencies were established to not only protect and advise consumers on affordable purchases but also educate them about ethical and social concerns. Some like the Consumers' Association even collaborated with international NGOs like Oxfam and War on Want. They offered consumers information about how to ethically use their purchasing power to advance domestic and international causes.

In the 1960s nonprofits, especially international aid organizations, embraced the consumer-citizen as their target audience. Informing consumers about their causes became a way of recruiting Britons to become part of the development project as much as it was about funding them. They did so through a variety of creative events: from walkathons to fundraisers for charity, to collaborations with children's television shows like *Blue Peter*, which invited children to create their own "bring and buy" sales.[76] They produced and broadcasted commercials on national television.[77] The rapid growth in charity shops was one successful manifestation of how consumer culture became connected to morality. Charity shops offered a material presence on the British high street for ethically minded shoppers to use their power as consumers and support their choice of charity. In turn, charity shops were one place where an active citizenry came into being and formulated its desires. The consolidation of charity shops engendered new ethical and economic subjects, from the volunteers who ran the shops, to donors, to those who shopped in them.

The first to change was the pool of donors. Working alongside advertising and marketing agencies, NGOs sought to include large swaths of the public in the charity economy through the donation of goods. In a 1963 appeal in the *Daily Mail*, a popular newspaper for middle-class Britons, Oxfam told readers how ordinary Britons of all ages and classes took part in Oxfam's mission: there was the unmarried elderly lady of eighty who gave her "dearest earthly treasure," her mother's engagement ring, or the Crufts' habitué who gave her pedigree poodle puppy to be sold in the shop.[78] The appeal showed the public that anyone of any age group could find something to donate to the shops and become a humanitarian. "Our army of supporters," an Oxfam report on the shops stated, "including the platoons of the young, grows daily."[79]

The formation of a charity donor was not an abstract exercise. Nonprofits like Oxfam taught people to think of donations in terms of economic aid. Ads and leaflets often specified the value in aid for each item donated to the shop: "Beautiful Silverware like this," read one pamphlet, "provided 2,000 bottles of enriched milk powder for new born babies in the New East." And below another image: "These Soapstone Carvings presentation mugs, spoons and necklaces are equivalent to 10 large fishing nets for one of our fishery programmes in India."[80] Donated decanters and candlesticks financed irrigation projects in Southern Rhodesia; sapphire rings bought medical supplies for childcare programs in the Middle East.

What's more, the shops created a day-to-day presence for international and domestic aid initiatives and became the physical and local representation of aid organizations. They were a meeting place for local community organizing and lobbying activities on behalf of NGOs. Shops even had their own local newsletters in which they could advertise to the community about their various appeals and sales. The shops encouraged local participation in the broader, often international missions of charities.

Take, for example, the story of David Caynes, a semi-retired sixty-year-old farm worker from Paignton, a small seaside town on the coast of southwest England. In the early 1970s, Caynes used the Oxfam shop as a space to generate a local crowdsourcing venture for the work of the broader organization. He decided to donate £100 of his annual savings to Oxfam in order to help the hungry people of the world, no small amount relative to his earnings. Indeed, it was almost 62 percent of his annual income. He gave £50 immediately. The rest, he said, he would donate if twenty other people from the area would be willing to match the amount.[81] As one local commentator put it, Caynes's donation—at least relative to his earning—was quite a "sacrifice."[82] And yet in October that year, when he saw the success of this crowdsourcing venture, Caynes entered the Oxfam shop once more to offer an additional £500 from his life savings. Caynes's name may not be remembered in the annals of twentieth-century philanthropy, but his so-called "extreme altruism," as it might be termed, depended on the physical presence of the Oxfam shop in Paignton.[83]

Once donated items arrived at a charity shop, they were sorted by a large group of volunteer workers and priced by a professional charity worker. The growth of charity retailing in the 1960s was, in fact, largely sustained by a new group, voluntary charity workers, who operated alongside the professional regional organizers and commercial advisors to the charity. While professional charity workers were in charge of the pricing, bookkeeping, and regional coordination of goods and sales, volunteers were entrusted with sorting and cleaning the constant flow of donated items, organizing shop stock, dressing shop windows, and running a shop's everyday operations. Charity retail thus held an important and growing place in Britain's own informal economy.

More often than not, these volunteers were women, either retirees or housewives with extra hours to spare when their children were at daycare and school. Olive Tenant, a housewife from South London, admitted that after her children left home, volunteer work at a charity shop in Sheen was an alternative to "stagnating." "I was getting quote neurotic," she said in an interview, "always having aches and pains, but now I haven't any. The work does me good . . . you feel you're helping someone as well as yourself."[84] Volunteer work became an emotional as much as an occupational vocation. To some degree, volunteer work at charity retail was part of what sociologist Nona Glazer would later call "work transfer" in the service industry.[85] For others, like the retired Dorothy Faithfull, volunteer work offered a solution to loneliness after she retired as headmistress of a nursery school in Deptford.[86] More generally, charity shops became a meeting place for the elderly community in the neighborhood. For others, like Irene Anderson, a housewife from Watford, volunteer work at the local charity shop was also a form of ethical engagement with the community: "I couldn't give any money, so I decided to give my time instead."[87] Anderson was one of many women who viewed volunteer work at their local charity shop as comparable to working for the Women's Institute or the local church. Inadvertently, the shop generated new forms of employment for those typically excluded from the marketplace.[88] Volunteer charity retail became part of a gendered economy.[89]

From the mid-1960s, charities like Oxfam and Save the Children also encouraged local groups of supporters from all ages to open and run their own temporary shops.[90] If the permanent shops created new forms of labor relations, "pop-up" charity shops also generated an opportunity for women to run their own local businesses. As one reporter noted, anyone "who thinks that women don't have a head for business ought to meet the ones who run the Oxfam Shop."[91] The temporary shop offered a formula that could be replicated across the country by anyone with little experience in shopkeeping. Make "the shops as attractive and interesting as the commercial concerns on either sides and the public will come in. Offer them reasonable merchandise, and they will buy it. No favours, no begging, just good business practice," one journalist urged.[92] As much as it allowed women to be ethical subjects aiding local and international communities in need, the temporary shop became a training ground for women outside the workforce to gain experience running a small business.

The development of the temporary charity shops enabled the rapid growth of charity retailing in the 1960s and expanded its consumer base beyond the typical middle-class women who frequented the Oxford shop in the 1950s. Temporary shops were opened on properties slated for demolition and often free of local property taxes. Commercial properties like old Tesco, Boots, and Co-ops stores were converted to temporary shops.[93] They became a highly localized form of community organization. Some were opened for only a few weeks and some were virtually permanent. The shops not only fundraised for charities but also provided a local point of active engagement with charity and community work. "The shops are also the foci or rallying points for home-front work, through which many supporters are introducers to Oxfam," one confidential Oxfam report read.[94] "Because the gifts are collected from and sold back to the same community, there is a feeling of mutual benefit," Joe Mitty added.[95]

The temporary charity shops nurtured a type of "grassroots activism" that encouraged a new form of local engagement with charity work. "We always wanted to try our hand at running a Gift Shop for Oxfam," stated Mabel Hickman, "but we had never found the opportunity." But then she and some friends "were offered a disused shop in a town three miles away," she continued. "We mentioned it to our Oxfam Regional Organiser Gordon McMillan and then we went with him to look at it. He thought it might do and a week later we held a meeting. Gordon said that we must circularise every house in the town and neighbouring villages, organise reception centres where gifts could be brought beforehand, contact the local VIPs etc."[96] Professionals like Cecil Jackson-Cole, in his work with both Oxfam and Help the Aged, provided clear guidelines and encouragement that helped standardize charity retailing. These guidelines included information on how to price items as well as how to dress the windows.[97] "Shops are hard work to run but the principle is simple," read the annual review of Oxfam for the fiscal year of 1967–68. "Find empty premises—perhaps rent free—invite the public to give you goods, then sell them. Almost all shops are run by a voluntary manageress with a number of helpers working on a rote system. Otherwise patterns vary."[98] By 1968, Oxfam alone ran 136 of these shops, allowing for the most efficient and profitable system for amateur fundraising, aside from the professional methods of large advertising campaigns in the media.[99]

The expansion of the shops through "pop-up" stores also meant that charity retailing came to target a much broader group of customers than it had in the 1950s. Temporary shops often took in items that were too low in value to justify being sent to permanent shops.[100] By the late 1960s, charity retailing came to include secondhand clothing, which up until the early 1960s was typically sent as a donation to refugee and other impoverished communities. What Mitty in the 1950s would consider a non-worthy item for his Oxfam shop at Broad Street Oxford would by the late 1960s become a popular commodity with a quick turnaround in most shops, since it appealed to a new, less affluent clientele. The shops were transformed from a down-market version of an antique shop into an upscale-market version of a jumble sale, taking donations like books, toys, and clothing. Suddenly, one journalist commented, there were "gift shops in nearly every town in the British Isles, raising money for many different charities, selling everything from TV sets to old shoes."[101]

Located on the high streets of newly up-and-coming neighborhoods like Stoke Newington,[102] the pop-up shops of organizations like Oxfam, Save the Children, and Help the Aged attracted high pedestrian traffic and made strange bedfellows, ranging from white youth and the urban poor to migrant communities. "Youth" had been a growing subculture since the postwar period.[103] By the late 1960s, it came to symbolize Britain's relative affluence, with its distinctive consumer culture and spending. Its aesthetics and lifestyle joined what the historian Raphael Samuel called the culture of "retrochic" or the "nostalgia industry," which looked for alternative forms of consumerism where "free time counted for more than money, and style leaders were drawn from the culturally privileged rather than the wealthy."[104] The proliferation of charity shops selling secondhand clothing, old books, and records "brought the humours of the flea market to the shopping parade, allowing a 'concerned' middle class to experiment with style and at the same time perform a simulacrum of social service."[105] Through "Bring and Buy" sales, new pop-up shops engaged younger citizens as consumers and activists.[106] Youths could participate in this new consumer activist culture by either shopping in temporary shops or running their own.

At the same time, temporary shops offered bargains that were particularly attractive to an emerging urban clientele. Today we often speak about "gentrification" of urban spaces, but the term itself had its origins in the 1960s. "Gentrification," the British sociologist Ruth Glass wrote in 1964, was a process through which "many of the working-class neighbourhoods [are] invaded by the middle-classes—upper and lower." Glass, who studied Islington and London, coined the term in that decade to describe social and economic transformations in British urban society. "Once this process of 'gentrification' starts in a district it goes on rapidly," she argued; "the whole social character of the district is changed."[107] Although Glass did not write directly about the charity shops, it is worth locating them within this broader context of affluence, urbanization, and gentrification, especially of London.

Yet at the time charity shops spread throughout deindustrializing Britain in the 1970s, urban landscapes—not just in London—were becoming ethnically and economically diverse.[108] It was during this period that charity shops expanded from a middle-class venture to one that catered to a much more diverse community of working-class customers. The shops served both the global poor and economically disadvantaged populations in Britain. As Oxfam's annual review from 1969–70 stated, an Oxfam shop "is not only a profitable enterprise. In some areas it serves a genuinely social need."[109] Commonwealth migrants as well as white working-class communities from rapidly deindustrializing areas came to rely especially on the shops. Pricing itself was suddenly based on the customer's ability and need rather than on a general profit system. The local clientele, the *Daily Telegraph* claimed, "permanently hard up and bringing up large families, found it a boon."[110]

Vanda Golder of Save the Children was proud of this transformation. "It is a great joy to see the almost incredulous delight of pensioners, on being able to afford a pretty frock, a warm coat, a carpet or a comfortable armchair," she stated. "Another great source of satisfaction is seeing some of the poor children of the district go about dry shod, or warmly clothed, clutching a previous toy, all of which have been bought from our shop at a modest price."[111] Unlike the official Oxfam shops in the 1950s, by the 1970s temporary volunteer-managed charity shops served local customers who were the urban poor of Britain, especially in places like Croydon, Nottingham, and Manchester.[112]

That the shift described by Golder happened during a period of mass inflation and stagnant growth in both the British and the global economy was instrumental to the shops' success. After stagflation hit Britain in 1974, the shops' business provided the bulk of many charities' revenue. Charity shops came to serve Britons even as they provided funding for various international causes. They shaped British retail markets and became an integral part of the country's informal economy.

The Charity Tax

If the changing nature of British capitalism was one underlying factor of the "economization" of charity in the 1960s, another was the way charity transformed the British taxation system. In the second half of the 1960s, NGOs initiated a series of exemptions for their retail and trading ventures. Selling Christmas cards, secondhand goods, and, later, fair-trade products to fund their own operations, NGOs operated like any other retail body, generating their own revenue even though the profits were distributed to various charitable causes.

Nonprofits, of course, have long enjoyed a special status in the British economy. Since 1803 they have been able to claim, under their status as charities, parts of the incomes of the British taxpayer through deeds of covenant, which were transferred to these organizations by both an annual gift provided by the individual taxpayer and the tax they would have had to pay on it.[113] During the 1960s, however, NGOs decided to connect these deeds of covenant to a mission of helping newly independent economies. Through a series of campaigns, ads, and leaflets, NGOs promoted a new marketing strategy that connected growing affluence in Britain to a responsibility to help former colonial territories. "This little boy comes from Botswana, the former British protectorate in southern Africa," read one Oxfam leaflet:

> If he's lucky, he'll go to primary school and then, if he's luckier still, he might get a job. . . . The trouble is that in poor agricultural areas, there aren't enough places at school, let alone jobs for school-leavers. Most of them settle for dead-end jobs in mines far from home with very low pay

indeed. That's no way to build a new country. Making it a place to live and work in is an urgent task for the people of Botswana.[114]

Oxfam suggested to the British wage earner that the deed of covenant was "not so much 'charity' as a very real investment—an investment in people's own determination and hard work."[115] The deeds of covenant, usually set for seven years, forged connections between the income and tax of Britons and the newly independent economies. By 1987, the government even introduced direct payroll deduction, thus giving the British wage earner a direct path to tie their paycheck to donations, and in doing so receive tax relief on their income.[116]

NGOs also began to appeal to emerging British industrial interests through new "company covenants." In the 1960s, many British businesses were already contributing goods to nongovernmental organizations. Companies like Land Rover, for example, used their donations to NGOs as an informal way to establish a foothold in new markets in Third World economies. The new campaigns of "company covenants" offered British industry a way to expand its impact and to receive tax benefits and tax exemptions in the process. The covenants would allow companies to be "fully deductible for Corporate Tax Purposes." In 1964, for example, companies with less than £100,000 net income contributed a total of £20 million in covenants to Oxfam. By the late 1960s, about 85 percent of British companies, among them those with at least £500,000 capital employed, had signed such agreements.[117]

In 1965 nonprofits like Oxfam appealed to every public company on the London Stock Exchange, emphasizing the tax benefit of working with charities as the income from these sponsorship schemes was tax free. These appeals allowed nonprofits to set up a new industrial section with the aim of developing commercial schemes that benefited both sides by persuading companies either to set up businesses in underdeveloped areas or to send skilled British craftsmen abroad.[118] Company covenants also enabled nonprofits to establish collaborations with other parts of industry such as the Co-operative Movement and Trade Unions. The covenants became increasingly important revenue for NGOs.[119]

More important than deeds of covenant was the growth of charity trading in the 1960s, which expanded the definition of charitable work and further increased exemptions. From the mid-1960s, the proliferation of charity shops meant that the national government and local councils had to create new regulations, tax relief schemes, and new methods to account for a shop's income. Charity shops, in other words, had to create their own legal personhood within existing economic regulations and charity laws. From income tax and the new sales tax, introduced in 1973, to an exemption from property tax for many of the temporary shop premises, the shops generated a new status in the British economy for NGOs in general and international aid agencies in particular.

In the mid-1960s NGOs had to find ways to carve out exemptions for their charity shop business during a period of serious reforms in British tax law. Despite Labour's marginal win in the 1964 elections, the party committed to a progressive but radical tax reform that ended up affecting charity trading just as it was beginning to boom. Spearheaded singlehandedly by Labour's economic advisor Nicholas Kaldor, the reform was part of the party's overall modernization program. It aimed to generate higher taxation that would boost the British economy by integrating taxation of profits and income. But it also received criticism from various directions, immortalized by the Beatles song "The Taxman."[120]

The tax reform focused on two types of income tax: the corporate tax and the capital gains tax. It was the former that posed a risk to charity shops' revenue. Traditionally, NGOs enjoyed a tax exemption on any donation from the general public, but under the Finance Act of 1965 these organizations would be liable for income tax on any sales earnings, much like any other corporation.[121] The law offered an exemption only on the grounds that "a trade is exercised in the course of the actual carrying out of a primary purpose of the charity or that the work in connection with the trade is mainly carried on by the beneficiaries of the charity."[122] For many NGOs, the tax posed a serious threat to their income. Since the late 1950s, organizations like Oxfam and Save the Children as well as smaller, domestic charities had relied on charity retailing as well as charity Christmas cards for much of their revenue.[123] Christmas cards were a major source of income for small as well as large NGOs, without which, as one newspaper argued, many "would virtually collapse."[124] Many organizations either sold the cards in their own charity shops or worked with large retailers and stationers. By the mid-1960s, many NGOs were "cleaning up" the bulk of the Christmas card market and selling cards at the commercial price, thus making a profit of at least £7 million a year on cards alone.

The new law contested this profit. It stipulated that because products like Christmas cards and secondhand clothes were not produced by the beneficiaries of the charities, their sale remained liable to taxation. According to Niall MacDermot, the financial secretary to the Treasury, there was no reason why charitable trading activities should not be taxed. "Anyone who buys a charity Christmas card and thinks of this as a donation to that charity is deluding himself," he argued. "He merely buys something which he will need anyways."[125] The Finance Act, in fact, raised the question of what constituted a charitable action. Was it possible for an action to benefit the consumer directly even as it fulfilled a charitable cause? For many NGOs, the economics of altruism did not negate self-interest. Consumers could both benefit from a purchase and authentically offer a charitable donation.

The Finance Act was in fact roundly criticized by both NGOs and the Tories, who described the charity tax as "deplorable."[126] "Compared with other countries," the *Daily Telegraph* complained, the British state "is extraordinarily stingy in its treatment of people who give to charitable organizations, granting them in general no relief from tax whatever."[127] For many charities in 1964, the sale of Christmas cards alone generated an average profit of more than £300,000.[128] The new tax system proposed to take around 43.75 percent of that.[129] Donald Powell, general secretary of the British Polio Fellowship, argued that "when people buy these cards they expect the money to go to charity, not to the tax man."[130] The Finance Act was perceived as a major blow to the income of many NGOs, from smaller ones that relied primarily on Christmas card income to larger ones that had a burgeoning empire of charity shops.

By the end of 1965, Labour had caved in to the pressure and added an amendment to the corporate tax code that allowed charities to receive an exemption by setting up their own subsidiary trading companies.[131] The idea was that the trading company would pay the profits back to the charity and thus help NGOs receive the full share of their charitable deductions. The solution, however, was favorable only to large charities like the humanitarian organizations Oxfam, Save the Children, and War on Want, who could afford it. Others were concerned that the trading companies would change the nature of charitable work and that they would not be able to compete under the conditions set up by the law.[132] Oxfam had been exploring the idea of setting up its own subsidiary company since 1964, in response to the pressure of the regulatory body of the Charity Commission.[133] The commission had questioned whether Oxfam could retain its status as a charity, even while expanding its retail venture to various developmental and fair-trade initiatives. The amendment to the Finance Act, in fact, opened a route for various organizations to not only manage their retail business but also escape the regulations of the Charity Commission altogether. Crucially, as we shall see, these trading companies reframed nongovernmental and humanitarian work as capitalist enterprise, generating their own economic knowledge and expertise about fair-trade markets.

The fight to retain income from charity retail did not end with the formation of subsidiary companies. In 1973, when Britain joined the European Economic Community (EEC), the Conservative government introduced Value Added Tax (VAT) as a general tax on the sales of goods and services.[134] VAT was a requirement for Britain's entry into the EEC, but it also suited the Conservatives' general fiscal policy: to move away from direct taxation on profits and income to indirect taxation, in order to introduce more flexibility into the tax system.[135] The new VAT exempted only essential goods, such as food, fuel, and housing, thus posing a serious challenge to charity businesses.[136] It was set to a rate of 10 percent on all goods, jeopardizing the shops' ability to offer cheap prices on charity retail.[137]

In September 1971, when news about the tax became public, the National Council of Social Services—acting in its traditional role as representing charitable organizations in the field of health, welfare, environmental, community, and youth services—formed an advisory group to examine the effect of the new proposed Finance Bill on British charities. The advisory group argued that the tax was defined as one on the individual consumer, but in the case of charitable retail it was the charity that should be treated as the consumer of goods (in this case the gift) rather than the individual shopper in their stores. VAT, the group argued, could have a "detrimental effect" on the services provided by charities. "Unless some relief is granted," it concluded, the VAT will "seriously erode" the resources of many NGOs in Britain and "reduce [their] ability to carry out [their] purposes." In its final recommendation, submitted to the financial secretary to the Treasury, the group suggested that "any organization that can show it is a legal charity should be entitled to recover VAT invoiced with all its inputs. . . . The criterion for relief should be charitable status and not function."[138]

In the summer of 1972, a number of domestic and international NGOs, led by Oxfam, launched a campaign to amend the tax to include zero rating for charitable services. "DepriVATion is uncharitable," read one of its pamphlets. The campaign explicitly argued against the taxation of charitable gifts given by the public, even if those gifts were in the form of secondhand goods to be sold in charity shops.[139] It claimed that charity shopping did not constitute a luxury purchase because it either traded in goods made by the communities it was set to aid or was donated by the general public.

Titled "Fight VAT Fast,"[140] the campaign appealed to national and local newspapers, shop customers, and organization supporters to write letters to their local MPs requesting that the government not "break with tradition" and continue to respect the special status charities had enjoyed in the British tax system, even for charity retail.[141] "The British people are wonderfully generous to a deserving cause," read one pamphlet.[142] "How many of them realise . . . that when Value Added Tax is introduced next April, 10% of the profit from [their] gifts will go to the taxman, instead of to the poverty-stricken." As for the government, it "will be practising a breach of faith with the public in doing this," the campaign concluded.[143] The campaign invited citizens to join various demonstrations against the tax that summer. Campaign supporters also met with various MPs and went to the House of Commons continuously over the summer and the fall of 1972 to lobby for the government to amend the bill.[144]

On March 6, 1973, the government responded to these concerns by amending the tax. According to the Conservative Chancellor Lord Barber, in response to the campaign run by various charities, the government "decided that the best course is simply to zero-rate the sale in a charity shop of all goods, both new and used, which have been given for resale to a charity established for the relief of the distressed."[145] The battle against the VAT for charity retail was won.

The battle for tax exemptions did not end with sales and income taxes, however. The brick-and-mortar shops also posed a challenge to local councils because charities claimed exemptions from local tax on their businesses as well. Many local municipalities feared that the shops would therefore create a loophole to avoid taxation on private premises.[146] In 1972, the Birmingham City Council made such a claim when it denied Oxfam a business rate relief on its nine shops in the city. The council contended that although the shops were occupied by the charity, they did not serve charitable purposes and therefore did not quality for relief. Under the 1967 General Rate Act, a business rate relief of 50 percent could be granted to charities if the premise "directly . . . facilitate[s] the carrying out of its main purpose."[147] But what constituted "charitable work" was a matter of much debate. Oxfam's lawyers charged that the charity shops were distinct from "ordinary trading" shops not least because "there was no buying but selling goods . . . [t]here was no paid labour . . . [and because] [i]t was possible that purchases of goods were motivated by desire to give to charity."[148] Although a charity might have used its profits to support various aid programs, on June 1, 1974, the High Court ruled in favor of the City of Birmingham, claiming that the shops' decision to raise money by trading was not a charitable purpose of the charity.

Throughout 1975, Oxfam appealed to the government to offer an amendment to the Rate Act, and by 1976 it was joined by other domestic and international organizations, among them Save the Children, Help the Aged, and the British Red Cross Society. Help the Aged, for example, argued that in 1975 the ruling against rate relief cost it around £50,000. Others had to close their shops.[149] In a letter from March 4, 1975, British prime minister Harold Wilson reassured Oxfam that he had "much sympathy with the position of Oxfam and other charities which have been affected . . . [and that] [t]he Government fully accepts that the decision should be reversed."[150] On July 7, 1976, the House of Lords put forward a Rating (Charity Shop) Bill that amended the law and restored to charities a rate relief of 50 percent even on trading activities. The shops thus became a discrete economic space free of tax and open for charitable trading.

New Market for Charity Retail

Sometime in the mid-1960s, charity shops began to sell small handicraft products made by communities in imperial or former imperial territories. The turn from local and national philanthropic markets toward imperial and postimperial ones was an important stage in the economization of charity work in the decade. It helped connect the growing network of new aid programs and fieldworkers in South Asia, and later Africa and Latin America (most of them with a former colonial background), to fundraising campaigns. Once the products from the various aid programs were added to the shops' stock, Oxfam and other organizations hoped that the shops would reshape economic life in Britain, forging a connection between local communities in Britain and postimperial communities abroad. It joined a broader turn in Western Europe toward ethical consumerism and the sale of handicrafts through what would be called on the Continent "Third World" shops.

The idea of selling handicraft products to British consumers was not entirely new; it had deep imperial origins. Beginning in the late nineteenth century, philanthropists and missionaries imported needlework, knitwork, and embroideries created by refugee communities across the South Asian and Near Eastern colonies in order to fund their aid work.[151] In the late 1950s, when charity shops began to expand their reach, NGOs built on this imperial tradition. The shops' network provided an opportunity to disseminate and fundraise for a variety of imperial and postimperial aid projects. The charity shop took these aid schemes, which essentially provided ad hoc relief to distressed communities, and developed them into a permanent source of revenue.

Oxfam was the first to utilize the shops' infrastructure for such fundraising activities. In 1956, Oxfam received a request to collaborate with the missionaries of the Lutheran World Federation's Department of World Services to sell pincushions and embroidered work by Chinese asylum seekers in British Hong Kong who had fled the revolution. The organization was skeptical, but the idea received support from Elisabeth Wilson, one of the founders of Huddersfield Famine Relief Committee and a member of Oxfam's Executive Committee and its Asia Grants Committee. Wilson, who at the time was working on behalf of Oxfam in India and the Far East, began to sell some of these items through the Huddersfield Famine Relief Committee operations in the north of England.[152]

By the late 1950s, when Wilson's efforts bore fruit, Oxfam decided to sell some of these items in its own shops. Imported by the Lutheran World Federation's Department of World Services director, Reverend Ludwig Stumpf, these handicraft items were sold in Oxfam shops across the British Isles in order to fund missionary aid work in British Hong Kong.[153] Oxfam had also paid the import duty for the items.[154] The exchange utilized the shops' modern network but bore the remnants of Victorian-style campaigns.

In the early 1960s, Oxfam decided to expand on this idea and stock its shops with handicraft work from the communities it supported. Oxfam had hoped "to obtain hand-made goods from under-developed countries for sale in our shops, particularly through those agencies overseas to whom we send grants."[155] Oxfam aimed to utilize the various projects it supported and marry them with its shops venture. The organization also lobbied HM Customs for an exemption on import duties.[156]

The person behind the idea was Lynn ten Kate, Oxfam's international appeals organizer and later its executive secretary, who also played a critical role in setting up Oxfam of Canada and Oxfam Belgique.[157] Ten Kate came to the organization with business experience; she had been running her

husband's engineering company for a couple of years before she began working for Oxfam in 1963. Before being sent to Canada, ten Kate initially worked
as a "gift organizer," hired to "fill the shops" with different items.[158] She quickly
garnered a reputation for obtaining great items and leaving the shops well
stocked. In late 1964, when ten Kate returned from her posts in Canada and
Belgium, she became the international appeals organizer. It was in this position that she came up with the idea of capitalizing on the connections between
the shops and the various development projects Oxfam supported. As she later
described it, it was "the beginning of what turned out to be the fair trade
movement."[159]

To make such an idea possible, ten Kate contacted Oxfam's first field director, T. F. (Jimmy) Betts, who had been working in Africa since 1961 to set up the
organization's own aid ventures across Britain's colonial and former colonial
territories.[160] Ten Kate had asked Betts to find various handmade items—
necklaces, musical instruments, ornaments, bowls—made by the communities
Oxfam had begun supporting in Africa that she could sell in the shops. At the
time, Oxfam was trying to grow its operations and supported a variety of projects across the decolonizing empire. These included not only the small-scale
projects it prided itself on but also state-led development programs.[161] The ad
hoc import networks that these experts utilized were not aimed necessarily at
generating revenue for the shops but rather at using them to extend the reach
of Oxfam's growing aid programs. But ten Kate hoped Betts could use his connections in Africa and bring back items that the organization supported—
whether through financial support or through direct projects it had begun
running—and that the shops would offer "a steady market" for the goods.[162]

The first items Betts's office acquired were handmade necklaces that
"looked exotic and attractive" and had been made by the Woman's Institute
(Maendeleo Ya Wanake) in Kenya in 1964, a year after the country had gained
independence by fighting against a violent counterinsurgency campaign led by
the British.[163] According to ten Kate, Oxfam bought the necklaces for "very,
very little" and was making a good profit on them.[164] The Kenyan necklaces,
in fact, generated a 30 percent profit for Oxfam.[165] But the operation was not
efficient enough for ten Kate's liking. It was "handled by the African members
themselves and quite frankly they are not capable of making up the parcels let
alone writing out the invoices or filling in the commonwealth Preference
form," she complained.[166] Ten Kate therefore asked Betts to step in and facilitate the purchase of the items. For ten Kate, Betts's position enabled him to
manage commercial exchanges that would benefit the shops as well as the aid
recipients. She similarly contacted and worked with Oxfam's other field directors across the decolonizing empire.[167]

Betts, the brother of Britain's first minister of overseas development Barbara
Castle, was one of many aid experts hired by Oxfam and other international aid
organizations.[168] The large informal aid empire of Oxfam's charity shops was

sustained, at least partially, by a growing body of aid workers hired across the former empire. With their knowledge of and emotional ties to the former colonial territories, these ex-colonial experts were ideal candidates for the expanding aid sector in the 1960s. They often had technical expertise in the fields of agriculture or irrigation. Some, like Betts, had even continued to collaborate and share their reports with the Colonial Office and later with the Ministry of Overseas Development (ODM), which inherited the Colonial Office's aid mandate in 1964. As historians have shown, these ex-colonial experts helped expand the nongovernmental aid sector in the 1960s exponentially.[169]

The newly created ODM would gradually help facilitate and support the fair-trade infrastructure created by Oxfam and other NGOs in Britain. Despite the mirage of nongovernmentality, Oxfam and other organizations maintained a close connection with the British government and ODM. The ministry not only financially supported nongovernmental economic ventures, it also saw similarities between its own economic and educational mission and that of organizations like Oxfam. The ministry, Barbara Castle declared when she was appointed in 1964, "would have the task of educating our own people in the vital role which overseas aid plays in the life of the world, in the struggle for peace, in the development of new markets and in the fight for full employment."[170] For Castle, the various voluntary bodies—Oxfam, Voluntary Services Overseas, and others—would help the ministry reach these goals. NGOs capitalized on that idea. "The Ministry has an urgent and most necessary job to do in helping NGOs," wrote Peter Burns, Oxfam's first lobbyist and, later, general secretary of War on Want.[171] NGOs fashioned themselves as the popular arm of the government, bodies that represented and could mobilize the British public in support of various economic missions.

It was largely thanks to Oxfam's "overseas arm" of field directorates, as one of its workers once called them, supported by the ODM, that the network of Oxfam aid experts across the newly independent Third World became the basis for stocking the growing network of charity shops in Britain.[172] These experts were well trained and conscientious, had excellent report-writing skills and knowledge in foreign politics, and were dedicated to public service.[173] Their overseas experience was one of the main qualifications for their recruitment to Oxfam.[174] They laid the groundwork for Oxfam's effective delivery of overseas aid and used their colonial expertise as the basis and background for a new international career as humanitarian aid workers.[175] These experts were the "men-on-the-spot" in charge of coordinating Oxfam's aid with the local authorities. They sparked Oxfam's substantial growth over the decade and expanded its scope and reach as an international relief agency. By 1965, Oxfam had five field directors: three in Africa, one in India, and one in the Far East.[176]

The field directors' work of obtaining handicrafts was not always seamless. Officials like Betts did not necessarily see the connection between their own

FIGURE 2.3. Joe Mitty receiving handicrafts from Rwandan refugees for the Broad Street shop, 1963.

work and the shops' operation. Moreover, they struggled to find "genuine," "native made" handicrafts, as ten Kate had lamented in one of her reports. Ten Kate even encouraged some of the field directors to consider teaching some of the groups they supported how to produce their own broaches, necklaces, and handmade goods so they could generate some funds for their aid programs. In the end, Oxfam often "resorted to buying foreign goods from wholesalers" in Britain itself, later marketing the items as handicraft goods.[177]

For appeal organizers like ten Kate, the problem of obtaining handicraft goods raised the question of whether it was even right to encourage their import as a form of development aid. "In this commercial world," she wrote in one of her memos, "a man is unlikely to make much headway if it takes him a whole day to carve one wooden animal perhaps, we should encourage semi-mass production articles. Perhaps instead of buying from existing sources we should co-operate with the Overseas Aid Department in encouraging new enterprise."[178] The shops' operation not only opened up the possibility of creating local and national philanthropic markets. It presented a lucrative opportunity to rethink the nature of development aid and to connect it to postimperial markets. The question for people like ten Kate was how to materialize this opportunity.

In the late 1960s, activists arrived at various solutions. After Oxfam set up its trading company, Oxfam Activities Ltd. (later renamed Oxfam Trading), the organization rethought its small handicraft venture and attempted to develop it into a postimperial market. The company's infrastructure and organization, as well as its new business and retail expertise, offered Oxfam an opportunity to reconceptualize the connections between the organization's charity shop empire and the growing number of aid programs it not only supported but also had begun to run independently. The result was one of several attempts to create alternative, fair-trade markets that would sell the promise of an "authentic" connection between the consumer and producer through the shops' operation. The "economization of charity" in the 1960s provided concrete models for how nongovernmental activists might realize this alternative form of development.

Consumer Desire

"In the past few years," wrote the activist Jane Leathley in *The Guardian* in 1975, "a changed attitude to and by charity has altered the face of fund-raising in this country." Throughout the 1960s, NGOs came to embrace a new economic mentality in their work. From secondhand charity shops, to limited liability companies, and, finally, to handicrafts from various Third World communities, changes in approaches to charity were not limited to fundraising. Through charity trading, NGOs and humanitarian organizations in particular became their own economic agents. "The need industry," to use Leathley's formulation, has adopted "the advertising and marketing skills used by big business."[179]

The transformation of NGOs into "big business" had some of its origins in the introduction of new charity workers and advertising expertise in 1950s, but it was in the 1960s that the "economization of charity" really took shape. In the 1960s, nonprofits turned to the consumer-citizen as their main constituent. Nongovernmental work was assembled and quantified into economic activity through charity trading. Charity shops were consolidated into economic spaces that engaged a range of social actors, from donors to consumers, volunteers, and, eventually, postimperial producers. They became a key site for nongovernmental markets—at first local and eventually postimperial ones.

In the 1960s NGOs designed charity trade to transform consumerism into a meaningful act, allowing British citizens to transcend the commodification of consumption, the alienation and exploitation of the global market. Charity retail carried an emotional potential: it could gratify local, intimate acts of shopping with global, compassionate exchange of money and labor. When an English woman in Kent went to a charity shop to buy a real leather purse made in Morocco, "a country famous for its leather work," she became connected to the Moroccan leatherworker who made the purse.[180] Similarly, when a young girl in York bought a beaded necklace, she knew the money would go to a worthy cause. Charity trading packaged shopping as an ethical and pleasurable activity. Their products carried a new type of "commodity fetishism," if it can be called that, in which the objects to be consumed carried an ethical worth that transcended their aesthetic or normal exchange value. Through the charity trade a British housewife in Kent could buy a leather purse not merely because it was fashionable but also because it fulfilled an ethical imperative.

Some products even had an educational value aimed at globalizing the minds of young consumers. Such was the rag doll kit advertised in a 1969 charity shop catalogue. Dressed in the traditional style of Bolivia, India, Ghana, or Korea, it helped British girls learn about distant cultures and traditions for the small price of 5s. 6d.[181] These kinds of items had a specifically pedagogical goal: to create a new kind of global subject with a new sense of ethical obligation. Other objects were displayed in a "Festival of India," an exhibition touring London, Cardiff, Glasgow, Sheffield, and Bradford, as well as "Man Exhibition" at the Hayward Gallery.[182] Handicrafts were seen authentic, their production as ethical.

In 1970, an Oxfam brochure explained to the consumer the philosophy behind the shops. "In a country which is becoming more and more mechanical and where commercialism roars on every side," it emphasized,

> Oxfam shops are a refreshing reminder that *people* matter. In them the paper-back or the mandolin—or whatever you buy—represents not only value for money but a contribution towards someone's *life*. Oxfam's work is not only headline-hitting rescue operations at time of earthquake and flood but much more concerned with helping people in simple ways to free themselves from the yoke of poverty and hunger to which they were born. It is precisely here that the everyday purchases of ordinary British people in Oxfam shops are helping the everyday lives of people in less fortunate areas of the world.[183]

By emulating a key ingredient of the market economy, Oxfam framed freedom of choice as a way to constitute one's subjectivity as an ethical consumer, a choice that goes beyond what one wants but rather is focused on what one ought to purchase. It created capitalism with a human face, which at the level of consumption offered an "authentic" shopping experience.

By the mid-1970s around 90 percent of the British population was giving something to charity annually, according to Leathley. "Strangely," she observed, despite the recession, "individual belt-tightening does not make people less generous."[184]

In the 1970s the growth of charity trading shaped economic life among not only affluent donors but also impoverished communities in deindustrialized Britain who had come to rely on charity shop products during the recession. Charity trading helped NGOs develop their own economic and moral approach to development, one based in some of Schumacher's economic philosophy. Chapter 3 traces how in the 1970s nonprofit activists attempted to use charity trading to generate fairer markets that would end inequalities between Britain and the world. It shows how the ethical consumer, created by charity shops and retail in the 1960s, became connected to a network of producers in the former colonies in the 1970s and how, in the process, nonprofits aimed to remake the meaning of work after empire.

CHAPTER THREE

Can Trade Be Fair?

IN AN INTERNAL MEMO dated March 1, 1973, Roy Scott, a manager at Oxfam Trading, wrote that "the present system of trade discourages rather than encourage[s] poor people in development countries." According to Scott, workers "are exploited by profit-oriented forms of business. Profiteering and clumsy distribution systems also increase prices for consumers." The entire system of international trade hinged on monopolies and disadvantaged Third World producers, and it was not serving British consumers either. The solution Scott proposed was to forge a nongovernmental trade agency that would bypass the official channels of international trade. This agency would help create new trading structures to "bridge" the gap between British consumers and Third World producers and would "provide a healthy framework for developing *responsibility* among both groups."[1]

During the 1970s a new generation of activists in Britain came to believe that the nonprofit sector had a central role to play in the fight against global inequality. Instead of promising more "philanthropic paternalistic sentimentality," they called for the formation of nongovernmental markets that would restructure economic relationships between Britain and its former colonies.[2] Echoing the economic philosophy of E. F. Schumacher, activists sought a fairer trading system that would not serve governments but "focus instead on *people*."[3] They strove for a decentralized trade system that would be based on the principles of solidarity and mutual aid. Trade had a key role in this vision because, advocates believed, all participants in fair-trade markets would benefit equally, consumers as well as producers.[4] Their programs marked a critical moment in the search for ethical capitalism.

This chapter locates the turn to this decentralized, fair-trade vision within the postimperial politics of development in the 1970s. It shows how, in this decade, activists like Scott took the infrastructure of charity trading and connected it to burgeoning nongovernmental, development programs. To such activists, these programs offered a direct and ethical solution to the contemporary crisis of global capitalism because they enabled nonprofits to generate decentralized, grassroots markets independent from formal international and bilateral trade. Already in the 1960s British NGOs became invested in the project of development. But in the 1970s their embrace of fair trade enabled them to expand on these programs and to shape labor and production patterns. They aimed to move production from large factories to small workshops and to sell directly to British consumers what they considered authentic "indigenous handicrafts."

The history of ethical capitalism has largely been told as a story about the consumer movement and the politics of globalization from the late 1980s onward; this chapter demonstrates that earlier, in the 1970s, ethical capitalism was also intertwined with efforts to remake labor after empire.[5] It joins new works that explore the relationship between fair trade and the end of empire and shows that, in Britain, fair trade was linked to a postimperial mission to transform Britain's role in the global economy.[6] Elsewhere in the 1970s, a new generation of activists were radicalized by calls to decolonize the world economy, driven in particular by the push for a New International Economic Order (NIEO) and the revolutionary spirit of 1968. Unlike their Western European counterparts, however, British activists had been shaped by more than a decade of imperial and postimperial political debates over international development. They believed that British NGOs had a particular role to play in solving the problem of international trade and global inequalities after decolonization.

This generation of activists, which came of age during the tumultuous decades of decolonization, had a complex relationship to empire and its contraction. Born around 1947, on the eve of Indian independence, it encountered the idea of development just as Britain lost the majority of its African and Caribbean colonies during the 1960s. Their understanding of development differed from that of their parents' generation. Unlike aid workers trained to govern an empire, the postwar generation was educated in the theories of economic development guiding the Third World during the years of independence: from technical knowledge of agriculture and irrigation to modernization theory. This generation's activism carried a postimperial mission infused with a particular moral undertone. When they encountered anticolonial calls to end economic domination, they interpreted them within a postimperial sensibility rooted in notions of the responsibilities and duties of British citizens. Their focus on development was almost exclusively centered around former colonial territories and Commonwealth nations rather than other geographies. The successes and failures of this generation's campaigns should not be measured against calls for radical, anticolonial politics but rather should be assessed in relation to this postimperial sensibility. Put simply, this generation revised rather than discarded the old imperial mission, ascribing to Britons a preeminent moral role in the global economy.

When the UN and other international organizations declared the failure of the modernization paradigm of development thinking in the early 1970s, this generation marshalled a new approach to development that emphasized decentralization and entrepreneurship. Amid a global economic crisis, aid workers and activists turned to fair trade as a grassroots solution to the problem of global unemployment. Fair trade became the answer to a broader, international question about the problem of global inequalities and the failure of international development to address them. Labeled "trade for the people" in one Oxfam pamphlet, fair-trade markets linking British consumers with Third World producers were this generation's answer to the problem of trade inequalities—a solution that would operate through nongovernmental channels. In this view, NGOs had a unique role to play as nonprofit organizations representing people rather than governments. Activists called it "people-centered development": a new microeconomic approach that made the poor themselves the drivers of growth. Rejecting macroeconomic growth as the solution to underdevelopment, they trained Third World producers to meet the demand of British consumers and to become entrepreneurs marketing their own "indigenous" products. Using the framework of nongovernmental subsidiary companies, these fair-trade programs aimed to shape both supply and demand.

The argument in this chapter is organized in four sections. The first locates the turn to fair trade within the broader politics of nongovernmental development of the 1960s. It shows how activists invested in development as part of a postimperial mission aimed at establishing a moral role in the international political economy. The second section charts the formation of one exemplary fair-trade market that emerged in the 1970s—Oxfam's handicraft market—and the solutions it was meant to offer to the problems of global unemployment and trade inequalities. The third section closely analyzes the political economy of this market and how it operated in practice. It argues that Oxfam's decentralized and unregulated handicraft market offered business opportunities geared toward satisfying consumer demand in Britain rather than addressing labor inequalities in the Third World. In some cases, it even supported poor working conditions while generating high profit margins for Oxfam. The fourth section briefly shows how in the 1980s Oxfam's market became an important model for fair-trade handicraft markets internationally. Untangling the postimperial legacies of these markets enables us to understand the successes and failures of this vision of ethical capitalism.

New Generation, Old Ideals

In a 1966 essay, the cultural theorist Stuart Hall claimed that the 1960s were defined by "the absence of political sensibility." According to Hall, in that decade the nature of politics had changed; it had become "unpoliticized."

To elucidate this somewhat abstract statement, he offered a specific example: Oxfam's development campaigns. Hall suggested that Oxfam and other international aid agencies had garnered huge support for their campaigns, especially among a new generation of young Britons, by treating the political issue of "the gap between the rich and poor nations" in "a non-political way." There was much to say in favor of the campaigns, Hall argued. They fought for a worthy cause and mobilized a new cohort of activists. Nonetheless, they "helped to depoliticize for some part of the British people the issue of poverty in the third world."[7]

In the early 1960s, during the rapid years of decolonization in Africa and the Caribbean, British NGOs embraced the project of development aid. From Oxfam to Christian Aid to War on Want, these organizations began to fund and eventually even run their own development programs. Development, of course, was not new to the 1960s. Since the late nineteenth century the imperial state used the framework of development to support its economy. But in the 1960s the nonprofit sector connected development with a postimperial mission to aid newly independent economies. Development, in fact, became the basis for the expansion of much of the nongovernmental sector in Britain in the 1960s.[8]

Development became the new frame to recruit supporters and teach the British public, especially young people, about their mission. British NGO campaigns devoted a huge part of their work to educating, informing, and even recruiting a new generation of British citizens to the cause of ending world poverty. Encouraged and funded by the British government, NGOs had hoped British youth would play a moral role in forging the path to postcolonial development. Their campaigns built on a long imperial tradition, which sought to ascribe to Britons a paternalistic role in international politics. Their campaigns often framed the politics of development in nonpolitical ways: instead of historical explanations for the causes of economic inequalities, they offered transhistorical depictions of a world divided between "rich" and "poor" nations. In short, they presented economic inequalities as disconnected from the political conditions that produced them.

The UN Freedom From Hunger Campaign (FFHC) had an important role in this story. Launched by the Food and Agriculture Organization (FAO), the FFHC enlisted over 75 international voluntary organizations to mobilize the support of the global public in the project of developing the Third World. Its main objectives channeled global Cold War politics, aiming to raise awareness of "the problem of hunger and malnutrition [which] pose serious threat to peace and orderly progress."[9] By the end of 1968 the FAO had implemented more than 400 development projects, costing about £20 million.[10]

While the FFHC was global in scope, it still played a critical role in the growth of aid organizations in Britain. The FFHC was embraced by all the main NGOs—including Oxfam, Christian Aid, Save the Children, War on

Want, and Save the Children—and it engaged them, for the very first time, in development work. It also advanced a collaboration between these organizations and the Colonial Office, which provided most of the funding for the FFHC campaigns.[11] The campaign received support from the Duke of Edinburgh, Prince Philip, who as the president of the Council for Volunteers Overseas stated that the British people had the responsibility "to fill the gaps in the developing fabric of the public, education and agriculture services in [newly independent and developing] countries, which they cannot fill themselves for the time being." "This is a great task," he continued, "which they set out to perform not only for the countries in which they will work but also for the good name of Britain."[12]

The FFHC helped Britain reclaim a global role as a postimperial nation of aid workers.[13] A huge part of the FFHC campaign involved educating the British public and marshalling a new generation of young people to support, and even volunteer for, development programs. "Idealism is the essence of youth," argued FAO director Binay Ranjan Sen, "but unless there is opportunity for the idealism to be expressed in concrete action, it often turns to anger and revolt."[14] Beginning in 1961, British NGOs issued various educational brochures, films, and booklets to schools and teachers across the country, all targeting adolescents as a key audience for new development ideas.[15] In 1965 they also launched Youth against Hunger, a scheme that was part of the FFHC's novel effort to recruit both middle- and working-class adolescents. The campaign collaborated with both the Boy Scouts and an array of church groups.[16]

By 1966, Oxfam and Christian Aid had taken over the work begun by the FFHC, creating their own education departments aimed at increasing awareness and understanding in Britain of global development issues. In the late 1960s, these departments began producing syllabi and conducting public examinations in schools and colleges of education to test how much "development" content had been made available to students and teachers.[17] For the large British NGOs, educational work was key to shaping a new generation of the British public into volunteers and supporters. Such educational work in Britain was viewed as intimately connected to the development project in the Third World.

Educational projects supported broader efforts to target young people by instilling a new aid culture on the streets of Britain. As the Liberal MP Jeremy Thorpe put it in 1969, youth represented "Britain's young volunteer army."[18] Activities like "fasts for famines" in Trafalgar Square marketed nongovernmental campaigns to young Britons. They aimed to make youth "feel" world starvation and act "in the cause of humanity."[19] Walkathons—in many ways the origins of today's sponsored charity marathons—were another way to mobilize young people on the streets.[20] Aid organizations even recruited celebrities like Twiggy and the Beatles to lend a trendy, young profile to humanitarianism.[21] NGOs hoped that British youth would "go out as our forefathers did in years gone by, not to conquer those countries, but to bring them up to the same standard of living, or prosperity and sophistication which we enjoy in this country."[22] The outreach to British youth was deeply connected to a discourse of imperial trusteeship.[23] It was a culture of aid that sought to appeal to the idealism of British adolescence and channel it to serve the post-imperial mission of development work.

The spread of a nongovernmental aid culture was supported by the British government and matched the government's postimperial aspirations. "We are in a new phase," announced the Conservative MP Charles Mott-Radclyffe in a speech to the House of Commons in February 1964. "The Colonial Empire has evolved into a series of independent Commonwealth countries and where the old administration left off [our] task begins. . . . There is still the absolute need for men of honesty, integrity and skill. We in the United Kingdom can still provide the personnel required."[24] Young people were a key element of the new postimperial personnel.

Youth was becoming an important social, political, and economic category, and not only for social scientists and policymakers.[25] Young people's work was itself embraced as part of the mission of the British welfare and developmental state in the 1960s.[26] "We need a plan to mobilise the enthusiasms of our youth, and to mobilise them in the cause of making their country a better country than it was when they were born into it," Lord Robertson declared in a 1965 speech to the House of Lords titled "Youth and Social Responsibilities."[27] In the same year, the new minister of overseas development, the Labour MP Barbara Castle, recognized the importance of adolescence in development aid by setting up a small government subsidy to help with education in development aid that particularly targeted youth. To both Conservatives and Labour, youth participation in development promised to provide Britain with a moral place in international relations.

The Ministry of Overseas Development joined a broader institutionalization of development work as a new field of knowledge and research in Britain by creating the Overseas Development Institute (ODI), a think tank founded in 1960 and funded by the UK government as well as the Ford Foundation, the World Bank, and British companies with overseas (and colonial) investments. During the 1960s and 1970s, the ODI became a central source for British expertise in development economics. It trained a young generation of economists, aid workers, and volunteers. "Volunteers' youth and enthusiasm," wrote one of its researchers, Adrian Moyes, in a famous 1966 report, "fit them well for these tasks."[28] But according to Moyes (who would later work for Oxfam), the new generation of volunteers needed to move from doing amateur aid work to becoming skills-based professionals. The ODI, which hosted a range of development and economic experts, played a crucial role in this professionalization. Many of the new generation of development thinkers and aid workers in nongovernmental and international organizations in the 1970s would go through the ODI.

Some activists—like Teresa Hayter—had been so radicalized by this postcolonial moment that they came to critique the entire field of development aid. Born in 1940 in Shanghai to a British diplomat, Hayter was hired by the ODI in 1963 for a three-year stint as a researcher on French Africa and Latin America.[29] During her tenure, and especially during her time working on Latin America, she came to see aid as perpetuating, and sometimes increasing, the "severe inequalities in the distribution of income and power" in recipient countries.[30] Her work on Latin America, financed by the World Bank and particularly critical of international aid mechanisms and the U.S. role within it, was censored by the ODI, which decided against publishing it. In the late 1960s, after a postgraduate course in political economy, Hayter became a Marxist and in 1971 published a series of critiques of international aid, which she titled *Aid as Imperialism.* The book was a direct attack on the ODI and what Hayter characterized as a native approach that assumed " 'aid' was good and that the major objective of 'aid' could reasonably be expected to be 'development' in, and for, the Third World."[31] For her part, Hayter embraced an alternative economics model articulated by postcolonial statesmen, which emphasized the dependencies of Third World economies on Western economies and called for a radical structural reorganization of global economic relations.[32] The majority of activists, however, working in Oxfam, Christian Aid, Save the Children, and even to some extent War on Want in the late 1960s absorbed the anticolonial critique of the period into an older framework of aid.[33]

The ODI was not the only hub for generating development knowledge in Britain, however. The burgeoning field of "development studies" became an independent subject in most British universities, not least the new "plateglass" universities founded in the 1960s. The field framed development as a moral mission that disguised old imperial aims. Most prominent was the Institute of Development Studies (IDS) at the University of Sussex. IDS was founded in 1966 by the economist Dudley Seers and partially funded by the Ministry of Overseas Aid. It became an important hub for training of British and international aid workers over the course of the 1970s and the 1980s. The IDS shared a similar postimperial mission to think tanks like the ODI, NGOs, and the British government. As Seers himself argued, although the British empire had ended, "Unspoken, perhaps, was the thought that a place of training in Britain was necessary to maintain British influence overseas."[34]

Seers, who together with his friend Schumacher was an ardent critic of the focus on economism and GNP-growth, directed the institute for the first five years and populated it with economists who shared his approach to development. These included Richard Jolly, who became the institute's director between 1971 and 1981 and later write an important report for UNICEF on social consequences of adjustments policies; Michael Lipton, who led a famous seminar at the institute on village economics; Hans Singer, who was best known for his Singer-Prebisch thesis, an important theory of dependency in development economics which argued (against modernization theory) for a structural reform in the global terms of trade; and Barbara Ward, who was affiliated with it. The institute also employed former colonial administrators such as Tommy Gee, who had served in Uganda and eventually became a Permanent Secretary of the Uganda Ministry of Education immediately before and after decolonization in 1962.

In the 1970s, IDS became an important international center, offering alternative approaches to modernization-doxa. Through its training seminars and MPhil program it promoted ideas such as a participatory approach to development; village studies; women and gender as integral to development; science and technology and transnational corporations; informal work and entrepreneurship; and alternatives to structural adjustment and debt relief. Importantly, in the early 1970s the institute established a unique partnership with the ILO on employment strategy and redistribution. This partnership produced a series of reports about employment beyond the industrial sector and the formal economy. It solidified the IDS' reputation for expertise in development policies during a period of deindustrialization and economic crisis. By the mid-1970s the IDS also played a critical role in generating new development strategies inspired by the NIEO's redistribution policies. IDS connected the egalitarian and anticolonial critique of the NIEO with a new cohort of aid workers in Britain and gave them a moral responsibility in implementing it.

In some cases, the moral role of development was often connected to a broader Christian religious mission.[35] A 1966 report by the British Council of Churches (to which the NGO Christian Aid was connected) was a case in point.[36] The report, *World Poverty and British Responsibility*, sought to appeal to the new constituency of British youth by connecting its religious mission to present-day egalitarian discourse. "We in Britain have to discover how to play a full part in a newly emerging world," it stated.[37] Britons had a particular moral duty toward the development of the Third World economy, one not connected to penance for their imperial past. Instead, the report argued, Britons had a moral duty to the Third World stemming from their so-called unique experience as the first industrial nation. It invited youth to join in a development partnership with the Third World: "Development is not something that we do for *them*, even if we devote *our* lives to doing it. It involves a working partnership between rich and poor, between donors of aid and the governments and peoples of countries striving to improve their lot."[38] Framing inequality in nonpolitical and ahistorical—but universal, religious, and egalitarian—terms, the report proposed a change in individual consumption patterns and an increase in Britain's aid budget. Such a frame informed much of Christian Aid's development programs: a language of partnership that was steeped in apolitical and moral messages.

The egalitarian discourse of the late 1960s shaped Oxfam and its future direction in similar ways. In 1969, the organization's deputy director, Reverend Nicolas Stacey, argued that Oxfam should shake off its "middle-aged image" and instead target "the imagination of the young professional and technocrat classes."[39] Stacey, who had come to Oxfam with experience doing social work in Woolwich, one of London's poorest neighborhoods, called on the organization to put aside its fundraising efforts and remake itself as an education and lobbying body. Stacey's specific proposal was rejected, but the organization did decide to reorient many of its activities toward youth and to invest 5 percent of its income in education, especially in the affiliated bodies run by the youth groups Young Oxfam, Third World First, and the World Development Movement.

By 1974, after the UN adopted the Declaration on the Establishment of a New International Economic Order, a number of young activists (many of whom had by then taken middle management positions at Oxfam) put forward a proposal that echoed aspects of the economic critique prevalent at the time. The proposal—which Oxfam would largely adopt—stated that the organization should focus on "a partnership of people rich and poor reaching across the barriers of power and oppression." It spoke about striving for "justice, freedom and equitable sharing of resources" and of Oxfam's role in "the developing process, firstly through financing of community project[s] . . . and secondly through the activities of the trading company in providing employment and markets."[40] It also made clear that Oxfam had a particular role in educating the British public and called for a department tasked with answering the question of "How the rich should live" and with shaping consumption patterns in Britain.[41] The younger generation of activists answered the call to decolonize the global economy by casting inequality in nonpolitical terms; they did not refer once to the imperial conditions that shaped global capitalism. Rather they used a universal egalitarian language decontextualized from the historic conditions that produced global inequalities. As we shall see, this depoliticized and moral framing also remade Oxfam into an organization devoted as much to reforming the British consumer and shaping public opinion as to running community development programs.

Parallel to this effort was the 1973 launch of a magazine devoted to development, the *New Internationalist*. It was founded by Peter and Lesley Adamson, University of Oxford students who were active in the student organization Third World First, one of many student associations shaped by FFHC. Volunteering for Third World First in order to fundraise for Oxfam, the Adamsons decided to create a publication that would "keep [students] involved."[42] The magazine originated in a Third World First campaign in 1969 and was initially distributed solely to Oxford students. By 1973, when it became a permanent (and broadly distributed) publication, the *New Internationalist* was receiving support from government officials as well as from all the major NGOs. It was financially backed by Devopress, a company established by Oxfam and Christian Aid with the specific aim of publishing the magazine. The *New Internationalist* framed the war against global inequality as one that had to be fought in both "rich" and "poor" nations. As the first issue stated: "It is the rich world which lays down the rules of world trade within which the poor must earn its living. It is the rich world which regulates the international monetary system within which the poor world must manage its finances. It is the rich world which commands 95% of the world's technological know-how and 90% of the world's income."[43] For the *New Internationalist* editorial team, the "second front" in the war against global inequality was development aid that would fight against the rich world's trade and monetary mechanisms. This redrawing of the global economic map worked against the historical conditions and the present-day political economy driving inequality between rich and poor countries.

The professionalization of a young generation of activists and aid workers through outlets like the *New Internationalist* won many British NGOs a seat at the table at international conferences on development aid throughout the 1970s. It was "the Decade of the Conference," as Peter Adamson himself put it in 1980.[44] British NGOs were invited and became active contributors to the various international conferences that established agendas for development work beyond modernization, from the World Conference on the Environment in Stockholm (1972) to the World Conferences on Food (1974), Women (Mexico City, 1975), and Employment (Geneva, 1976). Perhaps most importantly, it won them a seat at the three meetings of the United Nations Conference on Trade and Development (UNCTAD) in 1972, 1976, and 1979, which were crucial arenas for international discussions about the relationships between development and the international structures of trade.

Many activists and aid workers of the postwar generation in fact were confronted by the international politics of anticolonialism and its calls for a capacious economic restructuring of trade mechanisms at UNCTAD. "Trade not aid" was a slogan associated with UNCTAD as early as the 1960s.[45] The NIEO inherited these debates and used them to critique the field of development economics and the international aid structures that these activists participated in.[46] It saw development as a form of "neocolonialism," a dependency that cemented rather than negated the relationship of domination between the former metropole and the former colony. Although postcolonial leaders argued that their states succeeded in achieving political sovereignty, this success only deepened their economic dependence on financial mechanisms like trade agreements, aid, and debt. They called for a new international politics that would reclaim the ownership of national resources, remake international trade, and limit the hold of multinational corporations over their postcolonial economies.[47]

The political and economic critique of the NIEO coincided with a general crisis in the development framework (the only one that many activists had known). In the beginning of the 1960s there was optimism about the possibility of meeting development targets. The UN and the FAO set a minimum annual growth rate of 5 percent in aggregate national income by the end of the decade, but by the mid-1960s it was clear that many developing economies had stifled the growth of their economies. By the last half of the decade international organizations—from the FAO to the ILO and the World Bank—were recording high levels of unemployment and inequality within developing nations. In 1968, images of starving children from Biafra were appearing regularly in the British and European media. The failure of the UN First Development Decade brought new agendas and new ideas about the workings of the global economy and the role of aid. By 1973, the interconnected crises of energy, oil, currency, and, most importantly in the context of fair trade, unemployment only exacerbated these questions. It is within this context that many nongovernmental activists began to think about the nexus of anticolonial calls to decolonize the world economy, the failure of the international paradigm of development, and "the ethical aspect of the whole issue," and to tie them back to their nongovernmental campaigns.[48]

The NIEO's ideas challenged some of the moral language in which British NGOs framed development but did not revolutionize it altogether. The critique put forward by the NIEO was only one aspect of a longer institutional engagement with development aid. Instead, the younger generation of British activists was entangled in a postimperial project that attempted to find a new moral role for Britons—beyond the former imperial state—in the global economy. This generation—influenced by the postimperial politics of 1947 rather than 1968—drew direct connections between its members' positions as citizens of a former imperial metropole and the role of aid in repairing economic inequalities abroad. It was within this context that we should understand how, in the early 1970s, young aid workers in Britain turned to decentralized fair trade and the role of the British consumer—rather than the British state—as a response to the challenges laid out by the NIEO. In the minds of this generation, fair trade offered a solution to unequal development between the global North and the Third World. The turn away from structural revision at the state level was enmeshed within a longer politics of postimperial nongovernmental development and its dissociation from the British state. Oxfam's Bridge program, which we now turn to, serves as an instructive case study of how the 1970s nongovernmental turned to fair trade was rooted within this politics of development of the 1960s. Understanding this longer history of the 1947 generation and its moral engagement with development helps explain why more radical proposals to reform the world economy—as we shall see in the next section in the case study of Oxfam's Bridge program—never fully took hold.

Bridging the Gap between the Rich and the Poor

By October 1972, when Roy Scott first decided that Oxfam had a particular role to play in remaking international trade through its own fair-trade company, the organization was already involved in various trading schemes. Since the early 1960s a growing network of charity shops had been importing and selling small handicraft products like necklaces, ornaments, and embroideries made by communities around the world and supported by Oxfam through its field directors. These networks resembled and to a degree expanded on Victorian philanthropy.[49] But in 1965, after Oxfam set up a limited liability company, Oxfam Activities Ltd., the organization devised a new for-profit model and created Oxfam Trading. It handled all of Oxfam's ad hoc handicraft schemes for the shops and claimed tax relief for import duties as well as for the sale of the goods. Oxfam was of course not the only charity to forge such companies. Throughout the 1960s, other organizations like Christian Aid, Save the Children, and War on Want were undergoing a similar transformation. They became charities with for-profit sections aimed at both fundraising and development work.

But the economization of charity raised new questions about what nongovernmental work could entail. Were these import schemes part of a commercial fundraising effort or a form of development work? For many, the issue was whether Oxfam could justify making profits by capitalizing on the idea that its shops sold indigenous goods (or "native handicrafts" as they called these items).[50] Would it be capitalizing on someone's poverty and relative lack of economic power in the market? For proponents, handicrafts represented, on the one hand, an appropriate form of development aid and, on the other hand, a suitable source of fundraising. Yet the criteria used to judge success or growth were substantially different in each case. The question seemed particularly pertinent since most of the Third World handicrafts then sold in Oxfam shops were bought by commercial companies until, in 1966, Oxfam Trading's board of directors "decided that all purchases be made at source."[51] In other words, the company decided to commit to buying directly from the producers of the handicrafts. But the question of whether such transactions were commerce or development work continued to trouble Oxfam Trading and to influence its policies throughout the 1970s. It was a question that reflected the broader politics of development in Britain since the 1960s.

In 1969, Oxfam Trading appointed Guy Stringer as commercial director, and he formulated his own answer to the doubts surrounding charity work. The appointment was part of a larger institutional reorientation of Oxfam toward a more lucrative approach that would increase the shops' revenue and, in doing so, increase Oxfam's development budget.[52] Stringer came to the organization with a military and business background: a "commercial man with a conscience" is how one of Oxfam's biographers described him. He joined Oxfam after his wife, Mary, who ran one of Oxfam's charity shops in Dorset, persuaded him to try working for the organization.[53] Stringer brought a particular emphasis on entrepreneurial, commercial, and marketing strategies, which shaped Oxfam Trading, especially its fair-trade ventures, from the late 1960s through the 1970s.[54] Under his leadership, the company increased its annual sales from just under £300,000 in 1970 to nearly £750,000 in 1975.[55] He established various fundraising and tax-saving schemes for Oxfam, including Lifeline, a lucrative life insurance arrangement that gave its profits to Oxfam and afforded the

FIGURE 3.1. Koragrass weaving, southern India.
Oxfam's Helping-by-Selling poster, c. 1968.

insured tax-deductible benefits.[56] By 1983, when he became director at Oxfam, Stringer had initiated a collaboration with outside consulting firms for some campaigns, furthering his commitment to shape Oxfam Trading into a trade organization as well as the outpost of a charity.[57]

Stringer sought to connect Oxfam's commercial fundraising activities with its development programs. He did so through a fair-trade scheme called Helping-by-Selling, created in 1969.[58] The program, at least in its stated aim, would reorient Oxfam's existing handicraft imports toward a developmental goal rather than a fundraising one. "Profit is not the only parameter in this program," explained Stringer.[59] He believed that Helping-by-Selling would be better described as providing work and employment in handicraft production as "a form of aid."[60] The program concentrated on "stimulating small-scale industries, which can be one direct answer to unemployment."[61] It imported objects like dolls, jewelry, and mats made in Mexico, the Gilbert and Ellice Islands, Hong Kong, and elsewhere.[62] The idea was to utilize low-level technology, more "'labour-intensive' than 'capital intensive,'" as one promotional leaflet put it.[63] Stringer saw this as an "appropriate" form of development aid in both scale and scope.

Helping-by-Selling mirrored much of Schumacher's economic philosophy of "people-centered development" and his notion of "intermediate technology." In the early 1970s, when the First Development Decade failed to achieve its economic target and rates of unemployment in the Third World spiked, aid workers like Stringer took Schumacher's economics as a blueprint for an alternative form of aid. Schumacher's concept of intermediate technology was meant to provide a model set against modernization theory's notion that there was a single "appropriate" path to economic growth and its dogmatic emphasis on the transfer of large-scale technologies from the developing world to Third World countries. By contrast, advocates of intermediate technology proposed to advance indigenous manufacturing in rural communities in order to generate employment rather than merely increase GNP. As Schumacher stated in a 1964 report to the ODI, Third World countries required suitable technology "cheap enough to be accessible to a larger sector of the community" and easily implemented in rural communities as well as urban centers.[64] Activists like Stringer embraced Schumacher's economic philosophy because it celebrated indigenous manufacturing as a moral program rather than a political problem that needed more structural reorientation of international trade.

The scheme in fact was one of many solutions to the global unemployment crisis of the decade.[65] In the early 1970s, economists and policymakers had identified deindustrialization as a serious threat to national economies and global production systems.[66] According to a 1971 estimate, more than 75 million people in Third World countries were without jobs.[67] Rapid population growth in the Third World meant that the speed at which the labor force grew was outpacing the demand for labor, even in places where development agencies had poured funding into boosting national industries.[68] The global oversupply of workers grew further because of new redundancies in the agricultural sector in the aftermath of the Green Revolution. Even in places where food subsistence levels were met, there was chronic, weak demand for farm labor.[69]

Helping-by-Selling focused on handicrafts that utilized intermediate technology as a means to provide employment for large numbers of people.[70] One leaflet acknowledged that "Western-style highly mechanized factories may be appropriate for countries with rich consumer population and near-full employment."[71] But one factory did not fit the needs of all: "A handspun, handloom-woven run factory," the leaflet continued, "employs forty people full time to produce just five rugs a day."[72] Stringer's idea was to establish an importing company that would employ communities in the Third World through community development programs focused on self-help.[73] It aimed "to aid small scale industries in developing countries which directly benefited needy people, by providing an outlet, through Oxfam, for their useful and attractive products."[74] This was the practice of trade as aid.

Oxfam established a variety of outlets for supplying and marketing Helping-by-Selling products: these included mail-order catalogues and so-called "Third World shops" across Britain and its Commonwealth.[75] As Mary Trevena, an East Midlands organizer of such a shop, stated, "Some 30 per cent of the work force in most developing countries are unemployed. . . . This project [Helping-by-Selling] is an attempt to help the people to help themselves. It is not a charity in the conventional sense."[76] In 1969, the company was proving to be a commercially successful venture with sales of £28,000. By 1974, sales jumped to £343,564, that is, 47 percent of Oxfam's trading activities.[77] The sale of handicrafts in fact became a central point of growth for Oxfam Trading, expanding from only 9 percent of its shares in 1970 to 46 percent by 1975.[78]

In 1972, Roy Scott, a young Oxfam Trading manager working with Stringer, reviewed the program for Oxfam. According to Scott, Helping-by-Selling was focused on "short-term relief" rather than long-term development aims.[79] Still steeped in paternalist tropes, he argued that it did not offer a liberationist model to the Third World. While the program generated good revenue for Oxfam, Scott stated, its producer groups were not necessarily enjoying their fair share of the profits.[80] The program, in fact, financially benefited Oxfam much more than the producers, and only products considered to be commercially viable were supported.[81] Furthermore, while the program helped generate employment, it had not developed a way of assessing what kinds of working conditions it was actually promoting. "Is [Helping-by-Selling] arranged in the best possible interests of the people who are making the goods?" Scott asked. "Exploitation is normal in poor countries," he continued, "but we have wanted to break away from this pattern and work only with industries specially designed to avoid unfair treatment of the poor."[82] His assessment was that the program was not living up to its radical potential. Helping-by-Selling's products, he concluded, were "being made 'off the backs of the poor.' "[83]

Scott represented the new generation of British aid workers, who came of age in the 1960s. He tried to radicalize the approach of Helping-by-Selling, suggesting an alternative model in which Oxfam Trading would act as a "bridge" between producers from Third World communities and consumers in Britain. It would offer a market for indigenous goods through its shops and mail-order catalogues in order to assure a more equal and direct relationship between producers and consumers than international organizations did. In so doing, it would better support the producers who had been running the organization's production line by creating a more equal relationship. "We are, after all, trying to devise a form of international trade which best serves the interest of the people at the two ends of the trading system," explained Scott, "the producer and the consumer."[84] His vision was to create a nongovernmental cooperative model that would benefit both Third World producers and British consumers. He called this proposed program: Bridge.

Scott's proposal for Bridge built on a long imperial and postimperial tradition of using cooperatives as a technique for community development. Since the late nineteenth century, the British had used cooperatives as a development strategy to govern rural communities, first in British India and later in Britain's African and Caribbean territories.[85] By the second half of the twentieth century, cooperatives were reappropriated by the Asian and African independent states as a means of connecting their national targets for modernization with rural communities. In Britain, many Commonwealth migrants reprised the cooperative ideal as a solution to their exclusion from the country's welfare and financial services. Cooperatives, in other words, were entangled in imperial and postimperial history and were part of the history of community development long before they became a popular method of providing foreign aid.[86]

Oxfam had been investing in projects that aided cooperative communities in Third World countries since the early 1960s as part of its involvement in the FFHC. But Scott wanted to connect these cooperative ventures to domestic consumer politics, with the emphasis on consumer rights and consumer sovereignty that had been central to British political culture since the 1960s.[87] For Scott, cooperatives need not remain local or even rural. The cooperative ideal, he proposed, could be extended to fair-trade schemes that would operate globally, connecting consumers in Britain with producers in the Third World. On the one hand, Oxfam's trading company as a cooperative would serve Third World producers by offering them employment and income. On the other, it would serve "the needs of the consumer for high standards, quality, and fair price."[88] As an international, nongovernmental cooperative, the program would be based on "a partnership."[89] For Scott, such a decentralized model would shift development from the former imperial state to consumers and producers. This was a progressive vision, but it nevertheless, inadvertently, cemented a global division of labor between the West (as the consumers) and "the rest" (as producers) in the global economy.

In a period of stagflation in Britain and a global economic downturn in Third World countries, Scott's vision of Bridge had the chance of being a "near 'perfect'" trading structure if it could respond to the demands of people in developing countries "and in consumer circles here."[90] Scott's proposal was that Bridge would be comprised of democratically elected representatives of producers and consumers with equal voting rights for control of the executive committee. "The total population of producers and consumers is the supreme authority of Bridge," he explained.[91] Each group would be equally represented on a board of trustees. Furthermore, dividends would be shared fairly. Scott devised a system that distributed the profits of Bridge between producers, who would receive a permanent minimum of 25 percent, and consumers, receiving a permanent minimum of 5 percent (as "a bonus for shoppers"). The remainder of the profits would be invested in the expansion and development of the cooperative itself.[92] Scott's proposal, in other words, was to create an international company reliant on shared ownership between the main stakeholders of the company—producers and consumers—and independent of bilateral trading mechanisms.

What propelled Scott's radical proposal? To some extent, Scott's interest in fair trade was a response to broader discussions about international development. Since the late 1950s, international organizations had been thinking about how to make trade central to their development aims. "Trade not aid" was a slogan particularly associated with UNCTAD.[93] In fact, since 1968 UNCTAD and the General Agreement on Tariffs and Trade (GATT) had jointly administered the International Trade Centre (ITC), which aimed to promote all types of Third World exports, including handicrafts, as a form of development aid.[94] Trade was also a major priority for the launch of the UN First Development Decade in 1961. By the late 1960s, trade had become a central rallying cry for the Group of 77 (or G-77), the lobby of postcolonial nations that would push the UN to adopt the Declaration of the New International Economic Order (NIEO) in 1973. The G-77 called for "trade liberalization" that would afford Third World countries "unrestricted and duty-free access to the markets of all the developed countries for all manufactures and semi-manufactures from all developing countries."[95] In doing so, it made trade central to the NIEO campaigns.

But the inspiration for Scott's proposal came from beyond these postcolonial debates about decolonizing international trade. More importantly, his proposal was a response to the ongoing crisis of international development. In the early 1970s, when it had become clear that the UN's First Development Decade had failed to reach its target, both international and nongovernmental agencies had accepted that most development projects and blueprints with a focus on economic growth had had a negligible impact in solving global inequalities. In response, these agencies reoriented their development policies. While some, like the World Bank and the ILO, turned to a "basic-needs" approach that focused on meeting a humanitarian minimum, activists like Scott sought a nongovernmental approach to grassroots development that would connect consumers and producers directly through small-scale development programs. Scott's idea was to invest in microeconomic programs rather than large macroeconomic and structural reforms that did not reach the very poor. This meant rejecting large-scale, state-led development projects, but it also led to a departure from anticolonial calls to radically reform power in the global economy. Instead of reshaping the structures of international trade through trade agreements—as the NIEO advocated—Scott sought to use Oxfam's for-profit venture to directly connect people rather than their governments and elites. It was "people-centered development," which focused on generating decentralized markets rather than boosting the GNP of national economies.

In 1973, Scott tied these international discussions about development and trade to his nongovernmental trading vision: Bridge could offer an alternative, radical trading structure that would open a new handicraft market and generate employment for Third World producers independently from states. For Scott, handicrafts allowed Third World economies to diversify their export market from the grassroots and to move beyond reliance on primary commodities and raw materials. It was, in his mind, a way of addressing an international discussion underway throughout the 1960s about the imbalanced structures of international trade. Moreover, handicrafts were connected to discussions about the textiles market, one in which Third World countries could compete on a level playing field. Textiles were central to many development initiatives within Third World countries because they provided employment to many skilled and semi-skilled laborers.[96] Scott believed that Bridge could offer a nongovernmental route that would bypass bilateral and international trading agreements, which de facto restricted the export of handicrafts, particularly textiles and clothing, from the Third World to Western markets as well as limiting the access of Third World producers. Under the Generalized System of Preferences (GSP) negotiated by UNCTAD and GATT in 1968, handicrafts could be traded internationally without restriction or duties, but bilateral agreements nevertheless restricted the import of such products. Scott believed that NGOs had an advantage in correcting for economic inequalities because they were not bound by the same restrictions as the British or any other government. Echoing the antistatism of the ethical socialism of the 1950s, Scott depicted NGOs as operating on the level of the village rather than that of the state.

Scott suggested that Bridge be linked with the charity and fair-trade shops that were mushrooming in Britain, Europe, and the United States:[97] these ranged from the London-based Project Hand, which supplied wholesale handicrafts to Christian Aid and War on Want shops, to the Dutch Catholic youth group that founded SOSWereldhandel and the Belgian Associatie voor de Verkoop en de Aankoop van Produkten uit de Drede Wereld (perhaps not the most catchy name) to the German Dritte Welt Handel and the American SELFHELP Crafts of the World.[98] He met, for example, with SOSWereldhandel to explore such a merger, although by the end of 1973 the proposal was dead.[99] Initially, however, Scott thought the Bridge cooperative could become a transnational and nongovernmental empire that would repair trading relationships globally.[100]

What distinguished Scott's proposal from other European fair-trade initiatives was the role it envisioned for NGOs. The Bridge cooperative, in Scott's mind, should become more of a "service" rather than "a fund-raiser."[101] He proposed that NGOs could offer marketing services for Bridge products: helping Third World producers capture the hearts and pockets of European consumers, offering consumers a cheap deal on goods and at the same time providing Third World producers with access to a new Western market. In this vision, NGOs would offer marketing expertise and not just an import service or a physical venue to sell Third World products. With this model, nongovernmental or voluntary work had a more significant economic role to play in the global economy and, in particular, the labor market.

Scott even suggested that Oxfam could eventually withdraw its involvement from the venture, making Bridge an independent entity. That entity, according to Scott, would initially be funded and shepherded by Oxfam but eventually would be self-financing. It would be run completely by producers and consumers under a separate limited liability company, Oxfam Bridge Ltd., and would employ nongovernmental volunteers who would offer these marketing services. As Scott wrote, "a producer does not want to have his product bought out of charity or because of its educational or political message. . . . Producers are trying to break away from charity (and want to have their) production bought simply because the products are good articles at [an]attractive price."[102] Scott hoped that this kind of nongovernmental cooperative would allow producers to reach self-sufficiency and free them from the paternalistic model of aid.

From Producers to "Entrepreneurs"

In 1975, Oxfam established a new subsidiary company, Oxfam Bridge Ltd. The company, as one of its promotional leaflets explained, was committed to "Trade for the People."[103] The company maintained some of Scott's vision of NGOs as marketing experts and facilitators. It was founded with its own board of management and with the aim of promoting decentralized fair-trade markets. Oxfam, however, did not implement the more radical portions of Scott's proposal. For the business-minded Guy Stringer, who was pushing Oxfam toward a more commercialized model, the idea of making Bridge a cooperative governed exclusively by its stakeholders negated the entire mandate of its trading company to generate revenue for the organization's development programs. Control therefore remained in Oxfam's hands rather than being handed over to the stakeholders. The trading company, in fact, enabled Oxfam to expand its development work beyond the purview of what the Charity Commission might have allowed it if it had done so directly through its charitable status.[104]

The new subsidiary company, Oxfam Bridge Ltd., championed a commercialized model of a decentralized, fair-trade handicrafts market. It promised to offer an alternative form of trading—a "system of cooperative trading"—that would liberate Third World producers and provide the "best possible value for money" to British consumers. Over 40 percent of the price of Bridge items "is a direct payment to the workers who made your products," or so at least the company told its consumers.[105] Bridge sought first and foremost to increase employment in Third World communities "by providing a marketing operation in the UK for Oxfam shops' operation and the mail order services." In addition, Bridge aimed "to earn income and profits out of its activities which are then covenanted back to the charity" and to "enhance" Oxfam's work in shaping public opinion and educating the public through its goods.[106] It sought to connect Third World producers with British consumers by creating an alternative market that in practice was sometimes manipulated by Oxfam: "The economies of direct buying/direct selling enable Bridge to pay producers better and still sell to you at fair price."[107]

Oxfam's handicraft market aimed to generate large amounts of revenue that would fund future development work through trading activities across Asia, Africa, and Latin America. The idea was that the profits from the program would be returned to the producers in "the form of development grants and social dividends."[108] Twenty-five percent was distributed to producer groups as a "Producer Dividend" and 70 percent went into the "Bridge Development Fund," which producer groups could apply to for grants or loans. The remaining 5 percent was used for promotional work in Britain. Bridge did not return the profit for each product directly back to the producer but instead used its profits to support a variety of community development programs across different regions. The company's mandate, in fact, enabled Oxfam to support much broader development and business projects than was allowed under existing charity laws, such as buying special equipment, seeking management training, or buying bigger storage units to warehouse producers' supplies and products.[109] Bridge thus became the sort of organization that in the 1980s would be called an alternative trade organization.

Oxfam Bridge Ltd., in fact, focused much of its development efforts on training producers as entrepreneurs. The company's primary goal was to help producers successfully sell their products in Britain (and later the United States) by offering them marketing expertise and product development advice. But to create that market, the company decided it needed to cater to consumer desire and consumer needs. As Maurice Zinkin, a commercial consultant hired by Oxfam Trade, said, "The products must be salable, in other words, they must be [of] a type [an] Oxfam customer wishes to buy, at a price the customer is willing to pay, and they must be available in adequate quantity at the time when the customer wishes to buy them."[110] Bridge prioritized sales over other things such as working conditions and community welfare.

Despite its continued emphasis on generating employment and working closely with producers to benefit their communities, Bridge's main focus was satisfying the consumer. When demand for its goods was not as high as it

Employment & Trade

Cottage industry and homecrafts can provide employment and supplement family incomes in many parts of the Third World. Oxfam's BRIDGE programme helps them do just this.

FIGURE 3.2. "Employment and Trade." Poster advertising Oxfam's Bridge program, c. 1970.

expected, Oxfam began a training program to work closely with producers on how to manufacture products to suit British tastes. One early example of this tactic was Oxfam's support of a local embroidery project run by Spanish nuns in the district of Gomtipur, India, an industrial suburb of Ahmedabad and the home of Mahatma Gandhi after he returned from South Africa in 1915. The project started in 1970, when Oxfam began sponsoring a women's training center that offered tailoring and needlework classes. At the time the center was not particularly unique in India and especially in Ahmedabad. It joined other, more grassroots, organizations like the Self Employed Women's Association (SEWA),[111] which was founded in 1972 under Gandhian ideals that aimed to support women in the garment industry who had been excluded from the main union, the Textile Labor Association—which Gandhi himself had founded in 1918—because they were working outside the textile mills. SEWA, like the Oxfam training center, valorized indigenous manufacturing (or "Khadi," that is, handwoven cloths) and saw it as an alternative mode of development for achieving self-sufficiency.[112]

But unlike SEWA, Oxfam's training center in Ahmedabad was not a grassroots cooperative organized around protecting the place of female producers in the Indian economy. Instead, it was oriented toward providing them with access to the British economy. The center initially was meant to supplement women's income by offering diploma courses, but because of Oxfam's involvement, by 1975 it had expanded into selling embroidery work. The first products were small wall hangings of elephants and peacocks designed on locally produced maroon-colored cloth. These were imported by Oxfam and sold in Britain through its shops and mail-order catalogue. When the products were not doing as well in the British market as Oxfam had expected, it decided to realign its development and aid work to match consumer demand. Oxfam sent aid workers to closely advise women on how to tailor their products to British taste. According to Oxfam, "the maroon cloth, for example, [did] not always fit with British fashion and decorating colors"[113] and did not yield enough of a high revenue. Oxfam expanded Bridge's work to advising local community projects on how to improve products in such a way that they could be sold globally.

Furthermore, to help the market succeed, Bridge invested in and designed consumer surveys. They sought to deeply examine the desires and needs of British and Western consumers in order to better understand what motivated them to purchase fair-trade merchandise. "An understanding of the motivation of existing customers will enable the organization to identify ways in which it can enhance or modify existing marketing strategies in order to increase the revenue generated from these sources," one Bridge report explained.[114]

In 1979, Oxfam's Bridge expanded this mission, launching a "producer assistance" program that formalized and expanded the ongoing work that Oxfam had been doing with some of its community development programs, like the one in Ahmedabad. The producer assistance program offered training and workshops on topics such as accounting, and the marketing, design, and packaging of handicraft goods. The idea was to tailor business advice to different producer groups and producer products. While Oxfam had invested in and supported the sale of these products in the areas in which they were manufactured, the producer assistance program was mainly geared toward finding international markets in Britain, Europe, and later the United States. The program helped Oxfam expand its work beyond the charity shop venture and to start marketing its products to other Western fair-trade groups such as the German Dritte Welt Laden and Gesellschaft zur Förderueng der Partnerschaft mit der Dritten Welt mbH.[115]

Producer assistance was geared toward making Third World producers into entrepreneurs. Instead of generating wage employment and cooperatives, throughout the 1980s the program shifted its focus to training Third World producers how to generate their own profit by creating an enterprise culture. The program was based on a microeconomic approach to development that focused on transforming the poor into the engines of economic growth. It used fair trade to expand the economic activities of individual producers beyond formal employment—the factory and the farm—through what came to be called the "informal economy."

The term "informal economy" had been coined by the British anthropologist Keith Hart in 1971 and had already been embraced by international and nongovernmental agencies like Oxfam. The term expanded the definition of work and became a solution to what some described as the "inadequacy of the concept of unemployment [as well as] 'underemployment' and 'disguised unemployment.'"[116] Hart researched income opportunities among the unemployed urban population in Accra, Ghana. For him, the real question was whether the unemployed "really constitute a passive, exploited majority in cities like Accra" or whether "their informal economic activities possess some autonomous capacity for generating growth in the income of the urban (and rural) poor."[117] In Accra, over half of the economically active population was "self-employed, non-wage earning" in a wide range of jobs, from farming and petty trading to shoe shining and selling matches. These so-called informal activities, Hart argued, had as much to contribute to economic growth as wage labor. He called for a new development policy that would factor in the contribution of this "sub-proletariat."[118]

In 1972, the economists Hans Singer and Richard Jolly at the Institute of Development Studies (IDS) incorporated the idea of the "informal economy" into a report they wrote for the ILO about the Kenyan economy. Singer and Jolly were influenced by Schumacher's critique of the dual economy model and a strain of economism that focused too heavily on GNP over other metrics.[119] Their report called for including in their analysis economic activities beyond wage employment and counting all enterprises that were "economically efficient and profit making."[120] According to Singer and Jolly, the problem with the informal economy was not that it was unproductive but that it was considered illegal. The self-employed population in Kenya had to operate outside the official economy, yet it offered important services for low-income segments of the population, including transportation and trade.[121] Based on Singer and Jolly's research, the ILO and nongovernmental organizations like Oxfam adopted the concept of the "informal economy."

The gradual recognition and acceptance of the informal economy brought to light not only new economic activities taking place beyond the space of the factory but also new subjects, especially women. As development economists started to consider the role of the informal economy as a space for economic growth, they paid new attention to perennial forms of labor done by women in agriculture and handicraft work within the home.[122]

It was in the context of this turn to informality that Oxfam's producer assistance program began to focus on training producers, especially women, to become entrepreneurs. The program gradually trained producers to manufacture, design, and package their products as well as to assess the changing patterns of demand. The turn to entrepreneurship was part of a larger reaction in Britain, the United States, and India to the nagging questions of economic crisis and deindustrialization in the 1970s. The entrepreneur was conceived, as Angus Burgin argued, as broadly accessible, meaning that "anyone, whether working within a large organization or as a sole proprietor, could display and should try to cultivate entrepreneurial role behavior."[123] But in the late 1970s it expanded beyond the model of the white male worker and came to include women and the global poor.[124] The idea in fact fit much of the general turn to small-scale, microeconomic programs taken by British nonprofits like Oxfam as early as the late 1960s. Bridge presented a model of development that connected older Gandhian ideals of indigenous manufacturing and more recent anticolonial critiques of trade and fused them with a new culture of entrepreneurship, one promoted later in the 1980s by neoliberal policymakers like Margaret Thatcher.

The expansion of Oxfam's trading venture into producer assistance meant that the organization now hired aid workers with business experience or who specialized in design, marketing, and accounting. Accountants led workshops on how to systematize accounting books and records according to English practice, in order to streamline the work these communities were doing with Oxfam.[125] Designers helped producers "with design problems, costings, packaging, shipping etc.," so that producers could become self-sufficient and sensitive to consumer taste and demand.[126] The commercial function of tailoring these kinds of handicrafts to the desires of British and American consumers, one Oxfam report stated, was to bring financial gain not only to the producers but also to Oxfam more generally. "Attractive items will bring customers into the shop and help the sales of the donated goods" as much as the sales of the handicraft products.[127]

The new aid experts worked alongside Oxfam's field directors, although not always in alignment with directors' own understanding of the purpose of community development. Field directors were often "concerned," as one Oxfam Trading manager reported, "that most Bridge groups were geographically not in their priority areas, or that the size of OT [Oxfam Trade] prevented

[Oxfam] from buying from small groups, or that the whole concept of exporting was wrong for small groups."[128] Producer assistance aid experts offered their own version of community development programs. The program carried the tensions inherent to the trading venture from its foundation: between its commercial and developmental aims.

The creation of the producer assistance program also coincided with the expansion of Oxfam's work in former colonial spaces like South Asia as well as Latin America. In 1979, for example, Oxfam India was opened in order, among other things, to more closely sustain Bridge work with producer groups from the country. The operation was managed by Julian Francis, a full-time officer hired by Oxfam in the early 1970s. Francis had been in his early twenties when he started working for Oxfam as a volunteer in a Gandhian village development project in Bihar in 1968, using his background in agriculture and animal husbandry to help the community in the aftermath of the famine of 1966–67. When the 1971 War of Liberation broke out in Bangladesh, Oxfam recruited Francis to work alongside Gandhian organizations to coordinate relief for the East Bengali refugees. His involvement was recorded in "The Testimony of Sixty on the Crisis in Bengal," a collection of eyewitness accounts of the crisis that Oxfam published in 1971 and was used to draw international attention and support to the region.[129] In 1979, the work Francis had done there alongside Oxfam's newly appointed field director for eastern India and East Pakistan, Raymond Cournoyer, won him the position of heading Oxfam India.[130] His responsibilities included a large share of Bridge work and were influenced by Gandhian ideas about indigenous manufacturing. India became one of Bridge's most prominent sites.[131]

During the 1980s, the office under Francis took on three more aid workers (Elizabeth Mann, Malesh Jhurani, and K. Panchaksharam), and it was soon joined by a station in Bangladesh, another in South East Asia, and later yet another in Central America. Field workers affiliated with the new stations sought to find new producer groups, and once suppliers had been approved by a Product Selection Committee in Britain, they collaborated closely with them on developing a successful business model. According to an Oxfam report from 1989, the field workers "provide the vital link between Bridge and its producers, helping them with everything from costing and design to marketing—both local and exports."[132] These field workers, in fact, connected Bridge's development mandate to Oxfam's refugee and disaster relief work and saw a direct link between handicraft work and these victims' rehabilitation.[133]

Many field workers had a business background and, when hired by Bridge, applied it to aid work. Consider Edward Millard, who came to Oxfam in the late 1970s when he was in his twenties with a background in business. As one Oxfam profile suggested, he had a knack for marketing honed at his family company, which imported children's clothing from Europe and Africa.[134] In 1976, after reading the *New Internationalist*, Millard decided to take a position as a deputy managing director of FRIDA Marketing Services, an organization for crafts and small-business promotion in Africa. By June 1977, he had opened a retail shop in London's Africa Center and soon afterward set up a wholesale company. In late 1979 he moved to Kenya, where he became responsible for the East Africa operation. Based on this expertise, he was hired by Oxfam in 1981 to work in India and later Latin America training producers on product development and marketing strategies. "I am interested in trying to use all our experience in the market place to prepare some good, practical programmes of assistance and this is the direction in which I want to see our programme moving forward," he commented in one interview.[135] The manuals he wrote for the organization served as the foundation for many fair-trade handicraft businesses even beyond Oxfam.

The work that aid workers like Millard did with communities in places like India, Morocco, and Brazil altered the emphasis of Bridge's aims toward generating profit and shaping products to fit consumer markets rather than providing employment and fair wages. As one policy memo explained, one of Bridge's main functions was the promotion of efficient and viable handicraft production. The provision of employment overseas was a prime factor, but it was essential that the enterprises were able, in time, to produce good-quality goods at a profit—with fair wages being paid. They also needed to be in "a position to sell to a changing market at a competitive price—e.g. things which Oxfam [would] buy and sell in the UK for a profit."[136]

The policy paper never specified what constituted a "fair wage" and clearly stressed that Bridge's primary goal was to work within a competitive global market. The emphasis was on production and sales rather than producers and their livelihoods. Projects that did not prove "commercially viable," as one Oxfam report termed it, were in fact eventually "phased out" and canceled.[137] The "collapse of [some] groups is inevitable," another report argued, "to support them is merely prolonging the agony."[138]

As a result, Bridge was first and foremost a commercially driven company focused on buyer needs rather than a cooperative scheme committed to improving the material conditions of the producers. The reality was that many projects depended on poor working conditions, child labor, and low wages. Often, project managers commented on the low wages of Bridge producers, but labor costs were almost always measured against the efficiency of production and the overall profitability of the product. Producers were often paid for the amount of product they produced per day rather than being given a salary. For example, producers working in a small workshop making handmade sandals in Palam, India, did not receive enough money to sustain their families. While producers worked with their families together in small units, they received just under $1 per day ($2.76 in today's dollars), "an adequate wage by local standards," claimed Dick Mellor, an Oxfam project manager, after visiting India.[139] And yet he also added that despite this pay, "a high proportion of families are in [constant] debt to local moneylenders for occasional heavy outlays such as a wedding."[140] Such comments suggest that impoverishment was seen as a result of cultural choices rather than unfair wages. In other cases, low wages for handicraft work by women were justified because their labor was seen as providing "peaceful escape from their poverty at home."[141] The benefits of work, in these cases, were viewed as emotional rather than material.

Working conditions were so awful that sometimes even Oxfam's project managers commented on them in their reports. "I queried whether the new tannery and soap factory going up alongside the sandal unit might not pass on intolerable smells to the workers, but [was] assured . . . that leather-workers are immune to this," wrote Dick Mellor in 1981.[142] The organization was aware of the labor conditions but decided to prioritize Bridge sales over the rights of Bridge's producer groups.

Oxfam also started purchasing products from postcolonial commercial firms, which did not offer any direct-aid benefits to specific local communities and often reproduced exploitive working conditions. "Some people I met," wrote an Oxfam trading accountant, "were against OT [Oxfam Trading] buying from such organizations. Several Bridge groups exist primarily to prevent workers from being exploited in the commercial sector and it can be argued that Oxfam could never satisfy themselves with the condition of workers in the commercial sector." And yet the accountant nevertheless was in favor of collaborating with commercial firms because they helped increase sales in the shops. "The [method] by which OT currently sells the vast majority of Bridge goods, the Oxfam shop model system and the mail order catalogue, does not lend itself easily to production by small producers," he explained. "Bridge producers will not be helped by OT disappointing customers due to their failure of supply," he continued. "I think it should be acknowledged that purchasing goods from commercial sources in order to supplement and back-up the range of goods available from producer groups is a desirable thing."[143] Programs were organized and advised by accountants and profitability was measured against sales in the global North. Consumer desire trumped the individual success of each program, according to Bridge's business model.

In the early 1980s, Oxfam looked to the American market. Under the name "Global Exchange Inc." it partnered with the American International Small Enterprise Development Center and opened a new trading and importing company based in Xenia, Ohio. Global Exchange brought Bridge handcrafts directly to the American consumer.[144] The transition to the American market helped the company move from sales of around £700,000 in 1975 to over £2.5 million in 1985, and by early 1990 Oxfam achieved £8.5 million in sales on Bridge products alone. By 1990, Bridge was working with 295 groups in 43 countries.[145] Oxfam eventually converted Global Exchange into a corporation, with the hope of making its shares accessible to churches, commercial organizations, and "individuals wishing to invest or grant capital for its development."[146] At the same time, Oxfam collaborated with international organizations like UNICEF to share the burden of distributing Bridge products globally.[147] It also partnered with British corporations like Sainsbury's & Co. and branched out to work with producers of food and coffee.[148] By the late 1980s, Bridge had expanded into a fair-trade empire.

Solidarity Markets

In the fall of 1987, Oxfam Trading wrote a feasibility study, commissioned by the International Trade Centre (ITC) and the United Nations Development Program, that explored the establishment of an International Marketing and Assistance Center for the benefit of medium- and small-scale enterprises. The ITC—administered by both UNCTAD and the GATT—had been invested in promoting Third World exports, including handicrafts, since the late 1960s. The Oxfam study examined the possibility of creating an international body that would facilitate a market between Western consumers and Third World producers. It used the experience of Oxfam's Bridge in South and East Asia as the basis for its research, including its experience in marketing training, market penetration, and product development. "Despite the fact that many countries visited were celebrating the anniversary of achieving independence from Britain," the report stated, "the most popular city [chosen by producer groups it surveyed] for the Centre is London."[149] The idea for such a center had the backing of fifty-seven Third World countries like India and China, as well as that of the EEC. In a follow-up report in June 1990, the ITC concluded that "there is a demand for a professional, commercially oriented marketing and assistance organization to supplement the limited resources possessed by developing countries." Oxfam's Bridge company became the model for the type of fair-trade development work that aimed "to provide export development and assistance services for small and medium sized enterprises."[150]

The study became the basis for the foundation of an international trading company, Artisan Link Ltd., owned by the charity Artisan Trust and based in London. Founded in March 1991, the company's primary function was "to provide market and technical information to small scale producers and help them to develop suitable merchandise and to reach their market."[151] It aimed to offer "general and technical advice on the establishment and operation of business enterprises."[152] Artisan Link mirrored Bridge's experience, particularly its producer assistance program, and included an Oxfam representative as one of its directors, alongside representatives from Africa, Asia, Latin America, and the Caribbean. The company was financially supported by the United Nations Development Program, the World Bank, and the EEC. It collaborated with stores and companies like Selfridges in Britain, Ikea in Sweden, and Karstadt in West Germany.

Artisan Link Ltd. was one prominent example of how Oxfam's Bridge company shaped international ideas about development and fair trade in the late 1980s. What began in the mid-1960s as a small number of imports of handmade ornaments and dolls had expanded by the 1980s into a lucrative fair-trade business model for alternative trade organizations globally. According to one Oxfam aid worker, the success of this model led to the formation of a "solidarity market," one motivated not only by consumer savings but also by moral consideration of the social consequences of purchases. In actuality, Bridge was a training ground for teaching Third World producers how to become global entrepreneurs. It joined a broader neoliberal movement that sought to solve the problem of employment by supporting a profit-driven enterprise culture. At a time when the fair-trade movement was growing in power and influence in Europe and the United States, Oxfam's trading company created its own commercially driven model of a "fair-trade" business focused on handicraft products. The following chapters examine how, as Oxfam's fair-trade empire grew, the idea of fair trade was simultaneously being extended beyond handicrafts into the fair trade of foods as well as to collaborations with private industries under the banner of corporate social responsibility.

CHAPTER FOUR

Hunger and the Sustainable Planet

ON MARCH 25, 1975, the tabloid the *Daily Express* published a letter from a housewife in Kent named Grace S. Barnes who had been following the news about the latest famine in Bangladesh. Barnes wrote: "We are told that if we give up the equivalent of one hamburger a week, the starving of India could be fed." Sheila Pott, a housewife from Longwick, Buckinghamshire, expressed a similar sentiment in a letter published in the *Daily Express* on the same day. She asked, "Is there anyone in Britain who would not willingly make such a minute sacrifice . . . ?" and then added, "but as for buying less at the butchers with starving Indians in mind, how does the meat you do not buy [actually] get to them?"[1]

Mrs. Barnes and Mrs. Pott were not alone. In the 1970s, less than three decades after Britain itself had suffered from severe food scarcity, dozens of humanitarian campaigns invited citizens, especially housewives, to imagine a personal, ethical connection between the meals on their dinner plates and hungry mouths around the globe. The "Meatless Sundays" that Mrs. Barnes and Mrs. Pott's letters alluded to were only one example of such campaigns. Throughout Britain, NGOs held a series of events and teach-ins in local charity shops, churches, and town halls. From fair-trade campaigns for coffee and sugar to public fasts, citizens were called upon to examine the ethical, economic, and environmental relationship between their own food consumption and the project of feeding the world.

In the 1970s, the idea of "the clean plate" came to stand for a broader set of economic and ecological theories about the politics of limited resources, especially food. In the words of one of Oxfam's campaign organizers, the clean plate invoked "a welfare planet" that connected economic life in Britain to the world of diminishing resources.[2] The question of who got a fair share of the plate became the centerpiece of a new international politics in the mid-1960s.

The rapid expansion of political membership of decolonized countries in international society generated a range of discussions about the world's economy. On the one hand, anticolonial political thinkers called for structural reforms and a redistribution of the world's resources from the bottom up "to undo the hierarchies that facilitated domination."[3] At the same time, a resurgence of neo-Malthusian anxieties that originated in the West, including Britain, seeped into debates about the planet as a finite sphere for a rapidly growing global population. The problem of resources could only be mitigated through family planning and population control.[4] How, then, could international development and nongovernmental aid programs carry on without solving the problem of diminishing resources? As the American ambassador Adlai Stevenson stressed in a 1965 address to the United Nations Economic and Social Council, "We travel together, passengers on a little space ship, dependent on its vulnerable reserve of air and soil."[5]

By the 1970s, food was at the center of these debates about the viability of the spaceship. As a means of subsistence as well as a commodity, food exemplified concerns about the limits of the earth to provide for its inhabitants. In the postwar period, the creation of the Food and Agriculture Organization (FAO) was an acknowledgment of the imperative of solving humanitarian and economic problems in order to provide global security and economic stability.[6] What changed in the 1970s was that certain methods of food production were recognized as being implicated in resource depletion and as impediments to development and aid. In 1970, an international food conference in the Hague announced food as the challenge to "the increasing problems of population growth in relation to economic development, and the conservation of man's environment."[7] Similarly, in 1972, following an earth summit in Stockholm, *The Limits to Growth: A Report for the Club of Rome's Project on the Predicament of Mankind* paid particular attention to the exhaustion of food as energy.[8] These international conferences joined a grassroots environmental movement in Britain, Western Europe, and the United States for more sustainable use of resources, especially local foods.

By 1973, a world food crisis was looming. Increasing grain scarcity in markets created an acute food shortage, eventually leading to famines in the Sahel and also affecting Chad, Mali, Gambia, Senegal, Burkina Faso, Niger, and Ethiopia, as well as eastern Brazil and Bangladesh. The failure of the Green Revolution added to the sense of crisis.[9] In November 1974, the World Food Conference met in Rome to discuss and coordinate food production, food security, and the trade of food commodities on an international scale, with the goal of mitigating global inequalities between the West and the Third World. The crisis mobilized humanitarian organizations on an international scale.

The 1970s have often been dubbed a period of crisis. The oil crisis, economic stagflation, and growing levels of debt sparked international debates about the global economy that eventually paved the way for its liberalization.[10] "The world economy," announced the economist Hollis B. Chenery in 1975, "is currently in a state of disequilibrium of a magnitude not seen since the after-math of World War II."[11] He was right, but the magnitude of the crises of the 1970s cannot be understood without accounting for the world food crisis of 1974. It created a new humanitarian urgency to reform the world's economy and marshal its limited resources. The crisis became critical for how the prob-lem of resources, particularly grain, was reframed in international debates. Suddenly, the politics of food moved beyond humanitarian discussions about feeding the Third World to include debates about changing production and consumption patterns in the West. Both progressive hopes about the fair trade of food and conservative fears about population growth shaped ideas about and programs for feeding the world's poor.

In Britain there was a proliferation of various nongovernmental solutions that sought to shape a new "welfare planet" by reforming economic life. Long before bucolic images of coffee plantation workers became the liberal heart of fair-trade campaigns, the nongovernmental efforts of the 1970s forged a new economy around the dinner plate that connected the British diet to plenary politics. This chapter traces how nongovernmental organizations built upon the 1960s debates about the economics of welfare and altruism to generate postimperial ideas about a "welfare planet." It analyzes two central alternatives that proposed their own solutions to the politics of hunger and the sustainable planet. The first alternative was advanced by the Haslemere Group—a radical lobby of activists, journalists, and aid workers—and took the form of structural reforms of the world economy through commodity agreements for specific foods. Influenced by the politics of decolonization, Haslemere aimed to create a sustainable yet egalitarian international trade system that would help post-colonial economies integrate into international markets. I chart the failures of their ambitious alternatives by closely examining their campaign on sugar exports of the former plantation Caribbean economies. The case of sugar exposed the tensions between Britain's economic obligations toward its former colonies and the country's attempts to create its own sustainable food supply that did not depend on them.

Against Haslemere's alternative of structural reforms stood another one: focused on consumer action. In response to the 1974 world food crisis such an alternative became particularly popular among large humanitarian NGOs. These NGOs taught Britons how to restrain their food consumption, challeng-ing them to eat less and waste less. They aimed to create new subjectivities of ethical citizens. I explore one prominent Oxfam campaign that focused on changing the "lifestyle" of British consumers and show how these campaigns were particularly gendered, targeting British housewives as the main eco-nomic agent of household food consumption and marketing them the idea that their own food consumption and even bodies were connected to the prob-lem of sustainability and world hunger. The persistence of some of these cam-paigns over others demonstrates the possibilities that were open and then lost in the global "shock" of the 1970s.

Toward Planetary Justice

In 1966, the Anglo-American economist Kenneth Boulding announced: "We are now in the middle of a long process of transition in the nature of the image which man has of himself and his environment."[12] Since World War II, the conception of the globe had shrunk from an open frontier to "a closed sphere." Man "must find his place in a cyclical ecological system." Instead of the old "cowboy economy," as Boulding termed it, with a limitless frontier and infinite possibilities for growth, economists would have to come to terms with the idea of the earth as "a single spaceship, without unlimited reservoirs of anything, either for extraction or for pollution." This new understanding of the earth required the development of new ecological and economic principles for the global economy, or the "econosphere," that would account for the inevitable limits of growth.[13]

Boulding was not alone in calling for a new "spaceman" economy. In a series of lectures that same year, the British economist Barbara Ward made the case for the development of new economic principles that would accommodate the ecological limits of the growth paradigm. Ward, one of the most influential yet understudied intellectuals of the twentieth century, argued that the problem with the paradigm of "growth" was that it was based entirely on an economic model originating in a colonial world system.[14] The Third World, she argued, has "long been enmeshed in an international trading system which both provides much of what wealth they have yet is designed to see that its benefits are unequally divided."[15] Impoverished, decolonized small economies still largely depended on financial structures, tariffs, and markets of primary products, which had all been set up entirely outside their control. Modernization theory failed to serve a "growing, increasingly interdependent international society" with limited resources.[16]

"All through the developing world," she argued, "economies with exploitable resources—above all, minerals—lie next door to mountains and deserts where wretched farmers and pastoralists scratch a living."[17] This "growth" economy did not take into account economies of scale. "Within sixty years, the world was cocooned round with a thickening web of investment and commercial exchanges, the shop collecting distant cargoes of wheat from Argentina, palm oil from the Niger Delta, tea from Calcutta, cotton from the Southern States and carrying back to ports or railheads all round the world the goods and machinery of the new technology."[18] To her mind, the "'Third World' of colonial and semi-colonial economies" became dependent on economic principles suited only for large, colonial powers.

Ward joined other critics in Britain who were rethinking the relationship between ecology and economics. Most prominently she joined the company of her friend E. F. Schumacher, who had been thinking about the economics of limited resources domestically through his work at the National Coal

Board as well as through his involvement in various development aid projects globally.

By the late 1960s, "ecology" had "become the Thing," as Robert L. Heilbroner put it.[19] There was a new urgency to rethink aid and development beyond the "growthmania" of the preceding decades.[20] In 1972, the Canadian oil and mineral businessman and former undersecretary general of the United Nations Maurice Strong even invented a phrase for it, "eco-development," to signal the type of economic and policy thinking that calculated the environmental degradation and effects of development efforts. Economists, activists, and policymakers in Britain and the United States became particularly concerned with the "diseconomics of growth," or what new economic principles of development beyond modernization might look like.[21] If the earth's resources were finite, what was the moral responsibility of people from affluent countries toward rising inequalities and hunger in the Third World? The new environmental and postcolonial economics suggested a global interdependency that could endanger the Western world as much as the Third World. "The biosphere is not infinite," wrote Barbara Ward in a 1973 report she coauthored for the UN.[22] She called for a new "planetary justice" that would transcend the "relentless pursuit of separate national interests" and instead mobilize the entire community of the earth to equally share its resources.[23]

The emergence of antigrowth economics and calls for "planetary justice" inspired a new generation of activists in Britain to look to Ward, Schumacher, Boulding, and postcolonial critics like Julius Nyerere for alternatives. Between the late 1960s and the mid-1970s, activists ran a series of campaigns to reform the economic relationship between Britain and the Third World, particularly its former imperial territories. For these activists, it was not only that "spaceship earth" had limited resources but also that these resources were unequally distributed between former colonized nations and former colonizers. They proposed creating a mass movement that would restructure the global economy from the bottom up, pressuring governments and international institutions to rethink the organization of the international trade system.

Such was the case for the coalition called the Haslemere Group, formed in the late 1960s. Its members came from a young generation of radical campaigners and aid workers from various NGOs who were disillusioned with developmental economics and modernization programs. The group included people like Peter Burns, Oxfam's first lobbyist, who had been working alongside trade unions and cooperative movements for several years; Teresa Hayter, who had previously worked for the British Overseas Development Institute but eventually went on to publish books like *Aid as Imperialism*; Nicholas Fogg, Christian Aid's Secretary to Universities and Colleges of Education; and Jonathan Power, a journalist who worked for newspapers like the *International Herald Tribune* and created documentaries for the BBC.[24] All had been intimately familiar with the institutional framework of aid work in Britain over the course of the 1960s and were unsatisfied with it. They searched for a path for planetary justice that would be both ecological and decolonial through fairer trade.

In January 1968, these activists met outside London in the small town of Haslemere to form an alliance focused on "the social and economic crisis facing the 'developing countries' of Africa, Asia and Latin America" as well as the "failure of rich industrialized nations to recognize their responsibility for this crisis."[25] The increasing poverty rates in so-called developing countries could not simply be mitigated through foreign aid. Overseas aid, they argued, was "largely a myth."[26] The real cause of poverty, the group suggested, was the economic domination of Britain and the Western world over the Third World. There was a direct connection between poverty and underdevelopment in the Third World and economic life in Britain. The group called for an entire restructuring of the global economy.

In March 1968, the group published the Haslemere Declaration, which elaborated its critique. The problem with poverty was "the international monetary and trading system," which was "devised by the rich to suit their needs; it ignores those of the poor."[27] Economic domination was written into the global economy through trade agreements and financial institutions. Its origins, according to the group, were imperial economies, and they could be traced back at least to the transatlantic slave trade of the eighteenth century: "To understand the nature of the relationship between the rich and the poor worlds we must go back into history."[28]

The declaration, which sold thirty thousand copies within less than a year, was a call to arms. Inequality could not be solved simply through the nationalization and modernization of Third World economies, or an increase in aid programs or loans, as was previously assumed. Inequality was a product of economic dependency. Haslemere was full of radical activists, far more radical than the overall aid industry at the time, yet its impact was significant. For instance, in 1973 Judith Hart, a Labor MP and the minister for overseas development, published the book *Aid and Liberation*, which cited Haslemere's declaration and echoed many of its ideas.

Haslemere's ideas drew on the work of the Argentinian economist Raúl Prebisch, who together with the German-born British economist Hans Singer advocated for a structural reform in the terms of international trade.[29] According to Prebisch, modernization theory could not account for development because it understood growth in isolation from a world economic system.[30] His theory of dependence instead suggested that the roots of inequality between industrialized and non-industrialized economies were based on the terms of trade between them, especially on the type of commodities they traded. Countries that traded in primary commodities and raw materials like sugar, coffee, and tea were unable to achieve the same rate of growth as economies that traded manufactured goods. The reason was that the terms of trade

for primary commodities had been deteriorating relative to that of manufactured goods. Inequality would only increase with the growth of trade instead
of being reduced, as modernization theorists suggested.[31] International trade,
therefore, was based on a commodity trap that prevented the agricultural
economies of the newly independent Third World from competing with the
industrialized West. The commodity trap became a symbol of the larger problem of the economics of growth.

In 1964, Prebisch made the theory the basis of a new type of postcolonial
politics at UNCTAD, when he published a report that famously called for
"trade not aid."[32] Prebisch claimed that aid could not be the sole solution to
the economic and social development of the Third World.[33] He called for a
new global strategy that would devise measures to promote the development
of exports. He helped transform UNCTAD into a forum of debate about how
to equalize the world economy by transforming it from a colonial trading
system to a more egalitarian one.[34] By the late 1960s, Prebisch was joined by
a growing and diverse postcolonial critique about the connection between
poverty, underdevelopment, and empire.[35] His theory of dependency became
part of broader calls for a New International Economic Order (NIEO) that
sought to rethink the political economy of trade and self-determination.[36] But
while the NIEO wanted to "undo hierarchical relations that facilitated domination" through a radical economic redistribution, Prebisch's theory remained
liberal in its scope. It focused on market integration.

Prebisch's postcolonial critique of the global economy was the basis of
Haslemere's activism.[37] The Haslemere Declaration directly drew on Prebisch's call for "a very profound economic revolution" in the Third World that
would connect social, moral, and political causes to economic domination.[38]
The declaration joined a series of fair-trade campaigns in Britain as well as
Europe and North America, though it offered a more radical critique than the
bulk of fair-trade campaigns in Britain. Drawing on Prebisch, Haslemere
sought structural reforms that would enable postcolonial economies to slowly
integrate into the global economy. Its campaigns focused on short-term protectionist measures that would allow postcolonial countries to diversify their
economies and compete in a market economy. The idea was to correct the
economic imbalances between postcolonial economies and Britain, which
were the legacies of imperialism.

For activists from groups like Haslemere, Britain had a unique ethical
responsibility toward the decolonizing Third World. Haslemere saw a close
connection between racism, postcolonial violence, and global poverty and
was particularly interested in Britain's own imperial legacies both internationally and domestically.[39] The "roots of exploitation," one pamphlet stated,
was "in *our* attitudes as individuals and in the institutions we have created
that reflect them."[40] It was perhaps not a coincidence that a large portion of
Haslemere's efforts was spent on campaigning against Rhodesian white

nationalism and apartheid in South Africa.[41] Because of economic dependencies, according to Haslemere, if Britain officially pulled out of these countries, the loss of British capital would cause their economies to suffer. Britain, therefore, was complicit in the racist policies of both governments.[42] The inequality of the global economy replicated a much deeper exploitative system in international politics.

The majority of Haslemere's campaigns focused on food as a resource. Haslemere saw food not only as a form of subsistence that would reduce the levels of hunger but also as a commodity that shaped the position of Third World countries, and former British imperial territories in particular, in the global economy. Their campaigns built upon a broader interest in food politics at the time, including the UN Freedom From Hunger Campaign and feeding schemes in Nigeria during its civil war. For many British NGOs, food was a key element for rethinking the welfare of newly decolonized societies. "Responsibility extends beyond the provision of a tractor or the equipment of a hospital," the director of Christian Aid argued in 1965. "We must be concerned about international agreements on commodity prices."[43] But while more established organizations like Christian Aid and Oxfam focused their campaigns in the 1960s on humanitarian and development work, Haslemere pushed for a restructuring of trade agreements for primary commodities like coffee, sugar, and tea. For Haslemere, the fair trade of food was a way to connect economic life in Britain with inequalities in the global economy.

Haslemere's understanding of fair trade in fact was more capacious and expansive than that of most NGOs at the time. It saw fair trade as a systematic reform of international trade that was connected to consumption habits but not dependent on it. Their campaigns aimed to utilize consumers as pressure groups that would call upon the British government and international organizations to restructure international terms of trade. Because of the legacies of the colonial world system, postcolonial countries like Ghana had received political independence, yet their economies were still deeply dependent on international terms of trade. "Many developing countries," explained the journalist and activist Jonathan Power in 1971, "are dominated by what are called 'one-crop economies.' This means that, apart from the crops they grow for subsistence, they tend to rely on one or two export crops. For example, Ghana relies on cocoa, Malaya on rubber, and Brazil on coffee. . . . There are 22 developing countries which are dependent on three primary crops for 70% of their export earnings."[44] For all their political independence, Third World economies had yet to be decolonized.

The further problem with "one-crop economies" was that they pitted postcolonial producers from different countries against each other. "In fact no one farmer can have any control over the prices he gets: he does not produce a large enough proportion of the total market to influence it," claimed Power.[45] Such was the case for coffee producers in Guatemala and Ghana, who had to compete with each other for their fair share of coffee trade in the global market. "The bulk of coffee is grown on small holdings farmed at little above subsistence level," Haslemere argued in a pamphlet.[46] Although farmers produced coffee for their own domestic consumption, the majority of their product went abroad to be sold by multinational companies as well as individual roasters in Europe and the United States, which "hold their own stockpiles of coffee to guard against price fluctuations."[47] Postcolonial farmers were not protected from speculations and the economic instability of coffee prices in the global market.

To right this economic injustice, Haslemere called for fair competition in and fair access to the international trading system at the General Agreement on Tariffs and Trade (GATT). For Haslemere, fair trade meant leveling the terms of access and competition in the global economy. Its campaign aimed to reform economic life in Britain and to create an international mechanism that would transcend the domain of the former colonial state. In a series of pamphlets, Haslemere suggested creating international regulatory mechanisms that would give postcolonial countries a fair stake in the global market of coffee, cocoa, tea, sugar, and bananas. It modeled these proposals on the International Coffee Agreement (ICA), an existing international mechanism that Haslemere deemed inefficient yet nevertheless had radical potential. Originally created in 1962, the ICA was signed by the producing and consuming countries in order "ostensibly to stabilize the market situation and to resolve the problems of over-production and price instability."[48] And while it had been "unable to effect even the mildest reforms" in shaping the prices of coffee,[49] Haslemere saw in it the capacity to serve as an international mechanism that would allow postcolonial producers to determine the price of their commodity, an innovation that would adjust the structure of prices and the quantities produced globally.

In fact, for Haslemere commodity agreements were part of a larger economic reform to expand postcolonial exports while stabilizing their prices internationally. It stood for a type of globalism that would eventually liberalize international trade. While at first glance the call for economic liberalization may sound peculiar, Haslemere was following ideas developed by policymakers like Prebisch at UNCTAD. As Johanna Bockman has argued, the postcolonial project at UNCTAD envisioned the formation of "a new international economic order that was based on markets" that had to be planned.[50] Similarly, Haslemere pushed for "structural adjustments" that would help reorganize global production and services, adjustments that substantially differed from the IMF-led policies of the 1980s but were nonetheless based on market globalism. Haslemere's activism, in other words, aimed to create a laissez-faire mechanism that would use temporary protectionist measures like commodity agreements in service of a larger, liberal goal of enabling Third World countries to fully participate in international trade.

Postimperial Obligations versus Self-sufficiency

The case of the 1972 Haslemere campaign against the Common Market and its impact on the British Commonwealth Sugar Agreement represents one of the richest examples of why Haslemere's activism failed. The campaign aimed to mobilize consumers to pressure the British government to protect sugar imported from former colonial countries, then providing almost two-thirds of British sugar, against new trading agreements with the Common Market. It argued that Britain had a particular obligation toward sugar and plantation economies because of the country's long imperial past. Its activists called for the creation of commodity agreements that would allow these economies to ease into the international trade system. The campaign, however, clashed with Britain's own economic quest for self-sufficiency after decolonization.

In 1969, Britain began a four-year negotiation process to join the European Economic Community (EEC), which included signing its Common Agriculture Policy (CAP). Under CAP, Britain would have to prioritize EEC products like sugar over sugar available through trade agreements with its former colonies. Furthermore, CAP controlled sugar surplus levels in Europe, thus determining sugar prices globally. Haslemere argued that Britain's commitment to CAP would be detrimental to postcolonial economies like Barbados, which were dependent on the British market through the Commonwealth Sugar Agreement. CAP would impoverish them and put their political independence in at risk.[51] The campaign became part of a larger discussion in Britain about the tensions between Britain's postimperial obligations toward its former colonies and the country's attempt to move toward self-sufficiency.

Haslemere's campaign about sugar was part of a larger coalition led by the World Development Movement, a consortium of NGOs across Britain established by Oxfam, Christian Aid, War on Want, the Overseas Development Institute, the Catholic Institute for International Development, and the Voluntary Committee on Overseas Aid and Development.[52] The World Development Movement lobbied the British government to increase its national aid budgets and lobbied against joining the Common Market. The coalition helped transform the sugar question into a popular political campaign. In the early 1970s it distributed leaflets and more than two hundred thousand packets of cane sugar to the public, as well as holding sugar-tasting competitions, to raise awareness about the centrality of former colonies in the Commonwealth to the British sugar bowl.[53] It also met with Prime Minister Edward Heath and MPs from across the political map to garner support. By 1971 it had collected over one hundred signatures for a Commons motion that called for extending the Commonwealth Sugar Agreement in 1974, after which Britain would join the Common Market.[54]

By the end of 1972, the World Development Movement had launched a broader program to help Third World producers negotiate a better trading position with the EEC. As its activists stated in one pamphlet, "We want to guarantee access to the rich markets for the EEC for goods from the Third World."[55] Dubbed "Europe '73," the program was launched in collaboration with other European NGOs and called for a reform in the CAP.[56] Once Britain joined, the lobby argued, the EEC would become "the largest and most powerful trading bloc in the world." It would have "considerable influence on the world economy and in particular on poor countries which rely so heavily on industralised countries."[57] Britain's membership in the EEC would have a tremendous effect on Third World commodities and trade, the World Development Movement argued, but especially on trading agreements like the Commonwealth Sugar Agreement. Britain, the lobby argued, had a particular duty toward the Commonwealth sugar industry, and it called on Britain to press the EEC on guaranteeing "continued access of cane sugar in quantities and at price at least equal to those present[ly] prevailing under the CSA."[58]

Sugar epitomized Britain's colonial legacies. As one journalist put it in 1973, sugar was "one of the most emotionally and politically charged commodities in world trade."[59] Sugar was a crop introduced in the eighteenth century to colonial territories in tropical and semi-tropical climates and relied on slave and, later, indentured labor. It transformed the entire South Atlantic economy.[60] It offered Britain raw materials for domestic consumption as well as for trade and became the basis for Britain's prominence in the global economy even up to the early twentieth century.[61] During the two world wars, sugar crops supported the British economy "against short-term expedients" and at the expense of impoverishing the colonial territories that produced it.[62] In the postwar period, the Labour government was committed to a new development policy that would support not only its domestic population through welfare but also its colonial territories.[63] The 1951 Commonwealth Sugar Agreement was the product of such policies. The agreement provided Britain with cheap sugar and, at the same time, was tied to late colonial development policy.

The agreement aimed to secure these development policies through fixed prices and quotas for sugar in fifteen colonial territories, including Barbados, Jamaica, St. Kitts, Guyana, British Honduras, and Mauritius as well as Kenya, Uganda, and Tanzania. It provided them income and employment but kept them dependent on the metropole. When these territories declared independence from Britain in the 1960s, the agreement was essential for sustaining their GDPs. In the case of Mauritius, 98 percent of its exports was made up of sugar cane and its by-product, and of that 60 percent was bought through the Commonwealth Sugar Agreement.[64] By the early 1970s, the agreement set a fixed price of £43.50 per ton from Commonwealth nations and sold sugar cane on to British sugar refiners at world market prices.[65] The agreement offered newly independent countries a secure market instead of relying on loans or aid.

It is for this reason that activists from Haslemere and the World Development Movement called upon the British government "to put pressure on its

Common Market partners to guarantee the developing Commonwealth sugar producers at least their present access to the UK market."[66] While campaigns for sugar also spread across the Continent, British activists argued that Britain had not only the negotiating power—now that it was about to join the EEC— but also a moral duty toward its Commonwealth sugar industry.[67] According to these activists, Britain had a moral as well as economic responsibility to maintain its commodity agreement with sugar-producing countries and to secure the UK market, if not also negotiate a unique place for Commonwealth sugar producers in the Common Market.[68] Haslemere called upon the government to resist "tough lobbying by the big sugar beet farmers of Northern France . . . farmers who were not peasants, but businessmen with considerable political say, running the most efficient beet farms in the Community."[69] To these activists, the Common Market represented a turn away from Britain's postimperial obligation toward a neoliberal policy that would advance the interests of European businessmen.

The sugar campaign was part of a broader British opposition to the Common Market. For many on the British left, the turn to the European community risked Britain's postimperial connection with its Commonwealth as well as the British economy itself.[70] At the same time, once in the Common Market Britain would surrender control of its food supply and no longer be able to set its own food prices. It would not only lose its special status in the world economy but also risk losing sovereignty over its domestic economy. These arguments arose from a particular form of imperial amnesia on the British left, since calling for the economic sovereignty of Britain erased the imperial formations that allowed for the primacy of the country's economy in the first place.

By the time Britain joined the Common Market in 1973, it became clear that such campaigns about Britain's postimperial obligations had reached their limit. Despite its commitment to overseas aid, the Common Market ended Britain's system of "imperial preference," established in 1932 and continued by Commonwealth commodity agreements in the 1950s. In the summer of 1974, Britain experienced a major sugar shortage, exposing the country's dependency on food imports. The Commonwealth Sugar Agreement was about to expire, yet the EEC was reluctant to make a decision as to whether or not it would renew it and give the fifteen sugar-producing countries a special trading preference. In September 1973, newspapers were warning that the "UK is likely to withdraw from its sugar agreement."[71] Sugar cane was a crop that took years to grow, and Caribbean producers became particularly concerned about getting the assurances necessary to secure enough credit for future crops.[72] Caribbean producers turned to more lucrative American markets; UK imports from the Caribbean dropped by more than a third.[73]

The sugar shortage that followed turned the NGOs' sugar campaign for the Commonwealth into a domestic issue about self-sufficiency and dependency on the former empire. The shortage affected British consumers as well as major British businesses like Tate & Lyle, which were dependent on Caribbean supplies for their refineries.[74] With the value of the pound plummeting, British supermarkets began to ration customers "to between two and four pounds of sugar."[75] Others allowed consumers to purchase sugar only if they spent more than £2 while shopping. Consumer associations and bakeries warned against a black market in sugar, as housewives were emptying the shelves of sugar in a panic.[76] Although the shortage was mitigated by autumn, the price of sugar remained high.[77] In November, the government introduced a price-equalizer scheme to support refineries and help consumers weather price fluctuations.[78] At the same time, it also announced a new initiative to encourage British farmers to sow sugar beet crops.[79] Commentators began to warn about Britain's reliance on the CAP and the world's primary commodities of food more broadly.[80] "At stake," as the historian Robert Saunders argued, "was not simply the price of food but Britain's ability to feed itself at all, as a declining economy in a world of scarcity."[81] Together with an ongoing oil crisis, and global scarcity in grain, the sugar crisis exposed that it was not only Commonwealth economies that were dependent on international trade; dependency went both ways.

While the Labour government, traditionally committed to overseas aid, had recognized Commonwealth dependency in primary commodities like sugar, it was nonetheless wary of Britain's high dependence on imports.[82] In April 1975, the Labour government released a White Paper titled *Food from Our Own Resources* that committed the country to increasing its self-sufficiency in agricultural products.[83] The White Paper aimed to reduce risks to the economy by nationalizing the production of food in Britain and decreasing its dependency on primary commodities in a period when food prices were rising globally as well as in the Common Market. "The levels of world and Community prices for major foodstuff between now and the early 1980s, and the risks of possible shortage and sharp price fluctuation," it stated, "justify [such] a policy."[84] *Food from Our Own Resources* proposed a five-year plan for expanding British national output by about 2.5 percent annually on net agricultural products. It placed special emphasis on crops like sugar beets in order to end its reliance on "substantial subsidies made available by the European Community for the purchase of sugar on world markets,"[85] as well as on milk and beef. The White Paper became part of a broader effort from the mid-1970s to increase food sustainability and self-sufficiency.[86] The policy marked a turn away from old imperial commitments and obligations toward postimperial economies and an attempt to claim Britain's own economic sovereignty.

The fate of international trade agreements like the one for sugar was no different. As part of the Common Market, the British government signed an international trade agreement at Lomé, Togo, between the EEC and seventy-one countries from the African Caribbean and Pacific, all former European colonial territories. The 1975 Lomé Convention solved the problem of the Commonwealth Sugar Agreement, but the fix was temporary.[87] It offered the seventy-one countries preferential access to commodities like sugar based on a quota system and a guaranteed price that would protect against fluctuations in world prices, as well as tariff-free access for most agricultural products and raw materials. And unlike previous EEC agreements, it did not demand reverse preferences for European goods. In addition, the Common Market committed to three billion European Currency Units (ECUs) in aid distributed through the European Investment Bank.[88] For some contemporaries, Lomé marked "a step which offers possibilities for a restructuring of the cooperation system, which contains assurances for the future and which promotes further progress towards a more just, New International Economic Order."[89] Some hoped it would be the beginning of an expansive new reform of the global economy and called to extend it to the entire Third World.[90]

By 1977, after the failed UN conference on sugar, the World Development Movement warned that Commonwealth sugar producers could not compete with European or American ones.[91] While the Lomé Convention was renewed three more times, in practice European, and particularly French, sugar producers did not respect their sugar quotas. The EEC, argued Minister of State for the Foreign and Commonwealth Office Frank Judd, was at risk of calling into question "the entire sincerity of the [trade agreements between the] EEC and the Third World."[92] In 1996, the Lomé Convention was effectively canceled when the United States made a formal complaint to the WTO against the preferential agreements of bananas imported from the Caribbean to the EEC. The WTO ruled that Lomé was incompatible with WTO trade regulations.[93] Lomé, created in the mid-1970s to amend the injustices of the protectionist Common Market, was now charged with being an unfair trade agreement that restrained the full potential of laissez-faire markets.

From Trade Agreements to British "Lifestyle"

In early 1970, a series of crop failures created a massive food shortage across the Third World. By 1972, cereal stocks had been reduced to their lowest levels since World War II, tripling the price of wheat.[94] The shortage was a result of bad weather as well as rising demand for grain, particularly from the Soviet Union, and an increase in meat consumption that required a higher volume of cereals. At the same time, it was exacerbated by the American, Canadian, and Australian governments, which subsidized and encouraged local farmers to decrease their grain production "and intentionally [run] down reserves to drive up prices" in order to benefit their national economies.[95] As a result, in early 1973 famines spread across Chad, Mali, Gambia, Senegal, Burkina Faso, Niger, and Ethiopia as well as eastern Brazil and Bangladesh. By the mid-

1970s, around two million people had died of disease and hunger, mainly in Bangladesh, Ethiopia, and the West African Sahel.[96]

The world food crisis of 1974 heralded a new age of scarcity. In February 1973, the FAO director-general Addeke Boerma warned of an impending food crisis. Within six months, at the 4th Summit Conference of Heads of State or Government of the Non-Aligned Movement, leaders from the Third World called upon "the international community [to] adopt as a matter of extreme urgency the measures dictated by this situation, which is now coupled with the unchecked rise in the prices of staple products."[97] In November 1974, only after the Americans backed the idea, the FAO held a World Food Conference aimed "to bring about a commitment by the world community as a whole to undertake concerted action towards resolving the world food problem within the wider context of development problems."[98] The conference invited 161 nongovernmental and humanitarian organizations, as well as 69 multinational businesses, to join the UN discussion table.[99] It was an unprecedented collaboration of international and nongovernmental activism. As a result of this work, in 1975 the UN issued the Universal Declaration on the Eradication of Hunger and Malnutrition, stating that "every man, woman and child has the inalienable right to be free from hunger and malnutrition in order to develop fully and maintain their physical and mental faculties."[100]

The crisis generated a new humanitarian urgency, and with it a new set of ethical dilemmas about the responsibility of those in the West toward the world's hungry.[101] While in the late 1960s activists discussed the problem of resources as part of postimperial politics of international commodity agreements, by the middle of the 1970s, at least for those in the West, food scarcity was suddenly understood according to the Malthusian idea of a world population growing rapidly amid diminishing global resources. The world food crisis altered the way that nongovernmental and international organizations approached the question of distribution of resources, particularly of food. It reframed the problem of limited resources as a consequence of population growth and consumption rather than a product of imperial economy. In so doing, it inadvertently marked a turn away from postimperial and structural critiques of the economy toward discussions about personal, individual responsibility, and altruism.

For Anglo-American liberal philosophers, for example, the crisis crystallized the necessity of accounting for ethical imperatives beyond national borders. In his famous 1972 essay "Famine, Affluence, and Morality," the utilitarian philosopher Peter Singer made the case that individuals—and not just governments—had a moral obligation to aid faraway strangers.[102] Singer's emphasis on voluntarism, as we have already seen, was shaped by welfarist debates in Britain and Titmuss' economics of altruism. But Singer scaled these welfarist ideas up to the global community. In an interconnected world, shaped by economic interdependence and technological advances, Singer made the case that individuals in the West had a duty to help the starving in the Third World, even if it just meant donating money to charity. Doing nothing effectively meant being complicit in their deaths.

Three years later, the British liberal philosopher Onora O'Neill joined Singer's company. Her 1975 essay "Lifeboat Earth" recognized the moral obligation prompted by the humanitarian emergency of the world food crisis, but O'Neill sought a solution that would move away from Singer's altruistic model. Trained under John Rawls, O'Neill wanted to anchor ethics in a more robust discourse of rights rather than charity, one that would be based on a political commitment to human rights rather than dependent on the structure of feeling.[103] To her, the humanitarian emergency of the period marked a transition from the earth as a realm of equality to one that was hierarchically divided between two classes of passengers: the saved and the forsaken. What she proposed was a minimal ethical principle anchored in rights discourse rather than altruist decisions: every person has the right not to be killed.

The lifeboat earth offered the perfect metaphor to test this principle.[104] O'Neill borrowed the term from the neo-Malthusian ecologist Garrett Hardin, who argued that the lifeboat better represented the survivalist threat than the spaceship metaphor. But while Hardin used the idea of the "lifeboat" to advance a racist critique against aiding the world's poor, O'Neill used it to consider seriously the ethical liability against doing exactly that.[105] Like Singer, she emphasized that contemporary "economic and technological interdependence" altered the ethical obligation to include people who lived beyond the boundaries of the state.[106] For O'Neill, the obligation meant that individuals had a duty to act not only through voluntary channels (as Singer would have it) but also as citizens by pressuring their governments to adopt moral economic policies. "If all persons have a right not to be killed and a corollary duty not to kill others," she wrote, "then we are bound to adopt pre-famine politics which ensure that famine is postponed as long as possible and is minimized. And a duty to try to postpone the advent and minimize the severity of famine is a duty on the one hand to minimize the number of persons there will be and on the other to maximize the means of subsistence."[107] O'Neill advanced a rights discourse based on a humanitarian minimum of bare life and a call to action for political pressure aimed at Western citizens.

The question of lifeboat ethics was in no way confined to intellectual circles. It was also on the minds of policymakers, diplomats, and aid workers who grappled with how to reform economic life in a world of limited resources. In his September 1973 address to the UN General Assembly, the West German chancellor Willy Brandt famously stated that "morally it makes no difference whether a man is killed in war or is condemned to starve to death by the indifference of others."[108] Security was no longer an issue exclusive to wars but was also a matter of access to resources and food. Everyone was responsible—not just governments and international organizations but also individual citizens. In 1977, Brandt chaired an international commission and, eventually, produced the ambitious report "North-South: A Programme for Survival."[109] But the politics of the report originated in the survivalist discourse of the 1970s and its connections to food and the scarcity of resources. The report suggested that there was a "mutual interest" between global North and South to end poverty and that the global North must move away from palliative and ineffective aid programs. While the report's proposals were never fully adopted by affluent countries, Brandt's critique nevertheless inspired environmental and humanitarian activists to apply his ideas to aspects of economic life beyond the state's purview.

In a public lecture for Oxfam on October 31, 1973, the former president of the European Commission, Sicco Mansholt, invoked Brandt's words to make a similar case for survivalist politics. Mansholt proposed adopting a new form of egalitarianism, a system of "distribution of the remainder of natural resources that mankind has left in the world."[110] He stated that "I do not think that we can deal with any problem of poor or rich in the world, or indeed the responsibilities of any nation of the Community of Europe, unless we fit such questions into the context of the overwhelming question of mankind's survival."[111] Speaking to an audience of Oxfam activists, Mansholt called for economic activism that would readjust Western consumption and production "to the level needed to restore the imbalance in the world" and go beyond the paradigm of modernization and economic growth.[112] Lifeboat ethics presented him with a moral duty to aid not only those hungry in the Third World but also future generations. It was an obligation of creating a world that would sustain its inhabitants and their children.

According to Mansholt, the problem with lifeboat earth was not only that the world's resources were diminishing but also that Western consumers were depleting them the most. He claimed there was no point in critiquing the policies of the European Common Market, as many of the activists in the room did, without reforming Western individual consumption patterns. "It's easy to say: 'Europe must do that, and that, and that,' but when in the meantime we all as citizens take no action . . . when we just sit around and say 'it should be' and are not willing to work for it," he argued. "So long as we continue in this way, Europe will never have the force to be a power in the world that can shoulder its responsibilities."[113] Although the problem of natural resources was discussed in radical circles in the late 1960s, it was approached through activism that focused primarily on structuralist arguments about economic production and postimperial dependency. For Mansholt and others, the world food crisis demanded new ways of thinking about the ethics and economics of Western consumption, not only production, in order to address environmental problems.

The politics of nonrenewable resources was also at the center of a 1974 BBC documentary called *The Other Way*, which prominently featured the economist E. F. Schumacher.[114] The film aimed to educate British viewers about the energy crisis and how it was connected to everyday life in Britain. "The continuing energy crisis has begun to make us realize that we have been burning up the world's limited resources of fuel too fast. And unlike wood, fossil fuels like coal and oil are nonrenewable," opened the documentary. "It's the price of our evolving in the West. . . . Almost everything from mass housing to transport, industry, and even food now depends on the vast use of energy." The documentary invited British viewers to assess the problem of resources through an image of one loaf of mass-produced, sliced bread. "Instead of casting today's [bread] loaf in pennies, cast it in energy," the narrator Ian Holm told viewers. The documentary divided the bread into six portions, each representing the energy that went into its production: the tractors and fertilizers behind the harvest of wheat; the power it took to mill the wheat; the energy it took to package the wheat, and then to transport it to the baker; the time it took to bake the bread; and finally, the energy it took to package and transport the bread from the bakery to the local supermarket. "The total energy put into this loaf would run an electric fire for about three hours," the documentary concluded. For each unit of energy Britons extract as food, the documentary suggested, these "laborsaving processes have burned out three units of energy in growing, baking, packing, and transporting the bread." The documentary turned to Schumacher, who explained the environmental economics of nonrenewable resources to the British viewer in simple terms: the consumption of energy and food of everyday life in Britain had a direct effect on diminishing resources in the Third World. It was part of a humanitarian economics. The documentary advocated for simpler, alternative technologies that would be more labor-intensive for the British consumer (or the Third World producer) but would save energy and be environmentally friendly.

By the mid-1970s, consumption patterns and the economics of altruism became the heart of nongovernmental campaigns in Britain. This focus was not entirely new for British NGOs, especially when it came to food.[115] But the world food crisis shifted activists' attention toward reforming consumption patterns in order to address environmental concerns about diminishing resources, especially of food and energy. Instead of looking at food consumption in the Third World, large British NGOs like War or Want, Save the Children, Christian Aid, and Oxfam turned their attention to reforming consumption patterns in their own backyard gardens and kitchens. These organizations joined a broader movement in Britain that emphasized the connection between the economy of what one ate at home and poverty in the Third World and were inspired especially by the work of Schumacher.

No campaign captured the idea of lifeboat earth more than Oxfam's "lifestyle" campaign. "The British people must get a hold of the fact that mankind sinks or swims together," explained Oxfam's director Brian Walker in one of the organization's press releases in November 1974. "Our economic plight and that of starving peoples of the world are part and parcel of the same issue."[116] Building directly on the work of Barbara Ward, E. F. Schumacher, Willy Brandt, and others, Walker wanted the organization to create an ethical consumption movement, especially concerning food, that would address the environmental economics of diminishing resources. "It is particularly pertinent for the British people to stick closely to this issue of food," he argued, "because as a nation, we import more food, by volume, than any other nation in the world."[117] Walker, in fact, saw the campaign as part of a broader reorientation of Oxfam toward environmental politics. He developed it alongside campaigns like "Wastesaver," which invited British households to recycle waste like tins, paper, and bottles at an Oxfam center which, in turn, sorted it and sold it back to consumers and to industry "after being granulated, pressed, or shredded."[118]

Walker, who had just returned from the World Food Conference in Rome in November 1974, also wanted Oxfam to push for a serious reconsideration of the structural connection between consumption in Britain and the growing grain crisis in the Third World. "Are they poor because we're rich?" asked Walker in an internal memo.[119] In the months that followed, Walker commissioned a study from a political scientist at the London School of Economics, A. N. Oppenheim, about how Oxfam could develop an effective set of campaigns that would use environmental economics and directly address the relationship between renewable and nonrenewable resources and the idea of global economic dependency. Among other things, Oppenheim's report included myriad proposals about commodity agreements and collaborating with Third World governments.[120]

Oxfam was particularly interested in how a campaign attuned to the scarcity of resources might look, and how citizens could make deep changes in their consumption patterns.[121] Drawing on Oppenheim's recommendations, Oxfam created the "lifestyle" campaign. Launched in April 1975 in the midst of an economic crisis in Britain, the campaign proposed a set of reforms and activities—from food labeling to diets—that would help British citizens shoulder the responsibility of global starvation and diminishing grain reserves. Its aim, as one Oxfam memo specified, was not merely "to make people *feel* as if they are living as world citizens." Instead, it should "create a structural change in the pattern of trade between the over-developed countries by influencing consumption habits in the rich countries."[122] The idea was to shape economic behavior rather than solve specific crises of food and poverty around the world. In the words of Walker, the goal of the "lifestyle" campaign was to help create "a welfare planet" with a more equitable distribution of resources.[123]

To do so, the campaign focused on reforming British food habits, diets, and consumption patterns. Consumption, Walker argued, could be used as a tool to change the patterns and lifestyles of people in "rich countries" and thereby was a way for ordinary citizens to reshape trade patterns. Walker, however, decided to center the campaign on consumer action. The idea was to use the power of the consumer as a global as well as a British citizen and to engage British consumers by creating a series of linkages between "our wealth—their poverty," that is, between Britain and the Third World. Walker hoped that decreasing consumer demand for primary raw materials could help determine import patterns and, through that, reform world inequalities. The campaigns were to pay special attention to grain, sisal, and mineral extraction. According to Walker, the rich countries were "using an increasingly unfair share of the world's resources and harvests." The solution, Oxfam proposed, was a total reduction of growth in Western economies and especially in Britain. This was, according to Oxfam, a fair-trade system that would combat resource depletion in "a finite plenary system."[124]

At the beginning of 1975, Walker appointed an Oxfam task force to consider making consumer action the heart of the campaign. Consumers, the task force argued, certainly had an advantage politically because they could use their power to increase the leverage of the producer in the global economy by choosing to buy their products over ones that came from Europe or the United States. Consumers could reshape the global economy from the "bottom up." Instead of relying exclusively on governmental or even international pressure, consumers could help producers in the Third World directly "to increase their power—e.g. through OPEC-type organisations"—as much as they could shape demand for certain products and commodities in Britain itself.[125] At the same time, the task force warned that there were clear limitations to using consumer power to reform world trade. "Market forces may be the wrong lever for effecting what are essentially social and political reforms," it purported. "The market communication system is not subtle enough to carry the message; child labour in the mines could not have been ditched by consumers refusing to buy coal mined with such labour."[126]

Despite these limitations, the task force saw a radical promise in the power of the consumer as a sovereign actor in a global community that could shape, at least partially, trading systems and commodity habits. "Your personal action," one of its campaign leaflets stated, "*in isolation,* will not help the hungry elsewhere. However, it does help to create awareness of world needs. If enough people in Britain become aware of their food-consumption patterns, they might be able to form a powerful political voice which could alter the government's attitude to aid." The idea was to mobilize consumers to pressure the governments especially on foreign policy: "Overseas aid does not get votes."[127]

The idea that consumption in the marketplace mirrored a choice at the ballot box had both conservative and progressive origins in the twentieth century.[128] The term "consumer sovereignty" itself was coined in 1931 by the conservative LSE economist William H. Hutt. Hutt used the term against socialist and fascist notions of state-led sovereignty. He argued that the freedom of the consumer as citizen represented the freedom to choose "between ends, over the custodians of the community's resources, when the resources by which those ends can be served are scarce."[129] Consumer sovereignty was the ideal democratic mechanism, according to Hutt, that would bypass the power of an authoritative state and maximize liberty and justice. It was this formulation that was as appealing to game theorists, neoconservative economists, and, in the 1940s and 1950s, neoliberal thinkers like Friedrich Hayek as it was to welfare thinkers like Anthony Crosland who sought to empower working-class communities through consumption.[130] Just as citizens made choices about which party or candidate to vote for, the market offered consumers a way to express their own preferences and politics through the items they purchased.

In 1960, that idea became the heart of the politician and sociologist Michael Young's vision of the Labour Party. In a pamphlet titled *The Chipped White Cups of Dover*, Young argued that "class based on production is slowly giving way to status based on consumption as the centre of social gravity."[131] The consumer represented a new form of global citizenship. From the way welfare services were set up to the organization of the family and gender relations, the consumer had become a "third force" in society.[132] As such, Young made the case that Labour should represent the consumer and, in doing so, forge a new domestic and international politics. The consumer, according to Young, afforded Britain a new moral position in the world economy: "For it is not as producers that we feel sympathy for Indian or Chinese peasants—rather the reverse since other producers are possible competitors. It is as consumers that we feel for them: they too are people, whose families are dying because they do not get enough to eat."[133] A consumer party would be able to move away from imperialist agendas and become a progressive, internationalist party that would encourage global solidarities. Later, Young also called upon Western consumers to donate 1 percent of their income to development projects directed by the International Organization of Consumers' Unions.[134] For Young, as the historian Pat Thane argued, welfare was both a domestic and an international project of responsibility on behalf of the affluent for the poor.[135]

Influenced by this vision, the Oxfam "lifestyle" task force met with consumer groups across Britain and the Third World. In particular, it hoped to team up with the Consumers' Association—established by Young in 1957—and publish information in its newsletter *Which?* In a meeting on October 1, 1975, with Eirlys Roberts, the association's deputy director, and Daphne Gross, the deputy of campaigning and representation, Oxfam made the case that it shared a common interest with the association in "the social effects of consumption."[136] For Oxfam, international and domestic consumer interests were connected rather than competing. "In buying, or not," Oxfam argued, "one has an effect on other people's employment, on pollution, on the use of energy, on the depletion of non-renewable resources, and on the prices people get from their work. Most of these effects take place within Britain . . . but some affect the poor in the Third World."[137]

The Consumers' Association, however, rejected Oxfam's suggestion and claimed that its members were primarily interested in what would give them the best value for money rather than political causes. Oxfam's proposal, the association argued, was unmanageable since it was "very difficult to work out the energy, or balance of payments, or pollution effects of most things, let alone the effects on employment in Guatemala."[138] The association worked less as a political or ethical movement than its founder Michael Young originally envisioned. Instead, by the 1970s it had become more of a utilitarian organization that focused on efficiency, design, and the safety of specific products.[139] "Michael Young, who after all, is the founder and President of Consumers' Association, has been pressing this sort of thing for years," the association admitted.[140]

Oxfam's lifestyle task force turned its attention to shaping consumer action directly through Oxfam's outreach programs. In the second half of 1975, it established a newspaper as well as local "cell" groups that would empower consumers and educate them specifically about the consumption of food. The newspaper provided guidelines "to all who wish to respond personally and joyfully to the urgent need to share the Earth's resources among the family of man; to conserve those resources for future generations; and to check inflation."[141] It was specifically set to engage the British household—rather than individuals—as a unit. It offered advice on what to buy, how to save, and how to recycle, as well as how to not be "persuaded by advertising to buy what in fact we do not want." The idea was to inform as well as offer support to the British housewife on how to adapt "our habits to eating and drinking to the needs of the human family."[142]

Oxfam's lifestyle task force also proposed creating a system to inform consumers about a product's benefits or harms to Third World economies. In a symposium about changing lifestyle habits, Walker suggested creating an "Oxfam seal-of-approval" tag that would include information about an item's connection to resource depletion and energy conservation, as well as the material conditions of the people in the product's country of origin. Oxfam would model the tag after a label made by the Conservation Society, and even considered collaborating with Friends of the Earth, though it worried that the organization was too radical.[143] The idea was to enlist specific conglomerates like Sainsbury's—middle-class brands—to use an "Oxfam seal-of-approval" indicating that consumers could purchase a product if they wished "to live as world citizens."[144] "Some marketers might be keen to co-operate on such a scheme," stated Walker, since "it would bring them extra customers."[145]

The fair-trade labels would serve a double purpose: to help create a brand of product as well as to encourage ethical consumers to shop at approved retailers.

Fair-trade labels, the task force suggested, could then be linked to a broader fair-trade business of Third World products, including the fair trade of coffee, as well as to development aid programs focused on farming. The task force made the case that some form of trade could benefit Third World producers: "Despite anti-trade and self-sufficiency arguments, some trade probably helps the poor whom we are trying to help."[146] In doing so, the task force directly sought to promote an economic activity that would be both sustainable and responsive to the antigrowth economics of the time.[147] Similar to the "bridge" handicraft venture that imported handmade clothes to be sold in charity shops, the lifestyle task force would identify products and raw materials like jute and sisal, "and then [see] how far [Oxfam] can maximize our import of them."[148] The idea was to utilize the power of the consumer to support sustainable Third World industries. "We would be encouraging the bits of fair (or fairer) trade in the world, and we would be educating people about the connection between their lifestyle and that of others," wrote the task force.[149] This fair-trade venture guaranteed both a fair-trade price and profits. It also factored in the economics of limited resources. It became the heart of the campaign throughout the second half of the 1970s and across Britain shaped local activism that sought to connect daily consumption habits with a global politics of diminishing resources.

Clean Your Plate!

It was, however, the idea of the clean plate that became central to Oxfam's "lifestyle" campaign in the last four years of the 1970s. The organization launched a series of proposals and activities that attempted to connect British food consumption with ecological concerns about food scarcity. The campaign sought to educate the British public about reducing food waste and, to a certain degree, to substitute parts of their diet—primarily meat—with more ecological solutions that could sustain the world's grain reserves. Altering the British lifestyle, in that sense, meant encouraging Britons to view their plate as something that represented finite resources shared between the West and Third World. The task force meant not only to foster solidarity and encourage sympathy for faraway starving people but also to create new attitudes, behaviors, and imaginations about the ethics of what one ate for dinner.

The idea of the clean plate was not an Oxfam invention. Its origins dated back to 1917, when the U.S. Food Administration ran a program to increase awareness of food shortages during World War I.[150] In World War II these ideas were used to support not only American soldiers but also the Allied powers. By 1943, local American youth organizations and the American Red

Cross had formed Clean Plate clubs in churches and schools.[151] "The average waste per person for the four-week period was 926 ounces," one such club reported. "Vegetables and bakery products competed for first place as major items of waste."[152] They called on American housewives to maximize their food consumption to help their European allies. In the 1960s, the FFHC adapted some of these ideas. It encouraged students in Britain and Europe to participate in public fasts and abstain from food luxuries during Lent in solidarity with the hungry in the Third World.[153] The campaign used the body to generate feelings of solidarity and sympathy toward people starving far away from ordinary British citizens. Food waste was seen not only as an offense against fellow Americans or even the European community. It was now also perceived as an injustice against the world's population as well as future generations.

There were three practical ways that Oxfam's "lifestyle" campaign connected personal consumption to global inequalities. First, the campaign encouraged Britons to have a "Family Added Tax," that is, to collect donations through little family boxes where housewives could put a penny for every cake, biscuit, or glass of wine the family consumed.[154] The purpose of the tax was not only to fundraise but also to make families aware of their diet and especially the particulars of their food intake. "This is the save-a-little-give-a-little approach," explained Oxfam. "Although it involves helping the poor through money and not through changing patterns of consumption, . . . [w]e could sell it as moderate lifestyle, befitting a world citizen—which would be internally satisfying, even if it had no direct effect on the poor."[155] The money would be donated to Oxfam to finance antipoverty and antiwaste programs. In other words, the tax served a symbolic as well as philanthropic purpose of reducing food waste in the West and food scarcity in the Third World.

Oxfam's "lifestyle" campaign also held events on food consumption to encourage the public to imagine the connection between their diet and diminishing resources in the Third World. One type of event was the "rich man-poor man" dinner. The dinners were both fundraising opportunities and social events. Members of the public who wished to participate had to pay around 50p a ticket, and based on a lottery selection, two-thirds of the participants received only a bowl of soup while the remaining third were served a lavish meal. "The idea is to bring home to people that only a third of the world have plenty of food," explained Derek Ingledew, the chairman of Saltburn Oxfam.[156] The dinners thus aimed to replicate the unequal distribution of resources. Some dinners even teamed up with Weight Watchers to encourage participants to check their weight and notice what Oxfam called "the crazy paradox that rich men pay to slim, and poor men have to fight to get enough food."[157]

The final goal of the campaign, and perhaps the most ambitious of all, was to alter the diet of British families by reducing their meat consumption. This was a concrete way for Britons to be educated about the global problem of

FIGURE 4.1. "Rich Man Poor Man Lunch," 1974.

food scarcity and limited resources. "We grow 10m tons of our feed grains and import 4m tons of cereals and 2m tons of protein meals," one Oxfam report stated.[158] While the campaign did not call for ecological vegetarianism altogether, it nonetheless aimed to educate Britons on how to reduce their weekly meat intake and urged them to alter their diet to rely more on vegetables and fruit. Meat production, the lifestyle task force argued, was one of the most wasteful industries, as it used excessive amounts of grain and land. As a sympathetic citizen and farmer from Dorset said in an Oxfam document, "If two people share a chicken produced under modern intensive methods, they are eating the meal of twenty people prepared to eat much the same stuff as bread and fishpaste."[159]

For Oxfam, the meat industry epitomized the transition from an organic economy of wood, wind, and water to a mineral economy that was based on the nonrenewable resources of coal, oil, and natural gas.[160] "In our affluent and modern industrial society, food and eating have become divorced from agriculture," the document stated.[161] Production suddenly relied on nonrenewable but energy-dense fossil fuels, which enabled food systems to expand in scale.[162] In a world where energy is limited, the "lifestyle" campaign suggested, meat production wasted an unnecessary amount of energy.[163] "If we buy less grain on the world market there will be more available for trade with the poorer countries such as India and Bangladesh, and assuming a decline in price more available for food aid," Oxfam stated.[164] The campaign proposed that reforming the British diet could pressure the food industry to restructure its production patterns.

To bolster this argument, Oxfam drew on the ideas of environmental activists like the American Lester R. Brown and his work on the environmental and moral dimensions of the world food problem. "It is no longer merely a matter of alms-giving, but of abstaining from excessive consumption when that consumption jeopardizes the very survival of human beings elsewhere in the world," Brown wrote in 1974. Limited resources presented a new challenge in international politics to think beyond altruism as a solution to scarcity. "For a man with only one crust of bread, the second crust may ensure survival, but one with a loaf of bread, an additional crust is of marginal value."[165] Brown called for affluent countries to reduce "the frivolous use of energy" and free up access to fossil-fuel supplies and particularly meat consumption in order for the Third World to expand its food production.[166]

The Oxfam campaign was also inspired by the American activist Frances Moore Lappé and her 1971 bestselling book *Diet for a Small Planet*. Lappé's book was one of the first to make the humanitarian case for a meatless diet. It was sponsored by the American Friends of the Earth organization. Lappé did not argue for full-fledged vegetarianism but advocated "a return to the traditional diet . . . in which animal foods play a supplemental role."[167] The book offered not only reflections on the detrimental effects of meat production on world hunger but also information about traditional cuisines—like Latin American and Asian diets—that relied primarily on grains and legumes for protein. Importantly, *Diet for a Small Planet* also included meatless recipes: from tofu spaghetti sauce and soy burgers to wheat-soy waffles and a tofu scramble breakfast. In 1973 it was followed by a similar book by Ellen Buchman Ewald titled *Recipes for a Small Planet*.

Oxfam's "lifestyle" campaign tailored these ideas to the British consumer by focusing on the British housewife in the majority of its dietary reform efforts. As the historian Emily LaBarbera-Twarog has argued, in this period the housewife became both "a political constituency group and an imagined ideal."[168] Between 1975 and 1977, Oxfam held special "meatless Sunday" events that invited housewives to reduce their reliance on meat for their Sunday cooking, encouraging them to give up the equivalent of one hamburger a week. The idea was to teach housewives how to adjust their family's diet and rely more on "protein-economy recipes."[169] The organization even collaborated with other agencies like Christian Aid and offered educational packets that included nutritional tables and alternative recipes based primarily on vegetables. A "person living in the United Kingdom can eat far more than the amount of protein and calories he actually needs," one educational packet argued. It also explained the dire nutritional situation of people in India and West Africa.[170]

In addition, the campaign explored the possibility of marketing soya-based meals through Oxfam charity shops, which would "ensure that the preparation for the soya foods were done in an ecologically sound way" and "without high technology processing."[171] It looked for ways to educate housewives "in economical and waste-saving methods of food preparation and cooking,"[172] such as suggesting how to substitute margarine and vegetable oil for butter. "Many of us over-eat either through an excessive intake of food, or—less obviously—by eating protein which has been produced by methods which are wasteful of agriculture and/or other resources,"[173] the campaign argued.

By establishing connections between the British diet and global hunger, the campaign made a direct link between individual bodies in Britain and worldwide hunger. If in the past charitable campaigns held fasts and vigils to encourage solidarities among a community of faith, the lifestyle campaign offered new ideas about redemption. It used a religious idea about abstaining from food and gave it a secularized meaning. Diet was now connected to a series of environmental, economic, and even nutritional ideas about hunger. The meatless diet it promoted offered consumers, particularly housewives, a recipe to save not only themselves but also the planet and its future generations.

At the time, nutritionists were also pointing to interconnectivity and dependency between dietary habits in Britain and in the Third World. "The European type of diet," wrote Moises Behar, chief of the Department of Nutrition of the World Health Organization, in 1976, "not only is not the best diet from [a] health point of view but is absolutely impractical in economic terms for the world population under the present circumstances."[174] Nutritionists argued that the globalization and industrialization of the Western diet not only wasted precious resources but also was unhealthy compared to more traditional diets. Oxfam deployed such nutritional research in its brochures and campaign leaflets but also went beyond its conclusions about dietary habits. It made a moral as well as material connection between the world food crisis and an unhealthy diet and, to some extent, even the obesity problem in Britain.[175] Simply put, Oxfam's campaign implied that in a world of limited resources, British obesity was not only unhealthy but also unethical.

FIGURE 4.2. Oxfam's Slimming Club poster, 1978.

These connections between British bodies and the politics of limited resources became the heart of the Oxfam campaign to reform British lifestyle habits. One striking example was the so-called "Slimming Clubs," organized by Oxfam in the 1970s, which invited women to diet for Oxfam and fundraise for their campaigns.[176] "With the arrival of the 'midi' dress . . . skirts which have been languishing in wardrobes for years are being resurrected and valiant attempts made to squeeze into former waistlines," suggested Betty Price, an Oxfam local organizer.[177] Oxfam emulated the technique of Weight Watchers, which emphasized the communal aspects of dieting.[178] It created local slimming groups that used their success as a way to solicit donations from friends and family. "It is crazy that half the world is unhealthy through eating too much while the other half is hungry from lack of food," noted one local Oxfam organizer.[179]

In the second half of the 1970s, the Slimming Clubs became more central to Oxfam's campaign. The "lifestyle" campaign suggested using these clubs to change consumers' mentality on a deeper level. It proposed that in a "welfare planet" there was a moral connection between what it meant to be overweight in Britain and world hunger.[180] Slimming Clubs became part of professional organizations that competed directly with commercial clubs like Weight Watchers, Silhouette, and the Society of Successful Slimmers, and combined group therapy as part of its work.[181] The clubs included recipes, caloric calculators, exercises routines, and information packs that aimed to educate the British consumer on their own nutritional health as well as in the causes of hunger in the Third World.[182]

Finally, as a way to supplement these campaigns with a series of pamphlets, Oxfam also lobbied the British government. In 1977, Adrian Walker proposed how to integrate the campaign into a new official policy on food and agriculture in Britain. In a report he published on behalf of Oxfam, Walker urged the government to adopt a food and agriculture policy that would include a more economical use of existing resources. The report argued that "the world must be regarded as a gigantic farm in which each country supplies its basic food needs and makes the best use of existing inputs."[183] Food production and food consumption should be considered together rather than separately.

As we have already seen, since joining the EEC the British government had been revising its own agricultural policy. The 1975 White Paper *Food from Our Own Resources* attempted to move Britain away from relying on the global economy and specifically the Commonwealth community. It was a pledge to move British food production toward self-sufficiency. For Oxfam, however, the White Paper did not fully deliver on its promise. The White Paper, Oxfam stated in a report, "remains based firmly on traditional economic considerations rather than on a reasoned appraisal of the nutritional needs of the population of this country."[184] Oxfam called on the British government to adopt a more ambitious food and agriculture policy that would not only increase British self-sufficiency but also account for British nutritional needs.

A large portion of the Oxfam report focused on British dietary needs rather than those of the Third World. "Perhaps as much as one third of the population of the UK suffer from diet-linked aliments such as obesity and digestive disorders," the report stated.[185] From excessive meat consumption to that of sugar, the problem of malnutrition was not only a story about the Third World. Instead, the report argued, the industrialization of food had produced a domestic challenge for the British population: "The UK government should . . . institute policies whereby agricultural production is geared to the dietary needs of the population of this country, the requirements of the less developed nations and to the optimum utilization of all agricultural resources both national and global."[186] Nutritional needs in Britain were connected to a global environmental agenda according to Oxfam.

The report called upon the British government to entrust a ministerial committee with integrating national and global food and agriculture strategies in a way that would improve the health of the British population. Moreover, the report stated that such a committee should be in charge of educating the British public on how to adopt a healthier and more ethical diet: "Housewives, especially, could adjust the diet of their families to changing economic and social conditions and should be educated in economical and waste-saving methods of food preparation and cooking."[187] The report suggested that the committee should help make significant changes to British taste and to modify its unhealthy consumption habits. What had begun as a global campaign to radically reform economic life in Britain had by the late 1970s turned to cultural activities focused on consumer lifestyle and the British body.

The Politics of "Good" Taste

In 1974, in response to the world food crisis, the Algerian president Houari Boumédiène said that "to speak only of the drought that is killing human beings by the thousands in the African Sahelian regions, one might recall that in order to meet their wheat needs these regions would have managed with one twentieth the amount of wheat that the [developed] countries use each year to feed their cattle."[188] For some postcolonial observers, the world food crisis epitomized the unequal relationship between the West and the Third World. There were those who even warned that the crisis was a product of particular market mechanisms created by the United States and Canada. "The politics of food," announced the young journalist and later historian Emma Rothschild, "is a game with winners as well as losers."[189]

On "the food front," announced Barbara Ward, "there is no absolute shortage." Ward argued that despite claims from politicians in the West, there was no grain scarcity; the problem was one of distribution. Grain was "simply being eaten by very well-fed people." Since 1965, estimated Ward, Americans had added 350 pounds per person to their annual diet, mostly in the form of beef and poultry, an amount almost equal to an average Indian's diet for the entire year: "Between the 1,900 lb of cereal consumed annually by each North American and the Indian's 400 lb, there is a margin to spare." She called for a global policy that would ration the West's food consumption. Organizations like the FAO, in cooperation with governments from Western countries like Britain, should restrain food consumption and cut the diet of wealthy countries. Otherwise, she warned, the "mega-deaths in the starving lands, watched on affluent people's television screens, could mark the end of any moral community of man."[190]

And yet, despite these warnings, by the second half of the 1970s politicians, intellectuals, and activists in the West came to see the world food crisis as no more than a humanitarian problem of limited resources. "Today's agricultural problems," President Nixon's International Economic Report famously claimed in 1974, "stem from adverse natural conditions and the worldwide economic boom. . . . In contrast, the petroleum crisis is wrought by man."[191] The mid-1970s marked a defining moment in the international politics of food. The world food crisis signaled the transition from a structural critique of the global economy—one that sought to revise international trade mechanisms—to one that focused on a minimal politics of aid concentrated on individual responsibility.

In the 1970s, British NGOs sought to remake the world economy by focusing on the politics of food consumption in Britain. Shaped by new economic theories, their campaigns connected ecological theories with economic life in Britain. Both radical and more established organizations sought to parse the way between the postcolonial economic revolt of the so-called Third World around fair trade and the concerns about population growth and resource depletion, advocated by those in the West and especially in Britain. While in the early 1970s nongovernmental campaigns focused on revising commodity agreements for specific foods—like coffee, sugar, and tea—in the mid-1970s many organizations turned their efforts to changing the British diet. By the late 1970s, activism around food consumption had lost its radical potential. Instead, nongovernmental campaigns relied almost exclusively on the symbolic power of the consumer, as a citizen of the world, to remake the global economy. The politics of food consumption, especially of meat, became connected to the economics of nonrenewable energy and diminishing resources.

In the mid-1980s, food scarcity became a cause célèbre of humanitarian campaigns. One of the most famous images of the period was the logo of the band that recorded the very first charity song. The British collective of singers and songwriters known as "Band Aid" advertised their efforts with a logo that portrayed the entire globe as a dinner plate with a knife and fork on either side of it, and above it the catchy slogan "feed the world." The logo signaled the shared faith of the earth's inhabitants during their journey in "spaceship earth." By then, the politics of food had joined campaigns like Oxfam's and Christian Aid's imported coffee efforts, which carried fair-trade labels that vouched for the labor conditions in which their products were produced. But the fair-trade and humanitarian campaigns of the 1980s had more capacious origins in the environmental politics of natural resources and food consumption of the 1970s. By the end of that decade, those politics had been hollowed out. Instead, the metaphor of the earth was replaced by individual ethical choices about the virtue of food consumption. And it was this individual ethic, a politics of "good" taste, that became the center of NGO campaigns in the 1980s and 1990s.

CHAPTER FIVE

The Responsible Corporation

DO BUSINESSES HAVE A social responsibility to their workers, consumers, and the community? That question was at the heart of "Ownership," a lesser-known essay by E. F. Schumacher included in his 1973 bestseller *Small Is Beautiful.* A revision of a paper he gave in March 1965 in New Delhi at the Seminar on the Social Responsibility of Business, the essay argues that the social responsibility of a business was a matter of its scale. The bigger the business, the bigger its labor force and its revenue, the more it is obligated to serve the interests and needs of its employees, consumers, and the community. In a way, a business belongs to them, not its owners or shareholders, because they are its stakeholders. Traditionally, Schumacher explained, the social responsibility of large corporations had been realized through the state. The nationalization of industry was one way of securing the social conduct of businesses. But there were other ways to achieve social responsibility. Drawing on the work of R. H. Tawney, Schumacher explained that nationalization was a "means to an end, not an end to itself."[1] He called for a new, decentralized model of ownership, one that was neither public nor private but that belonged to the stakeholders of industry.

Between the 1960s and the 1990s, the idea of corporate social responsibility was at the center of numerous nonprofit campaigns in Britain and part of a broader movement toward reshaping the global economy and especially international trade. Corporate social responsibility, especially for multinational corporations, was politicized in the United Nations through calls for the New International Economic Order and the creation of a UN Commission on Transnational Corporations, tasked with assessing the impact of corporations on the Third World. Calls for corporate social responsibility inspired a broad range of nongovernmental campaigns and grassroots activists across Britain, Europe, South Asia, Canada, and the United States. From transnational boycotts like the anti-apartheid movement to local campaigns for the fair trade of tobacco and tea, activists grew concerned with the social responsibility of the for-profit sector on a wide range of issues.[2] But in Britain there was more at stake: for many businessmen, NGO activists, and government officials, corporate social responsibility was connected to questions about ownership in British and Third World industry. The period saw the proliferation of campaigns that invited British businesses to become central actors in shaping the private sector of Third World economies through development aid.

The history of transnational campaigns for corporate social responsibility has largely been told as a story of the late twentieth century, connected to the history of globalization and its backlash. According to this narrative, global campaigns initially emerged from calls for a New International Economic Order at the level of the UN in 1975 and were only partially realized through the UN attempt to write a Code of Conduct for transnational corporations.[3] Those attempts, which failed in 1992, were then replaced by a grassroots antiglobalization revolt in North America, one that culminated in a series of protests in Seattle in November 1999 against the World Trade Organization. North American activists protested against economic and neoliberal forms of globalization in order to create a fairer global economy, or an "alternative globalization movement" as it has sometimes been termed.[4] They called for fairer working conditions and workers' rights and restraining multinational corporate power in the global economy. Although the chronology of this history has recently been stretched to consider the longer origins of the movement, the story has remained the same.[5]

There is, however, an earlier yet equally important episode in the transnational history of corporate social responsibility, one that emerged from mid-century statism rather than globalization. It was animated by domestic concerns about the question of ownership in industry as well as by Cold War anxieties about the role of British capitalism in the global economy. In 1960s Britain, it was British businessmen together with the nonprofit sector, and not anticorporate activists, that led the campaigns for corporate social responsibility. Amid wage inflation and the growing militancy of trade unions, these campaigns were designed to respond to an age-old question: who should represent the interest of workers in industry? Instead of state management of the economy and collective bargaining as means to hold industries accountable, these campaigns advocated mixed ownership in industry that would extend globally. This new model, which they called "industrial common ownership," was promised to be a more efficient, ethical, and democratic path to caring for the company's stakeholders than the state or the trade union. They invited British businesses to become central actors in shaping the private sector of Third World economies through development aid.

These campaigns, in fact, devised a business ethics that meant to further corporate power rather than limit it, albeit through a series of social and environmental commitments especially to its workers. They saw the corporation as a trust that carried, according to one businessman, an "inherent responsibility of business enterprise to its consumers, workers, shareholders, suppliers, and the community and the mutual responsibilities of these to one another."[6] They came to perceive corporations as trusts that could serve the local and global community and sought to transform corporations into social bodies that would lead the development of British and Third World economies. Their campaigns represented a wholesale reform of both British and Third World industries, creating an alternative to the welfare and the developmental state. Doing so, they purported, would create a more harmonious, democratic, and humane capitalism.

This chapter traces the intellectual and political origins of these British campaigns and how they came to transform the nonprofit sector. It shows that in Britain, ideas about the social responsibility of corporations emerged from a particular conjuncture of domestic industrial strife and the global politics of the Cold War and decolonization. In the early 1960s, as the first section charts, corporate social responsibility emerged as an alternative to the project of national ownership and was immediately linked to various development aid initiatives. I follow the formation of the chemical company Scott Bader Commonwealth, which sought to transform itself into a trusteeship that would offer not only welfare for its employees in Britain but also aid to the postcolonial community. The initiatives of the Scott Bader Commonwealth, as the second section demonstrates, became the basis for Schumacher's own nonprofit aid agency, the Intermediate Technology Development Group (ITDG), which pioneered an approach to the role of the for-profit world in development aid. ITDG focused on encouraging British businesses to provide postcolonial communities with small-scale technology and training to build rural industries in postcolonial economies. It became a model for for-profit philanthropy and development programs. By the early 1970s, nongovernmental campaigns led by the NGO War on Want built on these ideas to develop legal mechanisms—like social auditing—that would hold corporations accountable to their stakeholders. NGOs came to see their own role, as nonprofits, as important representatives of the stakeholders in the global economy, ones that represented not only consumers but also workers. The last section traces how through campaigns against British tea companies in Sri Lanka, War on Want aimed to create new codes of conduct for British and multinational businesses in the decolonized global economy. By the mid-1970s, these initiatives and campaigns joined larger transnational movements, including ones in the United States, against multinational corporations.

By recovering the historical origins of these shifts in Britain as part of a socialist story about the remaking of ownership amid the Cold War and decolonization, this chapter tells the history of social responsibility beyond the narrative of the globalization of the consumer movement. Instead, the story here reveals that in Britain the movement for social responsibility was interwoven with the story of collective bargaining, trade unions, and the state's role in representing workers. The turn to corporate social responsibility in the Third World was part of a movement against nationalization, making the private corporation a central agent in welfare, one that to some degree stood against the state and trade unions.

The Postcolonial Origins of Stakeholder Capitalism

Much of what E. F. Schumacher had thought about the social responsibility of businesses was a product of his long-standing friendship with Ernest Bader, a Swiss-born British businessman who had made his fortune running a successful chemical company that manufactured synthetic resins in the postwar years. Although Bader was twenty-one years older than Schumacher, the two men had much in common. Both were German speakers and immigrants to Britain who became invested in the British way of socialism: Schumacher through his work at the National Coal Board and Bader through his strain of Christian socialism. Moreover, both Schumacher and Bader were deeply influenced by Gandhi's economics. While Schumacher encountered Gandhian economics when he worked as a development advisor in Burma and India in the mid-1950s, Bader had learned about Gandhian philosophy in the 1940s from his friend Wilfred Wellock, a Labour MP and Gandhian socialist. In 1958, Bader traveled to India and met several of the most prominent of Gandhi's followers, including Vinoba Bhave and Jayaprakash Narayan.[7] Their Western socialism, fused with economic ideas about indigenous labor, welfare, and the small community, drew heavily on Gandhi's anticolonial thought and his non-violent philosophy.

Bader had been thinking about the social responsibility of businesses for more than a decade before he met Schumacher in 1959. In 1945, when Bader joined the Society of Friends, he began searching for a model that would reflect his Quaker ethics in business. In the aftermath of World War II, he hoped that industrial democracy would establish a truce between capital and labor. He researched various models of socially responsible industry: from the British cooperative movement of the 1840s and late nineteenth-century Quaker industrialists such as Cadbury to Gandhian economics. In 1945, Bader wrote a pamphlet that he distributed to his employees, in which he proposed to establish a Scott Bader Fellowship, an effort aimed at reforming his employees' "attitude to work" and offering them "social satisfaction."[8] Bader intended the fellowship to operate as a trusteeship that would facilitate "co-operation in a common aim, i.e. Christian service."[9] The idea never came to fruition, yet Bader remained committed to the ethics behind it, and in 1951, three years after his employees organized a strike, he made the radical decision to hand over 90 percent of the ownership of his company to its workers, with the remaining 10 percent retained by the Bader family. In 1963, Bader sold the remaining family shares to the company and transferred his voting powers to a board of trustees. The company—Scott Bader Commonwealth—became the model for what would come to be called the "industrial common ownership movement" in 1960s Britain.[10]

At the time Britain had a long cooperative tradition, but the Scott Bader Commonwealth was different from other forms of co-ownership. Unlike a similar initiative led by John Spedan Lewis (the founder of the cooperative department store John Lewis Partnership), the Scott Bader Commonwealth was not a company under co-ownership whose members are individual share-holders. Instead, capital was held collectively between the employees and management. All employees, in other words, exercised control as members rather than shareholders.[11] The commonwealth had a trade union branch but its model also negated the need for any external collective bargaining that would mobilize the union of chemical industry workers as a whole. Employees became eligible for membership in the commonwealth after twelve months of employment, which, in turn, entitled them to voting rights and participation in the organization's democratic governance bodies.

Bader's vision of worker participation in industry drew on Quaker egal-itarianism and Marxist revisionism. As his son Godric Bader later explained, the idea behind the commonwealth model was to remove "Marx's criticism of alienation, for work was done more in satisfaction of workers' own needs rather than being a kind of cannon fodder of industry to feed the capitalist machine."[12] Bader sought to create a capitalism with a human face. He was part of a transatlantic turn toward corporations' social role in democracy. In the United States, most famously, *The Concept of the Corporation*, the 1946 bestseller by the Austrian American management consultant Peter Drucker, talked about the responsibility of managers "to the people they manage, and to their economy and society."[13] According to Drucker, the real challenge for business was not mechanical or technical but social, because "the worker has not enough relation to his work to find satisfaction in it."[14] For Bader, this challenge was exactly the incentive to reform industrial relationships. His vision was to create "a new class of limited liability companies" that would allow a more holistic inclusion of the worker in the company, one that would mirror social democracy.[15] The Scott Bader Commonwealth was set to offer an alternative form of capitalism that could be emotionally and materially beneficial to workers and generate solidarities between them. It became the first collectively owned private enterprise to seek a "third way" capitalism in which industrial relationships were egalitarian and labor employed capital.[16]

Bader, in fact, saw the commonwealth as part of a broader ethical and religious mission to reform industrial relations globally. He created the Scott Bader Commonwealth not only as a profitable model of industrial co-ownership but also as one that was invested in the project of Third World economies. The profits of the commonwealth were shared between the employees and management, except for the 10 to 20 percent earmarked as donations for various charities, with all members deciding "to which charity this money shall go." The idea was that the commonwealth represented a micro-society of global citizens invested in local as well as global welfare. "Worthy causes in Asia and the Colonies have had preference over better known ones in Britain," as one pamphlet explained about the company's charitable investments.[17] For Bader, worker participation was central to making a responsible society as much as it was to shaping a responsible business.

Bader was not alone in his vision of industrial common ownership in the 1950s. He developed the idea alongside two friends. The first was George Goyder, an Anglican businessman and the managing director of British Industrial Paper Ltd., who made his fortune procuring, supplying, and rationing newsprint to the British press during World War II. In the early 1950s, Goyder assisted Bader with drafting the legal framework for the Scott Bader Commonwealth, but Goyder had been engaged with the question of industrial reform since the postwar years. He was an active member of the Christian Frontier Council, an organization that tasked its members with injecting Christian ethics into British business and industry.[18] In 1947, Goyder began working on a book published in 1951 as *The Future of Private Enterprise*, which argued that the primacy of shareholders in company law was "indefensible on the grounds of justice," as well as a "fiction."[19] Instead, he proposed revising it to include the active participation of, and accountability toward, workers, consumers, and the community.[20] Goyder's emphasis on the responsibility of industry toward something other than the bottom line was a novelty. His book made the case for a new form of corporate governance based not on radical socialist thought but instead on liberal ideas of economic stability tinged with Cold War anxieties. For him, the threat of communism, coupled with what he viewed as the destabilizing power of trade unions, necessitated a rethinking of the legal personality of companies in Britain and their ownership.[21] By the 1960s, Goyder was an active member of the Liberal Party and chaired a committee on industrial policy that would push for legal reforms of corporate governance in industry.[22]

A close friend of Bader's joined him in the cause of industrial common ownership: the Methodist and former Labour MP Wilfred Wellock. For Wellock, who had been thinking about the question of industrial democracy since the interwar period, social responsibility was anchored in his radical Christian socialism. "Most socialists rested their case solely on the economic argument, whereas I saw the basic error of capitalism in certain spiritual deficiencies," he explained in his 1963 autobiography.[23] Wellock believed that the path to achieving social solidarities in industry was a peaceful one that ran through reconciliation rather than class conflict.[24] But Wellock could not have been more different than Goyder. He was the son of a factory worker in Lancashire as well as a socialist who was politicized during World War I when he became a conscientious objector and a member of a pacifist organization called the Fellowship of Reconciliation. In 1920, Wellock joined the Labour Party and was briefly elected as an MP for Sturbridge in 1927 and 1929. In the 1930s, in the midst of the Great Depression and Labour's embrace of Keynesianism, he decided to leave formal politics in search of a more radical alternative. He thought that Labour's politics had "degenerated into a power struggle," with an agenda focused too much on material gains, pushed among others by trade unions, rather than ethical concerns.[25]

Wellock found an alternative in Gandhian anticolonial thought.[26] From Gandhi he learned about the limits of "Western industrialism and the importance of small agro-industrial communities" and was introduced to the principle of trusteeship, which emphasized the social responsibility of the rich for the welfare of their community.[27] For Wellock, industrial common ownership expressed a grassroots, decentralized socialism that offered an alternative to American hyper-individualism and totalitarian communism. In the late 1940s, amid Cold War anxieties and Third World anticolonialism, Wellock advocated for this model of decentralized socialism as a path to nonviolent democracy in Britain, India, and East Africa. Borrowing from what he had learned from Gandhi, Wellock argued that "economic and social changes are now required all for far-reaching measures of political, economic and industrial decentralization." He called on Britain to embrace a third way capitalism that encouraged "creative living and social responsibility" beyond the development models of Moscow and Washington.[28]

In the mid-1950s, Bader joined forces with Wellock and Goyder to spread the gospel of industrial common ownership as an alternative to nationalization. Essentially, the industrial common ownership movement argued that a company's stakeholders—the workers, the consumers, and the wider community in which the company operated—should actively participate in a company's management and governance. Stakeholder capitalism was positioned against shareholder capitalism, which had been at the heart of the liberal corporate order since the creation of the Limited Liability Act of 1855, which made shareholders the managers of corporations. Their understanding of stakeholder capitalism was set against national as well as private ownership of industry.[29] It was a model that called for decentralization and privatization of industry as an alternative to the state-led welfarist model of the Labour Party. The movement believed that both Labour and Conservative visions for an "affluent society" were insufficient. "Neither higher wages and shorter working hours at one end of the scale, nor luxurious living based on high profit, extravagant expense-account or the gains of speculation at the other, can give real and lasting satisfaction," the movement argued.[30] Rather, echoing Britain's long Christian socialist tradition, it called for the formation of industrial relations based on "a genuine built-in fellowship."[31]

Bader's, Wellock's, and Goyder's vision of stakeholder capitalism, in fact, had clear religious ambitions. It aimed to emulate the relationship between the Church and its community and to secularize it.[32] Stakeholder capitalism, as Bader later explained, had "spiritual implications." It was part of a Judeo-Christian mission, "a communal, national, universal, and DIVINE purpose for the advancement of humanity." Bader even equated stakeholder capitalism with the liberationist and humanitarian mission of eighteenth-century abolitionism. "If the Abolition of Slavery is considered the supreme example of reform," he wrote, "Wilberforce would turn in his grave if he could see the countless millions of slaves in everything but name, working today at jobs they hate as extensions to machines and factories. There is little quality of life about that."[33] Modern industry, he thought, was too focused on efficiency through labor-saving techniques. Stakeholder capitalism, instead, allowed for a more holistic and organic model of production. It encouraged creativity. Bader, Wellock, and Goyder hoped to replicate the model of industrial common ownership in Third World economies as much as in Western ones.

For the three men, the gospel of this stakeholder model was one aspect of a global mission. They invited to their cause the Anglican priest Canon John Collins (known later for his activism at the Campaign for Nuclear Disarmament), and together the four founded the Society for Democratic Integration in Industry, or Demintry, in 1958. The organization fused many of the ideas of Bader, Goyder, and Willock that had been percolating since the late 1940s: from Bader's and Goyder's religious ethics and business experience to Wellock's Gandhian socialism, with its emphasis on decentralization and trusteeship. They designed Demintry as a social movement that would enlist other companies and workers to reform industrial relations in Britain and the world, their goal being a socialist mixed economy based on the idea of worker participation in the governance and management of the company.

Demintry aimed to bridge the gap between employers, workers, consumers, and the community and to create "a new spirit and COMMON OWNERSHIP ENTERPRISE in industry as an alternative to a war-based economy."[34] Its basic principles, according to one of its pamphlets, included the idea that "every undertaking [of a company] should be carried on as a joint concern by all those working for it."[35] And it defined such an undertaking as "socially healthy" only if the company "treat[ed] every human being working it [sic] it as an individual [that is helped to] develop his or her full capabilities and talents within the discipline of shared purpose." It viewed workers as equal partners to capital in the management, duties, and rights of the company, "without any section having an exclusive right to ownership, control or profit," and called for the establishment of this partnership within company law. It also directly promoted the decentralization of activities "so that everyone in it can embrace it in his mind and imagination." For Demintry, size was a question of ethics: large companies needed to create decentralized mechanisms for fostering harmonious relationships between workers and management. Lastly, Demintry defined one of its core principles as promoting the development of a social relationship between a company and the larger community beyond its workers, "realizing that [a company] is part of a national and international community with responsibilities beyond its own immediate interests."[36] Demintry, in other words, aimed to create a socially responsible industry that would be more organically integrated with society.

For its founders, Demintry modeled a form of capitalism that would operate beyond the basic principles of Keynesianism and its "expanding economy."[37] Keynesianism, the group argued, generated perpetual growth that perhaps helped raise income but did not necessarily improve an individual's quality of life. Its "economic Dinosaurism," as Wellock labeled it in a 1958 Demintry booklet, was "intrinsically aggressive": it was "a war stimulating economy."[38] Britain had to choose between an economy that would lead to a "nihilistic war" and "a way of life that is simple, wholesome, peaceful, satisfying and free."[39] It sought to revolutionize industrial relationships from the inside rather than to impose what its members saw as a top-down totalitarian form of state ownership. Its basic principle was to establish "mutually helpful relations with those it specially serves (consumers) and with the local community within which it carries on its activities." No one entity—employers, workers, consumers, or the community—enjoyed an "exclusive right to 'ownership.'"[40] By the late 1960s, Demintry was transformed into a national industrial common ownership movement that lobbied for the revision of British company laws and welfare services.

In May 1959, a year after Demintry had been launched, Bader met Schumacher and introduced him to his ideas about the social responsibility of businesses. They met through a mutual friend, David Astor, the heir of the Astor fortune and editor of the *Observer*. Astor knew both had recently visited India and were influenced by Gandhian economics. He invited them to a meeting of the British Friends of Bhoodan, a British appeal that grew out of Quaker networks to support the grassroots welfare movement led by Gandhi's pupil Vinoba Bhave. The meeting also included socialists like the Quaker activist Donald Groom, the Hungarian British Jewish author and journalist Arthur Koestler, the anti-apartheid campaigner and activist Mary Benson, and the overseas aid organizer Lady Isobel Cripps.[41] At a later meeting the group also considered inviting public figures like the historian Arnold Toynbee and the South African leftwing activist Rita Hinden.[42] It aimed to fundraise for Bhoodan and to generate support in Britain for a new approach to economic and social development in postcolonial India.[43] "Britain is still concerned to prove that the link with the new India is a real one, more lasting and humanly concerned than any propaganda gesture made by our friends from the communist half of the world!" explained one of its early organizers in March 1956.[44] The initiative grew out of Cold War anxieties about the future of postcolonial Indian politics.[45]

The meeting did not manage to raise large sums of money for Bhoodan in Britain, but the Bhoodan campaign, and the welfare movement "Sarvodaya" of which it was a part, had a profound effect on Bader's and Schumacher's economic thought as well as on others in their circle like Wellock. For this group of British socialists, the Bhoodan movement actualized much of Gandhi's philosophy of Sarvodaya into real-time politics and posed an alternative to India's economy. Sarvodaya, or universal service, was a concept developed by Gandhi and his pupil Vinoba Bhave to articulate the notion of the collective uplift of village communities without state intervention, relying instead on public donations of money, labor, and skills. After Gandhi's assassination in January 1948, Bhave became an important figure in Indian antistatist politics and turned Sarvodaya into a central concept of his own politics. In 1951, the philosophy of Sarvodaya inspired Bhave to cross India on foot to convince landowners (zamindars) to gift some of their land to landless peasants, a campaign that came to be called Bhoodan (land-gift). Bhave then organized a Gramdan (village gift) movement that established what was in essence a cooperative village owned by the entire community that sought to establish a new socioeconomic and political order based on Sarvodaya philosophy. By the late 1950s, as the historian Benjamin Siegel has argued, Sarvodaya "had become the most important source of non-state authority in India, particularly outside its major cities."[46]

Both Bhave's Bhoodan campaign and the Gramdan movement epitomized the principle of Gandhian trusteeship in rural communities. As Wellock explained in a 1958 pamphlet that circulated in Britain and the United States, "In essence [in Gramdan] no one owns the land of the village, but in another sense every man owns the entire village, grasps it in imagination, sees himself responsible for part of it, and the village as a variable part of his own personality."[47] Wellock himself even collaborated later with Bhave and published regularly in *Sarvodaya*, the movement's monthly magazine.[48] For Bader, Schumacher, and others like Wellock, the Bhoodan-Gramdan campaign proved that the egalitarian ideas of common ownership and welfare did not depend on state intervention. Instead, common ownership could voluntarily be bestowed from the wealthy to the poor. If the Bhoodan-Gramdan campaign, as the Quaker magazine *The Friend* suggested in 1959, was launched in an industrial society like Britain, it would involve "persuading factory owners to give their factories to the workers," which "might go some way to solving social problems in such a society."[49] The magazine noted that the Scott Bader Commonwealth had helped generate support for Bhave and the Sarvodaya movement in India and elsewhere, not the least Britain.

The Bhoodan-Gramdan campaign inspired Bader to create an industrial model that would replicate these ideas in the world of development aid. He believed that the spirit of the campaign "demand[ed] that the donor should be in personal touch with the recipient and should actively cooperate in bringing his gift to fruition."[50] The campaign gave Demintry and the industrial common ownership movement in Britain a global ethics. "In India," as one of Demintry's pamphlets explained, "Vinoba Bhave is seeking to alleviate the social problem in the country-side by persuading land-owners to give some of their land to the landless peasants."[51] The industrial common ownership movement sought to emulate this goal in industrial Britain and the decolonized world. Its model of stakeholder capitalism was seen as part of a decolonized and decentralized vision of international society in both rural and urban economies.

In 1959, a year after Bader returned from India, where he met Bhave as well as the Gandhian political activist Jayaprakash Narayan (who in the 1970s would famously lead the opposition to Indira Gandhi), he searched for ways to demonstrate how "the Sarvodaya (General Welfare), Bhoodan (Land Gift) and Gram-dan (Village Community) movements could be followed in industry."[52] To him, the Scott Bader Commonwealth offered a model for industrial law and business management that fit within the Gandhian principles of trusteeship and could therefore be replicated in postcolonial countries like India through training and technical aid. He looked for ways to secure funding from the commonwealth—which had already devoted 10 to 20 percent of its earnings to charity—for development projects that would mirror the company's experience and reproduce it in the newly independent economy of India and colonial societies of East Africa. He worked on various ideas for aid schemes: from training centers in Britain that would globalize Demintry to establishing "a model or a 'teaching business' organization in India as an economic self-supporting industrial unit" that would draw on the commonwealth's expertise in synthetic resins.[53] He invited his new friend Schumacher, whom he also made an external board member of his company, to collaborate with him as well as other members of the British Friends of Bhoodan such as Donald Groom, who would later lead his own aid project to support Gramdan on behalf of the NGO War on Want.

One idea for an aid scheme that Bader outlined in the autumn of 1959, and which Schumacher helped develop, was a training center for small-scale industry on the company premises in Wollaston. He called it Ekistechnia Ltd., a name that fused the Greek words for economics ("ekistics") and technology. Bader drew, at least in part, on the Greek movement "ekistic," an urban planning method developed by the Greek architect Constantinos A. Doxiadis that became prevalent in development plans in Iraq and Pakistan in the late 1950s and emphasized small-scale technologies and self-help.[54] He then fused it with his ideas about common ownership and the principle of trusteeship. The scheme was intended to bring together both European and Third World youths and teach them how to become self-sufficient through technical training in "village craft industries."[55] In a period where most development projects concentrated on boosting large industries in order to increase the GNP of colonial and postcolonial economies, Ekistechnia was designed instead to utilize unskilled labor and help local communities build their own small-scale industries. Bader hoped that Ekistechnia would encourage the decentralization "of public work and light industry" while eliciting "native enterprise for undertaking the constructional work involved, and the acceptance of, the functional discipline required for their proper execution and maintenance." The idea was to raise not only the standard of living in both subsistence Third World and Western economies but also the "level of morale and initiative through undertaking such planned communal projects as will improve their own home surroundings."[56] The scheme was designed as a charitable trust registered under the company act at a crucial period when many aid NGOs themselves were undergoing a process of economization that linked international aid with trading ventures.

In the end, Ekistechnia did not come to fruition, mainly because of funding issues, but its ideas about technology and aid served as the basis of Strive (Overseas) Ltd., or the Society for Training in Rural Industries and Village Enterprises, which Bader founded in 1962. Strive was a training center owned by and hosted at the Scott Bader Commonwealth premises in Wollaston Hall for the purpose of creating "small-scale industry based upon modern technology."[57] The scheme was initially funded by the money Bader received from selling his remaining 10 percent shares to the commonwealth, and then supplemented by voluntary contributions from the commonwealth. Strive used the expertise of Bader's chemical company as well as that of nearby firms to train students from the Third World how to create local enterprises in their village communities. "One of the aims," according to Strive's mission statement, was "that the new industries introduced into developing countries ought to reflect the material needs of the village or region and its people and should not be merely the provision of 'employment' and the production of goods for 'exports.'"[58] As MP Robert Edwards, a member of the Scott Bader Commonwealth and Strive, argued, Strive was geared to "help people who need help so urgently in order to be able to perform the day-to-day tasks connected with living."[59] In practice, the majority of training offered was in resins and molding technique, the specialties of the Scott Bader Commonwealth, but for Bader the purpose of the scheme was not to offer just one form of specialization. From the outset the program tailored its aid "to the needs and . . . the culture of the people whose level of wealth the programme [was] attempting to raise."[60] Its first student was from Sri Lanka, and it soon hosted trainees from Ghana, Sierra Leone, India, Nigeria, and Kenya. They learned techniques in silk printing and wood work; methods for producing reinforced corrugated sheets from plastic; and how to can food.

Bader created Strive as a decentralized alternative and "a model for Democratic Industrial Community Development."[61] Rather than investing in large-scale industrial projects, Strive aimed to encourage the formation of stakeholder capitalism by creating small-scale industries that used low-skilled technologies. As Bader himself described it, Strive was a " 'teaching business' project in England and . . . overseas, on the basis of economic self-supporting industrial units, combining production with education, commercial and technical training."[62] To make development aid an effective as well as moral program for industrial societies, Bader believed that aid programs needed to cultivate small- and medium-sized industries rather than the large industrial projects of roadworks, dams, and factories. Strive emphasized small-scale production as a key aspect of industrial social responsibility.

Strive was designed as a public company with a charity status that connected British industrial experts with future Third World industrial experts. It essentially functioned as a voluntary agency like any other British NGO. It was sponsored and advised by prominent economists and industrialists such as Schumacher and Goyder as well as Arthur E. Morgan, the first director of the Tennessee Valley Authority, and Siddharaj Dhadda, the secretary of Sarva Seva Sangh, the largest organization to oversee the Sarvodaya movement's work in India.[63] Bader even hired Harold Sumption, the public relations guru of all the major NGOs in the 1960s, among them Oxfam and Shelter, the domestic charity for the homeless.

Bader saw Strive as a form of "Aid by Trade."[64] Almost two years before the United Nations Conference for Trade and Development (UNCTAD) would embrace the phrase as a slogan, Strive was forged as an alternative model of development aid.[65] Strive took its authority not from the economic theory of dependency, developed by the Argentinian economist Raúl Prebisch, but rather from Bader's Christianity.[66] He saw it as a solution to the problem of development programs being fixated on the technical and materialistic calculus of growth. " 'Growth,' " argued Bader, "is a purely quantitative concept and therefore quite meaningless until defined in qualitative terms. Some 'growths' are healthy, others are unhealthy, even deadly. Cancer is growth without meaning and purpose." He cited interwar socialists like R. H. Tawney, who in 1922 suggested that industry "must satisfy criteria which are not purely economic."[67] Postcolonial development, according to Bader, "require[d] a certain spiritual discernment . . . to distinguish between healthy and unhealthy growth." Such discernment, he thought, was the work of Christianity.[68] Strive was a manifestation of what he described as the "re-establishment of the influence of Christianity in the business affairs of Industrial Society."[69] It taught mutual aid and solidarity as a religious ethics embedded in capitalism. These ideas would serve as the basis for a political movement for industrial common ownership in the late 1960s.[70]

Corporate Social Responsibility and
Its Alternative to the "Dual Economy"

In an October 1962 pamphlet titled "Modern Industry in the Light of the Gospel," E. F. Schumacher warned against the plagues of modern industry. For Schumacher, who would declare in 1971 that he was religious and a convert to Catholicism, industrial society "has produced a folklore of incentives which magnifies individual egotism in direct opposition to the teachings of the Gospel." Infected with greed, its sole purpose is "private pecuniary gain." The pamphlet, which he wrote on behalf of Demintry, stated that "industrial society, no matter how democratic in its political institutions, is autocratic in its methods of management." Modern industrialism focused on productivity rather than the dignity of work. While some large companies had been restrained in their pursuit of profit—"largely owing to the 'counter-vailing power' of the Trade Unions in conditions of full employment"—modern industry had destroyed any idea of labor as a form of self-expression. Work, in fact, had been rendered "undesirable." Instead, Schumacher proposed the creation of an alternative society that would be "responsible not only to its shareholders, but also to its employees, its customers and the community as a whole"; it would be an industrial society "organised in much smaller units, with an almost infinite decentralisation of authority and responsibility."[71] Schumacher's words echoed much of the writing of Bader, Goyder, and Wellock on industrial common ownership and its model of stakeholder capitalism.

In the 1960s Schumacher took the idea of corporate social responsibility and folded it into his ethical critique of economics. He had been thinking about the limits of national ownership since the 1950s, as part of his work as the economic advisor of the National Coal Board (NCB). At the NCB, he increasingly became critical of a state-led economy and its commitment to what he saw as purely quantitative measures of growth. After he traveled to Burma and India in 1955 and 1958, he embraced what he called "Buddhist economics," an economic philosophy he developed based on Gandhian notions of the dignity of work. He became particularly convinced that Gandhian notions of indigenous manufacturing and local industries were a form of community development and universal uplift, or Sarvodaya (universal welfare), as Gandhi called it. Schumacher's introduction to the activism of Bhave in 1959 through the British Friends of Bhoodan furthered his ideas about the merits of a decentralized economy located in the village community over a large-scale centralized nationalized economy. What he gained from joining the Scott Bader Commonwealth in the late 1950s, when Bader appointed him as a board member, was a model of how a Gandhian ethics might look if applied to modern private industry. Schumacher's involvement with Demintry and Strive offered him a way to connect his own economic critique of Keynesianism and

Third World development with a broader commitment to corporate social responsibility.

By 1964, Schumacher began working on his own development agency, the Intermediate Technology Development Group (ITDG), today known as Practical Action. ITDG was focused on creating work opportunities in private industries for Third World communities, providing them with affordable technology or helping them develop their own. It collaborated with British and later Third World industries to develop and hone low-skilled technologies that could be the basis for community development. It used technology to frame an entire approach about labor and industry. Technology could allow workers to actively participate in the creation and management of private industries. The ITDG was a predecessor of sorts to the type of corporate and technological engagement developed by the Gates Foundation.

Schumacher initially conceived the idea for ITDG when he traveled to Poona, India, in 1961 to speak at a seminar titled "Paths to Economic Growth."[72] He argued that the development doxa of his time was overly focused on replicating the economic development of Britain and the West in Third World economies rather than devising solutions that were aligned with economic life in these countries. To Schumacher, the development paradigm was concentrated on "abstractions" like GNP rather than on qualitative measures like mitigating mass unemployment and hunger. As he put it, development did "not touch the people's heart." Development, he suggested, "induce[d] the imagination to turn to the actual—that which exists already, and exists most conspicuously in the rich countries— whereas it should be turned to the potential, namely, the unused labour power and creativeness of the indigenous population."[73] He called for the development industry to allow a more gradual, creative, and organic process of economic growth by harnessing the most valuable resource Third World economies had in abundance—labor—through the use of labor-intensive rather than labor-saving technology. For him, development aid should be tasked with supporting the creation of private and regional industries that provided work and encouraged self-help.

Schumacher conceived the concept of "intermediate technology" as a direct response to the "dual economy," the dominant theory of labor adopted by the development sector in the 1960s. The "dual economy" model was forged by the St. Lucian British economist Arthur Lewis as a solution to what he saw as the main obstacle to economic growth in newly independent economies: the problem of surplus labor. In a famous 1954 essay, "Economic Development with Unlimited Supplies of Labour," Lewis argued that many countries could not accumulate capital and increase their GDP because their economies had superfluous labor in either the agricultural or urban handicraft sector. He coined the term "disguised unemployment" to signal economies in which the "marginal productivity of labour [is] zero, or even negative."[74] In this model, labor received its value from its contribution to national productivity. The solution, Lewis suggested, was to move surplus labor to the industrial sector, which in many countries was short on workers. In Lewis's model, labor transfer would become an engine of growth and help accelerate industrialization.

Lewis's dual-sector model shaped development thinking within international organizations throughout the 1950s and 1960s. In a coauthored UN report published in 1951, Lewis elaborated on this model and pointed to "disguised unemployment" as one of the key problems of Third World economies.[75] His work cemented a vision of "productive labor" as the manufacture of large quantities of industrial outputs—as a key component of GDP—at the time the ultimate measure of a country's development.[76] Drawing on his ideas, the UN and nongovernmental aid agencies concentrated their efforts on building the industrial sector in many Third World economies, focusing on capital transfers, technical assistance, and job creation. In most cases, the path lay in large-scale lending.[77] In the early 1960s, the economists Gustav Ranis and John C. H. Fei took Lewis's model and developed it further. According to Ranis and Fei, boosting labor transfers to the industrial sector alone was not enough. They argued that it was equally important to invest in the agricultural sector in order to solve the problem of employment. Following their work, many aid organizations began to promote rural development through subsidized agricultural credit schemes aimed at improving food production and moderating the impact of labor migrations between the sectors. Here, too, the methods were large scale and structural, focused on resolving the broad issue of surplus labor. It was against Lewis's model as well as the subsequent work of Ranis and Fei that Schumacher set his nonprofit ITDG.

In the 1970s, a period of economic crisis and subsequent deindustrialization, the theory of dual economy would be challenged by development economists. But Schumacher had already roundly criticized it in the early 1960s. He argued that the dual-economy model had wrongly conceived of surplus labor as an impediment rather than an asset of Third World economies. Such an economy treated development aid as "a small sector of opulence surrounded by an ocean of misery."[78] According to Schumacher, development aid needed to invest in affordable, labor-intensive technology that would utilize labor surplus and provide small-scale, affordable technology for rural communities in particular. He urged aid organizations to move away from promoting the development of Western technology that was created for "the purpose of saving labor." The sector needed to create workplaces "where the people are living now, and not primarily in metropolitan areas into which they tend to migrate." It needed to concentrate production on "local materials for local use." "The task," he wrote, was "to establish a tolerable basis of existence for the 80 per cent by means of an 'intermediate technology' which would be vastly superior in productivity to their traditional technology . . . while at the same time being vastly cheaper and simpler than the highly sophisticated and enormously capital-intensive technology of the West."[79] Technology needed to be "appropriate" for the place and the community that used it. Schumacher envisioned "intermediate technology" as an alternative approach to the problem of mass unemployment, especially in rural areas. While Strive, Bader's aid agency, worked primarily in urban communities, Schumacher's "intermediate technology" was a regional, decentralized approach to development that focused on rural renewal.

Schumacher's concept of "intermediate technology" was rooted in broader debates about labor rights and collective bargaining in Britain in the late 1960s, debates with which Schumacher was already familiar through his work at the NCB. The 1960s has been known for what some historians have called the "high tide of trade unionism."[80] Since the 1950s, trade unions gained power in nationalized and private industries through practices like the closed shop, official and unofficial strikes, and "shopfloor bargaining," which is the negotiation of the terms and conditions of labor at specific factories and places of production.[81] But by 1964, when the Wilson government was elected, the legitimacy of these practices was challenged. Many politicians—and not just Conservatives—criticized the ability of industries like coal to maintain efficiency in light of what they saw as the constant production disruptions caused by the tactics of the National Union of Mineworkers. Collective bargaining practices were perceived as disruptive, as well as responsible for causing inflation. By 1965, the state increasingly intervened in trade union reform. While both Wilson's Labour government and the subsequent Conservative government of Edward Heath recognized the presence of trade unions in the British economy, they also tried to limit and regulate their power over Britain's industry.

It was during these debates that ideas about worker participation as a form of corporate social responsibility became prevalent on the British liberal left. Even before deindustrialization and Thatcherism, many on the left believed trade unions were too adversarial. They advocated for worker participation in national and private industries as a path to a more democratic industrial society, one that allowed workers to be represented and join in the management of companies. On this view, worker participation represented the advancement rather than the abolition of collective bargaining. For the traditional left, however, the model of worker participation was anathema because it reinforced a capitalist vision wherein workers had to collaborate with capital. But for its enthusiasts from both the Labour and Liberal parties, worker participation—especially through common ownership structures—was a more ethical approach to industrial relations than trade unions. They saw worker participation as a model that fit closely with Christian ideas about human dignity and efforts to regain a "sense of 'belonging'" lost in modern industrialism.[82] They returned to Tawney's idea that industry had a duty to serve a "social purpose" rather than a purely economic one, and to the old Morrison tradition of "worker's control" in the economy.[83] Worker participation offered people like Schumacher a possibility for "a new human relations," mainly democratization.[84] For its supporters, worker participation gave both private and public industry a sense of shared responsibility, community, and dignity.

The Scott Bader Commonwealth offered one version of worker participation in private industry through common ownership, but there were other alternatives. Some of them, like the joint production committees that included workers within the management boards of industries, predated this moment; they had emerged during World War II and continued in the postwar years.[85] But in the late 1960s, ideas about worker participation percolated across British politics and industry and were often conceived as alternatives to the trade union model. Among national industries, for example, the British Steel Corporation adopted a plan in 1967 that appointed worker directors to division boards. Many British politicians and economists paid particular attention to the Western and northern European models of codetermination, where coal and steel unions participated in corporate governance. The West German model of codetermination was seriously examined by both Labour and Liberals, including the Oxford professor and member of the Labour Party Hugh Clegg, who in 1967 would serve in a key Labour commission on industrial relations, and the Liberal MP Michael Forgery, who wrote extensively on the two models.[86] In the 1970s, codetermination was even considered as part of the fifth directive on company law of the European Community, though the directive never received enough support.

Worker participation was, in fact, often measured against the power of collective bargaining through trade unions. In 1966, the Labour Party produced a report which argued that it would be easier to introduce employee directors in nationalized industries than in private ones, and sought the means to do so. The report prioritized the primacy of trade unions in securing social responsibility, but it recommended "strengthening the principle of social accountability" either through legislation that would compel companies to provide information about working conditions in their business or through worker participation in their directorates.[87] In 1965, Wilson's Labour government also appointed a Royal Commission on Trade Unions and Employers' Associations (known as the Donovan Commission) that surveyed trade unions and employers' associations in order to reconsider labor law.[88] More specifically, the commission was tasked with placing legal constraints on unions in order to back up government price and income policies; although pressured by Clegg, who was one of its members and the de facto author of the report, the committee ended up backing collective bargaining. In 1969, Labour also published a White Paper called *In Place of Strife*, which echoed some of its dismay over the power of trade unions and their ability to represent workers' interests. Although the White Paper was never implemented, its idea about placing limits on the power of trade unions had more than a passing resemblance to the

Conservatives' Industrial Relations Act of 1971 and the subsequent, superseding Trade Union and Labour Relations Act of 1974.

The industrial common ownership movement and its model of stakeholder capitalism offered Schumacher a program for worker participation in Third World rural industry. It is also why the idea of "intermediate technology" received so much support in the late 1960s and throughout the 1970s, when the global crisis of unemployment became central in the minds of development agencies and experts. At its core, the industrial common ownership movement defined social responsibility of businesses around the dignity of work. "The great danger to the whole enterprise of development was 'alienation,'" explained Schumacher in 1968. "When people become alienated from their own traditions, even from their families, when fathers could not teach their sons anything any more, then society was bound to suffer." The concept of intermediate technology drew on the industrial common ownership movement in order to connect industry with the rest of society: "We must not think simply in terms of econometrics, what was most profitable, and so on. The whole population must be involved; and in order to do this we must have very cheap, simple, sturdy equipment that would enable people to help themselves."[89] Schumacher saw in the Scott Bader Commonwealth a model for rural communities of how workers could become full participants in industry. Intermediate technology meant to replicate it. As he would later write in *Small Is Beautiful*, the commonwealth was more than an experiment in human relations. It offered "a lifestyle," in which workers could participate in industry and make decisions about their working conditions. Workers did not need to take an adversarial position against industry—as trade unions did—but rather could become equal participants in the governance of industry. The commonwealth built "a real *community*."[90] Cultivating the idea of "appropriate technologies" meant shaping a Third World community in which workers and capital could be equal.

In February 1966, Schumacher launched the ITDG as a development agency for disseminating these ideas. He had two collaborators: George McRobie and Julia Porter. McRobie was a colleague and friend of Schumacher; the two had met through their work on the NCB. McRobie had been a miner himself before he was trained as an economist at the LSE and began working at the NCB. He was a founding member of two economic think tanks, the Other Economic Summit and New Economics Foundation. He had also been an associate fellow of the Institute of Development Studies at the University of Sussex and an honorary vice president of the Soil Association (a leading proponent of organic farming), two institutions with which Schumacher was closely involved. In the early 1960s, McRobie gained some experience in development economics when he worked for the Ford Foundation in India on a small industries project.[91] At ITDG he was a founding member and one of its directors.

Julia Porter came with a background in fundraising. She had worked as a regional campaigner for Oxfam and the Freedom From Hunger Campaign (FFHC) in Britain in the early 1960s, after spending ten years in Northern Rhodesia and Zambia with her first husband, a colonial officer and military man. Through her connections with Arthur Gaitskell (the brother of Labour MP Hugh Gaitskell), she took a position heading the African Development Trust, an organization that supported a multiracial cooperative farm near what is now Harare and called the Cold Comfort Farm. In 1967, after she started working with Schumacher at ITDG, she married her second husband, Robert Porter, the senior economic advisor to the then Ministry of Overseas Development (ODM).[92] It was partially for this reason that the ITDG has had a close connection with ODM as well as the FFHC. Its board included representatives from ODM, and its first project officer was Noel Paterson, from the FFHC, who like many aid professionals of his generation was a former colonial expert, having worked in the India Civil Service in the 1920s and the Andaman and Nicobar Islands in the 1940s.[93]

Schumacher, McRobie, and Porter also garnered the support of about twenty industry members and NGOs. ITDG also included representatives from the Overseas Development Institute, the consulting firm McKinsey & Co., and the conglomerate Shell International Chemical Co., as well as financial backing from Oxfam and War on Want. By 1974, its board of directors included representatives from all the major NGOs including Christian Aid, War on Want, and Oxfam.[94] The organization operated like many NGOs, but like Strive ITDG was registered as a private company with a charitable status. ITDG, in fact, had a close connection with the Scott Bader Commonwealth and Strive. ITDG shared a similar emphasis on technology and small-scale business. Strive also funded some of ITDG's operations in its first years. By the late 1960s, when Strive experienced financial troubles, the ITDG absorbed its operations.

From its inception, ITDG was meant to connect the aid world and private industry through a shared mission. One of its main projects was to assemble and publish data on "efficient labour-intensive techniques, suitable for small-scale application."[95] The resulting annual catalogue, *Tools for Progress*, provided information about specific industries that sold a variety of low-skill equipment for rural development.[96] The catalogue was meant to offer for the first time a guide for development work that would support and encourage small-scale industry in Britain and the Third World through the business of development aid. As Schumacher explained, "Such a guide had never been produced before in the western world. The Japanese had compiled something similar, and it had earned an export promotion award from the Japanese Government because this small-scale equipment, although it might look like peanuts, was available to two million villages and could become very big business indeed."[97] *Tools for Progress* was authored by George Gater, an economist from the National Economic Development Office whom ITDG employed from 1966 onward. (Gater arrived with two years of experience in India and Sri Lanka with the British imperial shipping company Peninsular and Oriental Steamship Navigation Company.) The catalogue was a collaboration between ITDG and the Scott Bader Commonwealth, Oxfam, War on Want, and the William Johnston Yapp Charitable Trust, which surveyed these companies and funded their research.

ITDG used the catalogue as a way to reach a wide range of British businesses, from Cadbury to IBM United Kingdom Ltd. "In the initial stages there could be an export market," one of ITDG's members explained, "even for the developing nations, in low-cost technology, although ideally the technology is best evolved in the developing country in question."[98] Ironically, although Schumacher's economic ethics emphasized the importance of grassroots indigenous manufacturing, ITDG's catalogues promoted primarily British-based ones. These included chemical farming technologies like DDT and inorganic fertilizers, a contradiction that McRobie partly acknowledged in 1981.[99]

It is perhaps partially for this reason that ITDG received such large support, as well as funding from the British government by the 1970s. The focus on small-scale industries rather than large-scale, national ones fit well not only with a new development philosophy but also with Britain's own involvement in overseas aid, especially in postimperial territories where direct support of national economies remained politically fraught. Partially due to ITDG's close relationships with the ODM and partially because of the important influence of the progressive MP Judith Hart, who headed the ministry in 1969–70, 1974–75, and 1977–79, the government embraced the idea of intermediate technology and encouraged it by funding like-minded projects. Beginning in 1973, ITDG lobbied and pressured the British government to run its own small-scale development projects that emphasized "the 'human factor' in production" instead of "transplanting highly capital-intensive, expensive and labour-saving technologies into the principal cities of poor countries."[100] The government increasingly collaborated with and supported some of ITDG's projects. Indeed, despite Schumacher's and ITDG's emphasis on decentralization, the group often worked with the state and relied on its support and funding.

ITDG helped British industry find a lucrative market at a time when many newly independent economies were nationalizing their industries. It supported British interests and, in the words of one government official, provided a "growing market for our products."[101] Many British companies had their origins in imperial rule and after formal decolonization had to reorient their markets.[102] ITDG offered these businesses an opening to Third World markets through the idea of technology transfer. The group's focus on rural development was especially lucrative, as the majority of development programs focused on urban centers and high modernism. By 1974, when the aid sector as a whole moved away from large industrialization projects and Judith Hart headed the ODM, ITDG's philosophy was fully embraced by the British government. ITDG for example began to hold teach-ins with the ODM when it established a new Rural Development Department in 1975.[103] ITDG's Industrial Liaison Unit, founded in 1976 "as a point of contact for inquiries from developing countries seeking information on labour-intensive technologies," was financed and monitored by the ODM.[104] The unit was tasked with advising British industry on how to develop and market intermediate technologies for Third World community development projects.[105] It joined a long-standing tradition in Britain that tied development aid in the Third World to economic development in Britain.[106]

The British government also supported projects such as the research program conducted by Strathclyde University "into the appropriate level of technology for industries in the varying circumstances and conditions of developing countries."[107] In 1978, the ODM opened its own unit, Intermediate Technology Industrial Service, in Rugby "as part of the British Government's increase[d] programme of assistance for the spread of appropriate technology in developing countries."[108] Schumacher also shaped ideas about domestic economic development, and ITDG even helped secure funding for an appropriate technologies project to generate small-scale manufacturing across the UK.[109]

In addition to producing the annual catalogue, ITDG had two aims. The first was to disseminate the concept of "intermediate technology" in both private industry and aid organizations through books, articles, and lectures and to remake foreign aid in Britain. The second was to assist specific projects that "demonstrate the possibility of poor people in poor communities HELPING THEMSELVES when furnished with technological and other assistance appropriate to their actual conditions."[110] The group collaborated with other organizations, British NGOs, and industries on various field projects that installed intermediate technologies in rural communities. These field projects became a large part of ITDG work during the 1970s.

For example, in 1971 ITDG teamed up with Christian Aid and Shell on a project that introduced animal-drawn implements and hand-operated machinery in the local farming system in Zaria, Nigeria. The project ran for two years and was deemed a success when the Institute for Agriculture Research at Ahmadu Bello University took over the local training.[111] Similarly, in 1974 ITDG worked with Oxfam on establishing a program to develop village-based lime and pozzolana industries in Arusha. The project utilized the volcanic ash from Mount Meru to manufacture a lime-pozzolana cement for building materials. (Lime-pozzolana technology for the production of a low-cost cementitious material was first an established technology in India and in parts of Indonesia.)[112] The project originated in the early 1970s, when the British ITDG and its sister Indian IT organization in India collaborated on utilizing and importing the technology to community development projects across the Third World. ITDG introduced the Arusha project as a pilot, and with the help of Oxfam ITDG created similar industries throughout Tanzania.[113] Through such projects ITDG hoped to establish a stronger connection between private industry and the aid sector.

ITDG was not the first or only agency to connect development aid with private industry in the mid-1960s. Nongovernmental and international organizations collaborated with private businesses on various development projects. One example is the Industry Cooperative Program (ICP) created by the FAO in 1965 that linked agribusiness companies and developing countries.[114] The ICP was created as a joint venture between transnational agribusiness corporations and the UN, bringing multinational business inside the UN system.[115] Its objective was to "demonstrate that far-sighted and responsible business contributes to social and economic development by means of fostering profitable private enterprise."[116] The program initially included eighteen multinational companies, mostly from the United States and Britain, like Booker McConnell (today the Booker Group), whose director (and later chairman) Sir George Bishop became the first chairman of the ICP. Like many other ICP multinationals, Booker McConnell was formerly a sugar production company in British Guyana that during the 1960s transitioned from being a colonial plantation company to a diversified food conglomerate mainly based in the UK. ICP, in fact, helped facilitate a smoother transition from an imperial economy to a global one for companies like Booker.[117]

One offshoot of ICP was a company called Mumias Sugar in Kenya in the late 1960s. The company was created through a collaboration between the Kenyan government and the British-based multinational Booker McConnell after Booker had to leave Guyana. With the financial support of ODM, Booker trained Kenyan managers and engineers, shared their technology and machinery, and by 1971 erected the first sugar factory in the country. Between 1977 and 1979, factory capacity more than doubled, from 125 to 300 tons of cane per hour. By 1979, Kenya had achieved self-sufficiency in sugar for the first time, with Mumias providing 45 percent of its supply.[118]

Such examples demonstrate that ITDG was not unique. What made it different, however, was its ethical commitment to and development approach of "appropriate technologies." Such technologies, according to ITDG, rested on four criteria: smallness, simplicity, capital cheapness, and nonviolence. These criteria were not merely technical fixes. They were part of an ethics of cultivating socially responsible industries in Britain and the Third World. While many ITDG ideas drew upon Schumacher's own "Buddhist economics"— including the British Christian socialist tradition, Gandhian economics, and ecological commitment to use nonrenewable resources—its commitment to social responsibility came from the industrial common ownership movement. ITDG aimed to support industries that were accountable to their workers, consumers, and the larger community and even its ecosystem so as not to create a burden on the community or generate "sociological, ecological, and resource problems."[119]

By the mid-1970s, the idea of "intermediate technologies" became a development doxa for the majority of aid organizations in Britain and internationally. The idea was important for the international conversation about development both in the United States (through USAID) and at international organizations like the World Bank and the ILO. The concept of "intermediate technologies" dovetailed with a larger move by international and nongovernmental organizations toward basic needs and people-centered development, as well as a turn toward rural development. For example, Schumacher's emphasis on labor spoke directly to a global unemployment crisis that was at the center of the ILO's work. This was due in part to the collaboration in the 1970s between British economist Dudley Seers, one of ITDG's vice presidents and the director of the Institute of Development Studies, and the ILO. Schumacher's ideas about rural development, small-scale production, and intermediate technology became part of the Second Development Decade, helping to articulate the connections between environmental concerns and development programs.[120] ITDG helped disseminate Schumacher's ideas internationally. The agency collaborated with the World Bank, the ILO, and the United Nations Industrial Development Organization (UNIDO), which by 1976 had "all been considering how they may incorporate the concept into their programmes."[121] The organization also met with the European Development Fund and other bilateral agencies to advocate for investment in small-scale industries, and it advised the U.S. government on how to create its own appropriate technology organization. The idea of intermediate technology informed a new moment in development and nongovernmental thinking in the 1970s.

The Social Audit

In his 1961 book *The Responsible Company*, George Goyder suggested that industrial democracies needed to establish a legal mechanism that could function as a code of ethics and hold large corporations accountable for their social conduct. Goyder argued that traditionally the social responsibility of business was maintained "by the generally small scale of enterprise, and by its close relation to the local community." The small scale guaranteed some form of responsibility because the business was embedded in the local community. But in a large, industrialized society, a code of ethics was necessary for ensuring that corporations were behaving responsibly. One such mechanism Goyder suggested was the social audit, an annual check that would report to the public about the social conduct of a business. Matters to scrutinize would include: "(1) The company's pricing policies as they affect its consumers. (2) The company's labour policies as they affect the employees of the company and the

Trade Unions. (3) The company's community policies."[122] Goyder's idea of the social audit was part of his larger ethics, which focused on the responsibility of businesses toward labor, consumers, and the community. It was another means of achieving his vision of stakeholder capitalism.

In the 1970s, the idea of the social audit expanded beyond collaborations between nonprofits and businesses. The decade saw a vibrant discussion about the role of nonprofits in holding businesses accountable for their social conduct through codes of ethics. Here too, it was the industrial common ownership movement and the ideas put forth already in the 1960s by Bader, Goyder, and Schumacher that influenced British discussions about social responsibility. Even before the Third World calls for a New International Economic Order, politicians, economists, businessmen, social scientists, and activists turned their attention to formulating codes of ethics during a period of economic downturn at home and in Third World economies. The period saw increasing attention being paid to the role of corporations and multinational businesses in particular.

The turn to corporate accountability was not unique to Britain. In the United States, it was the subject of lively debate among progressives, neoliberals, and neoconservatives. For many, the corporation was a public entity and therefore morally obligated to account for its social responsibility, especially toward consumers and the community.[123] Similarly, in Malaysia consumer advocates led by the activist Anwar Fazal demanded that corporations account for their marketing practices toward local consumers. The Malaysian activists joined a growing global consumer movement.[124] In India, Tata, the country's largest corporation, investigated how to broaden its corporate outreach and accountability in ways not unlike the principle of industrial common ownership in Britain.[125] The European Economic Community, too, was debating how corporations should better represent their workers.

What set apart the discussions about codes of conduct and social audits in Britain was the heightened friction between trade unions and capital. While some of these discussions were animated by consumer activism,[126] the framing of social responsibility was inseparable from the question of how to represent workers as stakeholders in industry, whether through trade unions or industry-led mechanisms such as codes of conduct. In 1971, the controversial Industrial Relations Act, which sought to limit collective bargaining, included a code of conduct designed to complement the law by setting a minimum standard of "good practice" for companies toward their workers.[127] The code was strongly criticized by the Labour Party for its nonbinding standing and "paternalistic overtones."[128] But the code received support from individual companies and associations like the British Computer Society, the British Chambers of Commerce, the Confederation of British Industry (CBI), the British Institute of Management (BIM), and the Institute of Directors (IOD). By 1973, the Conservative government published a White Paper on company law which emphasized that "openness in company affairs is the first principle in securing responsible behaviour" and that "bias must always be towards disclosure, with the burden of proof thrown on those who defend secrecy."[129] This attention to corporate responsibility, however, was usually set against the intervention of trade unions and governments in the private sector. For Conservatives as well as for British businesses, embracing voluntary codes of conduct was a way to weaken the power of trade unions rather than to fully commit to a new relationship between management and labor in the workplace or toward consumers and the community.

Conservative policies garnered growing attention in the private sector when it came to codes of conduct. In 1971, the CBI established a Company Affairs Committee, which in the following year published an interim report stating that "there must be drawn up and published a code of corporate behaviour in business which will be adopted by as many public companies as possible."[130] The report was distributed among CBI, BIM, and IOD members. In July that year, the committee held a national conference in London and by 1973 published its final report, endorsed by the CBI. The report called for broadening company responsibilities toward "creditors, suppliers, customers, employees and society at large; and . . . strik[ing] a balance between the interests of the aforementioned groups . . . and the interests of the proprietors of the company."[131] It recommended formalizing the obligation toward social responsibility by collectively adopting codes of conduct but rejected the idea that companies should report to any external body about their compliance with social objectives.

Many private companies followed suit. By 1976, a study published by BIM reported that 31 percent of the 130 sampled companies had established codes of conduct, and an additional 20 percent were planning to implement a code in the near future. At the same time, bigger industry organizations such as the Chemical Industries Association, the Association of British Pharmaceutical Industries, and the Society of Motor Manufacturers also adopted codes. These efforts, the BIM study showed, focused on a wide range of areas such as "employees," "consumers," "the environment," "local community and society," "company shareholders," and "suppliers and other companies."[132]

The BIM study, in fact, was one of the many academic and business reports of the decade to focus on corporate social responsibility.[133] During the 1970s, social responsibility itself became an area of study in business and management schools. On September 24, 1975, the Public Relations Consultant Association, for example, held a national conference on the subject that featured academics, companies, and government representatives. The conference included participants from major British companies such as Tate & Lyle, Unilever, Booker McConnell, British Aircraft Corporation, Imperial Group, Marks & Spencer, and Shell UK. The conference discussed the topic of corporate responsibility against the role of trade unions. It paid particular attention to worker participation as a way to generate industrial democracy and enable employees, rather than "business executives," to define corporate responsibility.[134] There was also a discussion about responsibility toward consumers and community, with time devoted specifically to social audits.[135]

In the 1970s, the idea of formulating codes of conduct also became central to the work of the nonprofit sector through business-led charities like the Foundation for Business Responsibilities and the Christian Association of Business Executives (previously called the Catholic Industrialists' Conference in London).[136] The Foundation for Business Responsibilities was established in 1942 as an advocacy group opposed to nationalization. It was directly inspired by Goyder and his industrial common ownership movement. The Christian Association of Business Executives was a nondenominational nonprofit. In the 1970s, both of these groups published a series of reports and consultive documents on topics such as how to formulate a business code of ethics, how to create ethical marketing and advertising strategies, the responsibilities of trade unions, and the accountability of multinational corporations.[137] These publications opposed collective bargaining and nationalized industry. The corporation itself was presented as a public entity that could manage and regulate its own social conduct and behavior.

When Labour returned to power in 1974, it planned to enforce a more centralized code of conduct for business through the formation of a National Enterprise Board (NEB), which was originally tasked with nationalizing and organizing subsidies for the manufacturing industry as well as offering governmental financial assistance to companies that made their workplaces democratic.[138] The government, however, did not manage to pass the proposed plan, partially due to a countercampaign run by private companies, and so instead it partnered with industry and created semi-public bodies such as the Department of Industry's Industry/Education Unit. Established in 1976, it aimed to advise companies on industrial relations and social responsibility with workers, consumers, and the larger community.[139] In January 1977, Labour published the *Report of the Committee of Inquiry on Industrial Democracy* (also known as the Bullock Report).[140] Its immediate impact was an EEC proposal to include a codetermination model as part of the fifth directive on company law of the European Community, but Bullock was also part of a broader reaction to the labor disputes of the decade. It recommended the adoption of a worker participation model for companies with more than two thousand employees as a way to resolve industrial disputes, which some in the private sector criticized as government interference in industry. The recommendations were applauded by the industrial common ownership movement, which had lobbied for it.

Over the course of the 1970s, British activists working in nongovernmental aid agencies drew upon these domestic debates about industrial common ownership and collective bargaining to frame many of their campaigns for protecting the stakeholders of a global community. But their campaigns were also informed by a growing and lively debate about the power of corporations, especially multinational ones. More than anything else, nongovernmental activists were politicized by the New International Economic Order (NIEO) promoted by a coalition of Third World countries and passed in 1974 as a UN resolution. The NIEO placed the conduct of multinational corporations in the Third World at the heart of its international call to decolonize the global economy. According to the NIEO and its supporters, multinationals posed a challenge to the sovereignty of newly independent Third World economies.[141] Influenced by the calls for a NIEO, in 1972 the UN created the Commission on Transnational Corporations to study the role of multinational corporations and their impact on developing countries.[142] The commission's highest priority was the creation of a Code of Conduct on Transnational Corporations, which would include environmental protection, the safeguarding of human rights, and the adoption of high standards of corporate governance. In 1975, the UN began to work on a Code of Conduct, and although in 1992 negotiations were formally suspended, the issue remains an ongoing topic at the UN.[143] Similarly, throughout the 1970s and the 1980s, the International Labour Organization published a series of codes of practice for companies about providing safe and healthy working conditions in various industries, from mining and shipbuilding to manufacturing.

The NIEO sparked an international debate about the role of corporations in economic and social development. Acknowledging the growing power of multinationals, albeit suspicious of their influence, government officials, international organizations, and nongovernmental activists attempted to find ways to integrate corporations into more ethical forms of market exchange through international laws and institutions. In Britain, although NGOs had long collaborated with big businesses, the NIEO inspired organizations such as Oxfam, Christian Aid, and War on Want to redirect some of their domestic campaigns about the responsibilities of British and multinational business toward the Third World. They called upon British companies and banks to clearly outline their responsibilities toward their workers, consumers, and the global community.[144] Their campaigns merged with a growing agenda in shaping fairer trading structures and a fairer global economy. They advocated for global solidarities that would emulate the role of trade unions.

No organization was more focused on the question of social responsibility in the 1970s than War on Want. The organization was founded in 1954 and had close ties with the Labour Party. Throughout the 1960s, as we have seen, War on Want invested in village-based community development projects and was deeply influenced and was even consulted by Schumacher. Its approach to development was to implement much of Bhoodan's principles of decentralization into development programs and, with it, much of Schumacher's ideas of intermediate technologies. By 1973, when Peter Burns became its new general secretary (after working for Oxfam, the National Council for Civil Liberties, and Amnesty), War on Want embraced a lobbyist approach to mobilizing the British public to speak out against global economic inequalities. It became particularly known for its campaigns against British and multinational corporations, from infant formula and tobacco companies to Coca Cola and pharmaceuticals. The NGO saw itself as representing workers and consumers as stakeholders in the global economy.[145]

One of War on Want's earlier campaigns, launched in April 1974, sought to defend worker rights in British multinational tea plantations in Sri Lanka. Its campaign, called "The State of Tea," demanded that the British government and trade unions hold British tea companies accountable for the degrading working and living conditions, as well as the poor wages, of their plantation workers. It was framed around corporate responsibility, particularly that of British companies. War on Want launched the tea campaign after a 1973 exposé by the Granada television program *World in Action*, which reported on the deplorable working conditions in the industry and pointed in particular to plantations owned by the British Brooke Liebig estate and the Co-operative Tea Estate Society. The show interviewed the chairman of Brooke Bond Liebig, who argued that the conditions on their plantations were no worse than those on any other estate in the country, even those owned by the Sri Lankan government.[146] War on Want's campaign argued that almost 30 percent of the tea in Sri Lanka was grown by companies "with British connections," including those which ran their own plantations and those which exported tea from these plantations to Britain. The NGO linked Britain's responsibility to its imperial past. According to War on Want, despite independence, "the most profitable part of the [Sri Lankan] economy had been created by British capital investment, and the shipping, banking insurance, and export and import trade," which "were completely controlled by Britain." That included tea, the country's primary export commodity. In fact, as War on Want argued, the Sri Lankan tea industry was still rooted in its "colonial heritage."[147] Around 80 percent of the industry workers were of Tamil origins, many of whom were stateless and poor, and had been brought to Sri Lanka by the British empire as indentured laborers. War on Want's campaign suggested that British companies and the British government therefore had social and economic responsibilities toward the industry that dated to the late nineteenth century through independence.

The War on Want campaign aimed to rally the British public in general against the conduct of British businesses in Sri Lanka, but it targeted two bodies in particular, which the organization believed had the responsibility to represent stakeholder needs: the trade union movement as a representative of international workers, and the British government as the representative of British consumers. When it launched its campaign, the NGO approached the Trade Union Congress (TUC) as a natural ally and a potential collaborator in the campaign. As an NGO with close affiliations with Labour, War on Want saw trade unions as ideal interlocutors since they were already organizing on the domestic front. The TUC maintained a close connection with the International Labour Organization (ILO) and was a member of the International Confederation of Free Trade Unions (ICFTU). In 1971, influenced by calls for a New International Economic Order, the TUC supported the ICFTU Development Charter, which aimed to set international "fair labor standards" like "fair wages, unemployment benefits, safety, [and] workmen's compensation."[148] War on Want and trade union representatives therefore hoped that the TUC would join the campaign to pressure British tea merchants in Sri Lanka as an extension of their commitment to international solidarity and worker rights.[149]

TUC had known about the plight of the Sri Lankan tea workers even before War on Want had launched its campaigns. In October 1973, the ICFTU working party on multinational corporations appealed on behalf of the Ceylon Workers' Congress (CWC) to TUC to help them hold British multinational tea companies accountable and lobby the British government on behalf of these workers. For some at the ICFTU, British trade unionists had a particular stake in the campaign. "Tomorrow it may be necessary to call upon the same international labour solidarity to defend the interests of the British worker against the manipulations of multinational companies," the British representative at the ICFTU argued.[150] Yet the TUC avoided committing to any real campaign or action, deferring the responsibility to the CWC. The TUC's reluctance to support the Sri Lankan workers was at least in part due to their complex relationship with the ICFTU and its desire to retain the power of deciding which campaigns to support.

War on Want had hoped it would have better success with the TUC. The NGO directly addressed British trade unions, claiming that "it is the responsibility of the British Trade Unionists to ensure that co-workers employed by the same companies receive fair wages and are not exploited."[151] It called upon the TUC to mobilize against the employment conditions, the poor pay, and the health and sanitary conditions of the workers and their families. In 1975, when the Sri Lankan government decided to nationalize its tea industry, War on Want expanded its campaign and collaborated with the CWC, sending the TUC various international reports about working conditions in Sri Lanka and the British companies' mistreatment of workers. It hoped that the TUC would pressure the British government to include the plight of tea workers in negotiations for the compensation of the British businesses and that some of the compensation money would be "diverted back into Sri Lanka to be used by the United Nations or non-government agencies to help rehabilitate the tea workers."[152] In response to War on Want's appeal, the TUC stated that "the situation of the working people, most of them Tamils, on tea state has been kept under close review," but when War on Want inquired again, the TUC claimed that "not enough information was provided about the production process."[153]

In 1978, frustrated by the lack of commitment, War on Want published a scathing critique of the trade union movement and the TUC in particular. War on Want condemned the Anglo-British trade union movement for a lack of solidarity with Third World workers. It charged the TUC with condoning proto-imperialist and paternalistic measures and described the American ICFTU as a government-financed antisocialist organization. War on Want claimed that the TUC, instead of representing the plight of Third World workers as stakeholders in British multinationals and in the global economy, was a conduit of the Foreign and Commonwealth Ministry with a "non-political" policy. According to War on Want, the TUC should have encouraged a direct action "against multinational Third World exploitation at the place where it would count—at factory floor level in the home base of these companies." More specifically, War on Want was critical of the inability of the TUC and the trade union movement to respond to the rising power of multinational corporations: "Why is it left up to charities and newspapers to expose British company maltreatment of Third World labour when, through the ICFTU, we're meant to have a global exchange of worker information?"[154] According to the NGO, it was the TUC and not NGOs that needed to act on behalf of Third World workers and hold British companies accountable for their social conduct. As Carl Wilms-Wright, the British representative at the ICFTU in 1977, concluded, "The Sri Lanka experience illustrates the difficulties of organizing effective international labour solidarity."[155] War on Want was frustrated by the trade union movement's inability to establish "an effective countervailing power to offset the might of transnational capital," as Wilms-Wright termed it, on the international level.[156]

But War on Want's campaign did not end with the trade unions. It also pressured the government as the political body that represented British consumers and businesses to intervene on behalf of the tea workers on British plantations. The organization wrote letters to and met with the Foreign & Commonwealth Office (FCO), pressuring it to establish a committee to investigate the conduct of British-owned estates. War on Want also requested that the government intervene by negotiating an international commodity agreement for tea, which would ensure a fair price for what was one of the cheapest commodities in the British market at the time.[157] "The British Government and companies clearly have a major responsibility to improve conditions of the estate," Peter Burns stated.[158] The NGO also lobbied the government to establish a "fair" price that "would benefit the plantation workers."[159] The proposal received some consideration by the FCO, but the Department of Prices and Consumer Protection objected strongly to the campaign on the grounds that it would hurt "the average British worker," which would need to pay more for tea.[160] The Labour government, in other words, did not see a necessary connection between the plight of Sri Lankan workers and British ones.

In 1974, the FCO considered formulating a "code of conduct" for British businesses that would urge companies to "recognize their own interest in establishing a name as good employers in particular by keeping abreast of the best current practice in respect of pay and condition of employment." But, the FCO stressed, there was no way for the British government to enforce it. According to one FCO official, "responsibility for the control of company's conduct must rest with the country in which that company operates."[161] To make matters worse, the government was initially reluctant to even establish an official inquiry since, as one official later wrote, "an inquiry would have never served a useful purpose other than to confirm a difficult situation which was already well understood."[162] It was only after the government already had delegates in Colombo negotiating over the nationalization of industry with the Sri Lankan government and representing British businesses on the question of compensation that the FCO finally decided to send delegates to the British estates. The inquiry was a form of social audit that sought to make recommendations to British companies. In March 1975, the FCO sent a delegation of British officials to Sri Lanka.[163] They found that in the 1970s there had indeed been a decline in wages and a deterioration in workers' working and living conditions, especially during the world food crisis in 1974. Workers, the delegates reported, could not afford to purchase the allocated flour ration for a family. Similarly, the delegates found that "the situation of the children in the estate [was] very unsatisfactory."[164] Their report suggested that much of the responsibility for these conditions rested with the Sri Lankan government and local trade unions. The situation in the British estates, it argued, was compatible with the general standard in the tea industry in the country. Nevertheless, the delegates recommended that British companies should "take the lead" so that other employers in the industry would follow suit.[165]

By this point, War on Want was pressuring the government again to establish a commodity agreement. The NGO was joined by Oxfam and the World Development Movement as well as a student-led activist group called the Cambridge World Development Action. The Cambridge group suggested that due to its imperial past, Britain had a direct responsibility for "the underdevelopment of Sri Lanka." The legacy of Britain's imperial economy shaped the country's primary export commodity. British companies, it argued, had been "maintain[ing] their colonial privileges" even after political independence was achieved in Sri Lanka by migrating their operations to East Africa where taxes were lower and labor was cheaper.[166] It was for this reason, the group stated, "Britain must press for the successful completion of an international trade agreement."[167] In 1975, Granada broadcasted another program on the condition of estate workers in Sri Lanka. As with the Haslemere campaigns of the time, activists lobbied for a commodity agreement that would respond to the dependency of the Sri Lankan economy on the primary commodity of tea.

Since 1969, the government in London had been considering a commodity agreement with tea-producing countries, including Sri Lanka, through the auspices of the Food and Agriculture Organization (FAO) but was reluctant to commit to any binding agreement due to concerns about the effects on British consumers.[168] But the NGO lobby pressured its delegates in the FAO to make serious contributions to the negotiations. In 1976, when the tea industry had been nationalized in Sri Lanka, the fourth United Nations Conference on Trade and Development (UNCTAD) pushed for such a program by including tea as one of the main items of its Integrated Commodities program, which aimed to establish a stable price and export quotas on a range of products from developing countries.[169] By 1979, the British government agreed that tea was "a commodity suitable for an international agreement," and in 1982 a draft of such an agreement was approved.[170] The commodity agreement, however, left the question of multinational responsibility unresolved.

In the 1980s, the question of formulating a "code of conduct" for businesses was taken up by the Greater London Council (GLC) spearheaded by the London Labour MP mayor Ken Livingstone. The idea of formulating a code came up as part of a broader industrial strategy devised by the GLC's industry and employment branch, which, among many other things, aimed to connect the city's economy to Third World inequalities. For some members of the party and especially Livingstone, the GLC became a hyper-localized government aimed at combating Thatcher's monetary politics and their international implications, especially on Third World economies.[171] According to him, London had an obligation toward "the people in the south, in what we call the Third World." Livingstone sought to design an economic plan for London that would act upon it. "The great wealth of London," he argued, "was largely built upon the fortunes made in the colonial trade in sugar, tobacco, tea, cocoa, coffee, gold and other minerals and oil. Some part of these fortunes trickled down into the homes of Londoners as a whole."[172]

In February 1985 the GLC organized the "Third World and Technology" conference, which invited trade and development organizations from across Britain and Third World countries, especially from former colonial territories. The conference strove to create "a new international economic order," which included drafting "a code of labour for manufacturing industries in order to universalize best practices, such as the ILO code." It called for a labor solidarity between trade unions in the First and Third Worlds against the power of multinational companies as well as the formation of "joint projects of First and Third World producers" that would focus on alternative, small-scale technologies that aligned with the needs of people and their natural resources.[173] Doing so, it echoed much of Schumacher's philosophy of "intermediate technologies" and his ideas about corporate social responsibility.

Within less than a year the Thatcher government abolished the GLC, thus preventing any real possibility for drafting such a code. But the GLC did manage to fund and spearhead an alternative trading network, which was supposed to execute the GLC's internationalist vision of alternative economic order. It allocated £690,247 to cover the initial funds to form Twin Trading, a fair-trade company and an associated nonprofit, Third World Information Network (TWIN). Twin Trading aimed "to promote trade, development and technologic exchanges between persons and organisations in the less developed countries and regions of the world, on the basis of independence and mutual advantage." It did so both by running informational and educational workshops and by facilitating joint development projects with Third World countries and marketing their products. Livingstone and others—like the New Left activist Michael Barratt Brown, who chaired Twin Trading—believed that fair trade held the key to international labor solidarity and worker representation.

By 1991, however, it was nonprofits like Oxfam as well as Traidcraft, a Christian alternative trade organization founded in 1979, and not trade unions that ended up sponsoring much of Twin Trading's activities.[174] Influenced by these nonprofits, Twin Trading in fact ended up resembling much of Oxfam's Bridge as well as ITDG, which focused on consumer action in the capital rather than the restructuring of labor and industry. It imported handicrafts and foods—most famously by establishing fair-trade ventures Cafédirect in 1991 and Divine Chocolate in 1998—and did not work through trade union channels but instead focused on funding cooperatives and marketing their products to British consumers. The decentralized vision of corporate social responsibility took the form of an alternative trading organization (ATO) rather than an international labor solidarity movement. Twin Trading in fact joined a larger trend in the nonprofit world which, by the 1990s, took it upon themselves to become the representatives of the stakeholders of workers and consumers in the global economy, especially against multinational corporations. In doing so, it turned away from a vision of international trade unionism.

Labor Rather than Consumerism

In May 1996, Oxfam launched the "Clothes Code Campaign." It targeted large retailers like Marks & Spencer, the Burton Group, C&A, Sears, and Next, all of whom "exercise considerable power over the entire supply chain," and worked with them on formulating codes of ethics. The codes aimed to ensure that these retailers worked with South Asian and Latin American manufacturers "to bring about improved conditions—especially health and safety and compliance with existing labour law." It was set as a model for a larger program with other British NGOs that would collaborate with various UK companies on developing and adopting codes of conduct based on ILO standards for various manufacturing industries such as clothing, footwear, and toys.[175] As one Oxfam pamphlet stated, "good working conditions can help to create extremely good profits."[176] It sounded like a page taken from War on Want's campaign for a code of conduct.

The Oxfam clothing campaign represented the growing attention to corporate social responsibility in Britain and the world in the 1990s, often referred to as the decade of globalization. The period saw an even closer relationship between nonprofits and the for-profit world. Many nonprofits not only established a permanent office for corporate relations but also worked with businesses rather than against them on formulating codes of conduct in various industries.[177] These campaigns, in fact, joined what Naomi Klein, in her influential book *No Logo*, called "alternative models of globalization."[178] Yet in Britain, nonprofits' corporate social responsibility often became co-opted with a for-profit logic. It hinged upon the idea that corporate social responsibility could become a path to enhance the value of a brand in the eyes of future investors and consumers rather than a type of worker representation.

The history of corporate social responsibility has largely been told through the lens of the alternative globalization and consumer movement that culminated in such campaigns as Oxfam's.[179] In this story, the turn toward corporate codes of ethics was rooted in the globalization of consumer politics in the late twentieth century. Global consumers acted as global citizens in the effort to attack multinational corporations and large businesses where it would hurt the most: their brands. As Klein explained, "unlike governments, [corporations] are accountable only to their shareholders."[180] By connecting brands with labor and human rights violations, corporations were pressured to change their production practices. This was a type of activism that was rooted in the model of shareholder capitalism, aimed to injure the brand's reputation and share value. Shareholder activism became prevalent in the financialization of the 1990s.

But its story was only one episode in a longer history of corporate social responsibility. To focus exclusively on the history of consumer activism is to overlook a crucial aspect of how historically corporate social responsibility was intimately connected with the critique of collective bargaining and its replacement with the model of worker participation. In the 1960s, the idea of corporate social responsibility emerged from a story about labor rather than consumerism, an alternative model for development economics and the dual economy. For businessmen and economists-turned-activists, such as Bader and Schumacher, corporate social responsibility was part of a vision of worker participation and stakeholder capitalism, a way to remake economic development beyond nationalization and include worker representation in private industry. But their campaigns ended up curtailing the power of workers in industry. They garnered power and support because they were aimed against the militancy of trade unions in Britain and fused with Cold War anxieties. They proposed a model of mixed economy that was meant to replace the traditional model of state ownership. By the 1970s, NGOs like Oxfam, Christian

Aid, and War on Want came to connect these ideas of corporate social responsibility with a call for a New International Economic Order that focused on the power of multinational corporations. NGOs, in fact, used their role as nonprofits to represent the interests of the stakeholders in the global economy and to advocate in their behalf. Their embrace of campaigns for corporate codes of practice built upon and expanded the critique of trade union activism and collective bargaining, and instead assumed new methods of representing workers and advocating for their rights. This untold yet crucial story allows us to understand how corporate social responsibility not only emerged from consumer activism and the anti-globalization movement but also was deeply rooted within a critique of trade unionism.

CHAPTER SIX

Adjustment with a Human Face

IN 1989, FOUR years before he left to work as the NGO liaison for the World Bank, John Clark wrote a report for Oxfam titled "A Grass Roots View of the Debt Crisis." Clark, who had been working in Oxfam's Development Policy Unit since the early 1980s, declared that the "Debt Crisis is a macro-economic problem of Third World governments, Western based commercial banks and the international financial system stemming from a £1,000 billion Third World debt." Oxfam, however, although "the largest British private development agency," operated on the microeconomic level by supporting community organizations, popular movements, and individuals. The connection between the macroeconomic and the microeconomic levels, Clark suggested, "may sound obscure but it is as direct as the connection between drought and hunger." The debt crisis, Clark argued, was not "just an economic problem" but a "human crisis." According to Clark, the debt crisis brought austerity measures to Third World countries, pauperized the working class, and limited the aid these countries could offer their poor. Debt might sound like a technical subject, and many nonprofits steered clear of it, but "nothing could be further from the truth." Nonprofits had a major role to play in resolving the debt crisis.[1]

According to Clark, nonprofits like Oxfam had a unique "grassroots" perspective on the costs of structural adjustment policies. By contrast, he argued that international organizations had a limited perspective on the debt crisis. Their "*macro* approach is to fly over or climb an ivory tower and take a view from up high . . . the *aerial* view of the IMF showed that [a place like] Zambia had a major problem in making effective use of its scant foreign exchange reserves." Nonprofits, however, were interested in people, "and *people* is surely what development is about." Clark drew directly upon Schumacher's economic philosophy and argued that such an approach would be able to tackle both the problem of growth and the social costs of the crisis.[2] He called for a microeconomic approach focused on individuals and the social costs of adjustment.

The debt crisis originated in the 1970s, when rising oil prices and high inflation rates led to a global economic downturn. To counter the resulting economic challenges, Third World governments turned to commercial loans from Western banks which had large surpluses of dollar-denominated investments by oil-producing countries newly flush with cash. By 1979, the "frantic bout of borrowing," as one War on Want campaign put it, ran into difficulties.[3] That year, the second oil crisis, together with changing monetary policies at the U.S. Federal Reserve, drove up interest rates and pushed Third World economies into recession. Existing and future loans became pricier.[4] When payments came due, borrower governments had to turn to the International Monetary Fund (IMF) and the World Bank to stave off wholesale bankruptcy and defaults. In August 1982, for instance, Mexico, with over $80 billion in loans, half of which were due the following year, announced it would default on its debt. Instead, the country was pushed to rely on further loans to service its debts, with the IMF, stewarded primarily by the United States, becoming its main lender as well as the "financial policeman" of the country.[5] The IMF linked the granting of all loans, including its own and those of commercial and central banks, to conditions such as increased taxation, a reduction in imports, and spending cuts, especially on public welfare programs. The loans served essentially as a political intervention in Mexico's domestic economic policy.

The Mexican case launched a new era of lending shaped by what came to be known as IMF structural adjustment programs. By the late 1980s, countries from the Caribbean to Africa and South Asia all became subject to these forms of financial intervention, which aimed to service the debt acquired during the commercial borrowing of the previous decade. As had occurred in Mexico, structural adjustment programs were macroeconomic policies that obligated recipient nations to liberalize their trade and investment policies in return for loans that would bail out their economies. The programs included devaluation of currencies in order to enhance export earnings, while also discouraging imports, even in economies like Jamaica, which were completely dependent on imports of basic foodstuffs and oil. Such programs cut government budgets for health care, medicine, and public infrastructure. They were, to some extent, the top-down, neoliberal interpretation of the principle of trade not aid. Yet, as many activists have shown, instead of solving the debt crisis, they worsened it. For example, as Christian Aid has demonstrated, the total external debt among sub-Saharan countries rose from $84 billion in 1980 to over $220 billion by 1995, by which time the total Third World debt reached $2 trillion.[6] Structural adjustment programs locked countries across the Third World into chronic debt and plunged them into even greater crises of poverty and hunger.

When British nonprofits first undertook the project of making capitalism ethical in the 1960s, they could not have foreseen the debt crisis. Their ethical capitalism was meant to respond to Keynesian macroeconomics and the problem of state ownership during the period of decolonization. But the debt crisis, and the neoliberal structural adjustment programs that were meant to solve it, created a new framework for their work. Structural adjustment programs may have pushed the postcolonial state away from nationalization, but they nonetheless operated under a top-down growth paradigm that prioritized large-scale investments. They paved the way for multinational corporations rather than small businesses. Crucially, the programs' stringent repayment conditions consumed export earnings. Postcolonial countries had to restructure their economies to fit the IMF's conditions and in the process their currencies were devalued. Many Third World economies that depended on the importation of basic foodstuffs and oil reached new levels of crisis as prices of basic commodities rose. Third World consumers lost their purchasing power; unemployment rose and, with it, poverty and hunger were exacerbated. "Poorer people," stated one Oxfam report, "have no access to savings which they could use to cushion the effects of falling incomes."[7] Structural adjustment programs not only failed in their mission but impoverished the Third World even further. As many activists noted, the programs curtailed the postcolonial economic sovereignty of Third World countries. Some even argued that structural adjustment programs were a modern form of slavery.[8]

This chapter tracks how British nonprofits responded to the debt crisis and the financialization of the global economy between the mid-1980s and the 1990s. In this period, British nonprofits and church groups ran a series of campaigns that critiqued structural adjustment programs. Structural adjustments, they argued, accounted only for national economies and large corporations while ignoring the economic lives of individuals in Third World countries. It dragged individuals into perpetual poverty. Many nonprofits connected the debt crisis to the longer history of colonialism and structural adjustment, by association, to a form of neocolonialism. Drawing on Judeo-Christian ideas, they linked the biblical concept of Jubilee with the Millennium and with the urgent need to cancel the poorest countries' international debt. By the late 1990s, their campaigns, which began in Britain, had inspired a transnational grassroots movement in over forty countries led by consumers, pop singers, and politicians and which demanded a blanket debt cancellation by the year 2000.

But nonprofit campaigns to end the debt crisis did not mean these organizations did away altogether with debt as a form of aid. Nonprofits developed financial literacy and financial strategies to create an alternative form of financialization that would be more ethical and humane. Instead of large loan programs, they called for an "adjustment with a human face" and embraced the tools of microfinance and income-generation schemes. From the late 1980s onward, British nonprofits invited consumers to support small-scale, microfinance schemes that would directly help individuals and their families. While small credit schemes were nothing new in development work, microfinance initiatives generated loans aimed at supporting small enterprises. As the Bang-ladeshi economist Muhammad Yunus—one of the movement's key architects and the founder of the Grameen Bank, which became the model for many non-profit microfinance schemes—argued, wage employment did not guarantee an available or even stable income for everyone: "Creating favourable conditions for making a living through self-employment is [a] much more dignified way of solving [the] unemployment problem than instituting a system of doles and welfare payments."[9] The idea was popularized internationally by various aid organizations in the last decade of the twentieth century, not least because such initiatives encouraged Third World individuals to open their own business ven-tures and to generate their own income independently of the fluctuating labor market at a time when unemployment was skyrocketing.[10]

The turn to microfinance was not unique to British nonprofits, but it did dovetail with their search for an ethical capitalism. It was a microeconomic strategy that taught the poor how to manage, invest, and accumulate credit through small community-based solidarity networks. Instead of structural adjustment programs, it offered the poor the ability to build credit and manage their own debt. Its philosophy suited nonprofits' long-standing commitment to working on the very small scale, with microfinance serving as an "intermediate technology" that, at least in theory, empowered the very poor to be the masters of their own economic fate.

British nonprofits used microfinance to campaign against structural adjust-ment programs and to financialize existing facets of their fair-trade programs, in keeping with their general philosophy of decentralized aid. Unlike earlier fair-trade models managed directly by these nonprofits, microfinance allowed organizations to expand production through credit and help the very poor develop their own small business ventures. From microloans to "employment-generation activities" such as accounting and bookkeeping workshops, microf-inance carried the promise of educating the very poor in financial and business literacy, helping liberate them from precarious wage labor. The embrace of microfinance was, in fact, an aspect of the broader shift to employment-generation schemes that focused on encouraging self-employment instead of relying on wage work. For organizations like Oxfam, Save the Children, and Christian Aid, the turn to microfinance meant remaking existing fair-trade programs, which became a lucrative strategy for modifying, reforming, and enhancing flexible labor practices rather than abolishing them. By the 1990s, microfinance had been adopted by Third Way politicians in Britain itself in a similar effort to help ethnic minorities generate income through self-employment. What began as a decentralized international nongovernmental program was adopted by the British state as a domestic microeconomic welfare policy. As much as it fashioned economic lives in Third World communities, nonprofits' vision of ethical capitalism also played a role in remaking the post-imperial economy in Britain itself.

"The Most Potent Form of Slavery"

In a famous speech to the financial establishment of the City of London in March 1985, the Tanzanian president Julius Nyerere argued that the IMF and the World Bank were directly implicated in the widespread hunger and major famines on the African continent. Africa's crisis may have been brought to the world's attention through the widely televised Ethiopian famine the year before, but for Nyerere the dire conditions on the continent were tightly connected to an older story whose protagonist was the structural adjustment programs led by the IMF and the World Bank. Nyerere, who was central to anticolonial calls for a New International Economic Order in the mid-1960s, claimed that the IMF and the World Bank were part of a system that "transfers resources from the poor to the rich. It did it 20 years ago, and it is doing it now. It is a system of inbuilt exploitation." The debt crisis, he suggested, and its mismanagement through the IMF structural adjustment programs in the 1980s were embedded in a longer history of colonial domination. "Africa's debt burden is now intolerable," he declared. "We cannot pay. You know it and all the other creditors know it." He went on to ask: "Should we really let our people starve so that we can pay our debt?"[11] For Nyerere and other critics, the debt crisis and the stringent repayment policy enacted by the IMF and the World Bank not only generated misery but also curtailed Africa's sovereignty over key economic decisions.

As early as the 1970s, economists, academics, and aid workers began to warn about a looming default on Third World debt. In a 1971 book, the American academic Cheryl Payer drew similar links to those Nyerere drew between the IMF loans and the economic independence of Third World countries. She argued that international debates about trade dependency could not be understood separately from the issue of exchange rates and the repayment of loans to the IMF and World Bank.[12] The book became the basis of her more well-known *The Debt Trap: The IMF and the Third World*, which argued that Third World countries that had relied on loans since the 1940s were financially indentured to the IMF. "Since its founding," she argued, "the IMF has been the chosen instrument for imposing imperialist financial discipline upon the poor countries under a façade of multilateralism and technical competition."[13] The IMF, she concluded, was not only a bureaucratic and technical institution. It had a highly political role in determining the autonomy of Third World countries and the structure of their postcolonial economies.

Payer's work influenced British activists, especially at the World Development Movement, Oxfam, and War on Want. These activists were, of course, well acquainted with the IMF loan programs. In 1976 Britain itself took on an unprecedented loan of $3.9 billion from the bank, which compelled the government to reduce spending on welfare and partially privatize its national industries.[14] The British in fact followed the Chilean model instituted after

Pinochet's coup in 1973, which by the 1980s had taken the form of other structural adjustment programs. Yet, as activists soon pointed out, the impending default crisis posed a larger threat to poorer countries in the Third World that relied on exports for basic foodstuffs and energy. By 1979, the *New Internationalist* devoted an entire issue to the problem of loans. "The Third World has been on the receiving end of foreign aid from Western and Communist nations for over three decades. But with each passing year, debts of the poor world increase and economic self-reliance drifts further away," wrote coeditor Wayne Ellwood.[15] With exports remaining stagnant and the reduction of official aid in the late 1970s, Ellwood suggested, Third World countries were increasingly relying on loans to fill the gap. Dependence on loans halted the movement toward a New International Economic Order, which itself only briefly mentioned the monetary implications of global inequalities. As the global downturn hit, the situation became urgent, with many poorer Third World countries on the brink of default. Instead of drawing these countries into bankruptcy, Ellwood suggested, the West should increase and stabilize the prices for Third World commodities, reduce tariffs on their processed and semi-processed goods, and, importantly, implement a debt relief program that would free them from chronic dependency.

In the summer of 1980, Nyerere and Jamaican prime minister Michael Manley hosted a South-North conference in Arusha, Tanzania, titled, "The International Monetary System and the New International Order." The conference was based on a meeting convened in Kingston, Jamaica, in October of the previous year, which had questioned the IMF's legitimacy. "It cannot be a mere coincidence that the harshest IMF measures are reserved for those countries that appear to be striking out on a more independent economic path, which it surely must be their sovereign right to do," the delegates of the October 1979 meeting proclaimed.[16] For statesmen like Nyerere, the IMF was an institution directly connected with the history of colonialism. "The group of industrialized nations—which do act as a group when dealing with outsiders—control the levers of international exchange and finance, and also control the wealth accumulated through centuries of colonialism, gun-boat diplomacy, and an initial advantage in mass production techniques," he argued in a speech that same year to the countries of the G-77.[17] The economic crisis of the 1970s pushed Tanzania and Jamaica—which both led the calls for a New International Economic Order in the 1960s—to depend on the IMF's structural adjustment programs and their stringent conditions.

The Arusha initiative of summer 1980 was meant to provide a forum for discussing the political implications of the IMF's programs, which were cloaked in the guise of technical and "neutral" measures, and for proposing alternatives: "Those who wield power control money. Those who manage and control money wield power. An international monetary system is both a function and an instrument of the prevailing power structure."[18] Less than a year into the so-called Volker shock, when the U.S. Federal Reserve drastically increased interest rates at a pace that pushed Third World borrowers even closer to the brink of default, the Arusha initiative suggested that no one country or international institution should determine the fate of Third World economies. The forty delegates (which included parliamentarians, bankers, and economic researchers) called for a halt—in Nyerere's words—to the IMF's "meddling" and for the institution to remove the onerous conditionality of its loans.[19] It also proposed the establishment of a new international monetary system that would be managed by an extragovernmental community and include an international currency unit that would equalize international exchange rates. The Arusha initiative offered an alternative and updated the original ideas of the NIEO by addressing global monetary inequality.

In 1983, a year after Mexico announced it would default on its debt, the Brandt Commission published a report called *Common Crisis North-South: Cooperation for World Recovery.*[20] Since the late 1970s, the former German chancellor Willy Brandt had led an Independent Commission on International Developmental tasked with developing a plan to support Third World economies through a type of "global Keynesianism." The commission's first report in 1980 offered a program that would implement the conclusions of the NIEO, but despite attention from Third World countries it received "little favorable response from the International Monetary Fund and the World Bank."[21] The 1983 report was an updated version that directly addressed the IMF's structural adjustment programs. Much in the spirit of the Arusha initiative, the report called for reforming the outdated Bretton Woods institutions to include "attention to the question of power-sharing" and for "greater equality and partnership" especially between borrower countries and financial institutions. It directly attacked the IMF for losing sight of its "primary objectives" and demanded that the bank change its "adjustment policies or 'conditionality.' "[22] In 1985 Michael Manley followed up with a joint report with Brandt, written for the Socialist International Committee on Economic Policy, which more forcefully called on Western powers—and the Reagan administration in particular—to break from neoliberal structural adjustment policies and to accept the ideas of the NIEO.[23] The report connected the detrimental effects of these policies to a variety of issues such as common security and human rights, but, as scholars and commentators noted at the time, it did not offer a clear alternative to "monetarist-inspired capitalism."[24]

It was in this international context that, in the mid-1980s, nongovernmental activists in Britain turned their focus to the debt crisis and the IMF's structural adjustment policies. While as early as 1983 individual activists and aid workers campaigned in Britain for Third World debt relief, from 1984 on the debt crisis became the subject of national campaigns. The issue was picked up by three main NGOs in Britain: War on Want, whose campaign was led by John Denham (later a member of New Labour's shadow cabinets); Oxfam, whose campaign was run by John Clark (later the NGO liaison at the World Bank); and the World Development Movement, whose campaign was led by John Mitchell. They were joined by similar antipoverty groups across the United States and Western Europe who lobbied their governments and international organizations for debt relief in Third World countries.

What united the British campaigns, however, was their focus on the social and human costs of the debt crisis. Much like their earlier programs, the debt campaigns approached the Third World debt crisis with an emphasis on helping people, rather than institutions or the overall economy. These campaigns drew directly from economists like Schumacher and the nonprofit world's vision of ethical capitalism. The "economic and trade policies pursued by wealthier countries deepen this crisis" of world hunger and poverty, argued one of Oxfam's pamphlets, in the spirit of the Brandt report. It went on to note that "Oxfam's particular concern is that these attempts to solve the debt crisis are aggravating the world hunger problem."[25] In fact, all three NGOs focused on the connection between debt and hunger. They criticized structural adjustment programs for their detrimental effects on people, who they argued were not to blame for a government's reckless debt management policies. The latter decreased per capita income, raised unemployment rates, and reduced subsidies on basic foods and services. In responding to the debt crisis, the nonprofits aimed to connect the global debt crisis with the economic lives of everyday citizens, hoping to show that the present catastrophe was not only an abstract crisis of national governments but also one that directly shaped malnutrition and hunger in places like Jamaica and Sudan.[26] "The debt crisis is changing the geography of poverty," John Clark wrote.[27] These campaigns attracted the attention of the British public because they offered a reframing of world hunger and famines, issues popularized during the same years by the Band Aid and Live Aid concerts. "For every £1 the world contributed to famine relief in Africa in 1985, the West took back £2 in debt repayments," read one leaflet.[28] Their campaigns implied that it was debt, not natural disasters or internal political conflicts, that led to famines and hunger across the Third World.

The idea that structural adjustment should factor in the human costs of debt was further popularized by the British economist Richard Jolly. Jolly was a former fellow at the Institute of Development Studies and had worked with Dudley Seers on the "informal economy" report to the ILO in the early 1970s. In 1985 Jolly published a famous UNICEF report titled "Adjustment with a Human Face," which mirrored much of Schumacher's economic philosophy.[29] For Jolly, national programs for debt repayment were intimately connected to labor. As he later explained, "instead of moderating the human repercussions of recession in the industrial countries on the most vulnerable, the dominant economic forces tended to multipl[y] them."[30] The UNICEF report suggested that structural adjustments were inadequate because they did not account for the basic needs of Third World societies. UNICEF, together with NGOs like

Oxfam, War on Want, and the World Development Movement, emphasized the need to account for the nutrition, health, and welfare of vulnerable populations like children. Jolly also emphasized the need for "human development" over abstract metrics like GNP growth as measures of economic success. Jolly and British NGOs were later joined by other European organizations, which similarly stressed that, beyond abstract, economic consequences, structural adjustment policies also had human implications for recipient societies. "Among the social consequences spawned by the economic crisis," a joint report by international NGOs at the UN stated, "are rising infant mortality, decreasing access to food, increasing malnutrition, particularly among children and women, growing landlessness and employment, decline[s] in real wages, and curtailment in education, health and other social services."[31] The structural adjustment programs locked Third World subjects into perpetual poverty.

Alongside campaigns that emphasized the social costs of the crisis, British nonprofits also worked on exposing the connections between British banking institutions and the debt crisis. Britain under Nigel Lawson—who was responsible for the financialization of the British economy during this period—was in fact one of the leading supporters of structural adjustment policies. While the government committed to increasing its overseas aid programs in places affected by the debt crisis, such as Tanzania, it also tied its aid to the condition that these countries follow IMF policies.[32] The British government was the first country to support the IMF's new Enhanced Structural Adjustment Facility, which was introduced in 1987 and still held recipient countries to strict privatization policies, despite showing greater awareness of "basic needs." In 1988, as the World Bank warned against "debt fatigue," Lawson gave a speech at the IMF that laid out his infamous "Lawson Doctrine."[33] He argued that as long as a country preserved its fiscal balance, the size of its current account deficit did not matter because there could not be an external debt problem without a fiscal problem.[34] While Lawson supported the IMF's new program to ease the debt burden on sub-Saharan countries, his doctrine de facto endorsed the logic of structural adjustment, since it argued against including the private sector in calculations of the deficit.[35] The debt and balance of payments crisis of the following decade would prove Lawson's doctrine miserably wrong, but it nevertheless shaped the macroeconomic ideas and theories of the late 1980s and early 1990s.

British nonprofits, however, stressed that structural adjustment policies impoverished Third World societies while at the same time benefiting commercial banks in Britain and elsewhere. "Britain's big four high street banks—Lloyds, Midlands, NatWest and Barclays—made combined profits before tax of over £2.5 billion in 1985," one War on Want leaflet read. Nongovernmental activists argued that Britain's commercial banks were directly implicated in the crisis and suggested that Britons had a direct responsibility for mitigating it. "At the same time austerity measures were being imposed on Mexico's poor, Lloyds Bank International announced that profits had quadrupled in the six months after September 1982." They noted a "major boost" from countries that were being forced to reschedule their loans: "For many banks the fees involved in the Mexico rescheduling almost doubled the return on their lending."[36] Some activists even ran local campaigns that invited consumers to cancel credit cards issued by banks that profited from the debt crisis. Others called upon British banks to "lift this great burden off the backs of the world's poor by genuine debt cancellation."[37] These campaigns positioned their actions against the neoliberal IMF and the Thatcherite government that supported it in Britain.

In 1987, when the neoliberal Conservative Party was reelected, many of these organizations decided to directly lobby the British government to help relieve the debt. War on Want, for example, invited British citizens to write to the Chancellor of the Exchequer Nigel Lawson and request that the government buy out some of the commercial loans at a discount. Instead of the full price of the loans, the organization suggested that the government offer the commercial banks—which stood to lose massive profits as Third World countries were likely to default on their loans—nearly £1,000 million in tax relief.[38] The idea was to create a program that would benefit both the British economy and those of the Third World. While by 1989 the campaign's leader, John Denham, had left the organization for local politics, he continued to lobby the government for debt relief. When in 1992 he became an MP for Southampton, he brought the cause to the Labour Party and the House of Commons.

Similarly, Oxfam wrote letters to Minister for Overseas Aid Chris Patterson and to Lawson, urging both to invest more in aid to debt-ridden countries, especially in sub-Saharan Africa. That year Clark traveled to sub-Saharan Africa and the Caribbean to study the social costs of IMF structural adjustment policies. His findings—which showed the devastating effects of IMF policies on working- and even middle-class people—led the organization to place special emphasis on these regions in their campaigns. Oxfam's focus on sub-Saharan Africa in fact helped move British campaigns from general discussions about the debt crisis to a direct focus on the links between debt and rampant famine and hunger in Africa. In 1988, in preparation for the Annual Meeting of IMF and World Bank Governors in Berlin, the organization met with Lawson with the hope that the government would ask the IMF to change its conditionality policies. At the end of the meeting, however, the organization felt like Lawson was "uninterested in questions of quality of adjustment." Oxfam in fact was highly critical of Lawson and his "unwillingness to make the logical connection between reduced costs in debt burden for poor countries and increased resource for aid."[39] While Lawson led a special program that would translate all of the UK's loans into grants and that called for a rescheduling of loans to African countries, he nevertheless was a major supporter of the privatization measures advocated by structural adjustment programs.[40] In 1989 Oxfam, War on Want, and the World Development Movement joined a trans-European campaign aimed at members of the Common Market. They focused on European commercial banks and advocated a 50 percent reduction of Third World debts that would allow these banks to forgo their loans without losing too much money. They also lobbied the president of the EEC to support "a more radical action on debt reduction."[41] By 1991 John Clark had left Oxfam to join the World Bank and to act as liaison between the organization and NGOs on issues such as debt repayments and debt remission.

In 1988, when Oxfam and War on Want's main campaigners left to work in governmental and international agencies, the World Development Movement, Christian Aid, and the nonprofit New Economics Foundation formed a new alliance, the Debt Crisis Network.[42] The network added a new dimension to the campaigns around the debt crisis: they connected the idea of debt relief to Christian ethics. According to these activists, there were direct connections between the theology of the Old and the New Testaments and present-day debt remission. For example, in a 1988 booklet titled *Banking on the Poor: The Ethics of Third World Debt*, Christian Aid used Jesus's "preferential option for the poor" as the basis for calling upon Western consumers and governments to ensure that citizens in debt-ridden countries not bear the burden of the crisis. It encouraged indebted countries to push for remission of debt acquired on "imprudent terms" and called on the IMF and the World Bank for the "forgiveness" of debt. It also advised Western Christians to use their influence as shareholders to influence bank policies on Third World debt, while calling on Western churches to publicly declare the debt crisis a symptom of an unjust international order requiring fundamental change.[43] In 1990, Christian Aid was joined by the All African Council of Churches, which called for a year of Jubilee to cancel Africa's debt.[44]

By 1993, the connection between Christian ethics and debt became the heart of the "Jubilee 2000" campaign. The campaign was initiated by Martin Dent, a retired political scientist from Keele University and a former colonial officer, and Bill Peters, a retired British diplomat who served the Colonial Office in Ghana during the years of decolonization and later took posts in Cyprus, India, Bangladesh, Australia, Zambia, and Malawi.[45] Dent and Peters had both been interested in the relationship between debt and Christian theology for a number of years, and, after meeting at the "Unselfish Motivation in Economics" conference, they decided to establish a campaign that would call for debt forgiveness.[46] In 1995 they were joined by Isabel Carter at Tearfund, an evangelical Christian development agency, who helped them fundraise for their campaign. The idea behind the Jubilee 2000 campaign was to use the new millennium as a year for debt forgiveness in the spirit of Christian theology. Dent and Peters drew direct connections from the story of the Israelites, as told in Leviticus, where debt was considered a form of slavery and called for

debt forgiveness. They referenced the biblical notion of Jubilee, a time of celebration and relief every fifty years.

The Jubilee 2000 campaign moved beyond the issue of remission and
focused instead on debt forgiveness. While debt remission had already been
introduced by the IMF and the World Bank in 1989, the forgiveness campaign
emphasized that remission had little effect on poorer countries, especially in
sub-Saharan Africa. Under what was called Brady plan, the IMF and the
World Bank offered debt remission by replacing high-value commercial loans
with safer lower-value ones. But the plan had not improved the situation in
sub-Saharan countries, where debt was part of a crisis of development that
implicated national governments, banks, and multilateral agencies. Brady
bonds presented a fresh prospect for economies with the means to take advantage of them, yet for much of Africa this was not the case. The Jubilee 2000
campaign emphasized the importance of dropping a sizable portion of the
debt for such countries, which had no other means of extricating themselves
from the crisis. It called for the "cancellation of the backlog of unpayable debt
for the world's poorest countries—which either cannot be paid or can be paid
only with enormous human suffering."[47] It lobbied not only the British government but also international financial institutions, as well as the highly
industrialized nations in the Group of 8 (G-8): Canada, France, Germany,
Italy, Japan, Russia, the United States, and the UK.

The idea of the Jubilee 2000 received backing from clergy of various
denominations in Britain as well as nonprofits like Christian Aid, Tearfund,
the Catholic Agency for Overseas Development, and the Debt Crisis Network's chairman Ed Mayo. With the help of the Catholic Agency for Overseas
Development, Dent, Peters, and Carter even organized a tour of Britain by
African politicians, economists, and clergy that concluded with a conference
hosted by Cardinal Hume. Leaders from Latin America, Protestant clergy,
and financial experts were present, along with Michel Camdessus, the former
director of the IMF.[48] By October 1997, the director of Christian Aid Michael
Taylor helped form the Jubilee 2000 Coalition, which included more than
seventy organizations.

One of the main features of the Jubilee 2000 campaign was to draw associations between debt and slavery. For members of the campaign, the debt
crisis in Africa and the Caribbean was rooted in the history of eighteenth- and
nineteenth-century slavery. From its inception, the campaign evoked imagery
of chains and bondage. "Sauda is one day old," one pamphlet read. "She already
owes 30 times more than she will earn in her life."[49] The pamphlet concluded
with images of chains to mark Sauda's birth into debt bondage. In late 1996,
when the Debt Crisis Network and the New Economics Foundation took over
the campaign and appointed the South African–born British economist Ann
Pettifor to lead it, the campaign continued to evoke the connection between
slavery and debt. Debt, she argued, "is a form of slavery" not only because it

mired Caribbean and African countries in perpetual financial obligation but also because—through the market of trade in debt—it "removes choice from the governments of developing nations and denies people in these countries control over their own destinies."[50] On May 16, 1998, during the G-8 summit in Birmingham, the Jubilee 2000 campaign led a rally in the city that included a human chain of around seventy thousand people. The chain was meant to conjure the burden of debt as slavery as well as to symbolize the British and global community that stood against it. As Pettifor explained, "chains can also symbolize constructive links between people, and the power of such bonds to break bondage . . . the organizers believed that a human chain would be an innovative way of altering the dynamic between a large protest group and the authorities."[51] The idea was to demonstrate and emulate both the bondage of debt and the solidarity of a global community intent on dismantling it. "Break the chains of debt" was one of the campaign's slogans.[52]

The British Jubilee 2000 campaigners were, of course, not alone in making the connection between debt and slavery. The connection between the structures of the international economy and the long history of slavery was at the heart of the anticolonial critique emerging from the Black Atlantic in the 1930s, and it was central to the Black Power movement.[53] By the late 1960s it had become the basis for the calls for a New International Economic Order, and Manley and Nyerere invoked the comparison when critiquing the IMF in the early 1980s. In 1998, when the Jubilee Afrika secretariate was established to include the voices of African countries in the campaign, the historical connections between debt and slavery were cemented in the movement's rhetoric. As the Accra conference—called to celebrate the establishment of the secretariat—proclaimed, "the root-causes of these Debts lie in the History of Slavery and Colonialism."[54] In his keynote address to the conference, the South African Archbishop Ndungane of Cape Town even vividly compared the victims of the Middle Passage to those experiencing the bondage of debt in the present.[55] Emancipation from debt was thus viewed as one more chapter in the long struggle for liberty and self-determination.

But the parallels British campaigners drew between slavery and debt meant that they saw themselves as direct descendants of the abolitionist movement. From 1996 onward the British campaigners framed the Jubilee 2000 as part of a moral, humanitarian mission intimately connected with the long British tradition of abolitionism.[56] Dent wrote, for instance, that "there is a close parallel between the campaign in the last century to liberate people of African descent from the burdens of slavery, of a legal and coercive kind, and our campaign to free the 51 poorest countries of the world from the economic burden of debt slavery."[57] He also likened himself to William Wilberforce, the famed early nineteenth-century abolitionist. Similarly, in 1997 Christian Aid published a booklet titled *The New Abolitionists: Slavery in History and the Modern Slavery of Poor Country Debt*, which made the case that Jubilee 2000 activism emulated the moral cause of the antislavery movement. Even Pettifor, who took a more economic than moral or religious tone in her campaigning, evoked the comparison between the two. "As with the campaign against slavery," she noted, "religious and secular organizations are challenging the new bondage, and calling for drastic and urgent debt relief. They are calling for no less than a new economic order."[58] As a result, while the campaign aspired to become the first transnational grassroots mobilization to call for debt cancellation, it also linked itself to a long British tradition of humanitarianism.[59] For the African members of the campaign, by contrast, despite its success at mobilizing support and pressuring governments, Jubilee 2000 did not offer enough of a radical economic alternative.[60] Instead, it kept its campaign within the moral bounds of humanitarianism. The campaign often played on the paternalistic trope of the white savior in Africa.

The framing of the debt crisis as a moral, humanitarian calamity was further cemented when in 1999 Jubilee 2000 appointed U2 lead singer Bono as the campaign's ambassador. The campaign built on more than a decade of celebrity humanitarianism, especially the Live Aid concert in 1985 that connected the music industry with the humanitarian campaign to aid Ethiopia during a major (and highly televised) famine. The campaign's recruitment of Bono was part of a broader and conscious effort to reframe the campaign in "making the cause more mainstream."[61] In late 1998, one of Jubilee 2000's main campaigners and Christian Aid's media and communication specialist, Jamie Drummond, approached Mike Christie, a British television and music producer who at the time worked with bands like Suede and the Pet Shop Boys. Together, however, they decided to rebrand the Jubilee 2000 campaign; while maintaining its humanitarian impulse, they shifted away from the emphasis on the abolitionist legacy. "I thought slavery was the wrong message," said Christie in one interview.[62] Drummond and Christie decided to distill the campaign's message by using a more modern catchphrase: "Drop the debt" became the movement's new slogan.[63]

In 1999 Drummond and Christie contacted Bono through his record label and asked him to become the campaign's ambassador. They succeeded in wooing him by comparing Jubilee 2000 to Live Aid's mission: they told him that every week Africans were repaying around $200 million in debt, the same amount that his Live Aid concert raised in total. The connection to Live Aid convinced Bono, who for "over a decade" had been searching for a cause that would reinvolve him in an antipoverty campaign.[64] The campaign also commissioned a new music video, which it aired at the BRIT Awards on February 16, 1999. The video conveyed the same message given to Bono: "Live Aid raised 200 million. Africa repays that every week. Military spending costs you 316 pounds a year. Cancelling Third World debt would cost you 12 pounds a year. And save seven million lives. Every year."[65] The video included British artists like David Bowie, Jarvis Crocker, Cornershop's Tjinder Singh and Ben Ayres, and Prodigy's lead singer Keith Flint, who was seen tattooing "Drop the Debt" in gothic letters on his back. Moreover, the rock-singer-turned-humanitarian Bob Geldof, who was behind the Live Aid venture and its aid programs, joined Bono and shared his own expertise and experience with the Drop the Debt campaign.

By late 1999, the Jubilee 2000 or, as it was referred to more popularly, Drop the Debt campaign had garnered massive international support. One of its petitions, for example, gathered around six million signatories in Europe and six hundred thousand from the United States, the highest number on record for a public petition at the time. In Britain, the campaign received support from Prime Minister Tony Blair and Chancellor of the Exchequer Gordon Brown as well as from the rest of the New Labour government. In June 1999 the G-8 leaders agreed on a new Heavily Indebted Poor Countries (HIPC) initiative meant to provide an exit from the rescheduling process by reducing debt to "sustainable" levels compatible with growth. Blair then went on to lead a G-8 initiative that would write off $40 billion in debt to multilateral institutions. Bono also enlisted Bill and Hillary Clinton's support for the campaign. On September 29, 1999, Bill Clinton announced that the United States would forgive 100 percent of the debt owed to it by 36 poor countries, around $5.7 billion. It also committed to increasing its financial support of the HIPC initiative to forgive multilateral debt. At the end of 2001, according to its activists, the campaign had achieved around $110 billion in debt cancellation.[66]

But the Drop the Debt campaign can only be deemed a partial success. Debt remained a major burden on postcolonial economies, and structural adjustment programs continued to tighten their hold over governments. While the new HIPC initiative helped reduce debt, it also strengthened the links between debt reduction and structural adjustment. Under the new initiative, countries that benefited from HIPC had to demonstrate their strong commitment to major IMF and World Bank economic reforms for at least six years. For many African activists, such as the members of Jubilee Africa, the Drop the Debt campaign failed to disentangle debt relief and structural adjustment.[67] The Drop the Debt campaign, in fact, did not manage to transcend the charitable and humanitarian framing to achieve a structural reform that would match the aspirations of Nyerere, Manley, and the NIEO. Instead, like many of the programs to make capitalism ethical that emerged starting in the 1960s, it embraced much of the existing structural framework of the global economy and in some cases even strengthened it. "What's been lost in the Bono-ization is [the] ability to change these power structures," argued the journalist and antiglobalization activist Naomi Klein.[68] In the following years, in fact, Bono went on to launch several charities with the economist Jeffrey Sachs, an ardent supporter of what Klein called the "shock doctrine" of IMF structural adjustment programs.[69]

FIGURE 6.1. A Drop the Debt rally organized by Christian Aid in London.
Photo by Steve Eason/Getty Images.

Microfinance, Income-Generation Schemes, and "People-Centered Development"

"One of the most dramatic things that OXFAM has witnessed in recent years," wrote John Clark in 1988, "has been the way in which the constraints stemming from the debt crisis and stabilization measures and policies have impinged upon our work." Until recently, Clark suggested, NGOs like Oxfam had been working on the level of small-scale projects "in villages, slum communities, and so on." But structural adjustment policies had rendered such projects obsolete. Countries such as Jamaica, Zambia, and Tanzania, which had been deeply affected by the IMF policies, had experienced such shock to their economies and health services that Oxfam and other agencies were suddenly forced to focus much of their effort on basic relief. According to Clark, "nobody in their right mind would deny the fact that countries such as Zambia needed a major adjustment and stabilization programme," but many people with whom Oxfam had been working were "not getting any benefits" from the IMF's programs. The trickle-down economic model of the IMF was flawed. There was a need "to rethink adjustment and put the bottom first."[70]

In a booklet from the same year, Christian Aid expressed similar dismay at how structural adjustment affected their work. "The problem of Third World debt is not a problem [of] international finance. It is a human problem having a dire effect on millions [of] people all over the world." The IMF's stringent debt policies had opened Third World economies to the global market, yet in doing so they impoverished individuals throughout the Third World. Structural adjustment was "cancelling out the positive benefits of aid."[71] Many of the organization's programs in Jamaica, Tanzania, and Bolivia had been rendered ineffective, and "the payment of debt which was not contracted by the poor themselves is shuttering peoples' hopes and creating further misery."[72] Christian Aid's Debt Working Group was worried that the crisis would lead to the contraction of their development program in favor of minimal emergency relief schemes. Like Clark, they suggested that there was a need for an alternative model that would put the very poor at its center. By 1995 this model was called "people-centered development" and was placed at the heart of the UN World Summit for Social Development.[73]

When in the late 1980s British nonprofits' debt campaigns gathered momentum, they focused on more than advocacy work. While they lobbied the IMF, the World Bank, and the British and American governments for debt forgiveness, nonprofits also sought a new microeconomic approach to development that would respond to the demands of the financialized economy and, at the same time, empower the very poor. They turned in response to microfinance and what came to be called "income-generation schemes," both of which focused on generating self-employment through small enterprise and through education for financial literacy. These income-generation schemes emphasized "the economic aspect of people's lives using economic tools," mobilizing credit as well as "training or advice in skills or business management and other support services for small business such as assistance with marketing and the provision of temporary trained personnel."[74] Microfinance was part of a broader trend in international aid throughout the 1980s and 1990s. It was popularized by the Grameen Bank (created in Bangladesh by the economist Muhammad Yunus and funded by the Ford Foundation) and Accion (an American nonprofit that operated across Latin America), which were both created in the 1970s.[75] By the late 1980s, however, the model was adopted by British nonprofits seeking new avenues for social development and hoping to revive their small-scale programs that had been rendered almost obsolete by structural adjustment programs.

Microfinance and income-generation schemes provided small loans, financial and business education, and community support necessary to generate microenterprises. The idea was to transform the loan recipient into an autonomous economic agent capable of both managing debt and leveraging aid to increase the value of her own work. As Christian Aid's Debt Working Group explained, the schemes aimed at supporting literacy and building awareness "about existing schemes for cheaper borrowing," while also encouraging self-employment.[76] With microfinance as a tool, both the urban and rural poor would transition from sole reliance on wage labor to creating their own "employment opportunities."[77] Unlike the more typical credit cooperatives supported by various aid organizations in the 1950s and 1960s, such programs were seen as a solution to global unemployment that worked by offering new business opportunities. It also allowed organizations like Oxfam to expand production to the informal economy and to women, who had been traditionally excluded from aid programs and would now be taught how to develop their own small business ventures. Nonprofits sold microfinance with the promise of liberating Third World workers from the state-enforced servitude of structural adjustment and from wage work, depicting these programs as a type of adjustment from the "bottom up."

At the heart of microfinance and income-generation schemes was an alternative economic theory about how to generate growth. Financial education, savings organizations, and microloans were all aimed at helping the poor invest in their own human capital. "Human capital is after all the most important factor of production in developing and industrial capital alike," argued Jacques de Larosiere, the managing director of the IMF, in July 1986. "Safeguarding human needs may imply that credit flows be managed so that small-scale producers are not crowded out by large enterprises and the public sector."[78] The theory of human capital had been developed in the 1960s by American neoliberal economists like Theodore Schultz—who shared the Nobel Prize in Economics with Arthur Lewis in 1979—and his student Gary Becker. But it was only popularized in the 1980s, when the waning of earlier ideas about development and growth made way for new theories. Refuting the mainstream of development theory, Schultz and Becker argued that growth did not depend solely on investment in technologies, industries, and physical resources. They suggested that the real motor behind economic growth was the skills, knowledge, and abilities of the laborer. Workers who were more skilled would earn and spend more. In doing so, they would increase their consumption, including of education, which in turn would provide a further investment in their future income. For its theorists, human capital represented a type of investment that focused on "activities that influence future real income through the imbedding of resources in people."[79] Instead of labor power, what was central to the worker was his or her "capital-ability."[80] The idea of human capital became central to microcredit because it was based on investment in future pecuniary income.[81]

British nonprofits used these ideas as the basis of their microfinance and income-generation schemes. They focused on an array of issues: financial management and financial literacy; strategic and leadership skills, marketing, and accounting; and teaching the poor to save and build their own assets. "For people born into poor households, the development of skills and experience to improve their chances of successful income generation (often called 'human capital') is likely to be difficult," stated an Oxfam booklet.[82] A type of adjustment "with a human face" that provided financial and business training would develop the human capital of their aid recipients. As the development economists and activists Stephen Devereux, Henry Pares, and John Best explained, rather than focusing on national economies, aid organizations wishing to reach the very poor should use credit to directly target the individual unit of the household economy.[83] Devereux and colleagues likened the household economy to a tree, with the lower branches representing the basic needs of the family. Development economists had traditionally given priority to the higher branches, which represented long-term investments in human capital through education and technologies. Although families desperately needed to invest in the higher branches to be lifted out of poverty, most development programs focused, by contrast, on the family's basic needs. What poor households required were both flexible credit and training in how to save for investment in the "higher branches." Credit without such training was "not enough" and would lead recipients to become "chronically indebted" or to default on their loans.[84] Activists sought to equip the poor with the ability to develop their own income opportunities. Education, skills, and knowledge were capital inseparable from the person who possessed them.

Educating people to save, while also creating savings facilities, became a central tenet of many British microfinance schemes. "The poor *can* save, *do* save, and *want* to save money," argued Stuart Rutherford, a British consultant in financial services who worked with many British, American, and Indian NGOs like Oxfam, CARE, Save the Children, ASA, Proshika, and ActionAid. "They need these lump sums to meet life-cycle needs, to cope with emergencies, and to grasp opportunities to acquire assets or develop businesses."[85] The idea was that the very poor could not have easy access to banking facilities and therefore could not accumulate wealth to reinvest in their future income. At the same time, they were often driven to use credit to manage immediate, basic needs at the expense of longer-term and more lucrative investments. Many training programs sought to address this problem. Others were run through "saveway clubs," community groups that met on a weekly basis, shared financial knowledge, and set up collective objectives to benefit each saver.[86]

An early outlier was Save the Children's "Kiddy Bank" in northern Bangladesh. Aimed at younger children, the bank was part of a series of savings and credit programs that responded to the turmoil caused by the 1974 floods. Repurposing the idea of the "piggy bank," the Kiddy Bank was set up in 1980 as part of the organization's broader goal of teaching children to save for their own education. The idea, according to Azam Ali, the creator of the scheme, "wasn't just saving for its own sake." Ali wanted children "to aim at acquiring assets that would produce income. . . . a little inspiration to try to change their fate."[87] The project offered children a small loan which, if they managed to keep it for a certain amount of time, could be used to buy a goat kid. The child would then raise the kid, and its increasing value would fund the costs of the child's education.[88]

In one of its promotional campaigns, Save the Children highlighted the efforts of Firoza Begum, who was among the first children to participate in the Kiddy Bank. According to the organization, in the early 1980s Begum was identified by a Save the Children worker to be nutritionally at risk and was subscribed to the Kiddy Bank. With her savings, a meager 40 *taka*, Begum took out a loan for 300 *taka* and bought a sheep. Eight years later, in the last year of high school and needing to pay a fee to take her exams, Begum sold the sheep. Its offspring also financed Begum's younger brother's education. When Begum married, she left the latest batch of lambs as a gift to her parents, and eventually she herself became a Save the Children aid worker, a common trajectory in the 1980s. Begum, in fact, served as an ideal model of the scheme. She represented how human capital could be built through the financialization of aid. Through the Kiddy Bank, Bangladeshi children like Begum learned how to manage credit from an early age, as well as how to accumulate savings and manage their own debt.

In a report he wrote for the organization, Stuart Rutherford argued that "one of the charms of the scheme is that it was essentially self-financing."[89] Capital for the loans came from the project itself, including the children's savings, the sale of produce from the school's kitchen garden, Save the Children centers' registration fees, and bank interest. Save the Children was criticized for not offering interest on the children's deposits, but Rutherford maintained that the interest was unnecessary since most savers were also borrowers and benefited just as much from not paying interest on their loans. "Not paying interest also made the accounting transparently simple," Rutherford added.[90] This was a boon for the new efficiency-oriented activism.

In other examples, such as Oxfam's program in Zaire, British organizations used microfinance to fund existing rural development programs. The Zaire program, which ran throughout the 1980s and 1990s, gave small-scale cultivators credit to purchase intermediate technologies such as plowing equipment, thereby increasing by 350 percent the area of land each household could cultivate.[91] But credit was given under clear conditions: applicants must cultivate their lands communally, in groups of seven or more, for two growing seasons. They also had to prove their ability to market their produce by putting up 25 percent of the costs of the equipment themselves. Oxfam additionally provided these groups with training in veterinary and agricultural skills as well as carpentry, equipment maintenance, and bookkeeping, in addition to ongoing consultation services.[92] As Dr B. N. Okwuosa, an Oxfam advisor in Zaire, argued, "to have a successful credit programme, it will have to be an integral part of a rural development programme: i.e. there must be supporting services, a viable market, price incentives, good infrastructure and extension services."[93]

It was not only rural development programs that took on a pedagogical mission to develop the human capital of the poor. Nothing was more representative of the turn toward financialization than the work done with the handicraft sector in places like India, where handicraft work was "the second category of employment after agriculture."[94] The handicraft sector, which had already been the heart of British fair-trade programs in the early 1970s, now became the focal point of new training programs, workshops, and manuals in financial management geared to developing the human capital of its producers and making handicraft workers into independent entrepreneurs. In the handicraft sector, training had both financial and emotional goals. It was geared toward restructuring the "solidarity market," as one aid worker called it,[95] so as to make it more lucrative, but it also sought to build the confidence of producers, especially women, who were the main participants. The "lack of literacy skills," argued Devereux, Pares, and Best's manual, "may also reduce [poor women's] confidence and willingness to expand their economic activity to a level where it is of sufficient size to produce enough income to keep them and their dependents."[96]

Based on its experience importing handicraft work through its Bridge program, originally developed in the 1970s, Oxfam became the main facilitator of such training programs beginning in the late 1980s and throughout the 1990s. It worked with dozens of independent handicraft producers, as well as with local charities and microfinancial institutions in South Asia. Using financial knowledge and strategic management tools, it taught handicraft producers how to receive and manage microcredit loans, how to price and value their work, and, finally, how to sell their products on national and international markets.

A good example of this type of program was Oxfam's August 1991 workshop "Management of Handicraft Projects" for the rural and urban artisans of Orissa. The workshop introduced artisans to a representative of an export company, Anurag Mittal from Pushpanjali Exports, who had previously collaborated with Oxfam Trading and taught the participants how to export their products themselves. His panel covered export samples, the application process for the allotment of an Import-Export Code, registration with the Export Promotion Council for Handicrafts, registration with the Income Tax Authorities, and applications for various certifications (such as a GSP certificate). In addition, Oxfam introduced participants to new credit facilities, like the Small Industrial Development Bank of India, which funded microloans to handicraft producers without requiring a security deposit and offered flexible interest rates with a repayment period of ten years. The purpose was both to educate small producers on how to generate their own income by building a microenterprise and to directly put them in touch with potential microlenders.[97]

FIGURE 6.2. Mat weaving workshop in Cherthala, Kerala, India.

Another workshop, a four-day management training program held in February 1993, was billed as "the basic training for the manager of a small-scale income generation project."[98] It focused on basic accounting, cash flow management, quality control, cost management, pricing, packaging, and presentation. Practical rather than theoretical in emphasis, it included activities like solving common problems in production and in financial management, making charts and models and applying them to a specific business, discussions with experts in the field of marketing, and short explanatory videoclips on how to run a balance sheet. The workshop also included a special session with a manager from a local banking branch who explained how to negotiate for financial help and manage capital. On the final day, participants used the various tools they had acquired during the workshop and presented a poster about their products.

These training programs reshaped ideas about the value of handicrafts, the labor that produced them, and the markets where they were bought and sold. In the old fair-trade model, handicraft products derived their price from the labor of the producer and the time put into making the product. Training for financialization, however, taught producers to price their product based on their assessment of market demand—a prediction of a product's pecuniary value. The financialization of trade altered the value of labor. It was now the potential value of a product that established the amount a handicraft producer would be compensated for her or his labor. The financialization of handicraft work did not herald a reform in global labor relations (such as a minimum wage). Instead, it sought to turn handicraft producers and other precarious workers into entrepreneurs responsible for reading market trends and pricing their products accordingly. In other words, they moved the onus of ending inequalities to the poor themselves.

Microcredit and savings schemes may have provided the capital to invest in a product, according to Oxfam, but the success of the venture would depend on an artisan's ability to connect with consumers. "There is . . . no such things as a 'market,'" explained the manual. "Markets are defined according to the type of customers who use them."[99] The organization spent a great deal of energy training artisans to understand the various markets they operated in and the consumers they catered to. "Utility to the consumer, and competition from other products, are not the only factors influencing the market's perception of value."[100] It was the presentation, display, promotion, packaging, labeling, and display that raised a product's price on the market. "You must develop a marketing mentality when making plans," Oxfam explained.

Here Oxfam's activists drew on the field of strategic management, which had its roots in both military planning initiatives in the postwar United States and the discourse of managerialism that emerged in the 1950s. Strategic management was in fact strongly connected to what the historian Angus Burgin has called "the reinvention of entrepreneurship" in the United States, which emphasized that anyone, whether a large corporation or an independent trader, could cultivate entrepreneurial behavior and that "learning such behaviors should be a fundamental part of business education for the masses."[101] By the 1980s, strategic management had emerged as a distinct discipline that advised corporations on how to create long-term economic rents.[102] At its core, it emphasized the idea that value was constituted from what the customer sought. Its proponents preached the virtues of "competitive advantage," which started with "a company's existing attributes to 'design' an appropriate 'choice of products and markets' and a structure to support and deliver it."[103] For Oxfam, small-scale handicraft producers could utilize the lessons of strategic management in their own businesses. Activists called upon artisans to think about building their business through what strategic management literature called "a SWOT analysis," that is, "a summary of its main strengths, weaknesses, opportunities, and threats." Financialization here meant more than indebtedness and good saving habits: above all, charities like Oxfam pushed handicraft workers to value marketing over production and to market their product with an eye to consumer desire above all else.

Oxfam, then, was urging producers to minimize "traditional" utility and focus instead on the purpose a product might have for consumers. "Purpose is not to be confused with function; the purpose may be to produce something purely decorative," Oxfam explained.[104] What made the handicraft industry so distinct, according to Oxfam, was a product's decorative and emotional purpose. That purpose was "the only weapon available to handicraft producers to fight industrial competition."[105] The organization spent a great deal of its time on marketing assistance, with numerous workshops specifically aimed at teaching producers how to invest in printed labels, eye-catching packaging, and attractive displays that would enhance a product's value to consumers.

Nowhere was this value greater than in international and Western markets, according to Oxfam. While handicraft producers should sell to both domestic and international markets, Oxfam advisors wrote, Western markets had the potential of becoming the most lucrative. This was the key to the idea of competitive advantage. As an Oxfam handbook explained, "The market is far from being a passive entity."[106] The more sophisticated the market, the more a product's presentation would add to its overall value. In metropolitan and overseas markets, consumers would have less knowledge about the costs and labor that went into the production of a handicraft item. Instead, these consumers would be more interested in its aesthetic and emotional value.

Finally, Oxfam's approach to the market had a clear postimperial aim. At the heart of the organization's financial training was the goal of teaching artisans how to capitalize on their own value as Third World producers. According to Oxfam, "Designers have created belts, bags, clothing and soft furnishings from traditional pieces of textile work consistent with the best formula for export handicraft design: adapting what is traditional in the country of production to the taste in the country of sale."[107] Handicraft products could satisfy the Western desire to own an authentic piece of their "tradition," and tradition itself could be packaged and marketed. Handicraft producers, armed with new financial skills and credit to invest in their craft, could penetrate the Western, mass-produced market by capitalizing on their own heritage.

In some cases, "tradition" had to be manufactured: some of Oxfam's training programs included classes in traditional tie-dyeing methods because a number of producers were not familiar with them. Financialization returned to and reinvented traditional society, after various development programs— including the fair-trade imports of products—had tried to modernize them.[108] Handicraft products, Oxfam argued, had high value precisely because they sold the Western consumer the promise of an authentic traditional craft. As the organization explained,

> through harnessing the creative talents of artisans, there opens up a path for the future. *It is in the decorative, artistic tradition that the distinctiveness of a country's production lies.* . . . Countries wanting to export handicrafts should fight off competition from industry by studying their own unique traditions, and adapting these to the life-styles of modern consumers.[109]

FIGURE 6.3. "Shopping for a Fairer World," 1991.

So important was the halo of authenticity that Oxfam suggested including a personal note with information about the product and the people who made it. The organization offered the example of a small cooperative in Africa that sold wooden sculptures—"the design of which was rooted in the cultural tradition of the producers"—in some Oxfam shops. "Most people were not prepared to pay the price we were asking without getting that information."[110] Personalizing the product increased its value. While industrial and mass production focused on standardization, handicraft producers could offer the intimacy of their own cultural traditions, or at least what the Western consumer understood those traditions to be. The financialization of aid proposed a different form of globalization, one that repurposed fantasies about local, authentic traditions of Third World communities and distributed them on a global scale.

Microenterprise, Social Adjustments, and "Supply-Side Socialism"

In 1999 the New Economics Foundation, a nonprofit founded to confront the international debt crisis and that acted as manager of the Jubilee 2000 campaign and the Debt Crisis Network, published a booklet in collaboration with Oxfam titled *Poverty, Social Exclusion and Microfinance in Britain*. "Since the late 1970s, inequality in Britain has steadily grown, and poverty has become increasingly concentrated in certain geographical areas," the book opened. "The change to a New Labour regime in May 1997 signalled the start of a high-level government engagement with the challenge of countering poverty and social exclusion. At the same time, the anti-poverty lobby of non-government organisations and other civil-society groups, who had become used to working with a government which denied the existence of poverty in Britain, has continued to press the current government hard" to provide a plan for social development.[111] The book explored how the international experience of microfinance could serve as the basis for a new social and economic policy to tackle the problem of unemployment and social exclusion in Britain. The study was part of a new focus by the nonprofit sector, which traditionally concentrated on international aid abroad and the debt crisis in the Third World, on the role of microfinance in poverty alleviation and employment generation in Britain itself.

Between the mid-1990s and the early 2010s, microfinance, microenterprise, and income-generation schemes became popular strategies for solving the problem of poverty and unemployment in Britain. For its advocates, microfinance was perceived as "the missing link in the new monetized market."[112] "In the face of globalization," one activist argued, microfinance offered an alternative mode of "subsistence and participation for the poor."[113] Such approaches were conceived as a type of social adjustment that would respond to the challenges left by the Thatcherite neoliberal government over the long 1980s, which prioritized privatization, financialization, and the reduction of public services across Britain. Simultaneously, microfinance and income-generation schemes were embraced by nonprofits like Oxfam and the New Economics Foundation as well as by New Labour as part of a new social policy that focused particularly on women and ethnic minorities. "In Britain today, millions are still trapped in a cash economy," declared the New Labour prime minister Tony Blair.[114] While the neoliberal Thatcher government prioritized tax credits as a form of welfare, the New Labour government collaborated with nonprofits to place self-employment, entrepreneurship, and financial literacy—through microenterprise—at the center of the British welfare state.

The repurposing of "adjustment with a human face" for welfare policies was not an exclusively British strategy. Microfinance became especially popular after the fall of the Iron Curtain. In the 1990s, American, British, and

Western European organizations funded microcredit schemes in former Soviet countries, with the American-Polish Fundusz Mikro being perhaps the largest and most successful.[115] After the liberalization of the Polish economy in the early 1990s,[116] Fundusz Mikro was established to boost the Polish economy with microloans and to mitigate unemployment. The organization was headed by a British investment banker named Rosalind Copisarow, who had been working in Poland as J. P. Morgan's vice president and country officer. It was funded by the Polish American Enterprise Fund and set up by the Bush administration. With a budget of $240 million, it aimed to foster a private sector in Poland with similar outposts across the Eastern Bloc.[117] Modeled after nonprofit schemes in the Third World, Fundusz Mikro offered mutual guarantees to borrowers, "carpenters, hairdressers, stonemasons, metal workers, car repair mechanics, computer consultants, taxi drivers and stall/shop keepers" who could not otherwise access financial services.[118] Within four years, the organization had serviced around 25,000 loans worth $25 million, with a consistent repayment rate of 98 percent, and had thus become self-sustaining.[119] Based on this experience, Copisarow went on to found a similar organization in Britain, called Street UK, which supported a whole range of home-based businesses that were either too small or too risky to be supported by mainstream banking services.

Indeed, during the 1990s, microcredit schemes became the main model for welfare and development programs in the United States and Britain.[120] Microfinance, according to its champions, could emancipate and empower poor families in Chicago, Illinois, and Birmingham, UK, as much as it could those who lived in Dhaka, Bangladesh. Yet efforts to apply microfinance in the global North, experts argued, were not universal panaceas. They needed to be tailored to existing welfare services. While in the Third World microfinance was designed to reach the poorest of the poor, in the global North, aid workers and economists argued, microfinance was more suitable for working-class populations and ethnic minorities who had already begun some kind of business venture and were relatively educated (with at least a high school diploma). In the global North, experts claimed, the costs of self-employment were higher because of complicated business regulations, zoning laws, and higher taxes. They suggested making self-employment part of a larger portfolio of welfare services that targeted women, ethnic minorities, and refugee communities in particular.[121]

In the United States, as the historian Lily Geismer has shown, microfinance was first adopted in the 1980s as a strategy for urban development in Chicago and later by the Clinton administration as part of its various welfare programs.[122] In Chicago, it was the Ford Foundation that suggested that the ShoreBank Corporation—a community development program for urban regeneration run through Chicago's South Shore Bank—consult with Muhammad Yunus, one of the so-called fathers of microfinance in Bangladesh, on how to provide "creatively structured" finance and community-structured finance that would generate income through microenterprise.[123] The bank was set up as a holding company intended to help African American residents—"redlined" by traditional banking services—with small loans to purchase and rehabilitate housing units and to start local businesses. Based on this experience, the organization also founded the Women's Self-Employment Project in 1986 in Chicago. The latter was a microfinance organization focused directly on helping unemployed women. The program, called the Full Circle Fund, operated in churches and childcare centers to identify women who were already running a small, income-generating home-based business.[124] The majority of its clients were African American women and Latinas.

By the 1990s, microfinance was the basis of the Clinton administration's welfare reform as well as its international aid initiatives, and formed part of a broader financialized vision for a community development agenda that used tax breaks to incentivize private industries and employment in poor, urban communities, including self-employment through small businesses.[125] As Hillary Clinton later argued, microcredit projects could create a ripple effect "not only in lifting individuals out of poverty and moving mothers from welfare to work, but in creating jobs, promoting businesses and building capital in depressed areas."[126] Small-scale lending epitomized the new type of market-based politics that characterized the Clintons' vision of welfare policies.[127] It offered a model that fused community development and the promotion of self-help and individual empowerment with an approach to gender derived from second-wave feminism. Most broadly, microfinance offered a new vision of welfare that was based on a mixed economy of market-oriented aid. In 1996 it even became one of the work options available under the Personal Responsibility and Work Opportunity Reconciliation Act (PRWORA), which eradicated the Aid to Families with Dependent Children program and allowed welfare recipients the opportunity to retain their benefits for a set period while starting their own businesses.

In Britain in the late 1990s, microfinance became central for New Labour in its reimagining of the British welfare state. It was adopted by activists and New Labour politicians, who rejected the socialism-capitalism dichotomy and sought to fuse welfare with market liberalism.[128] For Third Way centrists, microfinance joined the turn to fiscal redistribution of welfare through transfer payments and the tax credit system.[129] Traditionally, Labour had made wage labor the centerpiece of its employment policy because the flexibility embedded within self-employment was seen as exploitative, precarious, and lacking social security. Labour policies therefore focused on promoting employment opportunities by supporting large-scale industries. After its defeat in the 1992 elections, however, Labour shifted its focus to relieving poverty outside the labor market. Even before it won the 1997 elections, New

Labour, as it was conceived by Tony Blair and Gordon Brown, had promoted "supply-side socialism," which looked for welfare measures that would soften the impact of deindustrialization instead of seeking to bring back old industries. If old Labour had focused on reforming the structure of the job market altogether, New Labour concentrated on shaping the aspirations of employees. Taking its cue from the Clinton administration's welfare reforms, especially PRWORA, New Labour devised a new welfare-to-work policy that would develop individual skills and boost entrepreneurial spirit.[130]

When the Blair government announced a New Deal for the unemployed in 1997, it designated a new role for the welfare state, at least rhetorically. The party abandoned redistribution as a means of tackling poverty and instead placed a strong emphasis on market inclusion as the primary goal of the welfare state.[131] Although in some ways their policies built on Conservative policies from the 1980s that made unemployment benefits conditional, New Labour additionally sought to expand individual opportunities while advancing social cohesion and community renewal. Their New Deal for the unemployed further aimed to respond to the malleable, precarious, and globalized job market. The British New Deal's welfare-to-work programs targeted specific social groups—such as young people and single parents—who had been excluded from the workplace. It provided them with resources, training, and personal advice—through, for example, Training and Enterprise Councils—in order to improve their chances of asserting themselves in the workforce. As Gordon Brown later stated, "globalisation can be for the people or against the people."[132] It was the role of the state to ensure the former by helping reshape individuals for increasingly global markets.

Among other measures, New Labour devised a strategy for community development, especially in poor urban areas. Known as the Social Exclusion Unit, the program mandated aid to individuals or regions that suffered from unemployment as well as high crime rates.[133] It sought to "bridge the gap between the poorest neighborhoods and the rest of Britain" through measures such as the creation of "employment zones."[134] The latter were modeled on the Clinton administration's "empowerment zones"[135] and were a collaboration between local councils and private businesses that used tax incentives and unpaid work experience to generate work opportunities in urban areas. "The renewal of deprived local communities," wrote Blair's advisor and Third Way idealogue Anthony Giddens, depended on "the encouragement of economic enterprise as a means of generating a broader civic recovery."[136] The zones specifically focused on the creation of business enterprise and aimed "to help with moving from welfare to self-employment," among other opportunities.[137] The program provided advice and training, including access to capital through "innovative approaches such as 'microcredit.'"[138] Indeed, while initially the New Deal did not offer microfinance through government funding,[139] the Social Exclusion Unit placed a strong emphasis on ending financial exclusion and "red-lining"[140] in order to widen access to financial services for people living in poor neighborhoods.

It was no surprise, then, that for activists like Ruth Pearson, microfinance fit perfectly within New Labour's New Deal. Since 1987, Pearson, who was previously a researcher at the Institute of Development Studies, had been running the Women's Employment, Enterprise and Training Unit, an organization in Norwich set up to lobby the government on behalf of unemployed and marginalized women and to provide them with employment, enterprise, and training opportunities. Many of the unit's programs—such as training in information technology—were based on collaborations with local businesses and were later officially adopted by local councils.[141] In May 1997, the same month that New Labour was elected, the Women's Employment, Enterprise and Training Unit began a microfinance scheme targeted at unemployed and socially excluded women in Norwich (a majority of them were likely white). The scheme, called the Full Circle Project, was headed by Pearson, funded primarily by Oxfam, and modeled after its Chicago counterpart and the microfinance programs in Bangladesh and India. It offered credit for low-income and socially excluded women who wanted to build their own businesses, as well as counseling, training, labor-market guidance, and business support. It worked with circles of four to six women and used the principle of joint liability for loan decisions and repayments.[142]

Pearson hoped that Norwich's Full Circle Project would serve as a model for the government's national welfare reforms. And indeed, within less than a year the project received support from the local council and was endorsed by several ministers from the UK Department of Employment. According to Pearson, microfinance was the missing link within New Labour's welfare-to-work policies: "The channelling of credit and entrepreneurial support services to the welfare-dependent can be seen as extending economic opportunity to the socially excluded."[143] While welfare-to-work policies focused on wage employment, Pearson argued that it neglected self-employment. For Pearson, microfinance could become a path to self-employment in a manner that would fit within the welfare-to-work program and "includes the option of training and credit for potential small entrepreneurs."[144] Pearson called on the government to develop a similar microfinance program, one that would not clash with existing benefit payments, which were the main subsistence income in the initial stages of establishing a small business.

Pearson also used Norwich's Full Circle Project as a model to lobby local and national governments to offer a "welfare waiver" that would protect the future welfare entitlements of those who took out microloans. In Britain, informal economic activities like microfinance are considered "something to be discovered, taxed, and probably eliminated rather than being considered as evidence of entrepreneurial activity which might contribute to local economic regeneration, earnings, and merit entitlements to training and financial and other support from the public purse."[145] In fact, she argued, while in the Third World the informal sector was considered "unemployment disguised as employment," in Britain the informal sector "is seen as employment disguised as unemployment."[146] The informal sector in Britain, she suggested, is criminalized and considered a way of "cheating" the welfare system. Without formal support from the welfare state, low-income individuals who chose the path of self-employment could be further marginalized and entrenched in poverty.

There were two overlapping, socially excluded groups that, according to Pearson, particularly benefited from microfinance programs: women and ethnic minorities. In the case of women, Pearson suggested that microenterprise was a particularly attractive path to self-employment because it offered women the flexibility of working from home even if they had small children. It was a project aligned with the agenda of second-wave feminism and supported businesses such as "office services, training, massage, children's clothing and party wear, knitwear and gardening board games."[147] The schemes were a perfect way, Pearson claimed, to include women in a precarious and global job market that was already becoming concentrated on the service sector. Quoting Giddens's *The Third Way*, Pearson suggested that microenterprise helped extend the reach of the welfare state and included support for new, more flexible forms of work beyond the traditional nine-to-five job.[148]

The second group that benefited from microfinance, according to Pearson, was ethnic minorities. Microfinance connected them to commercial banking providers, who had traditionally excluded them, at the same time that it helped them build a credit history. Microfinance also gave legitimacy to economic activities in the informal and so-called gray economy, which has often been occupied by ethnic minorities. "In the United Kingdom," according to Pearson, "the small 'corner shop' culture tends to be confined to the margins of the economy, particularly in localities where such activities have been the preserve of ethnic minorities. Self-employment and microenterprise has [*sic*] often been seen as 'cheating.' . . . This is compounded by the hostility towards new immigration from the Commonwealth."[149] Incorporating microfinance into welfare programs, according to Pearson, was a path out of financial exclusion as well as an opportunity to combat racial prejudice.

Furthermore, Pearson argued, microfinance offered a way to encourage some ethnic minorities, like Commonwealth immigrants, to take financial risks and open their own businesses. Microfinance's solidarity groups offered broad financial education and literacy, "essential for full social participation and survival." It increased the "employability and employment readiness" of groups such as ethnic minorities by taking them off of welfare benefits.[150] In fact, microfinance was a path to the labor market because it offered skills that "have transferability into the mainstream labour market and other aspects of modern life."[151] As such, it benefited both individuals and the wider community.

Eventually Pearson's advocacy for the financial inclusion of ethnic minorities joined a broader contemporary conversation, and in the 1990s microfinance took on an explicitly racialized and postimperial aim. For Third Way politicians, lending provided a solution to the problems of race relations in Britain at a time when the difficulties encountered by ethnic minorities in operating their own businesses were becoming national news.[152] "The use of credit by people from minority ethnic groups was more limited than was justified by their financial circumstances," claimed the Policy Studies Institute. "Cultural differences and the credit industry's lack of understanding of the needs of ethnic minority communities were also felt to limit access. There were also allegations of racism in the high street credit industry."[153] The problem of small credit and financial exclusion of ethnic minorities became the heart of the new political discourse. "Deregulation of financial services has widened access to banking services for most people in the UK, but a minority have needs that are largely unmet by a competitive market," explained the geographer Elaine Kempson from the Personal Finance Research Centre at the University of Bristol. "These needs include both personal and micro-enterprise banking."[154] She argued that research overwhelmingly showed that particular ethnic groups encountered disproportionate difficulty in obtaining loans for private enterprise.

Financial exclusion, according to Kempson and others, affected different ethnic groups in various ways. "People with an unstable work history, young people, women and people from African and Caribbean, Pakistani or Bangladeshi communities are especially likely to be excluded," she argued.[155] But each group had different access to financial resources. Since financial services in general, and credit in particular, were based on reputation and personal history, specific groups of ethnic minorities encountered different forms of informal and implicit discrimination. African and Caribbean people, she reported, "feel particularly disadvantaged in this respect . . . while Pakistani and Bangladeshi entrepreneurs believe that the high street banks often fail to understand the nature of the business they wish to run."[156] Creditworthiness and commercial microloans have often been based on racial stereotypes. According to Kempson, African and Caribbean people were almost entirely excluded from banking services, while the funding of Asian businesses was both highly selective and rooted in stereotypes, "so that those who are not running businesses that are considered typically Asian (such as take-away restaurants or corner shops) tend to be turned down for loans."[157] In other words, Indian, Pakistani, and Bangladeshi minorities were being seen as a model "entrepreneurial minority" in the commercial sector, but even they could not transcend racial profiling in lending. Nongovernmental organizations were making progress in combating these exclusions, but, as many argued, the support of the welfare state was indispensable in fighting such prejudices. By 1998, these calls were heeded when the government issued new guidelines that began to include microenterprise as one of the options for its welfare-to-work programs. In this way, microfinance became part of the welfare state's response to exclusion and inequality.

Credit Where Solidarity Is Due

When in the 1960s E. F. Schumacher developed his philosophy of "economics as if people mattered," he could not have anticipated the debt crisis and the rising importance of finance in the global economy. Instead, Schumacher was thinking about productive economies, the problem of unemployment and corporate monopolies, the structure of the welfare state and the limits of nationalization. Schumacher died in 1977, but his economic vision survived him in the logic of microfinance that emerged in the 1980s. Microfinance incorporated much of Schumacher's critique of the dual economy and the economics that focused on GNP growth. It was devised as a financial technology to empower individuals, generate employment, and create solidarity from the "grassroots." It reprised most of Schumacher's call for a "technology with a human face."[158]

The debt crisis and the centrality of finance in the global economy in the 1980s altered the nonprofit world's ideas about the purpose of fair-trade markets and what kind of economic subjects they were meant to create. In the early 1970s, when activists conceived of these markets amid international calls to decolonize the global economy, they sought to transform production from a localized, informal craft to a lucrative entrepreneurial activity. "The man of creative freedom is the entrepreneur," wrote Schumacher in an essay in *Small Is Beautiful* in defense of small-scale enterprise.[159] The ethical capitalism of British nonprofits was intended to unleash the creativity of Third World producers as entrepreneurs and to free producers from the constraints of state-led economies. By the late 1980s, in response to financialization and the "debt state," activists had shifted their attention to a different model that prioritized microenterprise.[160] The nonprofit sector embraced microfinance and income-generation schemes as a new ethical solution to the problem of global unemployment. Both approaches became part of ethical direct investment in people as human capital, rather than in their fair-trade products. By the late 1990s, microfinance had become an integral part of the financialized model of aid embraced by British Third Way politicians and a key part of the portfolio of services offered by the welfare state.

Epilogue

IN AN INTERNAL report that circulated in 1991, Oxfam's Corporate Relations Unit proclaimed that the nature of capitalism had changed. Nonprofits now operated in a new type of economy, in which social and environmental values, far from being antithetical to "healthy profit margins," were in fact integral to financial success. Historically, the report explained, there were only a few corporations that supported charities out of "altruistic" motives. The British multinational Cadbury was one well-known example. But the report pointed out that, in the economic conjuncture of the late twentieth century, "more and more companies are reassessing their activities in the light of growing public demand for ethical business practice." And it was not only corporations who were doing so. "A recent poll in the *Daily Telegraph* indicated that some 50% of [British] consumers [are] undertaking some form of product boycott," the report noted. "Ethical investments are growing and there are many examples of ethical products gaining a respectable niche in mainstream consumer markets." Consumers and investors were becoming equally concerned with ethical values. "Business today," Oxfam's report concluded, "is about 'adding value' in a crowded, ever more competitive marketplace and so is ripe for advocacy on behalf of the poor, not because it *threatens* . . . business but because it *enhances* it."[1]

Oxfam's report reflected dynamics also central to the growth of the fair-trade movement in the 1990s and the role of nonprofits within it. The decade saw the proliferation of alternative trade organizations and the growth of corporate partnerships with NGOs and charities. Fair-trade certified goods, new to the period, began to take up a sizable portion of the European, British, and eventually American consumer markets. Fair-trade coffee, for example, went from a minor 0.03 percent of the Dutch and French markets to around 5 percent in 1995. In Britain, Cafédirect (founded by Twin Trading), came to command 14 percent of the total market in the country by the new millennium. In the mid-2000s, activists and fair-trade advocates in the United States even managed to convince Starbucks to sell fair-trade certified coffee in 2,300 of its U.S. stores.[2] And it was not only coffee. Equally important were other products such as bananas, sugar, chocolate, and handicrafts. Many British and American businesses—from Nike and Coca Cola to Body Shop and Virgin Group—embraced some form of social engagement as part of their branding. More than half of British businesses, according to one survey, have at one time or another allied with charities to achieve specific corporate objectives.[3] The Hanley Centre for Business Responsibility reported that the "caring 90s" saw a cultural shift away from the materialism of the previous decades toward an increasing emphasis on ethical consumerism and environmental consciousness.[4] Ethical investments became the new frontier for a growing field of mass investments in Britain and beyond.[5] At the same time, the solidarity economy expanded beyond a few British nonprofits and their trading ventures to become part of a broader culture within financial capitalism, one that would increasingly come to shape the new millennium.

The formation of this new culture was not without opposition. In the early 2000s, the journalist and activist Naomi Klein famously criticized the new culture of corporate social consciousness for tricking consumers into buying a brand. Consumers, she argued, were repeatedly manipulated by a "global web of logos and products . . . couched in the euphoric marketing rhetoric of the global village."[6] For Klein, however, this new culture of capitalism provided transnational corporations with an alibi to further their exploitative practices. Companies like Nike sold their customers the illusion they were "enhanc[ing] people's lives through sports and fitness." The British Body Shop company framed its business mission around a "political philosophy about women, the environment and ethical business." Richard Branson—the head of Virgin Group (and a frequent collaborator with Oxfam and Save the Children)—bluntly admitted to Klein that his goal was to "build brands not around products but around reputation."[7] Klein, who was active in the antiglobalization movement of the early 2000s, argued that such ethical corporate branding enabled, and cloaked the exploitative nature of, the neoliberal capitalism of the period.

Klein's critique primarily targeted businesses rather than the NGOs that enabled them. Yet, as this book has shown, nonprofits—especially nongovernmental aid organizations—played an important role in paving the way for much of the economic and emotional transformation that shaped this new culture of capitalism. During the second half of the twentieth century, nonprofits used their welfare and development programs to form alternative fair-trade companies while also shaping consumer desire for ethically sourced food and goods from former colonies. Importantly, nonprofits trained producer groups across the former British empire to participate in new "solidarity markets" that would be tailored to consumer needs. Large nonprofits also partnered with the for-profit world, putting a humanitarian and sometimes environmental seal of approval on their products while recruiting these companies to assist in their development programs. These nonprofits carved out new tax exemptions in British law for many such collaborations and alternative trade activities. Nonprofits also helped shape consumer behavior: many organizations launched transnational boycotts against particular multinationals, urging consumers to abstain from products linked to world hunger, ecological degradation, labor exploitation, and even dubious advertising methods. With the introduction of microfinance, nonprofits also purported to offer British consumers a way to remedy the structural inequalities written into the debt crisis and to ethically invest in individual entrepreneurs in what was then called the Third World. By the 1990s, nonprofits had come to articulate their own "people-centered" approach to development, which was then embraced by other international organizations, businesses, and governments. This approach emphasized decentralization, supported entrepreneurship, and often encouraged private capital over state investment, all in the name of ethical capitalism. In some cases, this vision even became a pretext for disinvestment in social services in the name of building a society made up of voluntary organizations and businesses.

Today, many of the features that were central to the solidarity economy would commonly be associated with conservative neoliberal policies. From decentralization to privatization and the culture of entrepreneurship, these features became the main characteristics of the Thatcher-Major era and its disinvestment from the welfare and developmental state. We often identify them with conservative think tanks like the Institute of Economic Affairs rather than the work of nonprofits like Oxfam.[8] Historians have viewed these ideas as part of the neoliberal tool kit that captured the British left: the New Labour government that succeeded Thatcherism in the late 1990s is often depicted as the reluctant inheritor of neoliberalism, and scholars of New Labour have frequently explained the party's "modernization" since 1983 as a necessary if regrettable response to the Thatcherite and neoliberal challenge. In this narrative, New Labour's turn to "market socialism" and especially the party's abandonment of public ownership were part a series of concessions needed to win working- and middle-class voters. Rarely is this turn described as the product of the left's own *internal* discussions—ongoing since the 1950s and 1960s—about British capitalism rather than neoliberalism and the future of socialism.[9]

But what we might consider central tenets of conservative neoliberal thinking originated in part in left-wing conversations over fairness, redistribution, sustainability, and the responsibility of Britons to former colonial economies. Ideas about decentralization and entrepreneurship were embedded within socialist debates over the future of ownership and the meaning of work in Britain. Such ideas were not exclusive to the right-wing or neoliberal critique of state-led national economies, concerned with socialist authoritarianism and the encasement of markets. They were also part of a left-wing project animated by a socialist critique of the economism inherent in mid-century statism and national ownership.[10] The nonprofit sector took up these ideas as part of a project to make capitalism ethical—one that sidelined the responsibility of the state in delivering public goods in favor of decentralized and voluntary welfare aid. While nonprofits were perhaps not the main drivers of deregulation, they nevertheless helped legitimize it. The history of the solidarity economy opens new avenues for understanding the history of late twentieth-century capitalism and for revising the history of neoliberalism. It shows that what we might consider part of a conservative neoliberal project was instead part of a broader culture of capitalism of the late twentieth century, a fact that helps explain the extensive adoption of market ideologies.

A central thread in this story has been the sidelining of the state in the management of the national and global economy. While the search for ethical capitalism was never fully antistatist, its proponents turned away from the state as the central agent of economic development, instead favoring a voluntary, mixed, and decentralized economy. Between the 1940s and the 1990s, the nonprofit sector emerged as a central actor in the economy, and the project of making capitalism ethical positioned nongovernmental actors—both nonprofit and for-profit agencies alike—as agents as central to the transformation of twentieth-century capitalism as trade unions, policymakers, and intergovernmental agencies.

Vital to the success of this alternative, nongovernmental economics was its claim to operate from below. Of course, NGOs often worked closely with governments in both the former metropoles and the postcolonial states. They supported a variety of projects, including some that would be considered "top-down" or that followed more "macro" approaches to development aid. But the solidarity economy upheld nonprofits as the central agents of economic change and celebrated their work on a "grassroots" level. This approach allowed nonprofits to claim to represent Third World producers and British and Western consumers alike, and to protect both producers and consumers from predatory capitalism. Nonprofits thereby carved out a central place in the aid industry while remaining open to working alongside large international aid agencies like the World Bank and national and supranational bodies like the European Economic Community.

The nonprofit sector aspired to represent the overlooked stakeholders in the global economy: workers, consumers, and local communities. But they operated alongside rather than against the for-profit sector, and they elbowed aside the state agencies and trade unions that had previously represented workers and consumers in the economy. Positioning themselves as the advocates of cross-border, grassroots constituencies, nongovernmental activists sought to offer an alternative to both private ownership and nationalization. They touted "common" rather than public ownership as a more efficient, ethical, and democratic path to caring for each company's stakeholders, especially its workers.

Bader and Schumacher's nonprofit aid agencies—Strive and the Intermediate Technology Development Group (ITDG)—were a case in point. Both Strive and ITDG were created as development agencies aimed at boosting private industry in the Third World and the British economy. As a postimperial project they supported the liberalization of markets for the purpose of fostering social bonds rather than to free markets from them. But they did so against what Bader and Schumacher saw as the ineffective power of trade unions and nationalized economies in representing the interests of workers. Instead of looking to a state-managed economy and collective bargaining, Strive and ITDG designated corporations and businesses as agents of welfare. They focused on creating solidarity between workers and managers rather than on fostering and encouraging solidarity between workers across the entire private sector.

Nonprofits in fact joined and catalyzed a broader movement of international economic governance that banked on individual desire rather than state-led legislation to regulate the economy. Inspired by a postcolonial critique of international trade, the nonprofit sector supported the liberalization of markets, opposing contemporary preferential trade areas like the European Economic Community. Nonprofits instead aimed to create a laissez-faire mechanism that would free international trade from neocolonial lobby groups and enable Third World countries to fully participate in the global economy. Nongovernmental markets offered up the illusion of connecting consumers and producers from the "bottom up," without direct involvement by the state. These markets were meant to be regulated by individual desires, social sensibilities, and communal solidarities rather than by the price mechanism. This was a model of humanized capitalism set against the depersonalized image of a mass-produced, Fordist economy set forth by modernization theory. Fair-trade products even carried the "authentic" marker of the producers who made them. Positioning themselves as the advocates of cross-border grassroots constituencies, nonprofits reconnected former colonies and former imperial metropoles within a new framework of care and compassion. The nonprofit sector thus generated new myths about moral economy, forging an understanding of the market as not only potentially ethical but also emancipatory.

What this meant in practice was that the nonprofit sector helped cement postimperial inequalities, and new divisions of labor, between Third World producers and British consumers. In a period marked by deindustrialization and a crisis of unemployment, the solidarity economy not only mirrored the landscape of global labor relations but also contributed to it. Removing the state and the trade unions from the domain of the economy meant abandoning labor regulations. Instead, the nonprofit sector expected consumers to buy products that were "ethically sourced" while simultaneously failing to provide any mechanisms that would ensure decent labor conditions in their production. The legacies of this project are everywhere. From fair trade of coffee and tea to the clothes we buy, our contemporary global economy is riddled with so-called "solidarity markets" that sell us on the promise of an alternative, personalized, and ethical capitalism. Yet, like the solidarity economy in the 1970s, these markets often reproduce or even exacerbate poor working conditions.

Moreover, the neoliberal project of the nonprofit sector was one that altered the meaning of work. A common critique of neoliberalism is that it commodifies everything and reduces politics to consumer choice. But the solidarity economy teaches us that consumerism is a partial and indeed secondary story within a broader transformation whose primary effect was on production. The neoliberalism of the nonprofit sector remade the future of work, focusing on producers rather than consumers as the main subject of its politics.

This transformation of work and of the individual worker had deep roots. The nonprofit approach to markets originated in the changing political economy of the Cold War and decolonization and was shaped by ongoing debates about the nature of capitalism. Drawing on the ethical critique of modernization and growth, the nonprofit sector rejected the "national economy" as the main object of the development project. Its advocates were simultaneously informed by the ethical socialism of the 1960s, including the latter's suspicion of state-managed economies and nationalization as the main means of delivering public goods. Instead of the "national economy," they made the "people" into their primary object of economic development and economic thinking, seeking to place individuals rather than states and institutions at the heart of economic development.

The turn to individuals over the state meant that development projects now focused on "developing" people rather than providing them with more wage work. Initially, in the 1970s, this meant generating a culture of enterprise through fair-trade markets. Instead of large-scale modernization projects focused on infrastructure and factories—whose aim was to generate wage labor—activists emphasized helping Third World subjects generate their own employment. Concentrating on "people" rather than the state as the primary object of development, the nonprofit sector aimed to transcend the limits of the dual-economy model and move beyond wage labor during a decade of global unemployment.

Programs like Oxfam's Bridge aimed to help "people in simple ways to free themselves from the yoke of poverty and hunger to which they were born."[11] These were framed as projects that would liberate workers from the commodification of work by making them the owners of their own labor. When the informal economy was "discovered" this type of entrepreneurship was available to everyone, everywhere. Women, for example, who had not been traditionally deemed to have economic value, could now join the solidarity economy. In this way, long before the "gig economy" became a political question in rich countries, the nonprofit sector turned to entrepreneurship as a form of flexible self-employment. Schumacher even described entrepreneurship as the quintessential means of helping workers express their "creative freedom." Activists came to conceive of their work as facilitating, encouraging, and developing a culture of enterprise. Instead of engineers and bureaucrats, the nonprofit sector began to employ marketing experts and business advisors to help producers become entrepreneurs.

In the 1980s, when finance reemerged as the dominant sector in the global economy, activists realized that they need not confine their work to the sphere of production. Instead, the solidarity economy turned to microfinance as a way to help Third World subjects develop their own self-worth. It was a new form of ethical investment in people—now directly conceived as human capital—rather than in their fair-trade products. Activists encouraged Third World subjects to see themselves not only as workers but also as investees. They focused on educating them to increase their own employability and solvency through financial education and "solidarity circles." Hoping to reshape economic behavior, creditors like Oxfam often supervised borrowers and advised them on how to repay their loans. At the same time, they offered workshops on developing financial and business skills and taught debtors about financial risk and solvency.

Microfinance in turn created new economic subjects: indebted individuals committed to accumulation, improvement, and the effort to remake themselves as capital within the global economy. In so doing, the solidarity economy collapsed the presumed separation of production and reproduction.[12] It made the subject herself, the human, into a financial asset. It was an aid strategy that focused on teaching Third World subjects how to valorize themselves within a larger "Third World" brand ready to be marketed as a fair-trade good. By the late 1990s, both the British and American welfare services had brought these financial models home, using them to aid racial and ethnic minorities within their national boundaries. What began as an emancipatory model to help Third World producers in turn came to shape racialized and neoliberal forms of welfare provision in Britain and the United States. On both sides of the Atlantic, this financialized model of aid was embraced by Third Way neoliberals, who saw in it an approach capable of shifting the burden of poverty onto the poor—and especially ethnic minorities—themselves.

The economic crises of the past decade have caused many commentators to proclaim neoliberalism's demise.[13] Once again, economists, policymakers, and activists have argued that capitalism needs to account for ethical considerations beyond pure economic determinism. Progressive and liberal thinkers have called for new metrics to assess the well-being of people, their communities, and even their environment beyond the traditional measure of GNP. Once more we hear of the value of fair-trade markets, localism, and even deglobalization. In other quarters activists have suggested the importance of making economics fit planetary needs. Ethics, in other words, have returned to the heart of debates about the nature of capitalism.

The nonprofits' pursuit of ethical capitalism enables us to understand why such proclamations of neoliberalism's death, notably in 2016, 2019, 2021, and 2022, are premature and why a neoliberal rationality has continued to shape contemporary Britain and the world beyond it.[14] Neoliberalism's critics have explained its persistence by analyzing its authoritarian, illiberal, and amoral permutations.[15] Some have even talked about neoliberalism's zombie existence, a dead economic logic that continues to haunt us while we wait for an alternative.[16] These accounts offer important insights about neoliberalism but they nonetheless miss crucial aspects of its endurance. Neoliberalism's power lies, in part, in its capacity to offer false but inspiring hope for economic liberation and for humanized capitalism. Neoliberalism is sustained by a deeply moral vision and by the transformative promise of ethical capitalism. It is a fiction that continues to reproduce economic disparities even as it ceaselessly promises to overcome itself through new forms of nongovernmental solidarity. And so it endures, atomizing us further as we remain distracted by the false promise of the solidarity economy.

Introduction

1. That is the title of the English neoliberal journalist Samuel Brittan's collection of essays from 1995. See Brittan, *Capitalism with a Human Face*; Middleton, "Brittan on Britain."

2. Haskell, "Capitalism and the Origins of the Humanitarian Sensibility, Part 1"; Haskell, "Capitalism and the Origins of the Humanitarian Sensibility, Part 2." Haskell's account is limited for various reasons not least because his association between humanitarianism and capitalism inadvertently assumes that slavery was not central to the formation of British capitalism itself. See Williams, *Capitalism and Slavery*; Beckert, *Empire of Cotton*. As Chris Brown has shown, ideas about antislavery were rooted within imperial politics rather than new moral sensibilities. Bronwen Everill has also demonstrated that the ethical capitalism of the period emerged from a political economy of the broader Atlantic rather than European sensibilities. See Brown, *Moral Capital*; Everill, *Not Made by Slaves*.

3. Klein, *No Logo*.

4. See Harris, "Just Beans"; Žižek, *First as Tragedy, Then as Farce*.

5. For a good summary of some of this literature, see Burnard and Riello, "Slavery and the New History of Capitalism."

6. Getachew, *Worldmaking after Empire*; Ogle, " 'Funk Money' "; Vernon, "Heathrow and the Making of Neoliberal Britain"; Ward, introduction; Ward, *Untied Kingdom*.

7. See, for example, Hilton, "Ken Loach and the Save the Children Film"; Baughan, *Saving the Children*; Tusan, *Smyrna's Ashes*; Bailkin, *Afterlife of Empire*.

8. Cooper, *Africa since 1940*, 85.

9. Davies, Jackson, and Sutcliffe-Braithwaite, introduction to *The Neoliberal Age*.

10. Slobodian, *Globalists*; Jackson, "Currents of Neo-Liberalism"; Cooper, *Family Values*; Jackson, "Putting Neoliberalism in Its Place"; Harvey, *A Brief History of Neoliberalism*; Prasad, *The Politics of Free Markets*; Stedman Jones, *Masters of the Universe*; Gerstle, *The Rise and Fall of the Neoliberal Order*; Levien, *Dispossession without Development*; Andersson, "Neoliberalism against Social Democracy."

11. On "encasement," see Slobodian, *Globalists*. See also Arrighi and Silve, "Polanyi's 'Double Movement' "; Jeremy Adelman, "Polanyi, the Failed Prophet of Moral Economics," *Boston Review*, May 30, 2017.

12. Whyte, *The Morals of the Market*; Moyn, *Not Enough*; Sutcliffe-Braithwaite, "Neo-Liberalism and Morality in the Making of Thatcherite Social Policy."

13. Brown, *Undoing the Demos*; Slobodian, *Crack-Up Capitalism*; Mudge, *Leftism Reinvented*; Palley, "From Keynesianism to Neoliberalism"; Kus, "Neoliberalism, Institutional Change, and the Welfare State."

14. Two notable exceptions stand out: Offner, *Sorting Out the Mixed Economy*; Bockman, *Markets in the Name of Socialism*.

15. Gerstle, *The Rise and Fall of the Neoliberal Order*, 149.

16. Schumacher, *Small Is Beautiful*, 243.

17. Brown, *Fair Trade*, 158–59.

18. See also a discussion about the relationship between the Labour Party and the aid sector in Baughan, *Saving the Children*, 175–77.

19. Riley, " 'This Party Is a Moral Crusade, or It Is Nothing.' "

20. See, for example, Murphy, *Futures of Socialism*; Fielding, *The Labour Party*.

21. See Jackson, *Equality and the British Left*. Katrina Forrester also has a helpful discussion about the British liberal left and its influence on liberal philosophy. See Forrester, *In the Shadow of Justice*.

22. Burton, "Who Needs the Nation?"; Hall, "The Local and the Global"; Hall, *Cultures of Empire*; Hall, *Civilizing Subjects*; Levine, *Gender and Empire*; Bailkin, *Afterlife of Empire*; Shepard, *The Invention of Decolonization*.

23. Offner, *Sorting Out the Mixed Economy*; Immerwahr, *Thinking Small*; Raianu, *Tata*.

24. Schumacher, "Buddhist Economics."

25. Hein and Schwab, *Moderne Unternehmensführung im Maschinenbau*.

26. Prabhakar, *Stakeholding and New Labour*; Murphy, *Futures of Socialism*.

27. For modernization theory, see Gilman, *Mandarins of the Future*; Engerman et al., *Staging Growth*. For development, colonialism, and modernization, see Satia, "Developing Iraq"; Cooper, "Modernizing Bureaucrats, Backward Africans, and the Development Concept"; Mitchell, *Rule of Experts*.

28. Poulton, "On Theories and Strategies," in Poulton and Harris, *Putting People First*, 30.

29. Brown, *Fair Trade*, 158–59.

30. See, for example, Mitchell, "Fixing the Economy"; Tooze, *Statistics and the German State*. For how that space was ushered from imperial governance and appropriated by anti-colonial movements, see Goswami, *Producing India*.

31. Sewell, "A Strange Career."

32. Ward, *Untied Kingdom*.

33. I have chosen to use the term "Third World" instead of "global South" or "developing countries" because that is the term used most frequently in my archives. On the limits of the term "global South," see Sajed, "From the Third World to the Global South"; Prashad, *The Darker Nations*.

34. See Robinson et al., "Telling Stories about Post-War Britain."

35. Schumacher, *Small Is Beautiful*.

36. On "responsibilization," see, for example, Brown, *Undoing the Demos*, 133–44. On the liberal origins of this idea, see Helen McCarthy, " 'I don't know how she does it!' " in *The Neoliberal Age?* ed. Davies, Jackson, and Sutcliffe-Braithwaite, 135–54.

37. Hilton, *Consumerism in Twentieth-Century Britain*; Hilton, *Prosperity for All*; Trentmann, *The Making of the Consumer*; Benson, *The Rise of Consumer Society in Britain*; Rappaport, Dawson, and Crowley, *Consuming Behaviour*; Gurney, *The Making of Consumer Culture in Modern Britain*.

38. Millard, *Export Marketing for a Small Handicraft Business*, 94.

39. Schumacher, *Small Is Beautiful*, 243.

40. Meyerowitz, *A War on Global Poverty*.

41. Feher, *Powerless by Design*.

42. Following Stuart Hall, I approach the "postimperial" as a period that was informed by colonization but also shaped by the global and international politics that followed formal independence. See Hall, "When Was 'the Post-Colonial'?" See also Vernon, "The Worlding of Britain"; Satia, *Time's Monster*; Burton, "Who Needs the Nation?"; Hall, "The Local and the Global"; Hall, *Cultures of Empire*; Hall, *Civilizing Subjects*; Levine, *Gender and Empire*; Bailkin, *Afterlife of Empire*; Shepard, *The Invention of Decolonization*.

43. Burton, "Who Needs the Nation?"; Hall, "The Local and the Global"; Hall, *Cultures of Empire*; Hall, *Civilizing Subjects*; Levine, *Gender and Empire*; Bailkin, *Afterlife of Empire*; Shepard, *The Invention of Decolonization*.

44. Baughan, *Saving the Children*.

45. Ibid.; Hilton, "Charity, Decolonization and Development"; O'Sullivan, *The NGO Moment*.

46. Daunton, *Trusting Leviathan*.

47. Maier, *Leviathan 2.0*.

48. Figures are from Hilton et al., *Politics of Expertise*, 43.

49. Maier, *Leviathan 2.0*, 8.

50. Iriye, "A Century of NGOs"; Mazlish, *The New Global History*, 50; Manela, "International Society as a Historical Subject"; O'Sullivan, *The NGO Moment*.

51. Despite its antistatist rhetoric, the nonprofit sector was always part of a governmental project, funded by and collaborating with it. It also shared many of its experts and personnel. In postimperial Britain, many nongovernmental aid programs still received funding from the British government. On the politics of NGOs, see Feher, Krikorian, and Mckee, *Nongovernmental Politics*, 149–60.

52. Poulton, "On Theories and Strategies," in Poulton and Harris, *Putting People First*, 30.

53. Oxfam, *A Case for Reform*, 1–2.

54. Martin, *The Meddlers*.

55. Vernon, *Modern Britain*, 509.

56. Jennings, *Surrogates of the State*; Bailkin, *Afterlife of Empire*; Hilton, "Charity and the End of Empire"; Baughan, *Saving the Children*; Sasson, "From Empire to Humanity."

57. Jennings, *Surrogates of the State*.

58. Buzzacott, *Charities and Business*.

59. Tusan, "The Business of Relief Work."

60. See, for example, Jane Dudman, "Charity Shops: Bringing in the Cash, but Bringing Down the High Street?" *The Guardian*, September 11, 2017; Andrew Ellson, "Taxpayer's Charity Shop Subsidy Blamed for High Street Decline," *The Times*, January 12, 2019.

61. Brick, *Transcending Capitalism*.

Chapter 1

1. Schumacher, *The Roots of Economic Growth*, 29–42.

2. Cooper, *Africa since 1940*, 85. See also Mann, *In the Long Run We Are All Dead*, 75.

3. Schumacher, "The Making of Economic Society."

4. Schumacher, *Small Is Beautiful*.

5. Poulton and Harris, *Putting People First*, 31.

6. The only scholar who attempted to historicize Schumacher's thought has been the economist Robert Leonard, although he has not located Schumacher's work within British socialist thought. See Leonard, "Between the 'Hand-Loom' and the 'Samson Stripper.'" Histories of development only mention Schumacher in passing. See, for example, Immerwahr, *Thinking Small*, 168; Macekura, *The Mismeasure of Progress*, 77–78; Hilton et al., *Politics of Expertise*, 234.

7. "Keynesianism" is the term Schumacher and others examined in this chapter used to describe what we might today call state-led, modernization schemes.

8. Immerwahr, *Thinking Small*; Macekura, *The Mismeasure of Progress*.

9. Edgerton, *The Rise and Fall of the British Nation*.

10. Mitchell, "Fixing the Economy."

11. Harvey, *A Brief History of Neoliberalism*, chap. 3; Gerstle, *The Rise and Fall of the Neoliberal Order*. Against such accounts, Slobodian proposes that neoliberal thinkers' aim was to "encase" the market. Slobodian, *Globalists*, 13.

12. Gerstle, *The Rise and Fall of the Neoliberal Order*, 245.

13. See, for example, Harris, "Political Thought and the Welfare State"; Jackson, *Equality and the British Left*; Butler, *Michael Young, Social Science, and the British Left*.

14. Westad, *The Global Cold War*.

15. Holyoake, *The Co-Operative Movement To-Day*, 91.

16. Windel, *Cooperative Rule*.

17. Morris, *The Collected Works of William Morris*, 16:230; Thompson, *William Morris*; Bevir, "William Morris."

18. Rogan, *The Moral Economists*.

19. R. H. Tawney quoted in Thompson, *Political Economy and the Labour Party*, 58. See also Martin, "R. H. Tawney's Normative Economic History of Capitalism"; Passes, "The Christian Socialism of R. H. Tawney."

20. Neima, "Dartington Hall and the Quest for 'Life in Its Completeness,'" 124.

21. Quoted in ibid., 124, 117.

22. Dutta and Robinson, *Rabindranath Tagore*.

23. Young was educated in Dartington Hall and maintained a close relationship with the Elmhirsts. See Young, *The Elmhirsts of Dartington*. For Cole, see Wright, *G.D.H. Cole and Socialist Democracy*.

24. I say marginalized because they haven't completely disappeared. See Polanyi, *The Great Transformation*; Rogan, *The Moral Economists*.

25. Jackson, *Equality and the British Left*; Tomlinson, *Democratic Socialism and Economic Policy*, 280–83; Zweiniger-Bargielowska, *Austerity in Britain*, 203–26.

26. Mitchell, *Rule of Experts*; Edgerton, *The Rise and Fall of the British Nation*. For a similar story in Germany, see Tooze, "Trouble with Numbers"; Tooze, *Statistics and the German State*.

27. Sutcliffe-Braithwaite, *Class, Politics, and the Decline of Deference in England*.

28. Black and Pemberton, *An Affluent Society?*

29. Brick, *Transcending Capitalism*, 159–61; Brooke, "Atlantic Crossing?"; Jackson, *Equality and the British Left*, 155–57.

30. See also Haseler, *The Gaitskellites*.

31. Crosland, "The Transition from Capitalism," 42.

32. Chun, *The British New Left*; Kenny, *The First New Left*; Dworkin, *Cultural Marxism in Postwar Britain*; Foks, "The Sociological Imagination of the British New Left."

33. Sasson, "The Gospel of Wealth"; Thompson, *The Making of the English Working Class*; Thompson, "The Moral Economy of the English Crowd in the Eighteenth Century"; Satia, "Byron, Gandhi and the Thompsons." See also Götz, "Moral Economy."

34. Hall, "ULR Club at Notting Hill"; Hall, "Life and Times of the First New Left."

35. Cooper, "Modernizing Bureaucrats, Backward Africans, and the Development Concept." For a Caribbean example, see Natarajan, "Village Life and How to Improve It."

36. Natarajan, "Organizing Community."

37. Louis, *Ends of British Imperialism*, 696; Louis, "American Anti-Colonialism and the Dissolution of the British Empire," 409; Buettner, *Europe after Empire*, 54–56.

38. Quoted in Stuart Hall, "Interview," in *Rethinking British Decline*, ed. English and Kenny, 110.

39. D. H. Cole as quoted in Jackson, *Equality and the British Left*, 151. As Butler shows, Cole was somewhat ambivalent about Michael Young's own solution to the communitarian turn even though he was sympathetic to the move toward community more generally. Butler, *Michael Young, Social Science, and the British Left*, 80–83.

40. Richard Titmuss, introduction to Tawney, *Equality*, 10–11, 16.

41. Hall, "Crosland Territory," 4.

42. Immerwahr, *Thinking Small*. See also Sackley, "The Village as Cold War Site." The UN also began adopting a focus on community development. Midgley et al., *Community Participation, Social Development and the State*.

43. Michael Young, "For Richer, For Poorer: Report Prepared for Policy Committee," November 1952, 61, YUNG 02/001, Papers of Michael Young, Churchill Archives Center, Cambridge (hereafter CAC).

44. Young, *Small Man, Big World*.

45. Butler, *Michael Young, Social Science, and the British Left*, 78–83.

46. See ibid.

47. Young, "For Richer, For Poorer," 49.

48. Lawrence, "Inventing the 'Traditional Working Class.'"

49. Briggs, *Michael Young*; Thane, "Michael Young and Welfare"; Hilton, "Michael Young and the Consumer Movement"; Butler, *Michael Young, Social Science, and the British Left*, 119–22.

50. Young quoted in Butler, *Michael Young, Social Science, and the British Left*, 83.

51. Michael Young Notes, Sriniketan Institute of Rural Reconstruction, January 25, 1951, YUNG 4/1, CAC.

52. Ibid.

53. Mantena, "On Gandhi's Critique of the State."

54. Young also learned about the Tata family corporation more generally and their model of development and investment in social responsibility. Michael Young, "Summing Up of Impressions of India," January 11, 1951, YUNG 4/1, CAC. See also Butler, *Michael Young, Social Science, and the British Left*, 121; Raianu, *Tata*, 171–200.

55. Michael Young Notes, January 12, 1951, YUNG 4/1, CAC.

56. Michael Young Notes, January 18, 1951, YUNG 4/1, CAC.

57. Butler, *Michael Young, Social Science, and the British Left*, 122.

58. Michael Young, *Fifty Million Unemployed*, March 1952, 6, YUNG 4/1, CAC.

59. Ibid., 7.

60. Ibid., 11.

61. Ibid., 15.

62. Ibid., 11.

63. Young, "For Richer, For Poorer," 5.

64. Briggs, *Michael Young*, 281.

65. See also Butler, "Michael Young, the Institute of Community Studies, and the Politics of Kinship."

66. Young, *Fifty Million Unemployed*, 4.

67. Crosland, "The Transition from Capitalism," 52.

68. Kemseke, *Towards an Era of Development*, 243–55.

69. British Labour Party, "Talking Points September 1951," Pamphlet Box 125, 328.81, British Labour Party Archives, Manchester. I'm grateful to Charlotte Riley for sharing a copy of the pamphlet with me.

70. See Kemseke, *Towards an Era of Development*, 243–55.

71. Riley, "'This Party Is a Moral Crusade, or It Is Nothing.'"

72. Reisman, *Richard Titmuss*, 1.

73. See Welshman, "The Unknown Titmuss."

74. These included a 1955 essay about industry and family where he writes against the disconnect between factory life and communal life and a 1956 lecture about the welfare state and equality.

75. See also Abel-Smith, "Whose Welfare State."

76. Michael Harrington quoted in Greene, *America in the Sixties*, 69.

77. Reisman, *Richard Titmuss*, 30.

78. Titmuss, "Poverty vs. Equality," 132.

79. Titmuss, *Commitment to Welfare*, 114.

80. Titmuss quoted in Stewart, *Richard Titmuss*, 417.

81. Titmuss, "Social Policy and Economic Progress," 37, 39. Reprinted and slightly modified in Titmuss, *Commitment to Welfare*.

82. Titmuss, *Commitment to Welfare*, 50; Freeden, "Civil Society and the Good Citizen"; Marshall, *Citizenship and Social Class, and Other Essays*, 87; Moyn, "T. H. Marshall, the Moral Economy, and Social Rights"; Moses, "Social Citizenship and Social Rights in an Age of Extremes." On the limits of Marshall's welfarism, see Pedersen, *Family, Dependence, and the Origins of the Welfare State*. On Marshall's idea of social rights and the politics of race and empire in the Caribbean, see Putnam, "Citizenship from the Margins."

83. Reisman, *Richard Titmuss*, 2.

84. Titmuss, *Essays on "the Welfare State,"* 220, 225, 217.

85. Ibid., 222.

86. Together with his students Brian Abel-Smith and Tony Lynes he worked with the United Nations and the World Health Organization.

87. Titmuss, *Commitment to Welfare*, 128.

88. Myrdal, *Beyond the Welfare State*. See also Moyn, "Welfare World."

89. Titmuss, *The Health Services of Tanganyika*, 214.

90. Stewart, *Richard Titmuss*, 312–13.

91. Ibid., 314–16.

92. Piachaud, "Fabianism, Social Policy and Colonialism."

93. Doron, "Personal Welfare Services in Israel."

94. My translation, from Katz's eulogy in Katz, "Richard M. Titmuss."

95. Stewart, *Richard Titmuss*, 316.

96. Titmuss in the 1972 preface to Hebrew translation of his book *The Gift Relationship*.

97. Marmor and Marmor, *The Politics of Medicare*; Cohen et al., *Medicare and Medicaid at 50*. On the mixed economy of the War on Poverty, see Offner, *Sorting Out the Mixed Economy*; Cooper, *Family Values*; Hacker, *The Divided Welfare State*; Klein, *For All These Rights*.

98. Davies, "Promoting Productivity in the National Health Service."

99. Sloman, *Transfer State*, chap. 4.

100. Titmuss *The Gift Relationship*, 15.

101. Ibid., 212.

102. Coase, *The Problem of Social Cost*.

103. Titmuss, *Commitment to Welfare*, 139. See also Fontaine, "Blood, Politics, and Social Science"; Jackson, "Richard Titmuss versus the IEA."

104. Titmuss, *The Gift Relationship*, 206.

105. Ibid., 13.

106. See Titmuss's reference to Polanyi in Titmuss, *Commitment to Welfare*, 188. See also Adelman, "Polanyi, the Failed Prophet of Moral Economics"; Immerwahr, "Polanyi in the United States."

107. Titmuss, "Poverty vs. Equality," 132, 133.

108. Titmuss, *Essays on "the Welfare State,"* 39.

109. It also led to an inspection of commercial blood banks in the United States and prompted Secretary of State for Health, Education and Welfare Elliot Richardson to consult Titmuss personally on how to reform the system. Reisman, *Richard Titmuss*, 272.

110. Solow, "Blood and Thunder," 1696.

111. In the early 1960s the National Bureau of Economic Research under a grant from the Russell Sage Foundation ran a study of philanthropy in the American economy. See Box 59, Folder 516, Studies in Philanthropy, Russell Sage Foundation Archives, Rockefeller Archive Center, North Tarrytown, New York. See also Fontaine, "From Philanthropy to Altruism."

112. Boulding, "Economics as Moral Science," 6.

113. According to Phelps, the symposium was organized to investigate how "thinking about the economics of altruism has contributed to the rethinking of economics." Phelps saw the publication of Titmuss's book as an occasion to consider the increased interest in the theory of altruism at a moment when there was a "growing disenchantment with classical liberalism among economists as well as other social and political observers." Phelps, *Altruism, Morality, and Economic Theory*, 3.

114. See Fontaine, "From Philanthropy to Altruism."

115. Arrow, *Social Choice and Individual Values*; Arrow, "Uncertainty and the Welfare Economics of Medical Care"; Cherrier and Fleury, "Economists' Interest in Collective Decision after World War II"; Brick, *Transcending Capitalism*, 168–71.

116. Wollheim, "A Paradox in the Theory of Democracy," in *Philosophy, Politics and Society*, ed. Laslett and Runciman; Ewin, "Wollheim's Paradox of Democracy."

117. Nagel, *The Possibility of Altruism*, 118.

118. Nagel, "Poverty and Food."

119. Forrester, *In the Shadow of Justice*.

120. Singer, "Altruism and Commerce," 320.

121. See, for example, Wright, *The Psychology of Moral Behaviour*; Rescher, *Unselfishness*.

122. Singer, "Altruism and Commerce," 313–14. See also Singer, "Moral Experts"; Singer, "The Triviality of the Debate over 'Is-Ought' and the Definition of 'Moral.'"

123. Singer, "Famine, Affluence, and Morality," 232.

124. Ibid., 231–32.

125. Ibid., 231.

126. Singer, *Practical Ethics*, 162.

127. Schumacher, *Small Is Beautiful*, 40. The essay was first published in 1968.

128. Leonard, "E. F. Schumacher and Intermediate Technology," 263.

129. E. F. Schumacher, "Obituary of J. M. Keynes," *The Times*, April 22, 1946.

130. Faudot, "The Keynes Plan and Bretton Woods Debates."

131. As Robert Leonard argues, to the extent that Schumacher was concerned in the 1940s with so-called "Third World" economies, it was via his broader interest in the restoration of postwar trade and payments ("E. F. Schumacher and Intermediate Technology").

132. On the Shanghai Club, see Cockett, *David Astor and the Observer*.

133. Sir Edward Boyle in "Budget Proposals and Economic Survey," *Hansard*, House of Commons, April 16, 1951, vol. 486, cols. 1474–1592.

134. Wood, *E. F. Schumacher, His Life and Thought*, 116.

135. Balfour, *The Living Soil*.

136. Schumacher to Werner von Simson, quoted in Wood, *E. F. Schumacher, His Life and Thought*, 116–17.

137. Schumacher in McRobie and Schumacher, *Small Is Possible*, 3–4.

138. E. F. Schumacher, "Western Politics and Eastern Economics," 8, Box 5, Folder 3, World Politics, Schumacher Papers, Library, Schumacher Center for a New Economy, Great Barrington, Massachusetts (hereafter SPGB).

139. Ibid.

140. Edgerton, *The Rise and Fall of the British Nation*.

141. See Jevons, *The Coal Question*, 122, 125.

142. Gibbs, *Coal Country*, 26.

143. Sutcliffe-Braithwaite, "Tesco and a Motorway."

144. Edgerton, *The Rise and Fall of the British Nation*, 659.

145. On the Ridley Committee, which sought to devise a national fuel policy and market liberalization, see, for example, Hawkins, "Competition between the Nationalized Electricity and Gas Industries."

146. Gibbs, *Coal Country*, 29.

147. "National Coal Board (Report and Accounts)," *Hansard*, House of Commons Debate, July 20, 1955, col. 389. See also Clegg, "The Fleck Report"; Nelson, "The Fleck Report and the Area Organization of the National Coal Board."

148. Mitchell, *Carbon Democracy*, 139.

149. Schumacher, "Investment in Coal," in Schumacher and Kirk, *Schumacher on Energy*, 80.

150. Ibid., 81.

151. Ibid., 85.

152. Ibid.

153. Schumacher, Kessler, and Townend, *Britain's Coal*, 11–12.

154. Ibid., 16.

155. Schumacher and Kirk, *Schumacher on Energy*, 85.

156. Ibid., 82.

157. Schumacher also warned against the environmental consequences of nuclear energy, writing directly against his brother-in-law, the Nazi nuclear physicist Werner Heisenberg. See Leonard, "E. F. Schumacher and Intermediate Technology."

158. Schumacher, *Small Is Beautiful*, 31, 29, emphasis in the original.

159. Schumacher and Kirk, *Schumacher on Energy*, 131–32.

160. Clift and Tomlinson, "Tawney and the Third Way."

161. Schumacher and Kirk, *Schumacher on Energy*, 90, 133.

162. Ibid., 139–40.

163. Ibid., 140.

164. Leonard, "E. F. Schumacher and Intermediate Technology."

165. Black, "The Age of Economic Development."

166. See, for example, Cooper and Packard, *International Development and the Social Sciences*; Ferguson, *The Anti-Politics Machine*; Gupta, *Postcolonial Developments*; Li, *The Will to Improve*; Cullather, *The Hungry World*; Gilman, *Mandarins of the Future*; Engerman et al., *Staging Growth*; Unger, *International Development*.

167. Technical Assistance Administration, Request of Government of Burma, Job Description, April 12, 1954, Box 1, Folder 2: Burma Assignment, SPGB; see also Letter of Appointment, United Nations, July 27, 1954, E. F. Schumacher Archives, Box 1, Folder 2: Burma Assignment, SPGB.

168. Leonard, "E. F. Schumacher and the Making of 'Buddhist Economics,'" 167.

169. "Final Report by E. F. Schumacher, United Nations Economic Advisor to the Government of the Union of Burma, Economic and Social Board, Office of the Prime Minister," in Gillingham-Schumacher, Box 1, EFS, Articles & Pamphlets 1940–1959, SPGB.

170. EFS to Anna Maria Schumacher, March 2, 1955, SPGB. See also EFS to family, February 11, 1955, SPGB.

171. Quoted in Satish Kumar, foreword to Schumacher, *This I Believe*, 8.

172. Macekura, *The Mismeasure of Progress*, chap. 3.

173. Mishan, *The Costs of Economic Growth*.

174. International Labour Office, *Employment, Growth and Basic Needs*, 16. See also Hirsch, *Social Limits to Growth*.

175. Sharma, "The United States, the World Bank, and the Transformation of Development in the 1970s"; Brushett, "Partners in Development?"

176. Gandhi quoted in Weber, *Gandhi as Disciple and Mentor*, 224.

177. E. F. Schumacher, "Economics in a Buddhist Country," Rangoon, February 1955, pp. 1, 2, Box 5, SPGB, emphasis in the original.

178. The 1955 essay was published under the title "Economics in a Buddhist Country" and then republished with the new title in 1962. See Schumacher, *Roots of Economic Growth*.

179. Schumacher, "Economics in a Buddhist Country," 4.

180. Goswami, "From Swadeshi to Swaraj," 611.

181. Schumacher, "Economics in a Buddhist Country," 7.

182. Siegel, "The Kibbutz and the Ashram," 1182.

183. Association for World Peace, "War on Want"; Luetchford and Burns, *Waging the War on Want*, 14.

184. Battersby, "War on Want and the Bhoodan Movement."

185. Rigney, *Peace Comes Walking*; Luetchford and Burns, *Waging the War on Want*, 42–44. In 1967 the Bhoodan movement also received support from Oxfam. The Oxford Gramdam Action Programme aimed to develop economic infrastructure alongside social changes being promoted by the Gramdam movement. Hilton et al., *Politics of Expertise*, 229.

186. Donald Groom, "War on Want Projects in India," December 63/January 64, pp. 1, 7, Box 117, War on Want Collection, SOAS, University of London (hereafter WOW).

187. See, for example, War on Want, "Agrindus Project at Govindpur in Uttar Pradesh," Box 185, WOW; "Background Note to Adopt a Village Scheme," Box 185, WOW; India Development Group, News Bulletin and Report 1974, SPGB; Chatterjee, Prasad, and Śrīvāstavya, *Community Approach to Family Welfare*; Prem, *Agrindus Family Welfare Project*. The collaboration between Bhoodan and War on Want also gave rise to the Multipurpose Cooperative Association in India, among other ventures. See John Cunnington, "Cooperatives Create Change," Box 185, WOW.

188. Bader, "The Scott Bader Commonwealth"; Hoe, *The Man Who Gave His Company Away*.

189. Schumacher, *Roots of Economic Growth*, 23, emphasis in the original.

190. Ibid., 46.

191. Ibid., 47–48.

192. Ibid., 50, emphasis in the original.

193. Ibid., 53.

194. Ibid., 56.

195. Schumacher, *Small Is Beautiful*. The phrase "economics as if people mattered" was the book's subtitle.

196. Ibid., 29.

197. Schumacher, "Industrialization through 'Intermediate Technology,' " in *Industrialisation in Developing Countries*, ed. Robinson, 98.

198. Schumacher, *The Age of Plenty*, 18.

199. Verena Schumacher, "George McRobie Obituary," *The Guardian*, July 27, 2016.

200. Hoda also set up the India Development Group UK in 1968 with Schumacher, which runs rural development programs in India with the help of the Indian business community in Britain. See George McRobie, "Mansur Hoda Obituary," *The Guardian*, March 5, 2001.

201. George McRobie, "Obituary: Julia Porter," *The Independent*, August 30, 1992.

202. Draft submission, "Intermediate Technology Group," p. 2, OD 63/60, UK National Archives, Kew, London (hereafter TNA).

203. ITDG Annual Report 1973, Chairman's Report, October 1, 1973–September 30, 1974, p. 2, OD 63/60, TNA.

204. Schumacher, *Small Is Beautiful*, 68.

205. Minutes, "Meeting with Christian Aid and ITDG on March 21, 1975 re boat building project in South Sudan," March 24, 1975, OD 63/30, TNA.

206. "Oxfam Spinning Wheels": correspondence and papers relating to a low-cost spinning wheel designed by Oxfam, and handlooms, December 1974–February 1987, Oxfam PRG/7/3/7, Oxfam Archive, Bodleian Libraries, University of Oxford (hereafter OA).

207. Poulton and Harris, *Putting People First*, 32.

208. Oxfam, *Oxfam's Overseas Programme*, 17.

209. Hilton et al., *Politics of Expertise*, 230.

210. Schneider, *The Barefoot Revolution*, xiii.

Chapter 2

1. Special correspondent, "Business Approach Brings Charities Results," *The Times*, March 2, 1965.

2. Ibid.

3. Ibid.

4. Çalışkan and Callon, "Economization, Part 1."

5. Hilton, "Politics Is Ordinary," 238.

6. Prochaska, *Christianity and Social Service in Modern Britain*, 148–76.

7. The expansion of the NGO sector has been well documented. See, for example, Hilton et al., *Politics of Expertise*.

8. Hilton, "Politics Is Ordinary."

9. For the politics of mixed economy and their connection to the developmental state in the Americas, see Offner, *Sorting Out the Mixed Economy*.

10. Vernon, *Modern Britain*, 510.

11. Rose, *Making, Selling and Wearing Boys' Clothes in Late-Victorian England*; Richmond, *Clothing the Poor in Nineteenth-Century England*.

12. Mitchell, *Tradition and Innovation in English Retailing*.

13. Prochaska, "Charity Bazaars in Nineteenth-Century England"; Prochaska, *Women and Philanthropy in Nineteenth-Century England*, 47–72; Gurney, " 'The Sublime of the Bazaar' "; Waddington, " 'Grasping Gratitude' "; Shiell, *Fundraising, Flirtation and Fancywork*.

14. Hilton et al., *The Politics of Expertise*, 89–90; Koven, *Slumming*, 88–139; Ash, *Funding Philanthropy*. For secondhand clothing and religious organizations, see Rose, *Making, Selling and Wearing Boys' Clothes in Late-Victorian England*; Richmond, *Clothing the Poor in Nineteenth-Century England*.

15. Booth, *In Darkest England, and the Way Out*.

16. Murdoch, *Origins of the Salvation Army*; Gariepy, *Christianity in Action*; Sandall, Wiggins, and Coutts, *History of the Salvation Army*.

17. Tolen, "Colonizing and Transforming the Criminal Tribesman"; Bolton, *Booth's Drum*, 109. For the White Dominions, see Darwin, *The Empire Project*. For the Salvation Army in the United States, see Huyssen, *Progressive Inequality*.

18. Baughan, *Saving the Children*; Zahra, *The Lost Children*; Boucher, "Cultivating Internationalism"; Sasson, "From Empire to Humanity."

19. Quoted in "The Society of Friends' Relief Service in Berlin," December 1923, EJ132, A405, Save the Children Funds Archives, Cadbury Research Centre, University of Birmingham (hereafter SCFA). See also "The Clothes Problem in Germany," Save the Children Fund Report, c. Autumn 1923, EJ132, A405, SCFA.

20. Reinisch, "Internationalism in Relief."

21. McCarthy, *The British People and the League of Nations*.

22. Paul D. Sturge to the Friends Service Council, March 1949, DIR2/3/6/15, OA. See also R. H. Moxely, untitled, col. 1949, Acc 6235, Box 20, Folder 1: Oxfam Minutes, Cecil Jackson-Cole Papers, West Sussex Record Office (hereafter CJCP).

23. Whitaker, *A Bridge of People*, 18; Jones, *Two Ears of Corn*, 28.

24. Bishop and Green, *Philanthro-Capitalism*. For earlier origins of philanthro-capitalism, see McGoey, *No Such Thing as a Free Gift*.

25. Cecil Jackson-Cole, "Some of the Material for Helping Prepare the Book 'Ten Years Too Late,'" pp. 6, 10, 16, Acc 6259, Box 3, Folder 1, CJCP; Cecil Jackson-Cole, "Part Memories of C. Jackson-Cole Covering the Earlier Period of Oxfam: Chapter 3," November 8, 1978, Acc 6259, Box 3, Folder 3, CJCP.

26. Cecil Jackson-Cole, "Part Memories of C. Jackson-Cole Covering the Earlier Period of Oxfam," November 8, 1978, Acc 6259, CJC Autobiographical Writings, 1969–78, Box 3, Folder 3, CJCP.

27. Black, *Cause for Our Times*, 14.

28. Jarlert, *The Oxford Group, Group Revivalism, and the Churches in Northern Europe*.

29. Wilson, "Gilbert Murray and International Relations"; Collini, *Common Writing*, chap. 8.

30. Cecil Jackson-Cole, autobiographical account, 1974, p. 5, Acc 6259, Box 3, Folder 3, CJCP. Cole himself took an international turn in this period and even worked for UNESCO in the postwar years. Holthaus, "G.D.H. Cole's International Thought."

31. Cole was one of the signatories of a letter sent to the national press that called on the British government to end the war and aid famine-stricken Europe. See Whitaker, *A Bridge of People*, 15.

32. Jackson-Cole, "Part Memories of C. Jackson-Cole Covering the Earlier Period of Oxfam," November 8, 1978.

33. Ibid.

34. Ibid.

35. Ibid.

36. Cecil Jackson-Cole, "Whither Help the Aged: And Action in Distress?" September 20, 1976, p. 4, Acc 6259, Box 15, (2) AID (ii), CJCP.

37. Quoted in Field, "Consumption in Lieu of Membership," 983.

38. "Oxfam Shop Founder Dies Aged 88," BBC News, October 2, 2007; "Joe Mitty," *The Telegraph*, October 3, 2007; "Joe Mitty," *The Times*, October 4, 2007; "Joe Mitty," *The Guardian*, October 9, 2007; "Joe Mitty Tireless Worker for Oxfam," *The Independent*, October 11, 2007.

39. Byron Rogers, "Salesman on the Side of the Angels," *The Guardian*, August 3, 1971.

40. Hilton, "Charity and the End of Empire."

41. Rogers, "Salesman on the Side of the Angels."

42. Ibid.

43. Quote is from Joe Mitty in "Introduction," in the Oxford Committee for Famine Relief, "Gift Shop News" (c. late 1950s), COM/3/1/16, OA.

44. Black, *Cause for Our Times*, 97.

45. Quote from "Shop Window" in the Oxford Committee for Famine Relief, "Gift Shop News" (c. late 1950s), COM/3/1/16, OA.

46. For electric saucepans, see, for example, Joe Mitty to Mrs. Bruce, October 6, 1952, DIR/2/3/6/15, OA.

47. See, for example, "Gift Shop Window," *Oxfam Bulletin*, no. 25 (Summer 1961), COM3/1/15, OA.

48. Rogers, "Salesman on the Side of the Angels."

49. Jackson-Cole, "Part Memories of C. Jackson-Cole Covering the Earlier Period of Oxfam," November 8, 1978.

50. Jackson-Cole, "Whither Help the Aged," 2–3.

51. Jackson-Cole, "Part Memories of C. Jackson-Cole Covering the Earlier Period of Oxfam," November 8, 1978.

52. Jackson-Cole, "Whither Help the Aged," 3.

53. Sumption interviewed in Jane Leathley, "Sidelines: The State of Donation," *The Guardian*, July 21, 1975.

54. Some of these rules built on earlier fundraising techniques. See, for example, Baughan, *Saving the Children*, 25–45.

55. Oxford Committee for Famine Relief, "Gift Shop News."

56. Obituary, "Harold Sumption: Put Out the World on Poverty," *The Guardian*, March 27, 1998.

57. Obituary, "Harold Sumption," *The Independent*, April 21, 1998.

58. Darwin, "A Third British Empire?"; Darwin, *The Empire Project*.

59. N. M. Haybittle to Joe Mitty, October 24, 1952, DIR/2/3/6/15, OA.

60. Joe Mitty to the Crown Staffordshire Pottery Co., October 30, 1952, DIR/2/3/6/15, OA.

61. G. R. Margason to Joe Mitty, November 25, 1952, DIR/2/3/6/15, OA.

62. Patrick Stoddart, "Business Is Booming in the Tragedy Trade," *Watford Evening Echo*, July 13, 1971.

63. Christopher Driver, "Phenomenal Oxfam," *New Society*, no. 35 (October 3, 1963): 9.

64. Ibid.

65. "Where Charity Begins: About 100 Needy Organisations Have Mail Order," *The Guardian*, November 17, 1981; on the development of mail-order catalogues in the 1960s, see O'Connell, *Credit and Community*, 88–130.

66. Shirley Lewis, "Charity for the Stay-at-Homes," *The Guardian*, October 22, 1970.

67. For Shelter, see Sasson, "The Problem of Homelessness in Post-war Britain."

68. Hilton et al., *The Politics of Expertise*, 267.

69. Figures in Butler, *Michael Young, Social Science, and the British Left*, 160.

70. Eley, *Forging Democracy*, 353.

71. Gunn, "The Buchanan Report, Environment and the Problem of Traffic in 1960s Britain," 524.

72. Daunton and Hilton, *The Politics of Consumption*; Hollow, "The Age of Affluence Revisited." For the parallel American story, see Cohen, *A Consumers' Republic*.

73. Black, *Redefining British Politics*, 8.

74. Hilton, *Consumerism in Twentieth-Century Britain*.

75. On consumerism, gender, and the family, see Butler, *Michael Young, Social Science, and the British Left*.

76. Philip Howard, "Lennon to Smile for Charity," *The Guardian*, October 25, 1969; Stanley Bonnet, "The Boy Who Thought Big," *Daily Mirror*, July 16, 1969; "The Boy behind the March," *Sunday Times*, July 8, 1969; "Sun Hits Oxfam's Walk," *Daily Express*, July 14, 1969; Frank Howitt, "What a Blisterer," *Daily Express*, July 14, 1969; Brian Cashinella, "50,000 in Walk for Oxfam," *The Times*, July 14, 1969.

77. "Perspective: The Professional Approach Pays Off for Charity," *Advertiser's Weekly*, April 24, 1960.

78. Black, *Cause for Our Times*, 97.

79. Confidential report, "Daily Mail—Oxfam Campaign, Christmas 1963," c. 1964, COM/3/1/17, OA.

80. Oxfam pamphlet, "Your Gift Can Save a Life," c. 1960, p. 39, COM3/1/15, OA.

81. *Western Morning News*, August 20, 1970, COM/3/2/50, OA.

82. G. C. Maddever to Oxfam, August 20, 1970, COM/3/2/50, OA.

83. MacFarquhar, *Strangers Drowning*.

84. Quoted in "Shopkeeping for Charity," *Family Circle*, June 1971.

85. Glazer, *Women's Paid and Unpaid Labor*.

86. Ibid.

87. Stoddart, "Business Is Booming in the Tragedy Trade."

88. For women's employment in postwar Britain, see McCarthy, "Social Science and Married Women's Employment in Post-War Britain."

89. On emotional labor, see Hochschild, *The Managed Heart*.

90. As such they also served as a precedent for today's shops, which—based on the local Government Act of 1988—get 80 percent rate relief on their property. "Oxfam at Home," Annual Review 1965/66, COM/3/1/15, OA; "Oxfam's First Twenty-five Years—And the Next," *Oxford Mail*, September 29, 1967.

91. "Oxfam Shop at Bordon Rakes in Business," *Peterfield Post*, October 15, 1970.

92. Stoddart, "Business Is Booming in the Tragedy Trade."

93. "Good News for Charity," *Acton Gazette*, October 29, 1970; "New Oxfam Shop Needed," *Tunbridge Wells Advertiser*, October 28, 1970.

94. Supplementary Report, Confidential, "Report of the Working Party on Fundraising," Oxfam, May 1974, Acc 6259, Box 22, CJCP.

95. Mitty quote is in Mabel Hickman, "A Shop for Six Days," *Oxfam Bulletin*, Autumn 1964, COM/3/1/15, OA.

96. Ibid., 14.

97. See, for example, pricing policy in Supplementary Report, Confidential, "Report of the Working Party on Fundraising."

98. "Oxfam at Home," Annual Review 1967/68, COM/3/1/15, OA.

99. Ibid.; Report to Ad Hoc Committee, 5; "Temporary" Gift Shops, February 1964, COM/3/1/15, OA.

100. Hickman, "A Shop for Six Days."

101. Margaret Bennion, "Serving a Good Cause—Behind the Counter," *Daily Telegraph*, January 20, 1968.

102. Minutes of a meeting of the Gift Shops Committee held at 139 Oxford Street, London, W1, on Tuesday, April 9, 1974, Acc 6259, Box 15, CJCP.

103. Hall and Jefferson, *Resistance through Rituals*.

104. Samuel, *Theatres of Memory*, 211–12.

105. Ibid., 215–16.

106. Pop-up "Bring and Buy" shop at 58 Victoria Street by Save the Children was opened May 7, 1963, by Moire Lister and Ian Carmichael; Save the Children, "Minutes of the 17th Meeting of the London Committee: Save the Children Fund," May 19, 1963, A1218, 4: London Headquarter Branch, SCFA. The shop became permanent in June 1963. See Save the Children, "Minutes of the 18th Meeting of the London Committee: Save the Children Fund," June 25, 1963, A1218, 4: London Headquarter Branch, SCFA.

107. Glass, *London*.

108. Bailkin, *Afterlife of Empire*; Abel-Smith and Townsend, *The Poor and the Poorest*.

109. Oxfam Annual Review 1969/1970, p. 18, COM/3/1/15, OA.

110. Bennion, "Serving a Good Cause—Behind the Counter."

111. Vanda Golder, "Shop," *World's Children* 47 (Spring 1967): 15, A676, SCFA.

112. See, for example, "Oxfam Gift Shop Opened by Gateway Director," *Cheshire Observer*, October 23, 1970; "Oxfam's New Premises," *Nottingham Evening Post*, October 26, 1970; "Rate Cut for Oxfam Shop," *Sutton and Cheam Advertiser*, November 12, 1970.

113. See, for example, pamphlet, "Did You Ever Hear the Story of the Happy Tax-man?" 1973, Save the Children, A92.5, SCFA; John Gaselee, "Charities Can Profit by Your Tax," *Daily Mail*, May 3, 1967, 15; Lindsay Duncan, "Consequences of Covenants to Charity," *The Times*, May 29, 1971, 7; Clifford Longley, "Why Big Business Gives to Charity," *The Times*, May 7, 1971, 4; Our Taxation Correspondent, "The Best Ways to Help a Charity," *Financial Times*, August 15, 1964, 7. See James, *The Nonprofit Sector in International Perspective*, 267–85.

114. "How to Make the Government Give More Money to the Hungry," Oxfam (c. early 1970s), DIR/1/6/2/4, OA.

115. Ibid.

116. Neville Russel, "Tax Efficient Fundraising," London, December 1991, SCF/FR/3/3/3/NEV/1, SCFA.

117. Oxfam and Company Covenants, "An Operational Guide," DIR/1/6/2/4, OA.

118. Special correspondent, "Business Approach Brings Charities Results," *The Times*, March 2, 1965.

119. "Oxfam at Home," 1964, COM/3/1/17, OA.

120. Pemberton, "Taxation and Labour's Modernisation Programme"; Daunton, *Just Taxes*, 279–301; Whiting, *The Labour Party and Taxation*, chap. 4.

121. While some of the taxation system in the 1940s had already specified that income from trading activities had to be taxed, it was not fully enforced by the Inland Revenue. See Niall MacDermot quoted in "Tax and Charity Cards," *The Times*, June 22, 1967, 6.

122. "Tax Man May Swoop on Charity Cards," *Daily Mail*, December 13, 1965, 3.

123. The modern Christmas card market supplemented an older charitable tradition in England where charities would send tacks of cards to known supporters to sell to their neighbors.

124. Insight, "Sorting Out the Charity Chaos," *Sunday Times*, December 29, 1968.

125. Daily Mail Reporter, "Charity Tax Stays," *Daily Mail*, June 22, 1967, 7.

126. Duncan Guthrie quoted in "Charity Card Tax Plan 'Deplorable,'" *Financial Times*, November 22, 1966, 11.

127. "Taxed Charity," *Daily Telegraph*, December 14, 1965, 12.

128. "Tax Man May Swoop on Charity Cards," 3.

129. "Few Charities Escaping Tax on Card Sales," *The Guardian*, November 4, 1966.

130. Quoted in "Tax Man May Swoop on Charity Cards," 3.

131. Smith, *100 Years of NCVO and Voluntary Action*, 141–42.

132. "Few Charities Escaping Tax on Card Sales."

133. Oxfam, "Oxfam Report to the Executive Committee: Setting Up of Trading Company," June 4, 1964, COM3/1/23, OA.

134. Schenk, Thuronyi, and Cui, *Value Added Tax*.

135. Daunton, *Just Taxes*.

136. Ambrose Appelble Partners to Cecil Jackson-Cole, "Value Added Tax," May 9, 1973, Helping Hand Gift Shops, Acc 6259, Box 15, CJCP; Helping Hand Gift Shops Limited and Voluntary and Christian Services (A Charity), Value Added Tax, Report, May 1973, Helping Hand Gift Shops, Acc 6259, Box 15, CJCP.

137. Schenk, Thuronyi, and Cui, *Value Added Tax*.

138. National Council of Social Services, Charities and Value-Added Tax, June 26, 1972, DIR/1/6/2/3 VAT, OA.

139. "DeprіVATion Is Uncharitable," War on Want pamphlet, DIR/1/6/2/3 VAT, OA.

140. "Fight VAT Fast," July 4, 1972, DIR/1/6/2/3 VAT, OA.

141. Leslie Kirkley, letter to member, June 29, 1972, DIR/1/6/2/3 VAT, OA.

142. "To Editor of Local Paper," July 1972, DIR/1/6/2/3 VAT, OA.

143. Ibid.

144. VAT Parliamentary Lobbying, July 6, 1972, DIR/1/6/2/3 VAT, OA; "Director's Report to the Executive Committee," December 14, 1972, Acc 6259, Box 22, CJCP.

145. "VAT and Charities," *Hansard*, House of Commons, March 6, 1973, vol. 852, cols. 272–73.

146. "Gift to Charity," *Financial Times*, December 23, 1961, 5. Today there is a lot of criticism surrounding exactly such activity: some people argue that charity shops in fact contribute to the collapse of the small high-street trading activities.

147. Quoted in Oxfam v. Birmingham City District Council, Chancery Division, 1972, O. No. 4340, 1169.

148. Oxfam v. Birmingham Corporation, House of Lords, February 6, 10, 11, 12, Rate Case—Summary of Argument, COM/3/1/16, OA.

149. "Charity Shops: Rating," *Hansard*, House of Lords, March 29, 1976, vol. 369, col. 981.

150. Ibid., col. 985. See also Rating (Charity Shops) Bill [Lords], *Hansard*, House of Commons, July 7, 1976, vol. 914, cols. 1559–76.

151. Michelle Tusan, for example, shows how already in the late 1880s missionary philanthropy came to link "Christian service to commerce" ("The Business of Relief Work," 635); Tusan, *Smyrna's Ashes*, 100–105. For similar schemes at a later period, see Baughan, *Saving the Children*, 136–37.

152. On Elisabeth Wilson, see Andrews, *Lifetimes of Commitment*, 84–85.

153. Leslie Kirkley to W. J. Harward, "Aid Refugee Chinese Intellectuals Inc.," May 2, 1956, DIR/2/3/2/1, Folder 15, OA.

154. Daniel Nelson to Leslie Kirkley, March 18, 1959, DIR/2/3/2/1, Folder 15, OA.

155. General Manager's report, Gift Shops Sub-Committee, December 1963, TRD/4/1/1, OA.

156. Black, *Cause for Our Times*, 100.

157. Obituary, Clifton Hughes and Kerry Ten Kate, "Lynn Ten Kate: BBC Radio Presenter and Oxfam Organiser Whose Innovation Improved the Lives of Millions," *The Independent*, December 25, 2017.

158. Lynn ten Kate, interview by Dominique Marshall, Hampshire, August 11, 2010, part 1. I am grateful to Dominique Marshall for sharing the interview with me.

159. Ibid.

160. "Annual General Meeting: Chairman's Speech," December 13, 1962, R8105, OA.

161. For the connections between Oxfam and the state-led development projects in decolonizing Africa, see Hilton, "Charity, Decolonization and Development."

162. Report by Lynn ten Kate, December 1965. I thank Oxfam's archivist, Chrissie Webb, for sharing this report with me.

163. Ten Kate interview. In the interview ten Kate describes (from memory) handmade dolls but the archives show it was handmade necklaces. Report by Lynn ten Kate, December 1965. On British counterinsurgency campaigns, see French, *The British Way in Counter-Insurgency*; Elkins, *Imperial Reckoning*; Ocobock, *An Uncertain Age*; Bell, " 'A Most Horrifying Maturity in Crime' "; Linstrum, *Ruling Minds*, 155–88. On the connections between NGOs and the British counterinsurgency campaign during the Mau Mau uprising, see Hilton, "Charity, Decolonization and Development"; Baughan, "Rehabilitating an Empire."

164. Ten Kate interview.

165. Report by Lynn ten Kate, December 1965.

166. Ibid.

167. For example, she worked with Mavis Howard, the wife of Oxfam's field director in India. Ibid.

168. Jennings, *Surrogates of the State*; Hilton, "Charity, Decolonization and Development."

169. See, for example, Hilton, "Charity, Decolonization and Development"; Hodge, "British Colonial Expertise"; Baughan, *Saving the Children*, 178.

170. Peter Burns, "The Ministry of Overseas Development and Non-governmental Organisations," November 5, 1964, DIR/1/6/2/3, OA.

171. Ibid. On Burns, see also Hilton et al., *The Politics of Expertise*, 112–13.

172. Gill, *Drops in the Ocean*, 12.

173. Maggie Black, "Brierly Obituary," *The Old Radleian* (2011): 73; Hodge, "British Colonial Expertise."

174. See, for example, Nicolas Stacey, Ken Bennet, and Patrick Kemmis, "Relief Team for Nigeria/Biafra," August 8, 1968, DIR/2/3/2/33, OA.

175. See, for example, Lempell, deputy to Hug, and a Congo veteran, "Letter Gooch to Stamp," September 23, 1968, DIR/2/3/2/34, OA.

176. Ibid.

177. Oxfam Activities "Report and Plans," November 1966. I thank Oxfam's archivist, Chrissie Webb, for sharing this report with me.

178. Report by Lynn ten Kate, December 1965.

179. Leathley, "Sidelines: The State of Donation."

180. See, for example, item number 32 in Oxfam, "When Next You Pass an Oxfam Shop—Pop In!" Oxfam Activities, pamphlet, 1970, Oxfam Cards and Gifts, X.519/41135, British Library, London.

181. "Buy a Doll—All in a Good Cause," *Daily Express*, September 16, 1969. For similar venture by Save the Children, see "SCF around the World: The World's Most Traveled Dolls," *World's Children* 46 (Summer 1966): 46, A676, SCFA.

182. Oxfam Trading, Managing Director's Report, March 5, 1982, PRG/2/3/8/10, OA.

183. Oxfam, "When Next You Pass an Oxfam Shop—Pop In!"

184. Leathley, "Sidelines: The State of Donation."

Chapter 3

1. Roy Scott, "What, Why, How: Bridge Summarized," March 1, 1973, DIR/2/3/6/23, OA.

2. Roy Scott, "Give Us a Break, Folks: We Don't Want Your Charity Forever," April 8, 1974, DIR/2/3/6/23, OA.

3. Ibid.

4. Hirschman et al., *The Essential Hirschman*, 60, 67.

5. See, for example, Trentmann, "Before 'Fair Trade'"; Anderson, *A History of Fair Trade in Contemporary Britain*; Glickman, *Buying Power*; Quaas, "Selling Coffee to Raise Awareness for Development Policy"; Wheeler, *Fair Trade and the Citizen-Consumer*.

6. Van Dam, "The Limits of a Success Story"; O'Sullivan, *The NGO Moment*, 78. Matthew Anderson discusses Scott's proposal but doesn't root it within any specific politics in *A History of Fair Trade in Contemporary Britain*, 28–31.

7. Hall, *Selected Political Writings*, 85, 89.

8. Hilton shows that Oxfam's income, for example, grew from less than £10 million in 1960 to over £30 million by 1970. See Hilton, "Oxfam and the Problem of NGOs Aid Appraisal in the 1960s."

9. "Editorial: World Campaign against Hunger."

10. Stamp, *The Hungry World*, 53.

11. Hilton, "Charity and the End of Empire."

12. "Service Overseas by Volunteers: 1966," CA/I/3, file 2, Christian Aid Archives, Special Collection, School of Oriental and African Studies Library (hereafter CAA).

13. Hodge, "Writing the History of Development (Part 2: Longer, Deeper, Wider)"; Hodge, "Writing the History of Development (Part 1: The First Wave)."

14. Quoted in Bocking-Welch, "Youth against Hunger," 158.

15. See, for example, CA/I/3/2, CAA.

16. Bocking-Welch, "Youth against Hunger"; Brewis, *A Social History of Student Volunteering*; Gatrell, *Free World?*

17. "The Growth of Development Education: The Voluntary Committee on Overseas Aid and Development (VCOAD)," Centre for World Development Education Contribution, COM/3/1/19, OA.

18. John Dodd, "Britain's Young Volunteer Army," *The Guardian*, June 14, 1969.

19. "Soup and Roll Ends 100 Hour Oxfam Fast," *Daily Telegraph*, April 8, 1969; "Fast Begins 'Focus on Famine,'" *The Guardian*, October 25, 1969; "Fasters Join Starving Millions," *The Times*, October 25, 1969.

20. "Cold and Hungry in Piccadilly," *The Guardian*, December 20, 1969; Stanley Bonnet, "The Boy Who Thought Big," *Daily Mirror*, July 16, 1969; "Parsons Hit at Walk 'That Will Keep You out of Church,'" *Daily Mirror*, July 12, 1969; "The Boy behind the March," *Sunday Times*, July 8, 1969; "Sun Hits Oxfam's Walk," *Daily Express*, July 14, 1969; Frank Howitt, "What a Blisterer," *Daily Express*, July 14, 1969; Brian Cashinella, "50,000 in Walk for Oxfam," *The Times*, July 14, 1969; John Ezard, "40,000 Teenagers Limp Home with Honour," *The Times*, June 14, 1969; "Blisters for Oxfam," *Oxford Times*, June 27, 1969. For a similar example of a Save the Children sponsored walk, see Major J.B.A. Miller, "The Young Walkers," *World's Children* 46 (Autumn 1966): 57–58, A676, SCFA.

21. Philip Howard, "Lennon to Smile for Charity," *The Guardian*, October 25, 1969.

22. Quoted in Bocking-Welch, "Youth against Hunger," 160.

23. Ibid.; Bailkin, *Afterlife of Empire*, 55–94.

24. Charles Mott-Radclyffe, "Overseas Aid," *Hansard*, House of Commons, February 21, 1964, vol. 689, cols. 1568–1630.

25. Hall and Jefferson, *Resistance through Rituals*; Osgerby, *Youth in Britain*; Black, *The Political Culture of the Left in Affluent Britain*.

26. See, for example, the Albemarle Report (1960) and the creation of "Youth Work." In Ministry of Education, *The Youth Service in England and Wales*.

27. "Youth and Social Responsibilities," *Hansard*, House of Lords, March 3, 1965, vol. 263, cols. 1138–1246.

28. Moyes, *Volunteers in Development*, 50.

29. Nkrumah in fact cites Hayter's OAI report on France in *Neo-Colonialism*.

30. Hayter, *Aid as Imperialism*, 161.

31. Ibid., 9. In the 1980s she would go further and argue that governmental aid was a form of bribery that created poverty rather than mitigated it. See Hayter, *The Creation of World Poverty*.

32. For others—like a local councillor for North Kensington, Donald Chesworth—it was the exposure to domestic antiracist politics that informed them on the merits of decen-

tralized community-based development. In the aftermath of the Notting Hill white race riots of 1958, Chesworth was radicalized alongside many New Left students and worked in community development project in the area. In the mid-1960s Chesworth then worked in Tanzania alongside Bishop Trevor Huddleston to erect an agricultural school at a time when the country was undergoing a project of "villagization." In 1967, he served as an advisor to the ILO in Mauritius on a program to establish a minimum wage. By the early 1970s, he was serving as the chairman of the NGO War on Want. See "War on Want History: Interview with Derek Walker London," January 12, 2000, 2, Box 117, WOW; Hall, "Life and Times of the First New Left"; Hall, "ULR Club at Notting Hill"; Hall, Familiar Stranger, 259; Schofield and Jones, " 'Whatever Community Is, This Is Not It' "; see also Screene, "Archival Review."

33. On Save the Children and its ambiguous embrace of development, see Baughan, Saving the Children, 173–77.

34. Richard Jolly, "A Short History of IDS," IDS Discussion Paper 388, January 2008, p.11; Beloff, The Plateglass Universities; Mandler, The Crisis of the Meritocracy.

35. Price, Making Empire; Dussart and Lester, Colonization and the Origins of Humanitarian Governance.

36. British Council of Churches and the Conference of British Missionary Societies, World Poverty and British Responsibility, 7.

37. Ibid., 17.

38. Ibid.

39. Stacey quoted in Whitaker, A Bridge of People, 25.

40. Robin Sharp quoted in ibid., 29.

41. Ibid., 30.

42. Letters, New Internationalist, issue 1 (March 1973): 2.

43. "The Second Front," New Internationalist, issue 1 (March 1973): 1.

44. Peter Adamson, "The Art of Development," New Internationalist, January 2, 1980.

45. For a sophisticated analysis of the politics of UNCTAD and dependency theories, see Fajardo, The World That Latin America Created.

46. "Declaration on the Establishment of a New International Economic Order," resolution adopted at the Sixth Special Session of the UN General Assembly, May 1, 1974, United Nations, Official Records of the General Assembly, A/RES/3201(S-VI).

47. Getachew, Worldmaking after Empire, 144–45.

48. Malcolm Harper to Philip Jackson, UNCTAD 3, March 12, 1972, DIR/1/6/2/4, OA.

49. Tusan, "The Business of Relief Work." Relief through work was also a common method for the Colonial Office's famine relief efforts in Ireland and India and was imported to international aid organizations like Save the Children and the Red Cross. See, for example, Sasson and Vernon, "Practicing the British Way of Famine"; Sasson, "From Empire to Humanity." Emily Baughan also shows that they extended throughout the postwar period and were part of counterinsurgency campaigns. Baughan, Saving the Children.

50. Jonathan Stockland, "Bridge: An Evaluation," April 1986, 1, TRD/3/6/3, Folder 1, OA.

51. Ibid., 2.

52. Black, Cause for Our Times, 162–64.

53. Maggie Black, "Guy Stringer Obituary," The Guardian, July 27, 2009.

54. Stringer also played an instrumental role in launching the New Internationalist in 1973 having run Devopress, a company established by Oxfam and Christian Aid to publish the magazine. See "Goodbye to Guy," New Internationalist (September 2009): 425, 28. In 1971 Stringer became the company's deputy director and later, in 1983, director of Oxfam.

55. Black, Cause for Our Times, 165.

56. Display Ad, "If Oxfam Showed You How to Accumulate £1,333 Would You Begrudge Them £333?" *The Observer*, August 4, 1974, 21.

57. Ben Whitaker in his autobiographical account connects Stringer to a broader reorientation of the organization when Brian Walker became its director-general. Whitaker, *A Bridge of People*, 34.

58. The program had earlier permutations but Stringer expanded it.

59. Stringer cited in January 1970, in Stockland, "Bridge: An Evaluation," 3.

60. Ibid.

61. HBS brochure, "Helping-by-Selling Philosophy and Objectives," TRD/3/8/2, OA.

62. Ad, *The Time*, November 3, 1969.

63. Leaflet, "Oxfam as an Importer," Helping-by-Selling, DIR/2/3/6/23, OA; Anderson, *A History of Fair Trade in Contemporary Britain*, 27.

64. Clark et al., *India at Midpassage*, 33.

65. There were other ideas and strategies adopted by international organizations in the 1970s, most notably the "basic-needs" approach of the International Labour Organization. See International Labour Office, *Employment, Growth and Basic Needs*, 7, 16; Sharma, "The United States, the World Bank, and the Transformation of Development in the 1970s"; Brushett, "Partners in Development?"

66. Brenner and Seong-jin, "Overproduction Not Financial Collapse Is the Heart of the Crisis"; Brenner, *The Economics of Global Turbulence*, 108–14.

67. Callaway, "The Cambridge Conference on Development."

68. Bloom and Canning, "Global Demographic Change"; Dyson, *Population and Development*; Davis, "Planet of Slums."

69. On the Green Revolution, see Siegel, *Hungry Nation*. On the process of "de-agrarianization," see Benanav, "A Global History of Unemployment."

70. For example, Helping-by-Selling Project: Pendants Floor Mats from the Gilbert & Ellice Islands, which provided "more than ten hours of work" to the islanders. Oxfam COM/1/2/6, Folder 3.1, OA.

71. Leaflet, "Oxfam as an Importer."

72. Ibid.

73. Oxfam Information Department, Further Accommodation for Handicrafts Training, Vimala, Welfare Centre, Cochin, Kerala (Institute of Social Service), July 24, 1970, COM/3/1/16, OA.

74. Oxfam Annual Review 1969/1970, p. 18, COM/3/1/15, OA.

75. Ad, *The Time*, November 3, 1969.

76. Topic of the Day, "Oxfam Experiment for the City," *Nottingham Guardian Journal*, April 2, 1973.

77. Anderson, *A History of Fair Trade in Contemporary Britain*, 28.

78. Black, *Cause for Our Times*, 165.

79. Roy Scott, Report, August 15, 1972, DIR/2/3/6/23, OA.

80. Scott in April 8, 1974, cited in Stockland, "Bridge: An Evaluation," 3.

81. Roy Scott, "The Future of the Helping-by-Selling Project," September 20, 1972, DIR/2/3/6/23, OA.

82. Roy Scott to Brian Walker, Proposal to the Executive, December 31, 1974, DIR/2/3/6/23, OA.

83. Scott in April 8, 1974, cited in Stockland, "Bridge: An Evaluation," 3.

84. Scott to Walker, Proposal to the Executive.

85. Windel, *Cooperative Rule*.

86. Immerwahr, *Thinking Small*.

87. Hilton, *Prosperity for All*.

88. Bridge Cooperative, Basic Principles of the Cooperative, August 15, 1972, DIR/2/3/6/23, OA.

89. Bridge Cooperative, Constitutional Formula, August 15, 1972, DIR/2/3/6/23, OA.

90. Roy Scott, August 15, 1972, DIR/2/3/6/23, OA.

91. Bridge Cooperative, Constitutional Formula, August 15, 1972, DIR/2/3/6/23, OA.

92. Bridge Cooperative, Dividend Distribution, August 15, 1972, DIR/2/3/6/23, OA.

93. Prebisch, *Towards a New Trade Policy for Development*, 122; "Bicester-Based Charity Celebrates Anniversary: Oxfam Celebrates 25 Years of Fair-trade," March 14, 1990, COM/3/1/16, OA; Fajardo, *The World That Latin America Created*.

94. United Nations, "The Objectives of the Second Session of the Conference," *Proceedings of the United Nations Conference on Trade and Development Second Session New Delhi, 1 February–29 March 1968*, vol. 1, Report and Annexes (New York: United Nations, 1968), 11, https://unctad.org/system/files/official-document/td97vol1_en.pdf.

95. Group of 77 and United Nations Conference on Trade and Development, *Trends and Problems in World Trade and Development*, 15. See also van Dam, "The Limits of a Success Story"; O'Sullivan, *The NGO Moment*, 78; Anderson, *A History of Fair Trade in Contemporary Britain*, 28–31.

96. McKenzie, *GATT and Global Order in the Postwar Era*, 196.

97. Scott to Walker, Proposal to the Executive.

98. Van Dam, "Moralizing Postcolonial Consumer Society"; Die Erklärung von Bern, Vereinigung für solidarische Entwicklung, March 10, 1968, DIR/2/3/6/23, OA; New Proposal for Oxfam Activities Limited, Appendix B, "Notes on other organizations interested in the development of handicraft employment programmes," October 1974, DIR/2/3/6/23, OA.

99. Roy Scott, Bridge Cooperative Europe, first full discussion meetings between Oxfam and SOAS, Kerkrade, Netherlands, January 13–14, 1973, DIR/2/3/6/23, OA.

100. Scott to Walker, Proposal to the Executive.

101. Ibid.

102. Scott, "What, Why, How."

103. "Bridge: Trade for the People," Oxfam Activities Ltd., 1976, DIR/2/3/6/23, OA.

104. Anderson, *A History of Fair Trade in Contemporary Britain*, 31–32. In turn, in 1979 Scott established his own alternative trade organization, One Village, which aligned more closely with his full proposal.

105. "Bridge: Trade for the People."

106. Oxfam's Director General Report from October 1976 cited in Stockland, "Bridge: An Evaluation," 3.

107. "Bridge: Trade for the People."

108. "Bicester-Based Charity Celebrates Anniversary."

109. Oxfam Information Office, Tamil Nadu 25, Making Leather Sandals and Belts—Palam Rural Centre, November 11, 1980, COM/3/1/16, OA.

110. Maurice Zinkin, Bridge Seminar, July 9, 1986, COM/3/2/42, OA.

111. Webster, "Organizing in the Informal Economy."

112. Spodek, "The Self-Employed Women's Association (SEWA) in India."

113. The Information Department, "Bridge: Gujarati Mirrorwork," September 29, 1976, COM/3/1/16 OA.

114. Managing Director's Report, June 25, 1982, p. 2, PRG/2/3/8/10, OA.

115. Edgardo Garcia to Edward Millard, "Capiz Shellcraft Project," May 26, 1982, PRG/2/3/8/10, OA.

116. Morse, "Employment and Economic Growth," 666.

117. Hart, "Informal Income Opportunities and Urban Employment in Ghana," 61.

118. Ibid., 67.

119. For the dual economy model, see chapter 5.

120. International Labour Office, *Employment, Incomes and Equality*, 504–5; Benanav, "The Origins of Informality," 118.

121. Werlin, "The Informal Sector."

122. Standing, "Global Feminization through Flexible Labor."

123. Burgin, "The Reinvention of Entrepreneurship," 166.

124. I draw here on Geismer, "Agents of Change."

125. See, for example, James Rowland, Palam Rural Centre Tirupur, Report on Visit 5–8 December 1981, Oxfam PRG/2/3/8/10, OA.

126. Julian Francis, Lonavla F.Ds Meetings, November 12–17, 1981, PRG/2/3/8/10, OA; Julian Francis, "Bridge in the Indian Sub-continent 1981," Bridge Committee, November 12–17, 1981, Oxfam PRG/2/3/8/10, OA.

127. Bridge Policy, Annexure "A" in Francis, "Bridge in the Indian Sub-continent 1981."

128. Oxfam Trading, Report on Visit to Bridge Producers in India, November 21–December 24, 1981, PRG/2/3/8/10, OA.

129. Philip Jackson to All Area Directors and Regional Organizers, "Testimony of the Sixty," October 13, 1971, COM/3/2/19, OA.

130. Francis, "Working with the Refugees, 1971."

131. "Oxfam Bridge in India—Summary," Strategic Plan 1992–1995, Oxfam Bridge New Delhi, TRD/3/6/3, Folder 7, OA.

132. Annual Bridge Report 1989, 2, Oxfam COM/3/1/11, OA.

133. Elizabeth Mann, "Handcrafts: The Role They Can Play in Rehabilitating Disaster Victims," *Oxfam Newsletter for Craft Producers*, issue 4 (June 1989), COM/3/1/11, OA.

134. "Meet Edward Millard, Bridge Buyer for Africa and Latin America," October 1990, COM/3/1/11, OA.

135. Ibid.

136. Bridge Policy, Annexure "A."

137. Ibid.

138. John Ballyn to George Rogers, "Support of Small Production Units in South Asia," March 31, 1982, Oxfam PRG/2/3/8/10, OA.

139. Value calculated in 2019.

140. Dick Mellor, Tour Report, India, December 1981, Oxfam PRG/2/3/8/10, OA.

141. James Rowland, Vimala Welfare Centre, Cochin, "Report on Visit on 3 December 1981," Oxfam PRG/2/3/8/10, OA.

142. Dick Mellor, Tour Report, India.

143. James Rowland, Oxfam Trading Accountant, Report on Visit to Bridge Producers in India from November 21–December 24, 1981, Oxfam PRG/2/3/8/10, OA.

144. Oxfam Trading, Managing Director's Report, March 5, 1982, PRG/2/3/8/10, OA.

145. Oxfam Trading, Bridge Annual Report 1990, "The Bridge Program," 3, COM/3/1/11, OA.

146. Oxfam Trading, Managing Director's Report, June 25, 1982, PRG/2/3/8/10, OA.

147. Ibid.

148. Bridge Annual Report 1990, "The Bridge Program," 16.

149. John Pirie, "Introduction," International Trade Centre (UNPD), August 8, 1987–September 4, 1987, TRD/3/6/2, OA.

150. Oxfam Trading, Feasibility Study for the Establishment of a Marketing and Assistance Centre for Artisanal Products from Developing Countries, October 1990–July 1991, 3–4, TRD/3/6/2, OA.

151. Ibid., 11.

152. Memorandum of Association of the Artisan Trust, March 20, 1991, TRD/3/6/2, OA.

Chapter 4

1. Letters to the editor, *Daily Express*, March 25, 1975.

2. Brian Walker to Adrian Moyes, May 14, 1975, DIR/2/3/2/19, OA.

3. Getachew, *Worldmaking after Empire*, 2.

4. Bashford, *Global Population*; Connelly, *Fatal Misconception*; Ehrlich, *The Population Bomb*.

5. Department of State Publication, *American Foreign Policy, Current Documents*, 147.

6. Shaw, *World Food Security*, 3–111. For the interwar origins of food security, see Clavin, *Securing the World Economy*.

7. Editorial, "Second World Food Congress," 9.

8. Macekura, *Of Limits and Growth*.

9. Baranski, *The Globalization of Wheat*.

10. Ferguson et al., *The Shock of the Global*. On oil, see, for example, Dietrich, *Oil Revolution*; Garavini, *The Rise and Fall of OPEC in the Twentieth Century*.

11. Chenery, "Restructuring the World Economy."

12. Boulding, "The Economics of the Coming Spaceship Earth."

13. Ibid.

14. Gartlan, *Barbara Ward: Her Life and Letters*.

15. Ward, *Spaceship Earth*, 93.

16. Ibid., 121.

17. Ibid., 64.

18. Ibid., 85.

19. Robert L. Heilbroner, "Ecological Armageddon," *New York Review of Books*, April 23, 1970; Heilbroner, *Between Capitalism and Socialism*.

20. Daly, *The Stationary-State Economy*.

21. Hodson, *The Diseconomics of Growth*. On the creation of the Ecology Party and the environmental movement in Britain, see Rüdig and Lowe, "The Withered 'Greening' of British Politics"; Clapp, *An Environmental History of Britain since the Industrial Revolution*.

22. Ward, "Only One Earth."

23. Ibid.; Lazier, "Earthrise."

24. Black, *Cause for Our Times*, 107; Hayter, "The Purpose of Aid"; UNESCO, *International Understanding at School*, 75; Jonathan Power, biography, https://www.jonathanpowerjournalist.com/biography-1.

25. "The Haslemere Declaration: The Political Programme after the Convention" (Notting Hill Press, 1969), in MSS. AAM 885, Archives of the Anti-Apartheid Movement, Bodleian Archives, Bodleian Library. There are few mentions of the Haslemere Group although there is currently no comprehensive history of it. See, for example, Hilton, "International Aid and Development NGOs in Britain and Human Rights since 1945."

26. "The Haslemere Declaration: The Political Programme after the Convention," 4.

27. Haslemere Group, *Haslemere Declaration*, 4.

28. Ibid., 7.

29. Singer, "The Distribution of Gains between Investing and Borrowing Countries."

30. As Margarita Fajardo showed, much of the *dependistats* argument was based on a longer economic debate in Chile and Brazil dating to the 1950s. Fajardo, *The World That Latin America Created*.

31. Toye and Toye, "The Origins and Interpretation of the Prebisch-Singer Thesis"; Toye and Toye, *The UN and Global Political Economy*.

32. Prebisch, *Towards a New Trade Policy for Development*, 122.

33. See also Garavini, *After Empires*, chap. 1.

34. Bockman, "Socialist Globalization against Capitalist Neocolonialism."

35. For example, Rodney, *How Europe Underdeveloped Africa.*

36. Getachew, *Worldmaking after Empire*, 154. On the NIEO and international development, see Ogle, "State Rights against Private Capital."

37. Haslemere Group, *Exploitation of the Third World.*

38. Haslemere Group, *Haslemere Declaration.*

39. "The Haslemere Declaration: The Political Programme after the Convention."

40. Ibid., emphasis in the original.

41. Robert Hutchison, "Southern Africa. Notes Towards a Haslemere Campaign," June 18, 1969, MSS. AAM 885; Monica M. Tomkins, convener for North London Haslemere Group, to Alan Brook from the Anti-Apartheid Movement, "Haslemere Group Teach-In," January 21, 1970, MSS. AAM 885.

42. Hutchison, "Southern Africa."

43. Quoted in Bocking-Welch, "Imperial Legacies and Internationalist Discourses," 887

44. Power, *Development Economics*, 33.

45. Ibid., 45.

46. North London Haslemere Group, *Coffee*, 4.

47. Ibid.

48. Ibid., 3.

49. Ibid., 18.

50. Bockman, "Socialist Globalization against Capitalist Neocolonialism," 115; Group of 77 and United Nations Conference on Trade and Development, *Trends and Problems in World Trade and Development*, 15.

51. See, for example, similar arguments made by Robert Lightbourne, Jamaica's minister of trade and industry; see John Young, "Survival at Stake in Europe Decision," *The Times*, September 14, 1970, p. i. Similar arguments were also made by Conservative and Labour MPs; see David James and Edward Milne, "Commonwealth Sugar and the Common Market," *The Times*, January 25, 1971, 14.

52. Saunders, "British Humanitarian, Aid and Development NGOs"; Clifford Longley, "How the Sugar Lobby Is Preparing for Battle," *The Times*, February 15, 1971, 12; Cook, *The Routledge Guide to British Political Archives*, 414; Hilton, "International Aid and Development NGOs in Britain and Human Rights since 1945," 455.

53. Dennis Barker, "Sugar Protest Offers a Sweetener," *The Guardian*, April 30, 1973, 5; Longley, "How the Sugar Lobby Is Preparing for Battle," 12.

54. Longley, "How the Sugar Lobby Is Preparing for Battle," 12; Clifford Longley, "Sugar 'Concession' Fails to Satisfy Producers," *The Times*, May 12, 1971, 6.

55. Pamphlet, "Europe '73 Programme: A Europe for the Third World," 1973, CPN/4/4/1, Folder 1, OA.

56. Melvyn Westlake, "EEC Drive to Promote Third World Trade," *The Times*, January 16, 1973, 18.

57. Pamphlet, "Europe '73: Programme Guide," 1973, CPN/4/4/1, Folder 1, OA.

58. Ibid.

59. Melvyn Westlake, "Writing New Chapter to Sugar's Bitter History," *The Times*, September 13, 1973, 21.

60. Mintz, *Sweetness and Power.*

61. Southgate, *The Commonwealth Sugar Agreement*, 8.

62. R. J. Hammond quoted in ibid., 9.

63. See Southgate, *The Commonwealth Sugar Agreement*, 10.

64. Guy Sauzier, "Safeguard for Sugar," *The Times*, March 12, 1968, p. vi (London representative of Mauritius Chamber of Agriculture).

65. Haslemere Declaration Group, *Sugar Today, Jam Tomorrow?*

66. Ibid.

67. On a similar Dutch campaign, see van Dam, "In Search of the Citizen-Consumer."

68. Many British MPs shared this view. See "'Moral Commitment' on Commonwealth Sugar," *The Guardian*, May 18, 1971, 4.

69. Ibid.

70. Sarah Wells et al., "Plight of Poor Countries," *The Times*, October 5, 1974, 15. On similar domestic debates, see Rob Saunders on the 1975 EU referendum in Saunders, *Yes to Europe!* chap. 9.

71. From Our Own Correspondent, "UK Likely to Withdraw from Sugar Agreement," *The Times*, September 20, 1973, 2.

72. Peter Strafford, "Mr Rippon Says 'Gigantic Blunder' if British Entry Hits Stability of Commonwealth Sugar Producers," *The Times*, March 17, 1971, 6.

73. Figures in Saunders, *Yes to Europe!* 278.

74. Philippe Chalmin, *The Making of a Sugar Giant: Tate and Lyle, 1859–1989* (London: Taylor & Francis, 1990). See also "UK Sugar Men Look Sour about the EEC," *The Times*, March 10, 1971, 20; RS, "Crisis That Faces the UK Refiners," *The Times*, October 18, 1973, 23; Melvyn Westlake, "Ration Fear Sends Sugar Price Soaring," *The Times*, February 14, 1974, 25.

75. Brian Bennion quoted in Peter Hetherington, "Rationing Starts as Sugar Shortage Looms," *The Guardian*, July 9, 1974.

76. "Shoppers Blackmailed over Sugar, Woman MP says," *The Times*, July 29, 1974, 3; Alan Smith, "Bakers Are Paying Black Market Prices for Sugar," *The Guardian*, July 29, 1974, 18; Rosemary Collins, "'Rationing' of Sugar Blamed on Hoarders," *The Guardian*, July 24, 1974, 6; "Sugar May Be Scarce," *The Guardian*, July 5, 1974, 8.

77. "Next Week's Sugar and Next Year's," *The Times*, August 27, 1974, 11; "Mrs. Williams Says Sugar Price Might Double," *The Times*, September 10, 1974, 1.

78. "Price Equalization Scheme for Sugar Announced," *The Times*, November 1, 1974, 9; John Carvel, "Famine in Sugar Now Looming," *The Guardian*, November 5, 1974, 1; "Mr. Wilson Proposes Pact with Commodity Producers for Stabilization of Prices," *The Times*, February 10, 1975, 15.

79. "Government Encouraging Farmers to Expand Sowing of Beet," *The Times*, November 8, 1974, 6.

80. "CAP to the Rescue," *The Times*, September 20, 1974, 17; Hugh Clayton, "Why the Sugar Shortage Meant Embarrassment for the Government," *The Times*, December 6, 1974, 14.

81. Saunders, *Yes to Europe!* 279.

82. Riley, "Monstrous Predatory Vampires and Beneficent Fairy-Godmothers."

83. Ministry of Agriculture, Fisheries and Food, *Food from Our Own Resources*.

84. Ibid., 17.

85. Ibid., 7.

86. Edgerton, *The Rise and Fall of the British Nation*, 667–729.

87. Frey-Wouters, *The European Community and the Third World*; Lister, *The European Community and the Developing World*, 58–166.

88. European Investment Bank, *European Investment Bank Operations under the Lomé Convention* (Luxembourg: OPOCE, 1975); "European Investment Bank: Annual Report 1976," https://www.eib.org/attachments/general/reports/ar1976en.pdf.

89. Frans A. M. Alting von Geusau and Joshua C. Anyiwo, eds., *The Lomé Convention and a New International Economic Order* (Leiden: Sijthoff, 1977), 7.

90. See, for example, Robbins and Ansari, *The Profits of Doom*, 10.

91. "Sugar Workers Meet Cane Cutters," *Spur*, issue 41 (July/August 1977): 1.

92. "Sugar Empire for the French Beet," *Spur*, issue 43 (October 1977): 4.

93. See, for example, Tangermann, "European Interests in the Banana Market."

94. Van Rooy, "The Altruistic Lobbyists," 176.

95. Gerlach, "Famine Responses in the World Food Crisis."

96. Figures from ibid. See also Emma Rothschild, "The Politics of Food," *New York Review of Books*, May 16, 1974.

97. 4th Summit Conference of Heads of State or Government of the Non-Aligned Movement, Algiers, Algeria, September 5–9, 1973, 65.

98. "FAO Endorses Unanimously World Food Conference in 1974," January 3, 1974, FCO 61/1059, TNA.

99. World Food Problems and the United Nations, House of Lords, January 9, 1974: 179–80, FCO 61/1059; "FAO Endorses Unanimously World Food Conference in 1974"; Draft, Written Parliamentary Question, Background Notes, December 5, 1974, FCO 61/1059; draft notes, c. December 1974, FCO 61/1059.

100. "Universal Declaration on the Eradication of Hunger and Malnutrition," World Food Conference, November 1974, UN.

101. On liberal philosophy, see Moyn, *Not Enough*, chap. 6; Forrester, *In the Shadow of Justice*, chap. 6.

102. Singer, "Famine, Affluence, and Morality."

103. Moyn, *Not Enough*; Forrester, *In the Shadow of Justice*.

104. O'Neill, "Lifeboat Earth."

105. Forrester, *In the Shadow of Justice*, 193.

106. O'Neill, "Lifeboat Earth," 279, 279n2.

107. Ibid., 290.

108. Brandt was quoted frequently in Oxfam's internal correspondence about the "lifestyle" campaign.

109. Independent Commission on International Development and Brandt, *Common Crisis North-South*.

110. Sicco Mansholt, "Europe's Responsibility in the World," Gilbert Murray Memorial Lecture for Oxfam, Oxford Union, October 31, 1973, 4 MS Oxfam COM/1/5/2, OA.

111. Ibid., 1.

112. Ibid.

113. Quoted in Sharp and Whittemore, "Europe and the World Without," 4.

114. Mansfield, *The Other Way*.

115. "The Growth of Development Education: The Voluntary Committee on Overseas Aid and Development (VCOAD)."

116. "Oxfam's New Bid to Help Hungry," *Oxfam Mail*, November 18, 1974.

117. "Oxfam Launches National Fund-Raising Drive—Feed *All* the Family," *News from Oxfam*, November 17, 1974, DIR/2/3/2/19, OA.

118. Black, *Cause for Our Times*, 207.

119. Brian Walker to Adrian Moyes, May 14, 1975, 1–8, DIR/2/3/2/19, OA.

120. Oxfam memo, A. N. Oppenheim, "Changing Consumption Patterns," March 1, 1975, DIR/2/3/2/19, OA.

121. See also Elizabeth Stamp to Harford Thomas, "Conference: Mature Growth," April 14, 1976, DIR/2/3/2/19, OA.

122. Memo from Adrian Moyes, "Lifestyle Symposium," April 21, 1975, DIR/2/3/2/19, OA; emphasis in the original.

123. Walker to Moyes, May 14, 1975.

124. Ibid.

125. Moyes, "Lifestyle Symposium."

126. Ibid.

127. "What Can We Do?" in "Nutrition Paper 2 Part A," Oxfam DIR/2/3/2/19, "Food for Thought."

128. For the longer history of consumer activism, see Trentmann, *Free Trade Nation*; Hilton, *Prosperity for All*.

129. Hutt, "The Concept of Consumers' Sovereignty," 66. See also Hutt, "Economic Method and the Concept of Competition"; Hutt, *Economists and the Public*; Olsen, *The Sovereign Consumer*.

130. Slobodian, *Globalists*, 118–20. In the 1950s Crosland suggested that consumerism held the key to the end of social hierarchies. Jackson, *Equality and the British Left*, 194; Reisman, *Crosland's Future*, 54–55.

131. Young, *The Chipped White Cups of Dover*, 11.

132. Hilton, *Consumerism in Twentieth-Century Britain*, 274.

133. Young, *The Chipped White Cups of Dover*, 9.

134. Hilton, *Consumerism in Twentieth-Century Britain*, 242.

135. Thane, "Michael Young and Welfare."

136. Elizabeth Stamp and Adrian Moyes, "Lifestyle and the Consumers' Association," internal memo to lifestyle group, October 24, 1975, DIR/2/3/2/19, OA.

137. Ibid.

138. Ibid.

139. Black, "Which? Craft in Post-War Britain."

140. Stamp and Moyes, "Lifestyle and the Consumers' Association."

141. From the Dean of Bristol Horace Dammers, "Life Style News Letter 1975," Life Style Offers, DIR/2/3/2/19, OA.

142. Ibid.

143. Philip Jackson to Brian Walker, "Life-Styles," October 28, 1975, DIR/2/3/2/19, OA; Malcolm Harper to Brian Walker, "Lifestyle Planning Group," March 9, 1976, DIR/2/3/2/19, OA.

144. Adrian Moyes to Lifestyle Group, "Lifestyle Theme," December 22, 1975, DIR/2/3/2/19, OA.

145. Walker to Moyes, May 14, 1975.

146. Adrian Moyes to Lifestyle Group, "The Complexities of Changing Our Lifestyles," December 31, 1975, DIR/2/3/2/19, OA.

147. See Adrian Moyes's (ibid.) direct reference to economists like Barbara Ward and Lester Brown as well as to politicians like Willy Brandt.

148. Ibid.

149. Ibid.

150. Wood, *Out of My Mind*, 142; Leuchtenburg, *Herbert Hoover*, 34.

151. War Food Administration, "Outline of Clean Plate Club," Washington, D.C., November 15, 1943.

152. War Food Administration, Food Fight for Freedom, "Procedure for the Development of the Clean Club Campaign for the Midwest Region," Chicago, December 9, 1943.

153. On fasts, see, for example, "Soup and Roll Ends 100 Hour Oxfam Fast," *Daily Telegraph*, April 8, 1969; "Fast Begins 'Focus on Famine,'" *The Guardian*, October 25, 1969; "Fasters Join Starving Million," *The Times*, October 25, 1969. On walks, see Stanley Bonnet, "The Boy Who Thought Big," *Daily Mirror*, July 16, 1969; "Parsons Hit at Walk 'That Will Keep You out of Church,'" *Daily Mirror*, July 12, 1969; "The Boy behind the March," *Sunday Times*, July 8, 1969; "Sun Hits Oxfam's Walk," *Daily Express*, July 14, 1969; Frank Howitt, "What a Blisterer," *Daily Express*, July 14, 1969; Brian Cashinella, "50,000 in Walk for Oxfam," *The Times*, July 14, 1969.

154. "Oxfam Launches National Fund-Raising Drive—Feed *All* the Family"; "Save a Little, Give a Little during Oxfam (and every other) Week," pamphlet, c. 1976, DIR/2/3/2/19, OA.

155. Walker to Moyes, May 14, 1975.

156. "One in Three Will Get a Full Meal," *Darlington & Stockton Times*, May 18, 1974. See also "Oxfam Week," *Oxford Time*, September 23, 1977.

157. "One in Three Will Get a Full Meal."

158. Adrian Walker to Dr. H. C. Pereira, November 11, 1975, Oxfam DIR/2/3/2/19, OA.

159. "Eating in Britain" in "Nutrition Paper 2 Part A," Oxfam DIR/2/3/2/19, OA.

160. Penna, "The Coal Revolution: The Transition from an Organic to a Mineral Economy," in *A History of Energy Flows*, 53–83.

161. "Eating in Britain" in "Nutrition Paper 2 Part A."

162. Otter, *Diet for a Large Planet*; Otter, "Industrializing Diet, Industrializing Ourselves."

163. Walker to Moyes, May 14, 1975; Moyes, "Lifestyle Symposium."

164. "Eating in Britain" in "Nutrition Paper 2 Part A."

165. Brown and Eckholm, *By Bread Alone*, 251.

166. Lester R. Brown with Eric P. Eckholm, "Choices," in *War on Hunger*, ed. Rhoad.

167. Lappé, *Diet for a Small Planet*, 382–83.

168. LaBarbera-Twarog, *Politics of the Pantry*, 2.

169. "What Can We Do?" in "Nutrition Paper 2 Part A," Oxfam DIR/2/3/2/19, OA.

170. "Typical Diet in Three Countries" in "Nutrition Paper 2 Part A," Oxfam DIR/2/3/2/19, OA.

171. Harper to Walker, "Lifestyle Planning Group"; Lifestyle Planning Group, January 6, 1976, DIR/2/3/2/19, OA.

172. Walker, *One Crust of Bread*, 18.

173. "Eating in Britain" in "Nutrition Paper 2 Part A."

174. Behar, "European Diets vs. Traditional Foods"; Behar, "Nutrition and the Future of Mankind."

175. For more on obesity, see Offer, *The Challenge of Affluence*; Zweiniger-Bargielowska, "The Culture of the Abdomen."

176. See, for example, "Slimming for Oxfam," *Retail Newsagent*, June 6, 1970; *The Times*, September 11, 1970; "Slimming," *Financial Times*, September 12, 1970; "Oxfam £2,000 from Slimming," *National Newsagent*, January 16, 1971; "Lost Pounds Will Help Swell Funds," *Southern Evening Echo*, September 2, 1970; Philip Daley, "Slim for the Health of Others," *Oldham Evening Chronicle*, August 24, 1970; "Losing Weight to Help the Hungry," *Sheffield Morning Telegraph*, September 9, 1970; "Charity Will Benefit as You Shed Excess Weight," *Edgware, Mill Hill & Kingsbury Times*, September 25, 1970; D. Swithnmank, "Slimming for Oxfam," *Dunfermline Press*, September 11, 1970; Gordon McMillan, "Slimming for Oxfam," *Birmingham Post*, September 5, 1970; (Mrs.) D. C. Catt, "Slim for Oxfam," *The Dress and Journal*, Aberdeen, September 14, 1970; Alan Egglestone, "Slim for Oxfam," *North Wales Chronicle*, Bangor, October 8, 1970.

177. Betty Price, "Slimming for Oxfam," *Wimbledon Boro News*, September 11, 1970; Betty Price, "Slimming for Oxfam," September 4, 1970, COM/2/4/11, OA.

178. "Slimming Together: Extract From the Which Report on Slimming," in Betty Price, *Beginner Guide to Oxfam's Slimming Clubs*, 1978, CPN/7/1, Folder 1, OA.

179. McMillan, "Slimming for Oxfam."

180. "Lifestyle Planning Group," January 23, 1976, Oxfam DIR/2/3/2/19, OA.

181. "Oxfam Slimming Clubs—A Partnership for Mutual Benefit of the Overweight and the Underfed," in Price, *Beginner Guide to Oxfam's Slimming Clubs*.

182. See, for example, "Slimming—the Oxfam Way," in Price, *Beginner Guide to Oxfam's Slimming Clubs.*

183. Walker, *One Crust of Bread*, 6.

184. Ibid., 7.

185. Ibid., 11.

186. Ibid., 12.

187. Ibid., 18.

188. Quoted in Rothschild, "The Politics of Food."

189. Ibid.

190. Barbara Ward, "The Fat Years and the Lean," *The Economist* 253 (November 2, 1974): 19–25.

191. Quoted in Rothschild, "The Politics of Food."

Chapter 5

1. Schumacher, "Ownership," in *Small Is Beautiful*, 221–29.

2. Sasson, "Milking the Third World?"; Eckel, and Moyn, *The Breakthrough.*

3. Bair, "From the Politics of Development to the Challenges of Globalization"; Bair, "Corporations at the United Nations."

4. Solnit, Solnit, and Mittal, *The Battle of the Story of the Battle of Seattle*; Fernandez, *Policing Dissent*; Pleyers and Touraine, *Alter-Globalization.*

5. Kauffman, *Direct Action*; Adler, *No Globalization without Representation.* Two notable exceptions are Moreton, *To Serve God and Wal-Mart* and Raianu, *Tata.*

6. Goyder, *Trusteeship*, 10.

7. Ernest Bader, "Impressions from a Visit to Khadi and Village Industry Project, 1958," 1071/EB/Z/7, Modern Records Centre, University of Warwick (hereafter MRC).

8. Hoe, *The Man Who Gave His Company Away*, 80.

9. Blum, *Work and Community*, 6.

10. Bader, "The Scott Bader Commonwealth"; Hoe, *The Man Who Gave His Company Away.*

11. See also Watkins, *Industrial Common Ownership.*

12. Godric E. S. Bader of Scott Bader Co. Ltd., abstract of talk "Common Ownership—An Effective Means of Social Change," LSE/BHU/25, London School of Economics Archives.

13. Drucker, *The Concept of the Corporation*, 247.

14. Ibid., 135.

15. Quoted in extract from "A Case Study of Labour-Management Relations at the Godrej & Boyce Mfg. Co. Pvt. Ltd.," Bombay 1962, 1071/EB/PPS/2/5, MRC.

16. Bader, "The Scott Bader Commonwealth."

17. Quoted in extract from "A Case Study of Labour-Management Relations at the Godrej & Boyce Mfg. Co. Pvt. Ltd."

18. Jeremy, *Capitalists and Christians*, 196–209.

19. Goyder and Kellock, *The Future of Private Enterprise*, 25, 23.

20. Ibid., 82–87.

21. Ibid., 51.

22. Francis Boyd, "Liberal Party May Split over Workers' Control," *The Guardian*, June 2, 1967.

23. Wellock, *Off the Beaten Track*, 40.

24. Koven, *The Match Girl and the Heiress*, 295.

25. Wellock, *Off the Beaten Track*, 64.

26. Wellock had already been introduced to Gandhian ideas in the 1920s, but it was in the 1930s, when he became disillusioned with Labour's politics, that he turned to Gandhian economics.

27. Wellock, *Off the Beaten Track*, 53.

28. Wellock, *The Third Way*.

29. Taylor, *Creating Capitalism*.

30. Quoted in extract from "A Case Study of Labour-Management Relations at the Godrej & Boyce Mfg. Co. Pvt. Ltd."

31. Ibid.

32. Jeremy, *Religion, Business and Wealth in Modern Britain*. On business ethics and religious ambitions, albeit from a conservative perspective, see Moreton, *To Serve God and Wal-Mart*.

33. Ernest Bader, "The Spiritual Implications of Common *Ownership*," c. 1970s, 1071/EB/PPS/2/8, MRC.

34. Ad, "Demintry," *The Times*, February 25, 1958. See also Quarter, *Beyond the Bottom Line*.

35. Nigel Farrow, "The Profit in Worker Ownership," 1965 reprint from *Business*, the Management Journal, for Scott Bader & Company Limited, 1071/EB/DEM/2/51, MRC.

36. Ibid.

37. Wellock, *"Which Way America?" "Which Way Britain?"* 12.

38. Ibid.

39. Ibid., 31.

40. "Statement of Principles," in ibid., ii.

41. Notes on meeting in David Astor's office on September 30, 1959, 1071/SB/STR/1/1-25, MRC.

42. On Hinden, see Riley, "Writing like a Woman."

43. Suggested Letter to *The Times*, Bhoodan Fund, c. December 1959, MS62/MB1/R64, Hartley Library, University of Southampton (HLUoS). A similar organization also existed in the United States and was led by the former U.S. ambassador in India, Charles Bowles. See, for example, Charles Bowles to Mr. Rockefeller, July 24, 1955, MS62/MB1/R64, HLUoS.

44. Hallam Tennyson to Lady Mountbatten, Bhoodan Project Appeal, March 7, 1956, MS62/MB1/R64, HLUoS.

45. See also Engerman, *The Price of Aid*.

46. Siegel, "The Kibbutz and the Ashram," 1182.

47. Wellock, *India's Social Revolution Led by Mahatma Gandhi and Now Vinoba Bhave*.

48. See, for example, Wilfred Wellock, "India: A Meditation," *Sarvodaya* 17 (July 1967): 21–24, 1071/EB/PUB/ 1/30/1, MRC.

49. Quoted in Hoe, *The Man Who Gave His Company Away*, 165.

50. Memo, October 7, 1959, 1071/SB/STR/1/1-25, MRC.

51. Quoted in extract from "A Case Study of Labour-Management Relations at the Godrej & Boyce Mfg. Co. Pvt. Ltd."

52. "Ekistechnia Ltd.—a technical training center for small scale industry in underdeveloped countries. An outline and explanation," October 12, 1959, 1071/SB/STR/1/1-25, MRC.

53. "A practical proposal: Demintry Production-Cum-Training Centre in India, entirely supported by an in-built self-governed enterprise as a model for democratic industrial development," 1071/SB/STR/1/1-25, MRC; Hoe, *The Man Who Gave His Company Away*; "Ideas on a Commonwealth Centre for Study Development and Training," Fred Blum, 1071/SB/STR/1/1-25, MRC; A. D. Singh, "The Third Way in Industry for India," February 16, 1959, 1071/SB/STR/1/1-25, MRC.

54. Michael Ionides, "Object and Implications of Economic Development," Royal Institute of Public Administration, 1959, 1071/SB/STR/1/1-25, MRC; David Hardman, Notes on the memorandum entitled TEKISTICS, September 22, 1959, 1071/SB/STR/1/1-25, MRC; Gupta, "Staging Baghdad as a Problem of Development."

55. "Ekistechnia Ltd."

56. "Ekistics: A Note of Explanation," August 26, 1959, 1071/SB/STR/1/1-25, MRC.

57. David Billingsley, "Strive (Overseas) Ltd. Consideration of a Development Plan for a 'Strive' Centre at Wollaston Hall," March 19, 1964, 1071/SB/STR/2/1-112, MRC.

58. Ibid.

59. Robert Edwards, "Overseas Aid," *Hansard*, House of Commons Debate, February 21, 1964, vol. 689, cols. 1568–1630.

60. Billingsley, "Strive (Overseas) Ltd. Consideration of a Development Plan."

61. Ernest Bader, "Aid by Trade," February 1962, 1071/SB/STR/1/26, MRC.

62. Ibid.

63. For Arthur E. Morgan and community development, see Immerwahr, *Thinking Small*.

64. Bader, "Aid by Trade."

65. UNCTAD influenced discussions in Britain about a new overseas aid bill. During these deliberations MP Robert Edwards, who was a member of the Scott Bader Commonwealth, discussed Strive. See Edwards, "Overseas Aid."

66. Garavini, *After Empires*.

67. Ernest Bader, "Industrial Society" (c. 1964), p. 1, 1071/SB/STR/2/1-112, MRC. Bader quoted in Tawney, *Religion and the Rise of Capitalism*.

68. "Industrial Society Needs Help from the Churches," in Bader, "Industrial Society," 4.

69. Bader, "Industrial Society," 1.

70. Watkins, *Industrial Common Ownership*.

71. The pamphlet was based on a lecture Schumacher gave "to a group of young Christians studying industrial problems," in London, May 1961. See E. F. Schumacher, "Modern Industry in the Light of the Gospel," October 1962, Schumacher Center for a New Economics, https://centerforneweconomics.org/publications/modern-industry-in-the-light-of-the-gospel.

72. See also Leonard, "E. F. Schumacher and Intermediate Technology"; Alacevich and Boianovsky, "Writing the History of Development Economics."

73. Schumacher, *Roots of Economic Growth*, 35.

74. Lewis, "Economic Development with Unlimited Supplies of Labour." See Benanav, "The Origins of Informality," 110.

75. United Nations, *Measures for the Economic Development of Under-developed Countries*.

76. Tignor, "Unlimited Supplies of Labor."

77. Helleiner, *The Forgotten Foundations of Bretton Woods*.

78. E. F. Schumacher, "How to Help Them Help Themselves," *The Observer*, August 29, 1965.

79. Ibid.

80. Campbell and McIlroy, "The High Tide of Trade Unionism"; Goldthorpe, "The Current Inflation"; Reid, *United We Stand*.

81. Saunders, *Assembling Cultures*, 33.

82. J.R.L. Anderson, "A New Theory of Labour," *The Guardian*, October 27, 1964.

83. Tawney, *Equality* (1962), 242.

84. E. F. Schumacher, "The Problem of Ownership" (likely notes for 1965 conference in Delhi, "Social Responsibility of Business"), 1071/EB/PPS/2/1/1-12, MRC.

85. McElroy and Moros, "Joint Production Committees, January 1948."

86. Clegg, *A New Approach to Industrial Democracy*; Fogarty, *Company and Corporation*.

87. Labour Party, *Report of the Labour Party Working Party on Industrial Democracy*, 24.

88. See "Royal Commission on Trade Unions and Employers' Associations," in Terms and Conditions of Employment Act 1959: Recommendation made by the Donovan Commission, 1968, LAB 11/3082, TNA. See also Lane, "A Watershed Decade in British Industrial Relations," 28.

89. Conference Report, "The Further Development in the U.K. of Appropriate Technologies and Their Communication to Developing Countries," Intermediate Technology Development Group Ltd., January 1968, EB/ITDG/1/1-22, MRC.

90. Schumacher, *Small Is Beautiful*, 236, emphasis in the original.

91. Verena Schumacher, "George McRobie Obituary," *The Guardian*, July 27, 2016.

92. George McRobie, "Obituary: Julia Porter," *The Independent*, August 30, 1992.

93. For Noel Paterson, see Bocking-Welch, *British Civic Society at the End of Empire*.

94. "Intermediate Technology Development Group Ltd."

95. "The Intermediate Technology Development Group Ltd. Background—Formation—First Year's Work," April 1966/1967, ITDG Ltd. Annual Report 1967, EB/ITDG/1/7A, MRC.

96. *Tools for Progress* catalogue, 1967, in 1071/EB/PUB/2/4/2/1-2, MRC.

97. Schumacher quoted in Conference Report, "The Further Development in the U.K. of Appropriate Technologies and Their Communication to Developing Countries."

98. From Kenkare, "Technology for the Developing World."

99. McRobie and Schumacher, *Small Is Possible*, 49.

100. "Intermediate Technology Development Group," Science and Technology for Development, July 11, 1975, OD 63/60, TNA.

101. Conference Report, "The Further Development in the U.K. of Appropriate Technologies and Their Communication to Developing Countries."

102. On the involvement of businesses in decolonization, see, for example, Tignor, *Capitalism and Nationalism at the End of Empire*; Stockwell, *The Business of Decolonization*; Ogle, "'Funk Money.'"

103. "Intermediate Technology Development Group."

104. "Intermediate Technology Development Group," *Hansard*, House of Commons, December 6, 1977, vol. 940, cols. 669-70W.

105. "Intermediate Technology Development Group Ltd."

106. A.G.M. Report on the Industrial Liaison Unit, c. 1974, 1071/EB/ITDG/1/27A, MRC.

107. Judith Hart to Robert Hughes, May 1, 1975, OD 63/60, TNA.

108. Ministry for Overseas Development, "Helping Small-Scale Industries in the Third World"; "Mrs. Judith Hart Opens New Unit in Rugby," November 8, 1978, OD 63/60, TNA.

109. Intermediate Technology Development Group, "Annual Report and Accounts for year ended 30th September 1976, The Chairman's Report, 1 October 1975–30 September 1976," p. 9, OD 63/60, TNA.

110. "The Intermediate Technology Development Group Ltd. Background—Formation—First Year's Work," April 1966/1967, in ITDG Ltd. Annual Report 1967, EB/ITDG/1/7, TNA.

111. "Intermediate Technology Development Group Ltd."

112. UNCHS Habitat, "United Republic of Tanzania."

113. UNCHS Habitat, "Annex."

114. Gerlach, "Illusions of Global Governance"; Hamelink, *The Politics of World Communication*, 40-42.

115. Ad Hoc Meeting on FAO/Industry Relations, Rome, September 22–23, 1965, "FAO Cooperation with Industries, Volume II," Food and Agriculture Organization Archives, Rome.

116. George, *How the Other Half Dies*. See also A. H. Boerma, director-general, "Industry Cooperative Programme," 6th Session of the General Committee, March 23 and 24, 1970, 13–16, "FAO Cooperation with Industries, Volume II"; Solomon, *Multinational Corporations and the Emerging World Order*, 161–64.

117. Jonathan Taylor, "Obituaries: Sir George Bishop," *The Independent*, April 16, 1999. Bishop had worked at the Ministry of Food during the war and in the immediate postwar years served as undersecretary to the Labour minister of food John Strachey.

118. See "Sugar in Kenya, 1964–1966," DO 214/86, TNA; Abbott, *Agricultural Marketing Enterprises for the Developing World*, 93–96; Hazelwood and Holtham, *Aid and Inequality in Kenya*.

119. McRobie, "Intermediate Technology," 73.

120. Draft Discussion Paper, Science and Technology for Development, January 30, 1973, OD 63/57, TNA.

121. Intermediate Technology Development Group, "Annual Report and Accounts for year ended 30th September 1976," p. 3.

122. Goyder, *The Responsible Company*, 12, 109.

123. Some of these discussions later influenced consumer activism and campaigns against corporate secrecy in Britain. See Hilton, *Consumerism in Twentieth-Century Britain*, 275; Vincent, *The Culture of Secrecy*, 248–304. I thank Lise Bulter for drawing my attention to the connection between social audit and the opposition to secrecy laws.

124. Sasson, "Milking the Third World?"; Hilton, *Prosperity for All*.

125. Raianu, *Tata*.

126. For consumer activism and social audit, especially through the think tank the Public Interest Research Centre and its nonprofit the Social Audit Ltd., see Hilton, *Consumerism in Twentieth-Century Britain*, 275–76.

127. House of Commons, "Code of Industrial Relations Practice," *Hansard*, October 18, 1971, vol. 823, cols. 385–504.

128. See Barbara Castle's critique, for example, in House of Commons, "Code of Industrial Relations Practice," *Hansard*, October 18, 1971, vol. 823, cols. 385–504.

129. Quoted in Medawar, *The Social Audit Consumer Handbook*, 15.

130. De Paula, "The Six Commandments," 10.

131. Confederation of British Industry Company Affairs Committee, *The Responsibilities of the British Public Company*, 8–9.

132. Melrose-Woodman and Kverndal, *Towards Social Responsibility*, 5, 25. See also Kaplan and Kinderman, "The Business-Class Case for Corporate Social Responsibility," 148.

133. See, for example, Fogarty, *Company Responsibility and Participation*; Beesley, "The Context of Social Responsibility in Business"; Kempner, MacMillan, and Hawkins, *Business and Society*; Robertson, *Profit or People?*; Epstein, "The Social Role of Business Enterprise in Britain"; Beesley and Evans, *Corporate Social Responsibility*.

134. A. W. Fisher, "Notes on the Forum on Corporate Responsibility," September 24, 1975, Public Relations Consultant Association Limited, "Social Responsibility—For Whose Action?" 1974–1975, Papers of Alan Fisher Lectures 562/5/5, MRC.

135. See a talk by Denise Inchbald, "Social Audit as Means of Appraisal" in program draft, "Corporate Social Responsibility Forum, 1975," in Papers of Professor Kenneth William (Bill) Wedderburn, 972/1/6/26, MRC.

136. Mees, *The Rise of Business Ethics*.

137. Webley, *An Enquiry into Some Aspects of British Businessmen's Behaviour*; Webley, *Towards a Code of Business Ethics*; Fryers, *What Kind of Marketing Ethics?*; Basnett, *Trade Union Responsibilities*; Nicolson, *The Management of Change in British*

Airways; Ridley, *Company & Its Responsibilities?*; Morgan, *European Approaches to Responsibility*; Humble, *The Responsible Multinational Enterprise*; Williams, *Advertising and Social Conscience*.

138. Secretary of State for Industry, "The Regeneration of British Industry."

139. Department of Industry: Industry/Education Unit, BT 251/303, TNA.

140. Bullock, *Report of the Committee of Inquiry on Industrial Democracy*. See also Davies, "The Bullock Report and Employee Participation in Corporate Planning in the U.K."; Prentice, "Employee Participation in Corporate Government."

141. See also Vernon, "Economic Sovereignty at Bay"; Vernon, *Sovereignty at Bay*; Barnet and Müller, *Global Reach*; Gilpin, *U.S. Power and the Multinational Corporation*; Gilpin, "Three Models of the Future."

142. "United Nations Commission on Transnational Corporations."

143. Sen, *Multinational Corporations in the Developing Countries*; Bair, "Corporations at the United Nations," 159; Dunning and Nejad, *The UN and Transnational Corporations*.

144. See, for example, the anti-apartheid campaigns led by Oxfam and the World Council of Churches. World Council of Churches, *World Council of Churches and Bank Loans to Apartheid*, 11.

145. Luetchford and Burns, *Waging the War on Want*.

146. *World in Action*, 1973.

147. Bond, *The State of Tea*, 2.

148. International Confederation of Free Trade Unions Executive Board, *Towards a New Economic and Social Order*, 33; Alston, "International Trade as an Instrument of Positive Human Rights Policy."

149. War on Want was not the only NGO to consider collaborating with TUC in this period. See Anderson, *A History of Fair Trade in Contemporary Britain*, 94–97.

150. Carl Wilms-Wright, the British representative at the ICFTU, quoted in Anderson, *A History of Fair Trade in Contemporary Britain*, 92.

151. Bond, *The State of Tea*, 14.

152. Larson and Thompson, *Where Were You Brother?* 103.

153. Ibid., 104.

154. Ibid., 133–34. See also Anderson, *A History of Fair Trade in Contemporary Britain*, 94.

155. Wilms-Wright, *Transnational Corporations*, 14.

156. Ibid., 34.

157. Peter Burns to James Callaghan, April 1, 1974, FCO 37/1447, TNA.

158. War on Want Press Release, "The State of Tea," March 28, 1974, FCO 37/1447, TNA.

159. G. B. Chalmers to Mr. Ennals, "Meeting with the Ceylon Association in London," April 23, 1974, FCO 37/1447, TNA.

160. Ibid. For tea and British consumerism more generally, see Rappaport, *A Thirst for Empire*.

161. A. J. Cary to Miss Archbold (OMD), April 3, 1974, FCO 37/1447, TNA.

162. G. B. Chalmers to Mr. Wooland and Mr. Male, March 26, 1975, FCO 37/1581, TNA.

163. Report, W. T. Williams, "Sri Lanka Tea Estate," April 22, 1975, FCO 37/1582, TNA.

164. Ibid., 16.

165. Ibid., 30.

166. Cambridge World Development Action, Hamilton, Lawrence, Starkey, Starkey, and Tyler, *Tea: The Colonial Legacy*.

167. Ibid.

168. Possible International Tea Agreement, Memorandum of the International Tea Working Party, November 1969, FCO 37/590, TNA.

169. "Tea," Written Answers to Questions, House of Commons, *Hansard*, November 16, 1976.

170. Wiggin, "Tea," House of Commons, *Hansard*, February 6, 1980.

171. Ken Livingstone, "Monetarism in London," *New Left Review* 1, no. 137 (1983): 68–77.

172. Ken Livingstone, speech, Third World Trade and Technology Conference, February 18, 1985, in GLC, *Bridges Not Fences: Report of Third World Trade and Technology Conference* (London: Third World Information Network Ltd., July 1985).

173. Third World Trade and Technology Conference, "Draft Statement of Principles for Developing Trade and Technological Exchange," London, February 18–22, 1985, from the GLC's chief economic advisor Robyn Murray's website: https://static1.squarespace.com /static/5bc8924fb9144917ed082349/t/5e6b617b6d91381f59865257/1584095612643 /THIRD+WORLD+TRADE+AND+TECHNOLOGY+CONFERENCE.pdf.

174. On this point, see also Anderson, *A History of Fair Trade in Contemporary Britain*, 100–101.

175. Oxfam, "Clothes Code Campaign Strategy," April 15, 1996, CPN/5/3, Folder 2, OA.

176. "Sweat Shirts, Sweat Shops," Oxfam's Clothes Code Campaign Report, 1996, CPN/5/3, Folder 2, OA.

177. While many large NGOs have collaborated with large corporations, in the 1980s many of them appointed permanent staff designed to work with and recruit British corporations. Oxfam, for example, appointed its first "Corporate Appeal Executive" in 1987. Similarly, Save the Children (which had the largest share of the corporate market at the time) established in the 1980s a "Corporate Partnership and Activates" office. Oxfam, Corporate Relations Unit, "Engaging Companies in the Cause of the Poor," February 1991, pp. 6. 17, 27, 33, COM/3/2/32, Folder 3, OA.

178. Klein, *No Logo*, 723, 722.

179. Hilton, *Prosperity for All*; Trentmann, *The Making of the Consumer*.

180. Klein, *No Logo*, 53.

Chapter 6

1. John Clark, "A Grass Roots View of the Debt Crisis," c. 1987, COM/3/2/32, Folder 3, OA.

2. Ibid.

3. War on Want, *Profits out of Poverty?*

4. On the Volker shock, see Levy, *Ages of American Capitalism*.

5. War on Want, *Profits out of Poverty?*

6. Simms and Reindorp, *The New Abolitionists*, 13.

7. Kirton, *Jamaica*, 23.

8. Pettifor, *Debt, the Most Potent Form of Slavery*.

9. Yunus, *Credit for Self-Employment*, 5–6.

10. For example, Geismer, "Agents of Change"; Roy, *Poverty Capital*; Mader, *The Political Economy of Microfinance*; Fernando, *Microfinance*; Robinson, *The Microfinance Revolution*.

11. Victoria Brittain, "The Patient Vision of Julius Nyerere," *The Guardian*, March 21, 1985, 19.

12. Payer, *The Perpetuation of Dependence*.

13. Payer, *The Debt Trap*, x. Quoted also in Meyerowitz, *A War on Global Poverty*, 188.

14. Vernon, *Modern Britain*. See also Clift and Tomlinson, "Negotiating Credibility"; Rogers, *The IMF and European Economies*, 117–48; Harmon, *The British Labour Government and the 1976 IMF Crisis*; Burk and Cairncross, *Goodbye Great Britain*; Roberts, *When Britain Went Bust*.

15. Wayne Ellwood, "Keeping the Patient Alive," *New Internationalist*, issue 82 (December 2, 1979).

16. Dag Hammarskjöld Foundation, "The Terra Nova Statement on the International Monetary System and the Third World."

17. Nyerere, "Unity for a New Order," 56.

18. Dag Hammarskjöld Foundation, "The Arusha Initiative."

19. For the imperial origins of the "meddling" of international institutions, see Martin, *The Meddlers*.

20. Independent Commission on International Development and Brandt, *Common Crisis North-South*.

21. Willy Brandt quoted in Prashad, *The Poorer Nations*, 15.

22. Independent Commission on International Development and Brandt, *Common Crisis North-South*, 51.

23. Socialist International Committee on Economic Policy, *Global Challenge*.

24. Fulla, "A Discreet Alternative," 99; Clapham, "Understanding the Third World."

25. John Clark on "Hungry for Change" 1984 campaign, COM/3/2/32, Folder 3, OA.

26. Coote and Oxfam Public Affairs Unit, *Debt and Poverty*.

27. Clark, "A Grass Roots View of the Debt Crisis," 3.

28. Black, *Cause for Our Times*, 269.

29. Richard Jolly, Second Barbara Ward Memorial Lecture, "Adjustment with a Human Face," 18th World Conference of SID in Rome, July 1985, in Toye, "The Achievements of an Optimistic Economist."

30. Ibid.

31. Murray Silberman for UNIDO, "The Uses of Debt Conversion Mechanisms by Non-Governmental Organizations to Help Provide for the Capital Needs of Small Enterprises and Industrial Cooperatives," March 24, 1990, Vienna, United Nations Industrial Development Organization Online.

32. See, for example, the Minister for Overseas Development, Chris Patten, "Overseas Development," *Hansard*, House of Commons, October 24, 1986, vol. 102, cols. 1471–1500.

33. Christopher Huhne, "Bank Warns of 'Debt Fatigue,'" *The Guardian*, January 19, 1988.

34. Montes, *The Currency Crisis in Southeast Asia*, 15–20; James M. Boughton, "The IMF and the Silent Revolution: Global Finance and Development in the 1980s," International Monetary Fund, September 11, 2000, https://www.imf.org/en/Publications/Books/Issues/2016/12/30/The-IMF-and-the-Silent-Revolution-Global-Finance-and-Development-in-the-1980s-3687.

35. On the so-called "Toronto Agreement," which offered Western countries a variety of options to relieve debt to sub-Saharan countries, see Herbst, *U.S. Economic Policy toward Africa*, 53–59. On Lawson's commitment to reduce the debt of sub-Saharan African countries, see Black, *Cause for Our Times*, 269.

36. War on Want, *Profits out of Poverty?*

37. Phil Baker to Graham Dukes, "Oxford OXFAM Groups—Debt Campaigning," November 7, 1991, COM/3/2/32, Folder 3, OA.

38. "A Way out of Debt," *The Guardian*, July 31, 1987, 8; Marcel and Palma, "Third World Debt and Its Effects on the British Economy."

39. Wydham James, Campaign Unit, Notes on Meeting with Chancellor Lawson, July 6, 1988, COM/3/2/32, Folder 3, OA.

40. Oxfam, "African Debt: The Lawson Plan," internal memo, April 21, 1988, PRG/3/3/1/63, File 1, OA.

41. Denham, "The NGO Attitude to Debt Reduction."

42. For the parallel American Debt Crisis Network, see Adler, *No Globalization without Representation*, 98–100.

43. Christian Aid, *Banking on the Poor*.

44. Lysaught, "Roman Catholic Teaching on International Debt," 6.

45. Michael Smith, "Bill Peters: High-flying Diplomat Who Went on to Co-found the Jubilee 2000 International Debt Remission Campaign," *The Independent*, June 17, 2014.

46. Dent and Peters, *The Crisis of Poverty and Debt in the Third World*, 30–31.

47. Cited in Baillot, "A Well-Adjusted Debt," 224.

48. Also see Greenhill et al., *Did the G8 Drop the Debt*, 27.

49. Long, "Theological Reflection on International Debt," 42.

50. Pettifor, "The Economic Bondage of Debt," 121.

51. Ibid., 115.

52. Oxfam, "Drop the Debt—Global Chain Reaction," pamphlet, June 13, 1999, CPN/3/8, Folder 5, OA.

53. Getachew, *Worldmaking after Empire*; Gilroy, *The Black Atlantic*.

54. See Jubilee South 2000 National Coalition, Accra Declaration, April 19, 1998, https://www.jubileesouth.net/.

55. Baillot, "A Well-Adjusted Debt."

56. This tradition itself relied on imperial and racialized thought. See Hall, *Civilising Subjects*; Hall et al., *Legacies of British Slave-Ownership*.

57. Dent and Peters. *The Crisis of Poverty and Debt in the Third World*, 119.

58. Pettifor, "The Economic Bondage of Debt," 121.

59. See also Perry, *London Is the Place for Me*, 89–125.

60. Baillot, "A Well-Adjusted Debt."

61. Jamie Drummond quoted in Goldman, "From Margin to Mainstream," 92.

62. Mike Christie quoted in ibid., 98.

63. See ibid., 101.

64. Ibid., 110.

65. See Mike Christie's Vimeo page where he uploaded the video: https://vimeo.com/17186170.

66. Goldman, "From Margin to Mainstream," 2.

67. Baillot, "A Well-Adjusted Debt."

68. Brigid Delaney, "The Bono-ization of Activism," CNN, October 12, 2007.

69. Klein, *The Shock Doctrine*.

70. John Clark, "NGOs and Structural Adjustments," c. May 1988, Oxfam PRG/3/3/1/63, Folder 1, OA.

71. Christian Aid, *Banking on the Poor*, 5.

72. Ibid., 17.

73. UN, Department of Economic and Social Affairs, World Summit for Social Development 1995, https://www.un.org/development/desa/dspd/world-summit-for-social-development-1995.html.

74. Hurley et al., *Income Generation Schemes*, vii.

75. Yunus, *Banker to the Poor*; Meyerowitz, *A War on Global Poverty*, 259–61; Goenka and Henley, *Southeast Asia's Credit Revolution*.

76. Christian Aid, *Banking on the Poor*, 28.

77. Hurley et al., *Income Generation Schemes*, vii–viii; Eade and Williams, *The Oxfam Handbook of Development and Relief*, 610–11.

78. Jacques de Larosiere, address before the Economic and Social Council of the UN, Geneva, July 4, 1986, quoted in Jolly, "Adjustment with a Human Face."

79. Becker, "Investment in Human Capital," 9.

80. Foucault, Senellart, and Burchell, *The Birth of Biopolitics*, 225.

81. Levy, "Capital as Process and the History of Capitalism." Levy connects pecuniary value with a general theory of capitalism but the term relies on the financial logic of projected, speculative ability to generate future income.

82. Hurley et al., *Income Generation Schemes*, 12.

83. Devereux, Pares, and Best, *Manual of Credit & Savings*.

84. Ibid., 39.

85. Rutherford, *The Poor and Their Money*, emphasis in the original.

86. Devereux, Pares, and Best, *Manual of Credit & Savings*, 35–36.

87. Rutherford, "Learning to Lend," 11.

88. Ibid.

89. Ibid.

90. Ibid., 12.

91. Hoste, *Trypanotolerant Livestock in West and Central Africa*, 195.

92. Devereux, Pares, and Best, *Manual of Credit & Savings*, 39–40.

93. Quoted in ibid., 39.

94. Frank Rajan, Oxfam Bazaar, Bangalore, Sponsored by Development Commissioner (Handicraft) Government of India, May 8–17, 1992, p. 2, TRD/3/6/3, Folder 6, OA.

95. On the solidarity market, see Millard, *Export Marketing for a Small Handicraft Business*, 87.

96. Devereux, Pares, and Best, *Manual of Credit & Savings*, 49.

97. Oxfam, "Workshop on Management of Handicraft Projects for Rural and Urban Artisans of Orissa," Organized by Oxfam Bridge-New Delhi, August 1991, TRD/3/6/3, Folder 5, OA.

98. "Brief on Management Training Programme for Staff on IGP Units, Palmyrath Workers Development Society, Marthandam, Tamil Nadu," October 12, 1993, TRD/3/6/3, Folder 8, OA.

99. Millard, *Export Marketing for a Small Handicraft Business*, 32.

100. Millard, *Financial Management of a Small Handicraft Business*, 12.

101. Burgin, "The Reinvention of Entrepreneurship."

102. Tennent, "The Age of Strategy."

103. Quoted in ibid., 10.

104. Millard, *Export Marketing for a Small Handicraft Business*, 37.

105. Ibid., 38.

106. Eade and Williams, *The Oxfam Handbook of Development and Relief*, 506.

107. Millard, *Export Marketing for a Small Handicraft Business*, 123.

108. For the colonial invention of the "traditional," see Mantena, *Alibis of Empire*.

109. Millard, *Export Marketing for a Small Handicraft Business*, 90, emphasis in the original.

110. Ibid., 115.

111. Rogaly, Fisher, and Mayo, *Poverty, Social Exclusion and Microfinance in Britain*, 1–2.

112. Pearson, "Think Globally, Act Locally," 153.

113. Ibid., 154.

114. Tony Blair, " 'In Britain Today, Millions Are Still Trapped in a Cash Economy; Vulnerable, Extorted, Prey to Loan Sharks; In Britain Today, That Is Not Acceptable,' " *Observer*, May 31, 1998. See also Robin Stoddart, "Heading for a New World of High Risk: Gordon Brown's Emphasis on the Small Entrepreneur May Be the Most Important Element of His Strategy," *The Guardian*, March 25, 2000.

115. On similar programs in Hungary and Bulgaria, for example, see International Business Publication, *Bulgaria Investment and Business Guide*. For earlier examples, see Utting, *Social and Solidarity Economy*, 209–10.

116. Slay, *The Polish Economy*, 86–137.

117. Jane Perlez, "Polish Aid Fund Turns Profit, Posing a Problem," *New York Times*, April 27, 1998, sec. World. On the American Enterprise Fund, see also Birkelund, "Doing Good while Doing Well."

118. See Fundusz Mikro website: https://www.gdrc.org/icm/country/fundusz-mikro .html; Westall, Ramsden, and Foley, *Micro-Entrepreneurs*, 91.

119. Copisarow, "An Example of Micro-finance in the North," 53.

120. Aagaard, "The Global Institutionalization of Microcredit."

121. See, for example, Rogaly, Fisher, and Mayo, *Poverty, Social Exclusion and Microfinance in Britain*; Nelson, *Going Forward*. See also Jurik, *Bootstrap Dreams*, 57; Susan V. Berresford to Franklin A. Thomas, Recommendation for Grant/FAP Action, Program/U.S. and International Affairs Programs, Urban Poverty Related Investments, April 18, 1985, Ford Foundation Records, Rockefeller Archive Center, Sleepy Hollow, New York.

122. Geismer, "Agents of Change."

123. Pikholz and Grzywinski, "Communities Are Creditworthy," 72; Jurik, *Bootstrap Dreams*, 56; Balkin, "A Grameen Bank Replication."

124. Balkin, "A Grameen Bank Replication"; Geismer, "Agents of Change."

125. See, for example, in Memorandum for the President from the NEC-DPC Interagency Working Group on Community Development and Empowerment, "An Economic Empowerment Strategy," April 2, 1993, Clinton Digital Library (hereafter CDL); Memorandum for the President from the NEC-DPC Interagency Working Group on Community Development and Empowerment, "An Economic Empowerment Strategy," March 29, 1993, CDL.

126. Hillary Clinton, Remarks at Microcredit Summit in Washington, D.C., February 3, 1997, First Lady's Office, Press Office, and Lissa Muscatine, "[Speeches and Remarks] [binder]: [Remarks to the Microcredit Summit, 2/3/97] [Folder 2]," CDL.

127. Geismer, "Agents of Change"; Geismer, *Left Behind*.

128. Giddens, *The Third Way*.

129. Sloman, *Transfer State*.

130. For Thatcherism and enterprise culture, see Nigel Lawson, "The British Experiment," Mais Lecture at City University Business School, June 18, 1984, Margaret Thatcher Foundation, https://www.margaretthatcher.org/document/109504; Rieger, "Making Britain Work Again."

131. Levitas, *The Inclusive Society?* 128–58.

132. Chellakan, *Eradication of Poverty and Empowerment of the Poor*, 94.

133. Tony Blair quoted in Levitas, *The Inclusive Society?* 148.

134. Tony Blair in Great Britain, *Bringing Britain Together*, 8.

135. Cynthia Rice to Andrea Kane, "Re: Blair Visit," December 17, 1997, Box 058, Folder 023, CDL.

136. Giddens, *The Third Way*, 82.

137. Tim Jarvis Business and Transport Section, "Welfare-to-Work: The New Deal," November 12, 1997, Research Paper 97/118, House of Commons Library, 16, https://researchbriefings.files.parliament.uk/documents/RP97-118/RP97-118.pdf.

138. Great Britain, *Bringing Britain Together*, 62.

139. The government was exploring already in 1997 the idea of running microcredit schemes. See, for example, discussion in Giddens, *The Third Way*, as well as Great Britain, *Bringing Britain Together*, 62.

140. Great Britain, *Bringing Britain Together*, 73.

141. Lemire, Pearson, and Campbell, *Women and Credit*, 167–68.

142. Pearson and Watson, *Giving Women the Credit*, 52–57.

143. Pearson, "Microcredit Meets Social Exclusion," 813.

144. Ibid., 817.

145. Ibid., 818.

146. Pearson (quoting Connolly), ibid., 818.

147. Lemire, Pearson, and Campbell, *Women and Credit*, 173.

148. Pearson, "Think Globally, Act Locally," 157.

149. Ibid.

150. Ibid., 158.

151. Lemire, Pearson, and Campbell, *Women and Credit*, 176.

152. See, for example, Ward, "Ethnic Communities and Ethnic Business"; Jenkins and Ward, *Ethnic Communities in Business*; Metcalf, Modood, and Virdee, *Asian Self-Employment*; NatWest, *Afro-Caribbean Businesses and Their Banks*; NatWest, *Asian Businesses and Their Banks*; Fadahunsi, Smallbone, and Supri, "Networking and Ethnic Minority Enterprise Development"; Herbert and Kempson, *Credit Use and Ethnic Minorities*; Deakins, Hussain, and Ram, "Ethnic Entrepreneurs and Commercial Banks"; Jones, McEvoy, and Barrett, "Raising Capital for the Ethnic Minority Small Firm."

153. Herbert quoted in Rogaly and Roche, *Learning from South-North Links in Microfinance*, 35.

154. Kempson, "Bank Exclusion in the United Kingdom," 13.

155. Ibid.

156. Ibid., 16.

157. Ibid., 16–17.

158. Schumacher, *Small Is Beautiful*.

159. Ibid., 243.

160. Streeck, *Buying Time*.

Epilogue

1. Oxfam, Corporate Relations Unit, "Engaging Companies in the Cause of the Poor," February 1991, pp. 6, 17, 27, 33, COM/3/2/32, Folder 3, OA.

2. See, for example, Jaffee, *Brewing Justice*, 61.

3. Buzzacott, *Charities and Business*.

4. Quoted in Oxfam, Corporate Relations Unit, "Engaging Companies in the Cause of the Poor," 14.

5. Sparkes, *The Ethical Investor*.

6. Klein, *No Logo*, xxxiii.

7. Ibid., 23–24.

8. Davies, Jackson, and Sutcliffe-Braithwaite, *The Neoliberal Age?*; Jackson and Saunders, *Making Thatcher's Britain*; Djelic and Mousavi, "How the Neoliberal Think Tank Went Global"; Stahl, *Right Moves*.

9. For a helpful discussion of the historiography on New Labour, see Murphy, *Futures of Socialism*, 5–15. Murphy's account convincingly offers a narrative that counters the existing literature about New Labour yet his analysis is almost exclusively confined to internal and domestic debates within the party.

10. Weber, "China and Neoliberalism."

11. Oxfam, "When Next You Pass an Oxfam Shop—Pop In!"

12. On this collapse between production and reproduction, see Feher, "Self-Appreciation."

13. See, for example, Rana Foroohar, "After Neoliberalism: All Economics Is Local," *Foreign Affairs*, October 28, 2022; James Meadway, "Neoliberalism Is Dying—Now We Must Replace It," *Open Democracy*, September 3, 2021; Davies and Gane, "Post-

Neoliberalism?"; Tobias Debiel and Mathieu Rousselin, "Is a Post-neoliberal World Possible?" *International Politics and Society*, January 3, 2022; Ed Burmila, "Is the Neoliberal Era Over Yet?" *New Republic*, June 15, 2022, https://newrepublic.com/article/166742/neoliberal-era-end.

14. George Eaton, "Is the Neoliberal Era Finally Over?" *New Statesman*, June 16, 2021; Meadway, "Neoliberalism Is Dying"; Gary Gerstle, "The Age of Neoliberalism Is Ending in America; What Will Replace It?" *The Guardian*, June 21, 2021; Quinn Slobodian, "Is Neoliberalism Really Dead?" *New Statesman*, October 27, 2020.

15. Bruff, "The Rise of Authoritarian Neoliberalism"; Rose, "Still 'like Birds on the Wire'? Freedom after Neoliberalism"; Hendrikse, "Neo-illiberalism"; Brown, *In the Ruins of Neoliberalism*.

16. Quiggin, *Zombie Economics*; Duménil and Lévy, *The Crisis of Neoliberalism*; Mark Fisher, "How to Kill a Zombie: Strategizing the End of Neoliberalism," *Open Democracy*, July 18, 2013; Monbiot, "Neoliberalism"; Jaffe, "Zombie Neoliberalism"; Guzman, "Here Comes Zombie Neoliberalism"; Ross Douthat, "The Crisis of the Liberal Zombie Order," *New Statesman*, March 18, 2020.

BIBLIOGRAPHY

Archival Collections and Papers

Archives of the Anti-Apartheid Movement. Bodleian Archives, Bodleian Library. Oxford.
Bader, Ernest. Papers. Modern Records Centre. University of Warwick.
British Labour Party Archives. Manchester.
British Library. London.
Christian Aid Archives. Special Collection, School of Oriental and African Studies Library. London.
Food and Agriculture Organization Archives. Rome.
Ford Foundation Records. Rockefeller Archive Center. Sleepy Hollow, New York.
Hartley Library. University of Southampton, Southampton.
Jackson-Cole, Cecil. Papers. West Sussex Record Office.
Oxfam Archive. Bodleian Libraries. University of Oxford.
Papers of Alan Fisher Lectures. Modern Records Centre. University of Warwick.
Russell Sage Foundation Archives. Rockefeller Archive Center. North Tarrytown, New York.
Save the Children Funds Archives. Cadbury Research Centre. University of Birmingham.
Schumacher Papers. Library, Schumacher Center for a New Economy. Great Barrington, Massachusetts.
Sir Arthur Knight Seminar Papers. London School of Economics Archives.
UK National Archives. Kew, London.
War on Want Archives. Special Collection, School of Oriental and African Studies Library. London.
Wedderburn, Professor Kenneth William (Bill). Papers. Modern Records Centre. University of Warwick.
Young, Michael. Papers. Churchill Archives Center. Cambridge.

Online Collections

Clinton Digital Library
Hansard Parliamentary Debates, London
House of Common Library
International Monetary Fund
Margaret Thatcher Foundation
United Nations Industrial Development Organization Online
United Nations Official Records of the General Assembly
World Trade Organization

Newspapers and Magazines

Acton Gazette
Advertiser's Weekly
BBC News
Birmingham Post
Boston Review
Cheshire Observer

CNN
Daily Express
Daily Mail
Daily Mirror
Daily Telegraph
Darlington & Stockton Times
The Dress and Journals
Dunfermline Press
The Economist
Edgware, Mill Hill & Kingsbury Times
Family Circle (UK Magazine)
Financial Times
Foreign Affairs
The Guardian
The Independent
Inside/Outside
International Politics and Society Magazine
National Newsagent
New Internationalist Magazine
New Republic
New Scientists Magazine
New Society Magazine
New Statesman
New York Review of Books
New York Times
Nottingham Evening Post
Nottingham Guardian Journal
North Wales Chronicle
The Observer
Oldham Evening Chronicle
The Old Radleian
Open Democracy
Oxford Times
Peterfield Post, Hampshire
Retail Newsagent
Sheffield Morning Telegraph
Southern Evening Echo
Sunday Times
Sutton and Cheam Advertiser
The Telegraph
The Times
Tunbridge Wells Advertiser, Kent
Watford Evening Echo
Wimbledon Boro News

Published Sources

Aagaard, Peter. "The Global Institutionalization of Microcredit." *Regulation & Governance* 5 (2011): 465–79.

Abbott, John C. *Agricultural Marketing Enterprises for the Developing World: With Case Studies of Indigenous Private, Transnational Co-Operative and Parastatal Enterprise.* Cambridge: Cambridge University Press, 1987.

Abel-Smith, Brian. "Whose Welfare State." In *Conviction*, ed. N. McKenzie, 57–63. London: McGibbon & Kee, 1958.

Abel-Smith, Brian, and Peter Townsend. *The Poor and the Poorest: A New Analysis of the Ministry of Labour's Family Expenditure Surveys of 1953–54 and 1960*. London: Bell, 1965.

Adler, Paul. *No Globalization without Representation: U.S. Activists and World Inequality*. Power, Politics, and the World. Philadelphia: University of Pennsylvania Press, 2021.

Alacevich Michele, and Mauro Boianovsky. "Writing the History of Development Economics." In *The Political Economy of Development Economics: A Historical Perspective*, ed. Michele Alacevich and Mauro Boianovsky, 1–14. Durham: Duke University Press.

Alston, Philip. "International Trade as an Instrument of Positive Human Rights Policy." *Human Rights Quarterly* 4, no. 2 (Spring 1982): 155–83.

Anderson, Matthew. *A History of Fair Trade in Contemporary Britain: From Civil Society Campaigns to Corporate Compliance*. Basingstoke: Palgrave Macmillan, 2015.

Andersson, Jenny. "Neoliberalism against Social Democracy." *Tocqueville Review* 41 (2020): 87–107.

Andrews, Molly. *Lifetimes of Commitment: Aging, Politics, Psychology*. Cambridge: Cambridge University Press, 1991.

Arrighi, Giovanni, and Beverly Silve. "Polanyi's 'Double Movement': The Belle Époques of British and U.S. Hegemony Compared." *Politics & Society* 31, no. 2 (2003): 325–55.

Arrow, Kenneth J. *Social Choice and Individual Values*. New York: John Wiley & Sons, 1951.

———. "Uncertainty and the Welfare Economics of Medical Care." *American Economic Review* 53, no. 5 (1963): 941–73.

Ash, Susan. *Funding Philanthropy: Dr. Barnardo's Metaphors, Narratives and Spectacles*. Liverpool: Liverpool University Press, 2016.

Association for World Peace. "War on Want: A Plan for World Development." London: Association for World Peace, 1952.

Bader, Godric. "The Scott Bader Commonwealth: Putting People First." *Long Range Planning* 19, no. 6 (1986): 66–74.

Bailkin, Jordanna. *The Afterlife of Empire*. Berkeley: University of California Press, 2012.

Baillot, Hélène. "A Well-Adjusted Debt: How the International Anti-Debt Movement Failed to Delink Debt Relief and Structural Adjustment." *International Review of Social History* 66, no. S29 (April 2021): 215–38.

Bair, Jennifer. "Corporations at the United Nations: Echoes of the New International Economic Order?" *Humanity: An International Journal of Human Rights, Humanitarianism, and Development*, no. 1 (2015): 159–71.

———. "From the Politics of Development to the Challenges of Globalization." *Globalizations* 4, no. 4 (December 1, 2007): 486–99.

Balfour, Lady Evelyn Barbara. *The Living Soil: Evidence of the Importance to Human Health of Soil Vitality, with Special Reference to Post-War Planning*. London: Faber and Faber, 1943.

Balkin, Steven. "A Grameen Bank Replication: The Full Circle Fund of the Women's Self-Employment Project of Chicago." In *The Grameen Bank of Bangladesh: A New Direction in Poverty Alleviation*, ed. A. Wahid. Boulder, CO: Westview Press, 1993.

Baranski, Marci. *The Globalization of Wheat: A Critical History of the Green Revolution*. Pittsburgh: University of Pittsburgh Press, 2022.

Barnet, Richard J., and Ronald E. Müller. *Global Reach: The Power of the Multinational Corporations*. New York: Simon and Schuster, 1974.

Bashford, Alison. *Global Population: History, Geopolitics, and Life on Earth*. New York: Columbia University Press, 2014.

Basnett, D. *Trade Union Responsibilities*. London: Foundation for Business Responsibilities, 1974.

Battersby, Olwen. "War on Want and the Bhoodan Movement." *Aryan Path*, no. 34 (1963): 166–69.

Baughan, Emily. "Rehabilitating an Empire: Humanitarian Collusion with the Colonial State during the Kenyan Emergency, ca. 1954–1960." *Journal of British Studies* 59, no. 1 (January 2020): 57–79.

———. *Saving the Children: Humanitarianism, Internationalism, and Empire*. Oakland: University of California Press, 2022.

Becker, Gary S. "Investment in Human Capital: A Theoretical Analysis." *Journal of Political Economy* 70, no. 5, part 2 (October 1962): 9–49.

Beckert, Sven. *Empire of Cotton: A Global History*. Repr. ed. New York: Vintage, 2015.

Beesley, M. E. "The Context of Social Responsibility in Business." In *Productivity and Amenity: Achieving a Social Balance*, ed. M. E. Beesley. New York: Croom Helm, 1974.

Beesley, M. E., and T. Evans. *Corporate Social Responsibility*. New York: Croom Helm, 1978.

Behar, Moises. "European Diets vs. Traditional Foods." *Food Policy* 1, no. 5 (1976): 432–35.

———. "Nutrition and the Future of Mankind." *International Journal of Health Services* 6, no. 2 (1976): 315–20.

Bell, Erin. " 'A Most Horrifying Maturity in Crime': Age, Gender and Juvenile Delinquency in Colonial Kenya during the Mau Mau Uprising." *Atlantic Studies* 11, no. 4 (October 2, 2014): 473–90.

Beloff, Michael. *The Plateglass Universities*. London: Secker & Warburg, 1968.

Benanav, Aaron. "A Global History of Unemployment: Surplus Populations in the World Economy, 1949–2010." PhD thesis, UCLA, 2015.

———. "The Origins of Informality: The ILO at the Limit of the Concept of Unemployment." *Journal of Global History* 14, no. 1 (February 2019): 107–25.

Benson, Jon. *The Rise of Consumer Society in Britain, 1880–1980*. Harlow: Longman, 1994.

Bevir, Mark. "William Morris: The Modern Self, Art, and Politics." *History of European Ideas* 24 (1998): 175–94.

Birkelund, John P. "Doing Good while Doing Well: The Unheralded Success of American Enterprise Funds." *Foreign Affairs* 80, no. 5 (2001): 14–20.

Bishop, Matthew, and Michael Green. *Philanthro-Capitalism: How the Rich Can Save the World*. New York: Bloomsbury Press, 2008.

Black, Eugene R. "The Age of Economic Development." *Economic Journal* 70, no. 278 (June 1960): 266–76.

Black, Lawrence. *The Political Culture of the Left in Affluent Britain, 1951–64: Old Labour, New Britain?* Houndmills, Basingstoke: Palgrave, 2003.

———. *Redefining British Politics: Culture, Consumerism and Participation, 1954–70*. Houndmills, Basingstoke: Palgrave, 2010.

———. "*Which?*craft in Post-War Britain: The Consumers' Association and the Politics of Affluence." *Albion: A Quarterly Journal Concerned with British Studies* 36, no. 1 (Spring 2004): 52–82.

Black, Lawrence, and Hugh Pemberton. *An Affluent Society?: Britain's Post-War "Golden Age" Revisited*. London: Routledge, 2017.

Black, Maggie. *A Cause for Our Times: Oxfam: The First 50 Years*. Oxford: Oxford University Press, 1992.

Bloom, David, and David Canning. "Global Demographic Change: Dimensions and Economic Significance." *Population and Development Review* 34 (2008): 17–51.

Blum, Fred H. *Work and Community: The Scott Bader Commonwealth and the Quest for a New Social Order*. London: Routledge & K. Paul, 1968.

Boas, Taylor C., and Jordan Gans-Morse. "Neoliberalism: From New Liberal Philosophy to Anti-Liberal Slogan." *Studies in Comparative International Development* 44, no. 2 (June 1, 2009): 137–61.

Bocking-Welch, Anna. *British Civic Society at the End of Empire: Decolonisation, Globalisation, and International Responsibility*. Manchester: Manchester University Press, 2018.

———. "Imperial Legacies and Internationalist Discourses: British Involvement in the United Nations Freedom from Hunger Campaign, 1960–70." *Journal of Imperial and Commonwealth History* 40, issue 5 (2012): 879–96.

———. "Youth against Hunger: Service, Activism and the Mobilisation of Young Humanitarians in 1960s Britain." *European Review of History* 23, no. 1–2 (January 2, 2016): 154–70.

Bockman, Johanna. *Markets in the Name of Socialism: The Left-Wing Origins of Neoliberalism*. Stanford: Stanford University Press, 2011.

———. "Socialist Globalization against Capitalist Neocolonialism: The Economic Ideas behind the New International Economic Order." *Humanity: An International Journal of Human Rights, Humanitarianism, and Development* 6, no. 1 (March 16, 2015): 109–28.

Bolton, Barbara. *Booth's Drum: The Salvation Army in Australia, 1880–1980*. Sydney: Hodder and Stoughton, 1980.

Bond, Edith M. *The State of Tea: A War on Want Investigation into Sri Lanka's Tea Industry*. London: War on Want, 1974.

Booth, William. *In Darkest England, and the Way Out: Salvation Army Social Campaign*. London: Salvation Army, 1890.

Boucher, Ellen. "Cultivating Internationalism: Save the Children Fund, Public Opinion, and the Meaning of Child Relief, 1919–24." In *Brave New World: Imperial and Democratic Nation-Building in Britain between the Wars*, ed. Laura Beers and Geraint Thomas, 169–88. London: Institute of Historical Research, 2012.

Boulding, Kenneth E. "Economics as Moral Science." *American Economic Review* 59, no. 1 (1969): 1–12.

———. "The Economics of the Coming Spaceship Earth." In *Environmental Quality in a Growing Economy*, ed. H. Jarrett, 3–14. Baltimore: Johns Hopkins University Press, 1966.

Brenner, Robert. *The Economics of Global Turbulence: The Advanced Capitalist Economies from Long Boom to Long Downturn, 1945–2005*. New York: Verso, 2006.

Brenner, Robert, and Jeong Seong-jin. "Overproduction Not Financial Collapse Is the Heart of the Crisis: The US, East Asia and the World." *Asia-Pacific Journal* 7, issue 6, no. 5 (2009). https://apjjf.org/-Robert-Brenner/3043/article.html.

Brewis, Georgina. *A Social History of Student Volunteering*. New York: Palgrave Macmillan, 2014.

Brick, Howard. *Transcending Capitalism: Visions of a New Society in Modern American Thought*. Ithaca: Cornell University Press, 2015.

Briggs, Asa. *Michael Young: Social Entrepreneur*. Houndmills, Basingstoke: Palgrave, 2001.

British Council of Churches and the Conference of British Missionary Societies. *World Poverty and British Responsibility*. London: S.C.M. Press, 1966.

Brittan, Samuel. *Capitalism with a Human Face*. Cambridge, MA: Harvard University Press, 1995.

Brooke, Stephen. "Atlantic Crossing? American Views of Capitalism and British Socialist Thought, 1932–1962." *Twentieth Century British History* 2, no. 2 (1991): 107–36.

Brown, Christopher Leslie. *Moral Capital: Foundations of British Abolitionism*. Chapel Hill: University of North Carolina Press, 2006.

Brown, Lester R., and Erik P. Eckholm. *By Bread Alone*. New York: Praeger, 1974.

Brown, Michael Barratt. *Fair Trade: Reform and Realities in the International Trading System*. New York: Bloomsbury Academic, 1993.

Brown, Wendy. *In the Ruins of Neoliberalism: The Rise of Antidemocratic Politics in the West.* New York: Columbia University Press, 2019.

———. *Undoing the Demos: Neoliberalism's Stealth Revolution.* Brooklyn, NY: Zone Books, 2015.

Bruff, Ian. "The Rise of Authoritarian Neoliberalism." *Rethinking Marxism* 26, no. 1 (January 2, 2014): 113–29.

Brushett, Kevin. "Partners in Development? Robert McNamara, Lester Pearson, and the Commission on International Development, 1967–1973." *Diplomacy & Statecraft* 26, no. 1 (January 2, 2015): 84–102.

Buettner, Elizabeth. *Europe after Empire: Decolonization, Society, and Culture.* Cambridge: Cambridge University Press, 2016.

Bullock. Alan. *Report of the Committee of Inquiry on Industrial Democracy.* London: H. M. Stationery Office, 1977.

Burgin, Angus. "The Reinvention of Entrepreneurship." In *American Labyrinth: Intellectual History for Complicated Times,* ed. Raymond Haberski Jr. and Andrew Hartman, 163–80. Ithaca: Cornell University Press, 2019.

Burk, Kathleen, and Alec Cairncross. *Goodbye, Great Britain: The 1976 IMF Crisis.* New Haven: Yale University Press, 1992.

Burkett, Jodi. *Constructing Post-Imperial Britain: Britishness, "Race" and the Radical Left in the 1960s.* Houndmills, Basingstoke: Palgrave, 2013.

Burnard, Trevor, and Giorgio Riello. "Slavery and the New History of Capitalism." *Journal of Global History* 15, no. 2 (July 2020): 225–44.

Burton, Antoinette. "Who Needs the Nation? Interrogating 'British' History." *Journal of Historical Sociology* 10, no. 3 (September 1, 1997): 227–48.

Butler, Lise. *Michael Young, Social Science, and the British Left, 1945-1970.* Oxford: Oxford University Press, 2020.

———. "Michael Young, the Institute of Community Studies, and the Politics of Kinship." *Twentieth Century British History* 26, no. 2 (June 1, 2015): 203–24.

Buzzacott & Co. *Charities and Business: A Partnership of Interest?* London: Buzzacott & Co, 1989.

Çalışkan, Koray, and Michel Callon. "Economization, Part 1: Shifting Attention from the Economy towards Processes of Economization." *Economy and Society* 38, no. 3 (August 1, 2009): 369–98.

Callaway, Archibald. "The Cambridge Conference on Development: Prospects for Employment Opportunities in the 1970's." *Manpower and Unemployment Research in Africa* 4, no. 2 (1971): 3.

Callon, Michel. "The Embeddedness of Economic Markets in Economics." *Sociological Review* 46, no. 1 (1998): 1–57.

Cambridge World Development Action, John Hamilton, Tessa Lawrence, Hugh Starkey, Phyllis Starkey, and Geoff Tyler. *Tea: The Colonial Legacy.* Cambridge: Cambridge World Development Action, 1975.

Campbell, Alan, and John McIlroy. "The High Tide of Trade Unionism: Mapping Industrial Politics, 1964-1979." In *British Trade Unions and Industrial Politics: The High Tide of Trade Unionism,* vol. 2, ed. Alan Campbell, Nina Fishman, and John McIlroy, 93–130. London: Routledge, 1999.

Charities Advisory Trust. *The Public Perception of Charity Shops.* London: Charities Advisory Trust, 1997.

Chatterjee, Bishwa Bandhu, Hanuman Prasad, and Sureśacandra Śrīvāstavya. *Community Approach to Family Welfare: An Empirical Study, Report of an Evaluation of the Family Welfare Programme of the Agrindus Institute, Banwasi Seva Ashram, Govindpur, Mirzapur, India.* New Delhi: Shanti Publishers, 1973.

Chellakan, Amal Raj. *Eradication of Poverty and Empowerment of the Poor: Theology of Creation and the Newest Policies of Development in the Age of Globalisation.* Delhi: Indian Society for Promoting Christian Knowledge, 2007.

Chenery, Hollis B. "Restructuring the World Economy." *Foreign Affairs* (January 1975): 242–63.

Cherrier, Beatrice, and Jean-Baptiste Fleury. "Economists' Interest in Collective Decision after World War II: A History." *Public Choice* 172 (2017): 23–44.

Christian Aid. *Banking on the Poor: The Ethics of Third World Debt.* London: Christian Aid, 1988.

Chun, Lin. *The British New Left.* Edinburgh: Edinburgh University Press, 1993.

Clapham, Christopher. *Third World Politics: An Introduction.* London: Routledge, 1985.

——. "Understanding the Third World." *Third World Quarterly* 8, no. 4 (October 1986): 1425–32.

Clapp, B. W. *An Environmental History of Britain since the Industrial Revolution.* London: Longman, 1994.

Clark, William, K. B. Lall, Robert Neild, and E. F. Schumacher. *India at Midpassage.* London: Overseas Development Institute, 1964.

Clavin, Patricia. *Securing the World Economy: The Reinvention of the League of Nations, 1920–1946.* Oxford: Oxford University Press, 2013.

Clegg, H. A. "The Fleck Report." *Public Administration* 33, no. 3 (1955): 269–76.

——. *A New Approach to Industrial Democracy.* Oxford: Blackwell, 1960.

Clift, Ben, and Jim Tomlinson. "Negotiating Credibility: Britain and the International Monetary Fund, 1956–1976." *Contemporary European History* 17, no. 4 (2008): 545–66.

——. "Tawney and the Third Way." *Journal of Political Ideologies* 7, no. 3 (October 1, 2002): 315–31.

Coase, Ronald. *The Problem of Social Cost.* Chicago: University of Chicago Law School, 1960.

Cockett, Richard. *David Astor and the Observer.* London: André Deutsch, 1991.

Cohen, Alan B., David C. Colby, Keith Wailoo, and Julian E. Zelizer, eds. *Medicare and Medicaid at 50: America's Entitlement Programs in the Age of Affordable Care.* Oxford: Oxford University Press, 2015.

Cohen, Lizabeth. *A Consumers' Republic: The Politics of Mass Consumption in Postwar America.* New York: Vintage Books, 2004.

Collini, Stefan. *Common Writing: Essays on Literary Culture and Public Debate.* Oxford: Oxford University Press, 2016.

Confederation of British Industry Company Affairs Committee, *The Responsibilities of the British Public Company: Final Report.* London: Confederation of British Industry, 1973.

Connelly, Matthew James. *Fatal Misconception: The Struggle to Control World Population.* Cambridge, MA: Belknap Press of Harvard University Press, 2008.

Cook, Chris. *The Routledge Guide to British Political Archives: Sources since 1945.* London: Routledge, 2006.

Cooper, Frederick. *Africa since 1940: The Past of the Present.* Cambridge: Cambridge University Press, 2002.

——. "Modernizing Bureaucrats, Backward Africans, and the Development Concept." In *International Development and the Social Sciences: Essays on the History of Political Knowledge,* ed. Frederick Cooper and Randall M. Packard, 64–92. Berkeley: University of California Press, 1997.

Cooper, Frederick, and Randall M. Packard, eds. *International Development and the Social Sciences: Essays on the History and Politics of Knowledge.* Berkeley: University of California Press, 1997.

Cooper, Melinda. *Family Values between Neoliberalism and the New Social Conservatism.* New York: Zone Books, 2017.

Coote, Belinda, and Oxfam Public Affairs Unit. *Debt and Poverty: A Case Study of Jamaica.* Oxford: Oxfam, 1985.

Copisarow, Rosalind. "An Example of Micro-finance in the North: Fundusz Mikro (Poland)." In *Banking and Social Cohesion: Alternative Responses to a Global Market*, ed. Christophe Guene and Ed Mayo. Charlbury: Jon Carpenter, 2001.

Crosland, C.A.R. "The Transition from Capitalism." In *New Fabian Essays*, ed. R.H.S. Crossman, 33–68. London: Turnstile Press, 1952.

Cullather, Nick. *The Hungry World: America's Cold War Battle against Poverty in Asia.* Cambridge, MA: Harvard University Press, 2010.

Dag Hammarskjöld Foundation. "The Arusha Initiative." *Development* Dialogue, issue 2 (1980): 12.

———. "The Terra Nova Statement on the International Monetary System and the Third World." *Development* Dialogue, issue 1 (1980): 31.

Daly, Herman E. *The Stationary-State Economy.* Tuscaloosa: University of Alabama Press, 1971.

Darwin, John. *The Empire Project: The Rise and Fall of the British World-System, 1830–1970.* Cambridge: Cambridge University Press, 2009.

———. "A Third British Empire? The Dominion Idea in Imperial Politics." In *The Oxford History of the British Empire*, vol. 4, *The Twentieth Century*, ed. Judith Brown and W. Roger Louis. Oxford: Oxford University Press, 1999.

Daunton, Martin. *Just Taxes: The Politics of Taxation in Britain, 1914–1979.* Cambridge: Cambridge University Press, 2002.

———. *Trusting Leviathan: The Politics of Taxation in Britain, 1799–1914.* Cambridge: Cambridge University Press, 2007.

Daunton, Martin, and Matthew Hilton. *The Politics of Consumption: Material Culture and Citizenship in Europe and America.* Oxford: Berg, 2001.

Davies, Aled, Ben Jackson, and Florence Sutcliffe-Braithwaite, eds. *The Neoliberal Age?: Britain since the 1970s.* London: UCL Press, 2022.

Davies, Paul. "The Bullock Report and Employee Participation in Corporate Planning in the U.K." *Journal of Comparative Corporate Law and Securities Regulation* 1 (1978): 245–72.

Davies, Stephen M. "Promoting Productivity in the National Health Service, 1950 to 1966." *Contemporary British History* 31, no. 1 (2017): 47–68.

Davies, William and Nicholas Gane. "Post-Neoliberalism? An Introduction." *Theory, Culture & Society* 38, no. 6 (November 1, 2021): 3–28.

Davis, Mike. "Planet of Slums." *New Left Review* 26 (March–April 2004): 5–34.Deakins, David, Guhlum Hussain, and Monder Ram. "Ethnic Entrepreneurs and Commercial Banks: Untapped Potential." Working Paper and Research Report/Ethnic Minority Research Project. Birmingham: University of Central England, Enterprise Research Centre, 1994.

Denham, John. "The NGO Attitude to Debt Reduction." *IDS Bulletin* 21, issue 2 (April 1990): 82–83.

Dent, Martin, and Bill Peters. *The Crisis of Poverty and Debt in the Third World.* Milton Park, Oxfordshire: Routledge, 2019.

Department of State Publication. *American Foreign Policy, Current Documents.* Vol. 12. Historical Division, Bureau of Public Affairs, 1968.

De Paula, F. C. "The Six Commandments: A Code for Managers." *Journal of General Management* 1, no. 3 (March 1, 1974): 3–12.

Devereux, Stephen, Henry Pares, and John Best. *A Manual of Credit & Savings for the Poor of Developing Countries.* Oxford: Oxfam, 1987.

Dietrich, Christopher R. W. *Oil Revolution: Anticolonial Elites, Sovereign Rights, and the Economic Culture of Decolonization.* Cambridge: Cambridge University Press, 2017.

Djelic, Marie-Laure, and Reza Mousavi. "How the Neoliberal Think Tank Went Global: The Atlas Network, 1981 to Present." In *Nine Lives of Neoliberalism*, ed. Dieter Plehwe, Quinn Slobodian, and Philip Mirowski. New York: Verso, 2020.

Doron, Abraham. "Personal Welfare Services in Israel—Changes in Leadership and Its Implication on Designing the Israeli Welfare System." *Social Security (Hebrew edition)* 65 (March 2004): 11–32.

Drucker, Peter F. *Concept of the Corporation.* 1946. New Brunswick, NJ: Transaction Publishers, 1993.

Duménil, Gérard, and Dominique Lévy. *The Crisis of Neoliberalism.* Reprint, Cambridge, MA: Harvard University Press, 2013.

Dunning, John H., and Tagi Sagafi Nejad. *The UN and Transnational Corporations: From Code of Conduct to Global Compact.* Bloomington: Indiana University Press, 2008.

Dussart, Fae, and Alan Lester. *Colonization and the Origins of Humanitarian Governance: Protecting Aborigines across the Nineteenth-Century British Empire.* Cambridge: Cambridge University Press, 2014.

Dutta, Krishna, and Andrew Robinson. *Rabindranath Tagore: The Myriad-Minded Man.* London: Tauris, 2009.

Dworkin, Dennis L. *Cultural Marxism in Postwar Britain: History, the New Left, and the Origins of Cultural Studies.* Durham: Duke University Press, 1997.

Dyson, Tim. *Population and Development: The Demographic Transition.* New York: Zed Books, 2010.

Eade, Deborah, and Suzanne Williams. *The Oxfam Handbook of Development and Relief: Volume II.* Oxford: Oxfam, 1995.

Eckel, Jan, and Samuel Moyn. *The Breakthrough: Human Rights in the 1970s.* Philadelphia: University of Pennsylvania Press, 2013.

Edgerton, David. *The Rise and Fall of the British Nation: A Twentieth-Century History.* London: Allen Lane, 2018.

Editorial. "Second World Food Congress." *PANS Pest Articles & News Summaries* 16, no. 1 (March 1970): 9.

"Editorial: World Campaign against Hunger." *UNESCO Courier*, no. 7–8 (July–August 1962): 6.

Ehrlich, Paul R. *The Population Bomb.* Sierra Club-Ballantine Book. New York: Ballantine Books, 1968.

Eley, Geoff. *Forging Democracy: The History of the Left in Europe, 1850–2000.* Oxford: Oxford University Press, 2002.

Elkins, Caroline. *Imperial Reckoning: The Untold Story of Britain's Gulag in Kenya.* New York: Henry Holt, 2005.

Engerman, David C. *The Price of Aid: The Economic Cold War in India.* Cambridge, MA: Harvard University Press, 2018.

Engerman, David, Nils Gilman, Mark H. Haefele, and Michael E. Latham, eds. *Staging Growth: Modernization, Development, and the Global Cold War.* Amherst: University of Massachusetts Press, 2003.

English, Richard, and Michael Kenny, eds. *Rethinking British Decline.* Basingstoke: Macmillan, 2000.

Epstein, M. "The Social Role of Business Enterprise in Britain: An American Perspective: Part I." *Journal of Management Studies* 13, no. 3 (1976): 212–33.

Everill, Bronwen. *Not Made by Slaves: Ethical Capitalism in the Age of Abolition.* Cambridge, MA: Harvard University Press, 2020.

Ewald, Ellen Buchman, and Diane Coleman. *Recipes for a Small Planet: The Art and Science of High Protein Vegetarian Cookery*. New York: Ballantine Books, 1973.

Ewin, R. E. "Wollheim's Paradox of Democracy." *Australasian Journal of Philosophy* 45, no. 3 (January 1967): 356–57.

Fadahunsi, Akin, David Smallbone, and Salinder Supri. "Networking and Ethnic Minority Enterprise Development: Insights from a North London Study." *Journal of Small Business and Enterprise Development* 7, no. 3 (January 1, 2000): 228–40.

Fajardo, Margarita. *The World That Latin America Created: The United Nations Economic Commission for Latin America in the Development Era*. Cambridge, MA: Harvard University Press, 2021.

Faudot, Adrien. "The Keynes Plan and Bretton Woods Debates: The Early Radical Criticisms by Balogh, Schumacher and Kalecki." *Cambridge Journal of Economics* 45, no. 4 (July 1, 2021): 751–70.

Feher, Michael. *Powerless by Design: The Age of the International Community*. Durham: Duke University Press, 2000.

———. "Self-Appreciation; or, The Aspirations of Human Capital." *Public Culture* 21, no. 1 (January 1, 2009): 21–41.

Feher, Michael, Gaëlle Krikorian, and Yates Mckee, eds. *Nongovernmental Politics*. New York: Zone Books, 2007.

Ferguson, James. *The Anti-Politics Machine: "Development," Depoliticization, and Bureaucratic Power in Lesotho*. Minneapolis: University of Minnesota Press, 1994.

Ferguson, Niall, Charles S. Maier, Erez Manela, and Daniel J. Sargent, eds. *The Shock of the Global: The 1970s in Perspective*. Cambridge, MA: Belknap Press, 2011.

Fernandez, Luis. *Policing Dissent: Social Control and the Anti-Globalization Movement*. New Brunswick, NJ: Rutgers University Press, 2019.

Fernando, Jude L. *Microfinance: Perils and Prospects*. London: Routledge, 2004.

Field, Jessica A. "Consumption in Lieu of Membership: Reconfiguring Popular Charitable Action in Post–World War II Britain." *VOLUNTAS: International Journal of Voluntary and Nonprofit Organizations* 27, no. 2 (April 2016): 979–97.

Fielding, Steven. *The Labour Party: Continuity and Change in the Making of "New" Labour*. London: Palgrave Macmillan, 2003.

Fogarty, Michael. *Company and Corporation: One Law?* London: Chapman, 1965.

———. *Company Responsibility and Participation: A New Agenda*. London: PEP, 1973.

Foks, Freddy. "The Sociological Imagination of the British New Left: 'Culture' and the 'Managerial Society,' c. 1956–62." *Modern Intellectual History* 15, no. 3 (November 2018): 801–20.

Fontaine, Philippe. "Blood, Politics, and Social Science: Richard Titmuss and the Institute of Economic Affairs, 1957–1973." *Isis* 93 (2002): 401–34.

———. "From Philanthropy to Altruism: Incorporating Unselfish Behavior into Economics, 1961–1975." *History of Political Economy* 39, no. 1 (March 1, 2007): 1–46.

Forrester, Katrina. *In the Shadow of Justice: Postwar Liberalism and the Remaking of Political Philosophy*. Princeton: Princeton University Press, 2019.

Foucault, Michel, Michel Senellart, and Graham Burchell. *The Birth of Biopolitics: Lectures at the Collège de France, 1978–79*. Basingstoke: Palgrave Macmillan, 2008.

Francis, Julian. "Working with the Refugees, 1971." *Strategic Analysis* 45, no. 6 (2021): 530–37.

Freeden, Michael. "Civil Society and the Good Citizen: Competing Conceptions of Citizenship in Twentieth-Century Britain." In *Civil Society in British History: Ideas, Identities, Institutions*, ed. Jose Harris, 275–93. Oxford: Oxford University Press, 2003.

French, David. *The British Way in Counter-Insurgency, 1945–1967*. Oxford: Oxford University Press, 2011.

Frey-Wouters, Ellen. *The European Community and the Third World: The Lomé Convention and Its Impact.* Praeger Special Studies. New York: Praeger, 1980.

Fryers, G. *What Kind of Marketing Ethics?* London: Foundation for Business Responsibilities, 1973.

Fulla, Mathieu. "A Discreet Alternative: The Socialist International's Ill-Fated Battle for 'Global Keynesianism' and a New International Economic Order in the 1980s." In Michele Di Donato and Mathieu Fulla, *Leftist Internationalisms: A Transnational Political History.* London: Bloomsbury Publishing, 2023.

Garavini, Giuliano. *After Empires: European Integration, Decolonization, and the Challenge from the Global South, 1957–1986.* Trans. Richard R. Nybakken. New York: Oxford University Press, 2012.

———. *The Rise and Fall of OPEC in the Twentieth Century.* Oxford: Oxford University Press, 2019.

Gariepy, Henry. *Christianity in Action: The International History of the Salvation Army.* Grand Rapids, MI: William B. Eerdmans, 2009.

Gartlan, Jean. *Barbara Ward: Her Life and Letters.* London: Continuum International Publishing Group, 2010.

Gatrell, Peter. *Free World?: The Campaign to Save the World's Refugees, 1956–63.* Cambridge: Cambridge University Press, 2011.

Geismer, Lily. "Agents of Change: Microenterprise, Welfare Reform, the Clintons, and Liberal Forms of Neoliberalism." *Journal of American History* 107, no. 1 (June 1, 2020): 107–31.

———. *Left Behind: The Democrats' Failed Attempt to Solve Inequality.* New York: PublicAffairs, 2022.

George, Susan. *How the Other Half Dies.* Lanham, MD: Rowman and Littlefield, 1976.

Gerlach, Christian. "Famine Responses in the World Food Crisis 1972–5 and the World Food Conference of 1974." *European Review of History* 22, no. 6 (2015): 929–39.

———. "Illusions of Global Governance: Transnational Agribusiness inside the UN System." In *Food and Globalization: Consumption, Markets and Politics in the Modern World,* ed. Alexander Nützenadel and Frank Trentmann, 193–211. New York: Berg, 2008.

Gerstle, Gary. *The Rise and Fall of the Neoliberal Order: America and the World in the Free Market Era.* New York: Oxford University Press, 2022.

Getachew, Adom. *Worldmaking after Empire: The Rise and Fall of Self-Determination.* Princeton: Princeton University Press, 2019.

Gibbs, Ewan. *Coal Country: The Meaning and Memory of Deindustrialization in Postwar Scotland.* London: Institute of Historical Research, 2021.

Giddens, Anthony. *The Third Way: The Renewal of Social Democracy.* Cambridge: Polity, 2008.

Gill, Peter. *Drops in the Ocean: The Work of Oxfam, 1960–1970.* London: Macdonald & Co., 1970.

Gilman, Nils. *Mandarins of the Future: Modernization Theory in Cold War America.* Baltimore: Johns Hopkins University Press, 2003.

Gilpin, Robert. "Three Models of the Future." *International Organization* 29, no. 1 (1975): 37–60.

———. *U.S. Power and the Multinational Corporation: The Political Economy of Foreign Direct Investment.* New York: Basic Books, 1975.

Gilroy, Paul. *The Black Atlantic: Modernity and Double Consciousness.* Cambridge, MA: Harvard University Press, 1993.

Glass, Ruth. *London: Aspects of Change.* London: MacGibbon & Kee, 1964.

Glazer, Nona. *Women's Paid and Unpaid Labor: The Work Transfer in Healthcare and Retailing.* Philadelphia: Temple University Press, 1993.

Glickman, Lawrence B. *Buying Power: A History of Consumer Activism in America*. Chicago: University of Chicago Press, 2009.

Goenka, Aditya, and David Henley. *Southeast Asia's Credit Revolution: From Moneylenders to Microfinance*. London: Routledge, 2010.

Goldman, Paula. "From Margin to Mainstream: Jubilee 2000 and the Rising Profile of Global Poverty. Issues in the United Kingdom and United States." PhD diss., Harvard University, 2010.

Goldthorpe, John H. "The Current Inflation: Towards a Sociological Account." In *The Political Economy of Inflation*, ed. John H. Goldthorpe and Fred Hirsch, 186–213. London: Martin Robertson, 1978.

Goswami, Manu. "From Swadeshi to Swaraj: Nation, Economy, Territory in Colonial South Asia, 1870 to 1907." *Comparative Studies in Society and History* 40, no. 4 (October 1998): 609–36.

———. *Producing India: From Colonial Economy to National Space*. Chicago: University of Chicago Press, 2004.

Götz, Norbert. "Moral Economy: Its Conceptual History and Analytical Prospects." *Journal of Global Ethics* 11, no. 2 (2015): 147–62.

Goyder, George. *The Responsible Company*. Oxford: Blackwell, 1961.

———, ed. *Trusteeship: A Possible Solution to Problems of Power, Exploitation, Conflict and Alienation*. Mumbai: Leslie Sawhny Programme of Training for Democracy 1979.

Goyder, George, and J. M. Kellock. *The Future of Private Enterprise: A Study in Responsibility*. Oxford: B. Blackwell, 1951.

Great Britain, Social Exclusion Unit. *Bringing Britain Together: A National Strategy for Neighbourhood Renewal*. London: Stationery Office, 1998.

Greene, John Robert. *America in the Sixties*. Syracuse: Syracuse University Press, 2010.

Greenhill, Romilly, Ann Pettifor, Henry Northover, and Ashok Sinha. *Did the G8 Drop the Debt*. London: Jubilee Debt Campaign, 2003.

Group of 77 and United Nations Conference on Trade and Development. *Trends and Problems in World Trade and Development; Charter of Algiers*. Beograd: Međunarodna štampa Interpress, 1968.

Gunn, Simon. "The Buchanan Report, Environment and the Problem of Traffic in 1960s Britain." *Twentieth Century British History* 22, no. 4 (December 1, 2011): 521–42.

Gupta, Akhil. *Postcolonial Developments: Agriculture in the Making of Modern India*. Durham: Duke University Press, 1998.

Gupta, Huma. "Staging Baghdad as a Problem of Development." *International Journal of Islamic Architecture* 8, no. 2 (2019): 337–61.

Gurney, Peter. *The Making of Consumer Culture in Modern Britain*. London: Bloomsbury Publishing, 2017.

———. " 'The Sublime of the Bazaar': A Moment in the Making of a Consumer Culture in Mid-Nineteenth Century England." *Journal of Social History* 40, no. 2 (2006): 385–405.

Guzman, Rosario. "Here Comes Zombie Neoliberalism." *IBON*, August 30, 2019.

Hacker, Jacob S. *The Divided Welfare State: The Battle over Public and Private Social Benefits in the United States*. New York: Cambridge University Press, 2002.

Hall, Catherine. *Civilizing Subjects: Metropole and Colony in the English Imagination, 1830–1867*. Chicago: University of Chicago Press, 2002.

———, ed. *Cultures of Empire: Colonisers in Britain and the Empire in the Nineteenth and Twentieth Centuries*. London: Manchester University Press, 2000.

Hall, Catherine, Nicholas Draper, Keith McClelland, Katie Donington, and Rachel Lang. *Legacies of British Slave-Ownership: Colonial Slavery and the Formation of Victorian Britain*. Cambridge: Cambridge University Press, 2014.

Hall, Stuart. "Crosland Territory." *New Left Review* (March/April 1960): 2–4.

———. *Familiar Stranger: A Life between Two Islands*. Ed. Bill Schwarz. Durham: Duke University Press, 2020.

———. "Life and Times of the First New Left." *New Left Review* 61 (February 1, 2010): 177–96.

———. "The Local and the Global: Globalization and Ethnicity." In *Culture, Globalization, and the World-System: Contemporary Conditions for the Representation of Identity*, ed. Anthony King, 19–40. Minneapolis: University of Minnesota Press, 1997.

———. *Selected Political Writings: The Great Moving Right Show and Other Essays*. Ed. Sally Davison, David Featherstone, Michael Rustin, and Bill Schwarz. Durham: Duke University Press, 2017.

———. "ULR Club at Notting Hill." *New Left Review* 1, no. 1 (January–February 1960): 71–72.

———. "When Was 'the Post-Colonial'? Thinking at the Limit." In *Eleven When Was "the Post-Colonial"? Thinking at the Limit [1996]*, 293–315. Durham: Duke University Press, 2021.

Hall, Stuart, and Tony Jefferson. *Resistance through Rituals: Youth Subcultures in Post-War Britain*. 2nd ed. London: Routledge, 2006.

Hamelink, Cees J. *The Politics of World Communication*. London: Sage Publications, 1994.

Harmon, M. *The British Labour Government and the 1976 IMF Crisis*. New York: St. Martin's Press, 1997.

Harris, Jose. "Political Thought and the Welfare State, 1870–1940: An Intellectual Framework for British Social Policy." *Past & Present* 135, no. 1 (May 1, 1992): 116–41.

Harris, Malcolm. "Just Beans: What Was Ethical Consumption under Capitalism?" *The Drift* 8, no. 1 (November 2022). https://www.thedriftmag.com/just-beans/.

Hart, Judith. *Aid and Liberation: A Socialist Study of Aid Policies*. London: Gollancz, 1973.

Hart, Keith. "Informal Income Opportunities and Urban Employment in Ghana." *Journal of Modern African Studies* 11, no. 1 (March 1973): 61–89.

Harvey, David. *A Brief History of Neoliberalism*. Oxford: Oxford University Press, 2005.

Haseler, Stephen. *The Gaitskellites: Revisionism in the British Labour Party, 1951–64*. London: Macmillan, 1969.

Haskell, Thomas L. "Capitalism and the Origins of the Humanitarian Sensibility, Part 1." *American Historical Review* 90, no. 2 (April 1, 1985): 339–61.

———. "Capitalism and the Origins of the Humanitarian Sensibility, Part 2." *American Historical Review* 90, no. 3 (June 1, 1985): 547–66.

Haslemere Declaration Group. *Sugar Today, Jam Tomorrow?: A Study of the Sell-out over Commonwealth Sugar in the Common Market Negotiations*. London: Haslemere Declaration Group: Third World First, 1974.

Haslemere Group. *Exploitation of the Third World: Notes on Research and a Bibliography*. London: Haslemere Declaration Group, 1969.

———. *Haslemere Declaration*. London: Haslemere Group, 1968.

Hawkins, E. K. "Competition between the Nationalized Electricity and Gas Industries." *Journal of Industrial Economics* 1, no. 2 (April 1953): 155–73.

Hayek, F. A., ed. *Collectivist Economic Planning: Critical Studies on the Possibilities of Socialism*. London: Routledge, 1935.

Hayter, Teresa. *Aid as Imperialism*. Pelican Books. Harmondsworth: Penguin, 1971.

———. *The Creation of World Poverty*. London: Pluto Press, in association with Third World First, 1981.

———. "The Purpose of Aid." *New Internationalist*, September 22, 2009.

Hazelwood, Arthur, and Gerald Holtham. *Aid and Inequality in Kenya: British Development Assistance to Kenya*. New York: Routledge, 2010.

Heilbroner, Robert L. *Between Capitalism and Socialism*. New York: Random House/The Heritage Foundation, 1970.

Hein, Kroos, and Klaus Schwab. *Moderne Unternehmensführung im Maschinenbau*. Frankfurt/Main-Niederrad, DE: Maschinenbau-Verlag, 1971.

Helleiner, Eric. *The Forgotten Foundations of Bretton Woods: International Development and the Making of the Postwar Order*. Ithaca: Cornell University Press, 2014.

Hendrikse, Reijer. "Neo-illiberalism." *Geoforum* 95 (2018): 169–72.

Herbert, Alicia, and Elaine Kempson. *Credit Use and Ethnic Minorities*. London: Policy Studies Institute, 1996.

Herbst, Jeffrey. *U.S. Economic Policy toward Africa*. New York: Council on Foreign Relations Press, 1992.

Hilton, Matthew. "Charity, Decolonization and Development: The Case of the Starehe Boys School, Nairobi." *Past & Present* 233, no. 1 (November 1, 2016): 227–67.

———. "Charity and the End of Empire: British Non-Governmental Organizations, Africa, and International Development in the 1960s." *American Historical Review* 123, no. 2 (April 1, 2018): 493–517.

———. *Consumerism in Twentieth-Century Britain: The Search for a Historical Movement*. Cambridge: Cambridge University Press, 2003.

———. "International Aid and Development NGOs in Britain and Human Rights since 1945." *Humanity: An International Journal of Human Rights, Humanitarianism, and Development* 3, no. 3 (October 31, 2012): 449–72.

———. "Ken Loach and the Save the Children Film: Humanitarianism, Imperialism, and the Changing Role of Charity in Postwar Britain." *Journal of Modern History* 87, no. 2 (June 1, 2015): 357–94.

———. "Michael Young and the Consumer Movement." *Contemporary British History* 19, no. 3 (September 1, 2005): 311–19.

———. "Oxfam and the Problem of NGOs Aid Appraisal in the 1960s." *Humanity: An International Journal of Human Rights, Humanitarianism* 9, no. 1 (2018): 1–18.

———. "Politics Is Ordinary: Non-governmental Organizations and Political Participation in Contemporary Britain." *Twentieth Century British History* 22, no. 2 (2011): 230–68.

———. *Prosperity for All: Consumer Activism in an Era of Globalization*. Ithaca: Cornell University Press, 2009.

Hilton, Matthew, James McKay, Nicholas Crowson, and Jean-Francois Mouhot. *The Politics of Expertise: How NGOs Shaped Modern Britain*. Oxford: Oxford University Press, 2013.

Hirsch, Fred. *Social Limits to Growth*. Cambridge, MA: Harvard University Press, 1976.

Hirschman, Albert O., Jeremy Adelman, Emma Rothschild, and Amartya Sen. *The Essential Hirschman*. Princeton: Princeton University Press, 2013.

Hochschild, Arlie Russell. *The Managed Heart: Commercialization of Human Feeling*. Berkeley: University of California Press, 1983.

Hodge, Joseph M. "British Colonial Expertise, Post-Colonial Careering and the Early History of International Development." *Journal of Modern European History* 8, no. 1 (2010): 24–46.

———. "Writing the History of Development (Part 1: The First Wave)." *Humanity: An International Journal of Human Rights, Humanitarianism & Development* 6, no. 3 (Winter 2015): 429–63.

———. "Writing the History of Development (Part 2: Longer, Deeper, Wider)." *Humanity: An International Journal of Human Rights, Humanitarianism & Development* 7, no. 1 (Spring 2016): 125–74.

Hodson, H. V. *The Diseconomics of Growth*. New York: Ballantine Books, 1972.

Hoe, Susanna. *The Man Who Gave His Company Away: A Biography of Ernest Bader, Founder of the Scott Bader Commonwealth.* London: Heinemann, 1978.

Hollow, Matthew. "The Age of Affluence Revisited: Council Estates and Consumer Society in Britain, 1950–1970." *Journal of Consumer Culture* 16, issue 1 (2016): 279–96.

Holthaus, Leonie. "G.D.H. Cole's International Thought: The Dilemmas of Justifying Socialism in the Twentieth Century." *International History Review* 36, no. 5 (2014): 858–75.

Holyoake, George Jacob. *The Co-Operative Movement To-Day.* London: Methuen, 1891.

Horne, Suzanne, and Avril Maddrell. *Charity Shops: Retailing Consumption and Society.* London: Routledge, 2002.

Hoste, C. H. *Trypanotolerant Livestock in West and Central Africa.* Vol. 3, *A Decade's Results.* ILCA Monograph. Addis Ababa: International Livestock Centre for Africa, 1992.

Humble, John William. *The Responsible Multinational Enterprise.* London: Foundation for Business Responsibilities, 1975.

Hurley, Donnacadh, Steve Duke, Rebecca Francis, and Brian Pratt. *Income Generation Schemes for the Urban Poor.* Oxford: Oxfam, 1990.

Hutt, William. "The Concept of Consumers' Sovereignty." *Economic Journal* 50 (March 1940): 66–77.

———. "Economic Method and the Concept of Competition." *South African Journal of Economics* 2 (1934): 3–23.

———. *Economists and the Public: A Study of Competition and Opinion.* London: Honathan Cape, 1936.

Huyssen, David. *Progressive Inequality: Rich and Poor in New York, 1890–1920.* Cambridge, MA: Harvard University Press, 2014.

Immerwahr, Daniel. "Polanyi in the United States: Peter Drucker, Karl Polanyi, and the Midcentury Critique of Economic Society." *Journal of the History of Ideas* 70, no. 3 (2009): 445–66.

———. *Thinking Small: The United States and the Lure of Community Development.* Cambridge, MA: Harvard University Press, 2015.

Independent Commission on International Development and Willy Brandt. *Common Crisis North-South: Cooperation for World Recovery.* London: Pan Books, 1983.

International Business Publication. *Bulgaria Investment and Business Guide.* Vol. 1, *Strategic and Practical Information.* Washington, DC: International Business Publication, 2013.

International Confederation of Free Trade Unions Executive Board. *Towards a New Economic and Social Order: The ICFTU Development Charter: Adopted by the 70th Meeting of the ICFTU Executive Board, Hamburg, 17–19 May 1978.* Brussels: International Confederation of Free Trade Unions, 1978.

International Labour Office. *Employment, Growth and Basic Needs: A One World Problem: Report of the Director-General of the International Labour Office and Declaration of Principles and Program of Action Adopted by the Conference.* Geneva: CH, International Labour Office, 1976.

———. *Employment, Incomes and Equality: A Strategy for Increasing Productive Employment in Kenya.* Geneva: International Labour Office, 1972.

Iriye, Akira. "A Century of NGOs." *Diplomatic History* 23, no. 3 (1999): 421–35.

Jackson, Ben. "Currents of Neo-Liberalism: British Political Ideologies and the New Right, c. 1955–1979." *English Historical Review* 131, no. 551 (August 1, 2016): 823–50.

———. *Equality and the British Left: A Study in Progressive Thought, 1900–64.* Manchester: Manchester University Press, 2013.

———. "Putting Neoliberalism in Its Place." *Modern Intellectual History* 19, no. 3 (2021): 1–14.

————. "Richard Titmuss versus the IEA: The Transition from Idealism to Neo-Liberalism in British Social Policy." In *Welfare and Social Policy in Britain since 1870: Essays in Honour of Jose Harris*, ed. Lawrence Goldman, 147–61. Oxford: Oxford University Press, 2019.

Jackson, Ben, and Robert Saunders, eds. *Making Thatcher's Britain*. Cambridge: Cambridge University Press, 2012.

Jaffe, Sarah. "Zombie Neoliberalism." *Dissent*, Fall 2017.

Jaffee, Daniel. *Brewing Justice: Fair Trade Coffee, Sustainability, and Survival*. Oakland: University of California Press, 2014.

James, Estelle, ed. *The Nonprofit Sector in International Perspective: Studies in Comparative Culture and Policy*. Oxford: Oxford University Press, 1989.

Jarlert, Anders. *The Oxford Group, Group Revivalism, and the Churches in Northern Europe, 1930–1945: With Special Reference to Scandinavia and Germany*. Lund: Lund University Press, 1995.

Jenkins, Richard, and Robin Ward. *Ethnic Communities in Business*. Cambridge: Cambridge University Press, 1984.

Jennings, Michael. *Surrogates of the State: NGOs, Development, and Ujamaa in Tanzania*. Bloomfield, CT: Kumarian Press, 2008.

Jeremy, David J. *Capitalists and Christians: Business Leaders and the Churches in Britain, 1900–1960*. Oxford: Oxford University Press, 1990.

————. *Religion, Business, and Wealth in Modern Britain*. London: Routledge, 1998.

Jevons, William Stanley. *The Coal Question: An Enquiry Concerning the Progress of the Nation, and the Probable Exhaustion of Our Coal-Mines*. London: Macmillan, 1865.

Jolly, Richard. "Adjustment with a Human Face: A UNICEF Record and Perspective on the 1980s." *World Development* 19, no. 12 (1991): 1807–21.

Jones, Mervyn. *Two Ears of Corn; Oxfam in Action*. London: Hodder and Stoughton, 1965.

Jones, T., D. McEvoy, and G. Barrett. "Raising Capital for the Ethnic Minority Small Firm." In *Finance and the Small Firm*, ed. Alan Hughes and D. J. Storey. Routledge Small Business Series. London: Routledge, 1994.

Jurik, Nancy C. *Bootstrap Dreams: U.S. Microenterprise Development in an Era of Welfare Reform*. Ithaca: Cornell University Press, 2005.

Kaplan, Rami, and Daniel Kinderman. "The Business-Class Case for Corporate Social Responsibility: Mobilization, Diffusion, and Institutionally Transformative Strategy in Venezuela and Britain." *Theory and Society* 48, no. 1 (2019): 131–66.

Katz, Israel. "Richard M. Titmuss: Idealist, Scientist and Man of Action." *Social Security (Hebrew edition)* 6, no. 7 (1974): 141.

Kauffman, L. A. *Direct Action: Protest and the Reinvention of American Radicalism*. London: Verso, 2017.

Kempner, Thomas, Keith MacMillan, and Kevin Hawkins. *Business and Society: Tradition and Change*. London: Allen Lane, 1974.

Kempson, Elaine. "Bank Exclusion in the United Kingdom." In *Banking and Social Cohesion: Alternative Responses to a Global Market*, ed. Christophe Guene and Ed Mayo. Charlbury: Jon Carpenter, 2001.

Kemseke, Peter van. *Towards an Era of Development: The Globalization of Socialism and Christian Democracy, 1945–1965*. Leuven: Leuven University Press, 2006.

Kenkare, A. S. "Technology for the Developing World." *Chartered Mechanical Engineer* 2, no. 3 (March 1975): 87–90.

Kenny, Michael. *The First New Left: British Intellectuals after Stalin*. Manchester: Manchester University Press, 1995.

Kirton, Claremont. *Jamaica: Debt and Poverty*. Oxford: Oxfam, 1992.

Klein, Jennifer. *For All These Rights: Business, Labor, and the Shaping of America's Public-Private Welfare State*. Princeton: Princeton University Press, 2010.

Klein, Naomi. *No Logo: No Space, No Choice, No Jobs*. London: Flamingo, 2001.

———. *The Shock Doctrine: The Rise of Disaster Capitalism*. New York: Metropolitan Books/Henry Holt, 2007.

Koven, Seth. *The Match Girl and the Heiress*. Princeton: Princeton University Press, 2016.

———. *Slumming: Sexual and Social Politics in Victorian London*. Princeton: Princeton University Press, 2006.

Kus, Basak. "Neoliberalism, Institutional Change, and the Welfare State: The Case of Britain and France." *International Journal of Comparative Sociology* 47 (2006): 488–525.

LaBarbera-Twarog, Emily E. *Politics of the Pantry: Housewives, Food, and Consumer Protest in Twentieth-Century America*. New York: Oxford University Press, 2017.

Labour Party. *Report of the Labour Party Working Party on Industrial Democracy*. London: Labour Party, 1967.

Lane, Jacqueline Ann. "A Watershed Decade in British Industrial Relations, 1965 to 1974? The Donovan Commission Report, in Place of Strife and the Industrial Relations Act of 1971." PhD thesis, University of Huddersfield, 2017.

Lappé, Frances Moore. *Diet for a Small Planet*. Twentieth anniversary edition. New York: Ballantine Books, 1991.

Larson, R., and D. Thompson. *Where Were You Brother? An Account of Trade Union Imperialism*. London: War on Want, 1978.

Laslett, Peter, and W. G. Runciman, eds. *Philosophy, Politics and Society: (Second Series); a Collection*. Oxford: Blackwell, 1962.

Lawrence, Jon. "Inventing the 'Traditional Working Class': A Re-Analysis of Interview Notes from Young and Willmott's *Family and Kinship in East London*." *Historical Journal* 59, no. 2 (June 2016): 567–93.

Lazier, Benjamin. "Earthrise; or, The Globalization of the World Picture Earthrise." *American Historical Review* 116, no. 3 (June 1, 2011): 602–30.

Lemire, Beverly, Ruth Pearson, and Gail Campbell. *Women and Credit: Researching the Past, Refiguring the Future*. Oxford: Berg Publishers, 2001.

Leonard, Robert. "Between the 'Hand-Loom' and the 'Samson Stripper': Fritz Schumacher's Struggle for Intermediate Technology." *Contemporary European History* 31, no. 4 (November 2022): 525–52.

———. "E. F. Schumacher and Intermediate Technology." *History of Political Economy* 50, no. 1 (December 1, 2018): 249–65.

———. "E. F. Schumacher and the Making of 'Buddhist Economics,' 1950–1973." *Journal of the History of Economic Thought* 41, no. 2 (June 2019): 159–86.

Leuchtenburg, William E. *Herbert Hoover*. New York: Macmillan, 2009.

Levien, Michael. *Dispossession without Development: Land Grabs in Neoliberal India*. Oxford: Oxford University Press, 2018.

Levine, Philippa, ed. *Gender and Empire: Oxford History of the British Empire*. Oxford: Oxford University Press, 2004.

Levitas, Ruth. *The Inclusive Society?: Social Exclusion and New Labour*. 2nd ed. Basingstoke: Palgrave Macmillan, 2005.

Levy, Jonathan. *Ages of American Capitalism: A History of the United States*. New York: Random House Publishing Group, 2021.

———. "Capital as Process and the History of Capitalism." *Business History Review* 91, no. 3 (2017): 483–510.

Lewis, W. Arthur. "Economic Development with Unlimited Supplies of Labour." *Manchester School* 22, no. 2 (May 1, 1954): 139–91.

Li, Tania. *The Will to Improve: Governmentality, Development, and the Practice of Politics.* Durham: Duke University Press, 2007.

Linstrum, Erik. *Ruling Minds: Psychology in the British Empire.* Cambridge, MA: Harvard University Press, 2016.

Lister, Marjorie. *The European Community and the Developing World: The Role of the Lomé Convention.* Aldershot: Avebury, 1988.

Long, Adrian. "Theological Reflection on International Debt: A Critique of the Jubilee 2000 Debt Cancellation Campaign." PhD thesis, University of Birmingham, 2010.

Louis, William Roger. "American Anti-Colonialism and the Dissolution of the British Empire." *International Affairs* 61, no. 3 (July 1, 1985): 395–420.

———. *Ends of British Imperialism: The Scramble for Empire, Suez and Decolonization: Collected Essays.* London: I. B. Tauris, 2006.

Luetchford, Mark, and Peter Burns. *Waging the War on Want: 50 Years of Campaigning against World Poverty: An Authorised History.* London: War on Want, 2003.

Lysaught, M. Therese. "Roman Catholic Teaching on International Debt: Toward a New Methodology for Catholic Social Ethics and Moral Theology." *Journal of Moral Theology* 4, no. 2 (2015): 1–27.

Macekura, Stephen J. *The Mismeasure of Progress: Economic Growth and Its Critics.* Chicago: University of Chicago Press, 2020.

———. *Of Limits and Growth: The Rise of Global Sustainable Development in the Twentieth Century.* New York: Cambridge University Press, 2015.

MacFarquhar, Larissa. *Strangers Drowning: Impossible Idealism, Drastic Choices, and the Urge to Help.* New York: Penguin Books, 2016.

Mader, Philip. *The Political Economy of Microfinance: Financializing Poverty.* Houndmills, Basingstoke, Hampshire: Palgrave, 2015.

Maier, Charles S. *Leviathan 2.0: Inventing Modern Statehood.* Cambridge, MA: Harvard University Press, 2014.

Mandler, Peter. *The Crisis of the Meritocracy: Britain's Transition to Mass Education since the Second World War.* Oxford: Oxford University Press, 2020.

Manela, Erez. "International Society as a Historical Subject." *Diplomatic History* 44, no. 2 (2020): 184–209.

Mann, Geoff. *In the Long Run We Are All Dead: Keynesianism, Political Economy, and Revolution.* London: Verso, 2017.

Mansfield, John. *The Other Way.* BBC and Time-Life Films, 1975.

Mantena, Karuna. *Alibis of Empire: Henry Maine and the Ends of Liberal Imperialism.* Princeton: Princeton University Press, 2010.

———. "On Gandhi's Critique of the State: Sources, Contexts, Conjunctures." *Modern Intellectual History* 9, no. 3 (November 2012): 535–63.

Marcel, Mario, and J. Gabriel Palma. "Third World Debt and Its Effects on the British Economy: A Southern View of Economic Mismanagement in the North." *Cambridge Journal of Economics* 12, no. 3 (1988): 361–400.

Marmor, Theodore R., and Jan S. Marmor. *The Politics of Medicare.* London: Routledge & Kegan Paul, 1970.

Marshall, T. H. *Citizenship and Social Class, and Other Essays.* Cambridge: Cambridge University Press, 1950.

Martin, David A. "R. H. Tawney's Normative Economic History of Capitalism." *Review of Social Economy* 43, no. 1 (April 1985): 84–102.

Martin, Jamie. *The Meddlers: Sovereignty, Empire, and the Birth of Global Economic Governance.* Cambridge, MA: Harvard University Press, 2022.

Mazlish, Bruce. *The New Global History.* Abingdon: Routledge, 2006.

McCarthy, Helen. *The British People and the League of Nations: Democracy, Citizenship and Internationalism, c. 1918–45.* Manchester: Manchester University Press, 2011.

———. "Social Science and Married Women's Employment in Post-War Britain." *Past & Present* 233, issue 1 (November 2016): 269–305.

McElroy, Frank S., and Alexander Moros. "Joint Production Committees, January 1948." *Monthly Labor Review* 67, no. 2 (1948): 123–26.

McGoey, Linsey. *No Such Thing as a Free Gift: The Gates Foundation and the Price of Philanthropy.* London: Verso, 2015.

McKenzie, Francine. *GATT and Global Order in the Postwar Era.* Cambridge: Cambridge University Press, 2020.

McRobie, George. "Intermediate Technology: Small Is Successful." *Third World Quarterly* 1, no. 2 (April 1979): 71–86.

McRobie, George, and E. F. Schumacher. *Small Is Possible.* Harper Colophon Books. New York: Harper & Row, 1981.

Medawar, Charles. *The Social Audit Consumer Handbook: A Guide to the Social Responsibilities of Business to the Consumer.* London: Macmillan Press, 1978.

Mees, Bernard. *The Rise of Business Ethics.* New York: Routledge, 2019.

Melrose-Woodman, Jonquil, and Ingrid Kverndal. *Towards Social Responsibility: Company Codes of Ethics and Practice.* London: British Institute of Management, 1976.

Metcalf, Hilary, Tariq Modood, and Satnam Virdee. *Asian Self-Employment: The Interaction of Culture and Economics in England.* London: Policy Studies Institute, 1996.

Meyerowitz, Joanne. *A War on Global Poverty: The Lost Promise of Redistribution and the Rise of Microcredit.* Princeton: Princeton University Press, 2021.

Middleton, Roger. "Brittan on Britain: 'The Economic Contradictions of Democracy' Redux." *The Historical Journal* 54, no. 4 (2011): 1141–68.

Midgley, J., A. Hall, M. Hardiman, and D. Narine. *Community Participation, Social Development and the State.* London: Methuen, 1986.

Millard, Edward. *Export Marketing for a Small Handicraft Business.* Oxford: Oxfam, 1992.

———. *Financial Management of a Small Handicraft Business.* Oxford: Oxfam, 1987.

Ministry of Agriculture, Fisheries and Food. *Food from Our Own Resources, Etc.* (Parliamentary Papers. Cmnd. 6020). London: Her Majesty's Stationery Office, 1975.

Ministry of Education. *The Youth Service in England and Wales* ("The Albemarle Report"). London: Her Majesty's Stationery Office, 1960.

Mintz, Sidney W. *Sweetness and Power: The Place of Sugar in Modern History.* New York: Viking, 1985.

Mishan, E. J. *The Costs of Economic Growth.* New York: F. A. Praeger, 1967.

Mitchell, S. Ian. *Tradition and Innovation in English Retailing, 1700 to 1850: Narratives of Consumption.* Farnham, Surrey: Ashgate, 2013.

Mitchell, Timothy. *Carbon Democracy: Political Power in the Age of Oil.* London: Verso, 2011.

———. "Fixing the Economy." *Cultural Studies* 12, no. 1 (January 1, 1998): 82–101.

———. *Rule of Experts: Egypt, Techno-Politics, Modernity.* Berkeley: University of California Press, 2002.

Monbiot, George. "Neoliberalism: The 'Zombie Doctrine' at the Root of All Our Problems." *Common Dreams*, April 15, 2016.

Montes, Manuel F. *The Currency Crisis in Southeast Asia.* Singapore: Institute of Southeast Asian Studies, 1998.

Moreton, Bethany. *To Serve God and Wal-Mart: The Making of Christian Free Enterprise.* Cambridge, MA: Harvard University Press, 2009.

Morgan, J. Gwyn. *European Approaches to Responsibility.* London: Foundation for Business Responsibilities, 1975.

Morris, William, and May Morris. *The Collected Works of William Morris*. Vol. 2. London: Longmans, Green and Co., 1910.

Morse, David. "Employment and Economic Growth: An International Perspective." *Relations industrielles* 24, no. 4 (December 1969): 662–79.

Moses, Julia. "Social Citizenship and Social Rights in an Age of Extremes: T. H. Marshall's Social Philosophy in the *Longue Durée.*" *Modern Intellectual History* 16, no. 1 (April 2019): 155–84.

Moyes, Adrian. *Volunteers in Development*. London: Overseas Development Institute, 1966.

Moyn, Samuel. *Not Enough: Human Rights in an Unequal World*. Cambridge, MA: Harvard University Press, 2018.

———. "T. H. Marshall, the Moral Economy, and Social Rights." *Humanity: An International Journal of Human Rights, Humanitarianism, and Development* 11, no. 2 (2020): 235–40.

———. "Welfare World." *Humanity: An International Journal of Human Rights, Humanitarianism, and Development* 8, no. 1 (2017): 175–83.

Mudge, Stephanie L. *Leftism Reinvented: Western Parties from Socialism to Neoliberalism*. Cambridge, MA: Harvard University Press, 2018.

Murdoch, Norman H. *Origins of the Salvation Army*. Knoxville: University of Tennessee Press, 1994.

Murphy, Colm. *Futures of Socialism: "Modernisation," the Labour Party, and the British Left, 1973–1997*. Cambridge: Cambridge University Press, 2023.

Myrdal, Gunnar. *Beyond the Welfare State: Economic Planning and Its International Implications*. Storrs Lectures on Jurisprudence. New Haven: Yale University Press, 1960.

Nagel, Thomas. *The Possibility of Altruism*. Princeton: Princeton University Press, 1979.

———. "Poverty and Food: Why Charity Is Not Enough." In *Food Policy: The Responsibility of the United States in the Life and Death Choices*, ed. G. Brown and Henry Shue, 54–62. New York: New York Free Press, 1977.

Natarajan, Radhika. "Organizing Community: Commonwealth Citizens and Social Activism in Britain, 1948–1982." PhD diss., University of California, Berkeley, 2013.

———. "Village Life and How to Improve It: Textual Routes of Community Development in the Late British Empire." In *Reading the Postwar Future: Textual Turning Points from 1944*, ed. Kirrily Freeman and John Munro, 96–112. London: Bloomsbury Publishing, 2019.

NatWest. *Afro-Caribbean Businesses and Their Banks: Independent Survey Conducted for NatWest by Ethnic Response*. London: NatWest UK, 1996.

———. *Asian Businesses and Their Banks: Independent Survey Conducted for NatWest by Ethnic Response*. London: NatWest UK, 1996.

Neima, Anna. "Dartington Hall and the Quest for 'Life in Its Completeness,' 1925–45." *History Workshop Journal* 88 (October 1, 2019): 111–33.

Nelson, Candace. *Going Forward: The Peer Group Lending Exchange, November 2–4, 1993, Couchwood, Hot Springs, Arkansas*. Toronto: Calmeadow, 1994.

Nelson, J. R. "The Fleck Report and the Area Organization of the National Coal Board." *Public Administration* 43, no. 1 (1965): 41–58.

Nicolson, D. L. *The Management of Change in British Airways*. London: Foundation for Business Responsibilities, 1974.

Nkrumah, Kwame. *Neo-Colonialism: The Last Stage of Imperialism*. London: Nelson, 1965.

North London Haslemere Group. *Coffee: The Rules of Neo-Colonialism: A Study of International Coffee Trade and the International Coffee Agreement*. London: Third World First, 1972.

Nyerere, Julius K. "Unity for a New Order." *Black Scholar* 11, no. 5 (1980): 55–63.

Ocobock, Paul. *An Uncertain Age: The Politics of Manhood in Kenya*. Athens: Ohio University Press, 2017.

O'Connell, Sean. *Credit and Community: Working-Class Debt in the UK since 1880*. Oxford: Oxford University Press, 2009.

Offer, Avner. *The Challenge of Affluence: Self-Control and Well-Being in the United States and Britain since 1950*. Oxford: Oxford University Press, 2006.

Offner, Amy C. *Sorting Out the Mixed Economy: The Rise and Fall of Welfare and Developmental States in the Americas*. Princeton: Princeton University Press, 2019.

Ogle, Vanessa. " 'Funk Money': The End of Empires, the Expansion of Tax Havens, and Decolonization as an Economic and Financial Event." *Past & Present* 249, no. 1 (November 1, 2020): 213–49.

———. "State Rights against Private Capital: The 'New International Economic Order' and the Struggle over Aid, Trade, and Foreign Investment, 1962–1981." *Humanity: An International Journal of Human Rights, Humanitarianism, and Development*, no. 2 (2014): 211–34.

Olsen, Niklas. *The Sovereign Consumer: A New Intellectual History of Neoliberalism*. Cham: Palgrave Macmillan, 2019.

O'Neill, Onora. "Lifeboat Earth." *Philosophy & Public Affairs* 4, no. 3 (1975): 273–92.

Osgerby, William. *Youth in Britain since 1945*. Oxford: Blackwell, 1998.

O'Sullivan, Kevin. *The NGO Moment: The Globalisation of Compassion from Biafra to Live Aid*. Cambridge: Cambridge University Press, 2021.

Otter, Chris. *Diet for a Large Planet: Industrial Britain, Food Systems, and World Ecology*. Chicago: University of Chicago Press, 2020.

———. "Industrializing Diet, Industrializing Ourselves: Technology, Energy, and Food, 1750–2000." In *The Routledge History of Food*, ed. Carol Helstosky, 220–46. New York: Routledge, 2015.

Oxfam. *Oxfam's Overseas Programme, Objective and Strategies: From the Oxfam Field Directors' Handbook*. Oxford: Oxfam, 1980.

Oxfam, Policy Department. *A Case for Reform: Fifty Years of the IMF and World Bank*. Oxford: Oxfam Policy Department, 1995.

Palley, Thomas I. "From Keynesianism to Neoliberalism: Shifting Paradigms in Economics." In *Neoliberalism: A Critical Reader*, 20–29. London: Pluto Books, 2005.

Passes, Edwin Montague. "The Christian Socialism of R. H. Tawney." PhD diss., London School of Economics and Political Science, 1994.

Payer, Cheryl. *The Debt Trap: The IMF and the Third World*. New York: Monthly Review Press, 1975.

———. *The Perpetuation of Dependence: The International Monetary Fund and the Third World*. Boston: New England Free Press, 1971.

Pearson, Ruth. "Microcredit Meets Social Exclusion: Learning with Difficulty from International Experience." *Journal of International Development* 10, no. 6 (1998): 811–22.

———. "Think Globally, Act Locally: Translating International Microcredit Experience in the United Kingdom." In *New Roles and Relevance: Development NGOs and the Challenge of Change*, ed. D. Lewis and T. Wallace. Bloomfield, CT: Kumarian Press, 2000.

Pearson, Ruth, and Erika Watson. *Giving Women the Credit: The Norwich Full Circle Project*. Oxford: Oxfam, 1997.

Pedersen, Susan. *Family, Dependence, and the Origins of the Welfare State: Britain and France, 1914–1945*. Cambridge: Cambridge University Press, 1993.

Pemberton, Hugh. "Taxation and Labour's Modernisation Programme." *Contemporary British History* 20, no. 3 (2006): 423–40.

Penna, Anthony N. *A History of Energy Flows: From Human Labor to Renewable Power.* London: Routledge, Taylor & Francis Group, 2020.

Perry, Kennetta Hammond. *London Is the Place for Me: Black Britons, Citizenship, and the Politics of Race.* New York: Oxford University Press, 2016.

Pettifor, Ann. *Debt, the Most Potent Form of Slavery: A Discussion of the Role of Western Lending Policies in Subordinating the Economies of Poor Countries.* London: Debt Crisis Network, 1996.

———. "The Economic Bondage of Debt—and the Birth of a New Movement." *New Left Review*, no. 230 (July/August 1998): 115–22.

Phelan, D. "Working on the Chain Gang: Hard Labour for Charity Shops." *NGO Finance* 9, no. 6 (1999): 16–19.

Phelps, Edmund S. *Altruism, Morality, and Economic Theory.* New York: Russell Sage Foundation, 1972.

Piachaud, David. "Fabianism, Social Policy and Colonialism: The Case of Tanzania." In *Colonialism and Welfare: Social Policy and the British Imperial Legacy*, ed. James Midgley and David Piachaud. Cheltenham: Edward Elgar Publishing, 2011.

Pikholz, Lynn, and Ronald Grzywinski. "Communities Are Creditworthy: Shorebank (USA) and Bumblebees." In *Banking and Social Cohesion: Alternative Responses to a Global Market*, ed. Christophe Guene and Edward Mayo. Charlbury: Jon Carpenter, 2001.

Pleyers, Geoffrey, and Alain Touraine. *Alter-Globalization: Becoming Actors in the Global Age.* Cambridge: Polity, 2010.

Polanyi, Karl. *The Great Transformation: The Political and Economic Origins of Our Time.* London: V. Gollancz, 1945.

Poulton, Robin, and Michael Harris. *Putting People First: Voluntary Organisations and Third World Development.* Basingstoke: Macmillan, 1988.

Power, Jonathan. *Development Economics.* London: Longman, 1971.

Prabhakar, R. *Stakeholding and New Labour.* London: Palgrave Macmillan, 2003.

Prasad, Monica. *The Politics of Free Markets: The Rise of Neoliberal Economic Policies in Britain, France, Germany, and the United States.* Chicago: University of Chicago Press, 2006.

Prashad, Vijay. *The Darker Nations: A People's History of the Third World.* New York: The New Press, 2007.

———. *The Poorer Nations: A Possible History of the Global South.* London: Verso Books, 2013.

Prebisch, Raúl. "Global Strategy of Development and International Cooperation—Programme before UNCTAD-II." *Foreign Trade Review* 2, no. 4 (January 1, 1968): 359–71.

———. *Towards a New Trade Policy for Development: Report.* New York: United Nations, 1964.

Prem, Ragini. *Agrindus Family Welfare Project: Plans and Achievement, 1968–72.* New Delhi: Society for Developing Gramdans, 1974.

Prentice, D. D. "Employee Participation in Corporate Government: A Critique of the Bullock Report." *Canadian Bar Review* 56, no. 2 (1978): 277–304.

Price, Richard. *Making Empire: Colonial Encounters and the Creation of Imperial Rule in Nineteenth-Century Africa.* Cambridge: Cambridge University Press, 2008.

Prochaska, F. K. "Charity Bazaars in Nineteenth-Century England." *Journal of British Studies* 16, no. 2 (1977): 62–84.

———. *Christianity and Social Service in Modern Britain: The Disinherit Spirit.* New York: Oxford University Press, 2006.

———. *Women and Philanthropy in Nineteenth-Century England.* Oxford: Oxford University Press, 1980.

Putnam, Lara. "Citizenship from the Margins: Vernacular Theories of Rights and the State from the Interwar Caribbean." *Journal of British Studies* 53, no. 1 (2014): 162–91.

Quaas, Ruben. "Selling Coffee to Raise Awareness for Development Policy: The Emerging Fair Trade Market in Western Germany in the 1970s." *Historical Social Research* 36, no. 3 (2011): 164–81.

Quarter, Jack. *Beyond the Bottom Line: Socially Innovative Business Owners*. Westport, CT: Quorum Books, 2000.

Quiggin, John. *Zombie Economics: How Dead Ideas Still Walk among Us*. Princeton: Princeton University Press, 2012.

Raianu, Mircea. *Tata: The Global Corporation That Built Indian Capitalism*. Cambridge, MA: Harvard University Press, 2021.

Rappaport, Erika. *A Thirst for Empire: How Tea Shaped the Modern World*. Princeton: Princeton University Press, 2017.

Rappaport, Erika, Sandra Trudgen Dawson, and Mark J. Crowley, eds. *Consuming Behaviours: Identity, Politics and Pleasure in Twentieth-Century Britain*. New York: Bloomsbury Publishing, 2015.

Reid, Alastair J. *United We Stand: A History of Britain's Trade Unions*. London: Penguin, 2005.

Reinisch, Jessica. "Internationalism in Relief: The Birth (and Death) of UNRRA 1." *Past & Present* 210, no. suppl. 6 (January 1, 2011): 258–89.

Reisman, David. *Crosland's Future: Opportunity and Outcome*. London: Springer, 1996.

———. *Richard Titmuss: Welfare and Society*. Studies in Social Policy and Welfare. London: Heinemann, 1977.

Rescher, Nicholas. *Unselfishness: The Role of the Vicarious Affects in Moral Philosophy and Social Theory*. Pittsburgh: University of Pittsburgh Press, 1975.

Rhoad, David L., ed. *War on Hunger: A Report from the Agency for International Development, December 1975*. Distributed by ERIC Clearinghouse, 1975.

Richmond, Vivienne. *Clothing the Poor in Nineteenth-Century England*. Cambridge: Cambridge University, 2013.

Ridley, Nicholas. *Company & Its Responsibilities? The New Capitalism*. London: Foundation for Business Responsibilities, 1974.

Rieger, Bernhard. "Making Britain Work Again: Unemployment and the Remaking of British Social Policy in the Eighties." *English Historical Review* 133, no. 562 (2008): 634–66.

Righart, Hans. "Moderate Versions of the 'Global Sixties': A Comparison of Great Britain and the Netherlands." *Journal of Area Studies* 6, no. 13 (September 1, 1998): 82–96.

Rigney, Victoria. *Peace Comes Walking: The Life of Donald Groom, Quaker Peace Worker*. Carindale, Queensland: Glass House Books, 2002.

Riley, Charlotte Lydia. "Monstrous Predatory Vampires and Beneficent Fairy-Godmothers: British Post-war Colonial Development in Africa." PhD diss., University of London, 2013.

———. " 'This Party Is a Moral Crusade, or It Is Nothing': Foreign Aid and Labour's Ethical Identity." In *Rethinking Labour's Past*, ed. Nathan Yeowell, 195–212. New York: I. B. Tauris, 2022.

———. "Writing like a Woman: Rita Hinden and Recovering the Imperial in International Thought." *International Politics Reviews* 9, no. 2 (2021): 264–71.

Robbins, Christopher and Javed Ansari. *The Profits of Doom: A War on Want Investigation into the "World Food Crisis."* London: War on Want, 1976.

Roberts, Richard. *When Britain Went Bust: The 1976 IMF Crisis*. London: OMFIF, 2016.

Robertson, James. *Profit or People? The New Social Role of Money*. London: Calder & Boyars, 1974.

Robinson, Emily, Camilla Schofield, Florence Sutcliffe-Braithwaite, and Natalie Thomlinson. "Telling Stories about Post-War Britain: Popular Individualism and the 'Crisis' of the 1970s." *Twentieth Century British History* 28, no. 2 (June 1, 2017): 268–304.

Robinson, Marguerite. *The Microfinance Revolution: Sustainable Finance for the Poor.* Washington, DC: World Bank Publications, 2001.

Robinson, Roland, ed. *Industrialisation in Developing Countries: Impressions and Papers of the Cambridge Conference on the Role of Industrialisation in Development, 6–19 September, 1964, at King's College, Cambridge.* Cambridge: University of Cambridge, 1965.

Rodney, Walter. *How Europe Underdeveloped Africa.* London: Bogle-L'Ouverture Publications, 1972.

Rogaly, Ben, Thomas Fisher, and Ed Mayo. *Poverty, Social Exclusion and Microfinance in Britain.* Oxford: Oxfam in association with the New Economics Foundation, 1999.

Rogaly, Ben, and Chris Roche. *Learning from South-North Links in Microfinance.* Oxford: Oxfam GB, 2000.

Rogan, Tim. *The Moral Economists: R. H. Tawney, Karl Polanyi, E. P. Thompson, and the Critique of Capitalism.* Princeton: Princeton University Press, 2017.

Rogers, Chris. *The IMF and European Economies: Crisis and Conditionality.* Houndmills, Basingstoke, Hampshire: Palgrave, 2012.

Rose, Clare. *Making, Selling and Wearing Boys' Clothes in Late-Victorian England.* Farnham, Surrey: Ashgate, 2010.

Rose, Nikolas. "Still 'like Birds on the Wire'? Freedom after Neoliberalism." *Economy and Society* 46, no. 3–4 (October 2, 2017): 303–23.

Roy, Ananya. *Poverty Capital.* New York: Routledge, 2010.

Rüdig, Wolfgang, and Philip D. Lowe. "The Withered 'Greening' of British Politics: A Study of the Ecology Party." *Political Studies* 34, no. 2 (June 1, 1986): 262–84.

Rutherford, Stuart. "Learning to Lend: Informal Credit and Savings Schemes in Bangladesh." Working Paper (Save the Children Overseas Department). London: Save the Children, 1993.

———. *The Poor and Their Money.* Manchester: Institute for Development Policy and Management, University of Manchester, 1999.

Sackley, Nicole. "The Village as Cold War Site: Experts, Development, and the History of Rural Reconstruction." *Journal of Global History* 6, no. 3 (2011): 481–504.

Sajed, Alina. "From the Third World to the Global South." *E-International Relations*, July 27, 2020.

Samuel, Raphael. *Theatres of Memory: Past and Present in Contemporary Culture.* London: Verso, 2012.

Sandall, Robert, Arch R. Wiggins, and Frederick Lee Coutts. *The History of the Salvation Army.* London: T. Nelson, 1947.

Sasson, Tehila. "From Empire to Humanity: The Imperial Origins of International Humanitarianism and the Russian Famine of 1921–22." *Journal of British Studies* 55, no. 3 (July 2016): 519–37.

———. "The Gospel of Wealth." *Dissent* (August 22, 2018).

———. "In the Name of Humanity: Britain and the Rise of Global Humanitarianism." PhD diss., University of California, Berkeley, 2015.

———. "Milking the Third World? Humanitarianism, Capitalism, and the Moral Economy of the Nestlé Boycott." *American Historical Review* 121, no. 4 (October 1, 2016): 1196–1224.

———. "The Problem of Homelessness in Post-war Britain." In *Rescuing the Vulnerable: Poverty, Welfare and Social Ties in Nineteenth- and Twentieth-Century Europe,* ed.

Beate Althammer, Lutz Raphael, and Tamara Stazic-Wendt. New York: Berghahn Books, 2016.

Sasson, Tehila, and James Vernon. "Practicing the British Way of Famine: Technologies of Relief, 1770–1985." *European Review of History*, no. 2 (2015): 1–13.

Satia, Priya. "Byron, Gandhi and the Thompsons: The Making of British Social History and Unmaking of Indian History." *History Workshop Journal* 81, no. 1 (April 1, 2016): 135–70.

———. "Developing Iraq: Britain, India and the Redemption of Empire and Technology in the First World War." *Past & Present* 197, no. 1 (November 1, 2007): 211–55.

———. *Time's Monster: History, Conscience and Britain's Empire*. London: Allen Lane, 2020.

Saunders, Clare. "British Humanitarian, Aid and Development NGOs, 1949–Present." In *NGOs in Contemporary Britain: Non-State Actors in Society and Politics since 1945*, ed. Nick Crowson, Matthew Hilton, and James McKay, 38–58. London: Palgrave Macmillan, 2009.

Saunders, Jack. *Assembling Cultures: Workplace Activism, Labour Militancy and Cultural Change in Britain's Car Factories, 1945–82*. Manchester: Manchester University Press, 2019.

Saunders, Robert. *Yes to Europe!: The 1975 Referendum and Seventies Britain*. Cambridge: Cambridge University Press, 2018.

Schenk, Alan, Victor Thuronyi, and Wei Cui. *Value Added Tax: A Comparative Approach*. 2nd ed. New York: Cambridge University Press, 2015.

Schneider, Bertrand. *The Barefoot Revolution: A Report to the Club of Rome*. London: IT Publications, 1988.

Schofield Camilla, and Ben Jones. "'Whatever Community Is, This Is Not It': Notting Hill and the Reconstruction of 'Race' in Britain after 1958." *Journal of British Studies* 58, no. 1 (2019): 142–73.

Schumacher, E. F. *The Age of Plenty: A Christian View*. Lauriston Lectures. Edinburgh: Saint Andrew Press, 1974.

———. "The Making of Economic Society, by Robert L. Heilbroner; and The Great Ascent, by Robert L. Heilbroner." *Commentary* (July 1963): 81–83.

———. *The Roots of Economic Growth*. Varanasi: Gandhian Institute of Studies, 1962.

———. *Small Is Beautiful: Economics as If People Mattered*. 1975. London: Vintage Books, 2011.

———. *This I Believe: And Other Essays*. Repr. with corrections. Resurgence Book. White River Junction, VT: Green Books, 2004.

Schumacher, E. F., S. Kessler, and D.T.A. Townend for the National Union of Mineworkers. *Britain's Coal; Report of Study Conference*. London: National Union of Mineworkers, 1960.

Schumacher, E. F., and Geoffrey Kirk. *Schumacher on Energy*. London: Abacus, 1983.

Screene, Lorraine. "Archival Review: Donald Chesworth (1923–1991) Archives at Queen Mary, University of London." *Contemporary British History* 24, no. 2 (June 2010): 257–63.

Secretary of State for Industry. "The Regeneration of British Industry." *Challenge* 18, no. 1 (March 1, 1975): 53–59.

Sen, S. C. *Multinational Corporations in the Developing Countries*. Calcutta: Eastern Law House, 1978.

Sewell, William. "A Strange Career: The Historical Study of Economic Life." *History and Theory* 49, no. 4 (December 2010): 146–66.

Sharma, Patrick A. "The United States, the World Bank, and the Transformation of Development in the 1970s." *Diplomatic History* 37, no. 3 (2013): 572–604.

Sharp, Robin, and Claire Whittemore. *Europe and the World Without*. Oxfam Public Affairs Report. London: Oxfam Public Affairs Unit, 1977.

Shaw, D. John. *World Food Security: A History since 1945*. Basingstoke: Palgrave Macmillan, 2007.

Shepard, Todd. *The Invention of Decolonization: The Algerian War and the Remaking of France*. Ithaca: Cornell University Library, 2008.

Shiell, Annette. *Fundraising, Flirtation and Fancywork: Charity Bazaars in Nineteenth Century Australia*. Newcastle upon Tyne: Cambridge Scholars Publishing, 2012.

Siegel, Benjamin. *Hungry Nation: Food, Famine, and the Making of Modern India*. Cambridge: Cambridge University Press, 2018.

———. "The Kibbutz and the Ashram: Sarvodaya Agriculture, Israeli Aid, and the Global Imaginaries of Indian Development." *American Historical Review* 125, no. 4 (October 21, 2020): 1175–1204.

Simms, Andrew, and Jenny Reindorp. *The New Abolitionists: Slavery in History and the Modern Slavery of Poor Country Debt*. London: Christian Aid, 1997.

Singer, H. W. "The Distribution of Gains between Investing and Borrowing Countries." *American Economic Review* 40, no. 2 (1950): 473–85.

Singer, Peter. "Altruism and Commerce: A Defense of Titmuss against Arrow." *Philosophy and Public Affairs* 2, no. 3 (1973): 312–20.

———. "Famine, Affluence, and Morality." *Philosophy & Public Affairs* 1, no. 3 (April 1, 1972): 229–43.

———. "Moral Experts." *Analysis* 32, no. 4 (1972): 115–17.

———. *Practical Ethics*. Cambridge: Cambridge University Press, 2011.

———. "The Triviality of the Debate over 'Is-Ought' and the Definition of 'Moral.'" *American Philosophical Quarterly* 10, no. 1 (1973): 51–56.

Slay, Ben. *The Polish Economy: Crisis, Reform, and Transformation*. Princeton: Princeton University Press, 2014.

Slobodian, Quinn. *Crack-Up Capitalism: Market Radicals and the Dream of a World without Democracy*. New York: Metropolitan Books, 2023.

———. *Globalists: The End of Empire and the Birth of Neoliberalism*. Cambridge, MA: Harvard University Press, 2018.

Sloman, Peter. *Transfer State: The Idea of a Guaranteed Income and the Politics of Redistribution in Modern Britain*. Oxford: Oxford University Press, 2019.

Smith, Justin Davis. *100 Years of NCVO and Voluntary Action: Idealists and Realists*. Cham: Palgrave Macmillan, 2019.

Socialist International Committee on Economic Policy. *Global Challenge: From Crisis to Cooperation: Breaking the North-South Stalemate: Report of the Socialist International Committee on Economic Policy*. London: Pan Books, 1985.

Solnit, David, Rebecca Solnit, and Anuradha Mittal. *The Battle of the Story of the Battle of Seattle*. Edinburgh: AK Press, 2009.

Solomon, Lewis D. *Multinational Corporations and the Emerging World Order*. Port Washington, NY: Kennikat Press, 1978.

Solow, Robert M. "Blood and Thunder." *Yale Law Journal* 80, no. 8 (1971): 1696–1711.

Southgate, John. *The Commonwealth Sugar Agreement, 1951–1974*. London: C. Czarnikow, 1984.

Sparkes, Russell. *The Ethical Investor*. London: HarperCollins, 1995.

Spodek, Howard. "The Self-Employed Women's Association (SEWA) in India: Feminist, Gandhian Power in Development." *Economic Development and Cultural Change* 43, no. 1 (1994): 193–202.

Stahl, Jason. *Right Moves: The Conservative Think Tank in American Political Culture since 1945*. Chapel Hill: University of North Carolina Press, 2016.

Stamp, Elizabeth. *The Hungry World*. Leeds: E. J. Arnold, 1967.

Standing, Guy. "Global Feminization through Flexible Labor." *World Development* 17, no. 7 (July 1, 1989): 1077–95.

Stedman Jones, Daniel. *Masters of the Universe: Hayek, Friedman, and the Birth of Neoliberal Politics*. Princeton: Princeton University Press, 2014.

Stewart, John. *Richard Titmuss: A Commitment to Welfare*. Bristol: Policy Press, 2020.

Stockwell, S. E. *The Business of Decolonization: British Business Strategies in the Gold Coast*. New York: Oxford University Press, 2000.

Streeck, Wolfgang. *Buying Time: The Delayed Crisis of Democratic Capitalism*. Brooklyn, NY: Verso, 2014.

Sutcliffe-Braithwaite, Florence. *Class, Politics, and the Decline of Deference in England, 1968–2000*. Oxford: Oxford University Press, 2018.

——. "Neo-Liberalism and Morality in the Making of Thatcherite Social Policy." *Historical Journal* 55, no. 2 (June 2012): 497–520.

——. "Tesco and a Motorway: In the Coalfields." *London Review of Books* 43, no. 17 (September 9, 2021).

Tangermann, Stefan. "European Interests in the Banana Market." In *Banana Wars: The Anatomy of a Trade Dispute*, ed. T. E. Josling and T. G. Taylor, 17–44. Cambridge, MA: CABI, 2003.

Tawney, R. H. *Equality*. 1962. London: Unwin Books, 1964.

——. *Religion and the Rise of Capitalism*. New York: Routledge, 2017.

Taylor, James. *Creating Capitalism: Joint-Stock Enterprise in British Politics and Culture, 1800–1870*. London: Royal Historical Society, 2006.

Tennent, Kevin D. "The Age of Strategy: From Drucker and Design to Planning and Porter." In *The Palgrave Handbook of Management History*, ed. Jeffrey Muldoon, Anthony Gould, and Adela McMurray, 1–20. Cham: Springer International Publishing, 2020.

Thane, Pat. "Michael Young and Welfare." *Contemporary British History* 19, no. 3 (September 1, 2005): 293–99.

Thompson, E. P. *The Making of the English Working Class*. London: Victor Gollancz, 1963.

——. "The Moral Economy of the English Crowd in the Eighteenth Century." *Past and Present* 50 (February 1971): 76–136.

——. *William Morris: Romantic to Revolutionary*. Oakland: PM Press, 2011.

Thompson, Noel W. *Political Economy and the Labour Party: The Economics of Democratic Socialism, 1884–2005*. 2nd ed. New York: Routledge, 2006.

Tignor, Robert. *Capitalism and Nationalism at the End of Empire: State and Business in Decolonizing Egypt, Nigeria, and Kenya, 1945–1963*. Princeton: Princeton University Press, 1998.

——. "Unlimited Supplies of Labor." *Manchester School* 72, no. 6 (2004): 691–711.

Titmuss, Richard Morris. *Commitment to Welfare*. 2nd ed. London: Allen and Unwin, 1976.

——. *Essays on "the Welfare State."* 3rd ed. London: Allen & Unwin, 1976.

——. *The Gift Relationship: From Human Blood to Social Policy*. New York: Pantheon Books, 1971.

——. *The Gift Relationship: From Human Blood to Social Policy*. Hebrew translation. Tel Aviv: Am Oved, 1979.

——. *The Health Services of Tanganyika: A Report to the Government*. London: Pitman Medical Pub. Co., 1964.

——. *Income Distribution and Social Change: A Study in Criticism*. London: G. Allen & Unwin, 1962.

——. "Poverty vs. Equality: A Diagnosis." *The Nation* (February 8, 1965): 130–33.

——. "Social Policy and Economic Progress." In *The Social Welfare Forum, 1966: Official Proceedings, 93rd Annual Forum. National Conference on Social Welfare, Chicago, Illinois, May 29–June 3, 1966*. New York: Columbia University, 1966.

Tolen, Rachel J. "Colonizing and Transforming the Criminal Tribesman: The Salvation Army in British India." *American Ethnologist* 18, no. 1 (1991): 106–25.

Tomlinson, Jim. *Democratic Socialism and Economic Policy: The Attlee Years, 1945–1951*. Cambridge Studies in Modern Economic History. Cambridge: Cambridge University Press, 1997.

Tooze, Adam. *Statistics and the German State, 1900–1945: The Making of Modern Economic Knowledge*. Cambridge: Cambridge University Press, 2001.

——. "Trouble with Numbers: Statistics, Politics, and History in the Construction of Weimar's Trade Balance, 1918–1924." *American Historical Review* 113, no. 3 (June 1, 2008): 678–700.

Toye, John. "The Achievements of an Optimistic Economist." In *Towards Human Development: New Approaches to Macroeconomics and Inequality*, ed. Giovanni Andrea Cornia and Frances Stewart. Oxford: Oxford University Press, 2014.

Toye, John, and Richard Toye. "The Origins and Interpretation of the Prebisch-Singer Thesis." *History of Political Economy* 35, no. 3 (2003): 437–67.

——. *The UN and Global Political Economy*. Bloomington: Indiana University Press, 2004.

Trentmann, Frank. "Before 'Fair Trade': Empire, Free Trade, and the Moral Economies of Food in the Modern World." *Environment and Planning: Society and Space* 25, no. 6 (2007): 1079–1102.

——. *Free Trade Nation: Commerce, Consumption, and Civil Society in Modern Britain*. Oxford: Oxford University Press, 2008.

——, ed. *The Making of the Consumer: Knowledge, Power and Identity in the Modern World*. Oxford: Berg, 2006.

Tusan, Michelle. "The Business of Relief Work: A Victorian Quaker in Constantinople and Her Circle." *Victorian Studies* 51, no. 4 (July 1, 2009): 633–61.

——. *Smyrna's Ashes: Humanitarianism, Genocide, and the Birth of the Middle East*. Berkeley: University of California Press, 2012.

UNCHS Habitat. "Annex: Case Studies on Technology Transfer and Diffusion in the Building Materials Industry." In *The Use of Selected Indigenous Building Materials with Potential for Wide Application in Developing Countries*. Nairobi: Habitat, 1985.

——. "United Republic of Tanzania: Lime-pozzolana Project at Oldonyo Sambu." In *The Use of Selected Indigenous Building Materials with Potential for Wide Application in Developing Countries*. Nairobi: HABITAT, 1985.

UNESCO. *International Understanding at School; Circular*. Leiden: A. W. Sythoff, 1971.

Unger, Corinna R. *International Development: A Postwar History*. London: Bloomsbury Academic, 2018.

United Nations. *Measures for the Economic Development of Under-developed Countries: Report by a Group of Experts Appointed by the Secretary-General of the United Nations*. New York: United Nations Department of Economic Affairs, 1951.

"United Nations Commission on Transnational Corporations: Information Paper on the Negotiations to Complete the Code of Conduct on Transnational Corporations." *International Legal Materials* 22, no. 1 (January 1983): 177–91.

Utting, Peter, ed. *Social and Solidarity Economy: Beyond the Fringe*. London: Zed Books, 2015.

van Dam, Peter. "In Search of the Citizen-Consumer: Fair Trade Activism in the Netherlands since the 1960s." *BMGN—Low Countries Historical Review* 132, no. 3 (September 25, 2017): 139–66.

———. "The Limits of a Success Story: Fair-trade and the History of Postcolonial Globalisation." *Comparativ* 25, no. 1 (2015): 62–77.

———. "Moralizing Postcolonial Consumer Society: Fair-trade in the Netherlands, 1964–1997." *International Review of Social History* 61, no. 2 (August 2016): 223–50.

van Rooy, Alison. "The Altruistic Lobbyists: The Influence of Non-Governmental Organizations on Development Policy in Canada and Britain." PhD thesis, University of Oxford, 1994.

Vernon, James. "Heathrow and the Making of Neoliberal Britain." *Past & Present* 252, no. 1 (January 22, 2021): 213–47.

———. *Modern Britain, 1750 to the Present.* Cambridge: Cambridge University Press, 2017.

———. "The Worlding of Britain." *Journal of British Studies* 57, no. 3 (2018): 10–17.

Vernon, Raymond. "Economic Sovereignty at Bay." *Foreign Affairs* 47, no. 1 (October 1968): 110–22.

———. *Sovereignty at Bay: The Multinational Spread of U.S. Enterprises.* New York: Pelican, 1971.

Vincent, David. *The Culture of Secrecy: Britain, 1832–1998.* Oxford: Oxford University Press, 1998.

Waddington, Keir. " 'Grasping Gratitude': Charity and Hospital Finance in Late-Victorian London." In *Charity, Self-interest and Welfare in the English Past*, ed. Martin Daunton, 135–51. London: Routledge, 1996.

Walker, Adrian. *One Crust of Bread.* Oxford: Oxfam Public Affairs Unit, 1977.

Ward, Barbara. "Only One Earth." *The UNESCO Courier*, January 1973.

———. *Spaceship Earth.* New York: Columbia University Press, 1966.

Ward, Robin. "Ethnic Communities and Ethnic Business: An Overview." *Journal of Ethnic and Migration Studies* 11, no. 1–2 (1983): 1–9.

War on Want. *Profits out of Poverty?: British Banks and Latin America's Debt Crisis.* London: War on Want Campaigns, 1986.

Ward, Stuart. Introduction to *British Culture and the End of Empire*, ed. Stuart Ward, 1–20. Manchester: Manchester University Press, 2005.

———. *Untied Kingdom: A Global History of the End of Britain.* Cambridge: Cambridge University Press, 2023.

Watkins, David. *Industrial Common Ownership.* London: Fabian Society, 1978.

Weber, Isabella M. "China and Neoliberalism: Moving beyond the China Is/Is Not Neoliberal Dichotomy." In *The SAGE Handbook of Neoliberalism*, ed. Damien Cahill, Melinda Cooper, and Martijn Konings. London: Sage, 2018.

Weber, Thomas. *Gandhi as Disciple and Mentor.* Cambridge: Cambridge University Press, 004.

Webley, Simon. *An Enquiry into Some Aspects of British Businessmen's Behaviour.* London: Industrial Educational and Research Foundation, 1971.

———. *Towards a Code of Business Ethics: A Consultative Document.* London: Christian Association of Business Executives, 1972.

Webster, Edward. "Organizing in the Informal Economy: Ela Bhatt and the Self-Employed Women's Association of India." *Labour, Capital and Society* 44, no. 1 (2011): 98–125.

Wellock, Wilfred. *India's Social Revolution Led by Mahatma Gandhi and Now Vinoba Bhave.* Preston: Wilfred Wellock, 1958.

———. *Off the Beaten Track: Adventures in the Art of Living.* 2nd ed. Varanasi: Sarva Seva Sangh Prakashan, 1963.

——. *The Third Way*. Birmingham: Plaid Cymru, 1947.

——. *"Which Way America?" "Which Way Britain?": Abundance or Abundant Life*. London: Society for Democratic Integration in Industry, 1958.Welshman, John. "The Unknown Titmuss." *Journal of Social Policy* 33, no. 2 (April 2004): 225–47.

Werlin, Herbet H. "The Informal Sector: The Implications of the ILO's Study of Kenya." *African Studies Review* 17, no. 1 (April 1974): 205–12.

Westad, Odd. *The Global Cold War: Third World Interventions and the Making of Our Times*. Cambridge: Cambridge University Press, 2011.

Westall, Andrea, Peter Ramsden, and Julie Foley. *Micro-Entrepreneurs: Creating Enterprising Communities*. London: New Economics Foundation and Institute for Public Policy Research, 2000.

Wheeler, K. *Fair Trade and the Citizen-Consumer: Shopping for Justice*. Basingstoke: Palgrave Macmillan, 2012.

Whitaker, Ben. *A Bridge of People: A Personal View of Oxfam's First Forty Years*. London: Heinemann, 1983.

Whiting, R. C. *The Labour Party and Taxation*. Cambridge: Cambridge University Press, 2000.

Whyte, Jessica. *The Morals of the Market: Human Rights and the Rise of Neoliberalism*. London: Verso Books, 2019.

Williams, Eric. *Capitalism and Slavery*. Chapel Hill: University of North Carolina Press, 1994.

Williams, David. *Advertising and Social Conscience: Exploiting Products, Not People*. London: Foundation for Business Responsibilities, 1976.

Wilms-Wright, Carl. *Transnational Corporations: A Strategy for Control*. London: Fabian Society, 1977.

Wilson, Peter. "Gilbert Murray and International Relations: Hellenism, Liberalism, and International Intellectual Cooperation as a Path to Peace." *Review of International Studies* 37, no. 2 (April 2011): 881–909.

Windel, Aaron. *Cooperative Rule: Community Development in Britain's Late Empire*. Berkeley: University of California Press, 2021.

Wood, Barbara. *E. F. Schumacher, His Life and Thought*. New York: Harper & Row, 1984.

Wood, Martha B. *Out of My Mind: A Collection of Narratives*. Bloomington, IN: iUniverse, 2014.

World Council of Churches. *World Council of Churches and Bank Loans to Apartheid*. Geneva: World Council of Churches, 1977.

World in Action: The Cost of a Cup of Tea. ITV. 1973.

Wright, A. W. *G.D.H. Cole and Socialist Democracy*. Oxford: Oxford University Press, 1979.

Wright, Derek Stuart. *The Psychology of Moral Behaviour*. London: Penguin Books, 1971.

Young, Michael. *The Chipped White Cups of Dover: A Discussion of the Possibility of a New Progressive Party*. London, 1960.

——. *The Elmhirsts of Dartington: The Creation of an Utopian Community*. London: Routledge, 1982.

——. *Small Man, Big World: A Discussion of Socialist Democracy*. Towards Tomorrow. London: Labour Publications Dept., 1949.

Yunus, Muhammad, *Banker to the Poor: The Autobiography of Muhammad Yunus, Founder of Grameen Bank*. Karachi: Oxford University Press, 2001.

——. *Credit for Self-Employment: A Fundamental Human Right*. Dhaka, Bangladesh: Al-Falah Printing Press, 1987.

Zahra, Tara. *The Lost Children: Reconstructing Europe's Families after World War II*. Cambridge, MA: Harvard University Press, 2011.

Žižek, Slavoj. *First as Tragedy, Then as Farce*. London: Verso, 2009.

Zweiniger-Bargielowska, Ina. *Austerity in Britain: Rationing, Controls, and Consumption, 1939–1955*. Oxford: Oxford University Press, 2000.

———. "The Culture of the Abdomen: Obesity and Reducing in Britain, circa 1900–1939." *Journal of British Studies* 44, no. 2 (2005): 239–73.

ILLUSTRATION CREDITS

INDEX

Page numbers in italics refer to figures and tables.

A NOTE ON THE TYPE

THIS BOOK has been composed in Miller, a Scotch Roman typeface designed by Matthew Carter and first released by Font Bureau in 1997. It resembles Monticello, the typeface developed for The Papers of Thomas Jefferson in the 1940s by C. H. Griffith and P. J. Conkwright and reinterpreted in digital form by Carter in 2003.

Pleasant Jefferson ("P. J.") Conkwright (1905–1986) was Typographer at Princeton University Press from 1939 to 1970. He was an acclaimed book designer and AIGA Medalist.